LOVE OR GREATNESS

LOVE
OR
GREATNESS

Max Weber and masculine thinking
– A feminist inquiry

Roslyn Wallach Bologh

London
UNWIN HYMAN
Boston   Sydney   Wellington

Published by the Academic Division of

Unwin Hyman Ltd
15/17 Broadwick Street, London W1V 1FP, UK

Unwin Hyman Inc.,
8 Winchester Place, Winchester, Mass. 01890, USA

Allen & Unwin (Australia) Ltd,
8 Napier Street, North Sydney, NSW 2060, Australia

Allen & Unwin (New Zealand) Ltd in association with the
Port Nicholson Press Ltd,
Compusales Building, 75 Ghuznee Street, Wellington 1, New Zealand

First published in 1990

British Library Cataloguing in Publication Data

Wallach Bologh, Roslyn
  Love or greatness; Max Weber and masculine thinking
  a feminist enquiry.
  1. Sociology, Weber, Max 1864–1920
  I. Title
301.092

ISBN 0–04–301249–3
ISBN 0–04–301250–7 pbk

Library of Congress Cataloging in Publication Data

Applied for

Typeset in 10 on 12 point Bembo
Printed in Great Britain by the University Press, Cambridge

To Jean Lapides Wallach,
Max Wallach and George Uri Fischer

PART FOUR
An alternative world

Acknowledgments

I wish to thank first and foremost George Fischer for his friendship and continued mentoring. Without his help this book could not have taken shape as it did.

Joan Tronto read an entire draft and provided me with helpful and interesting comments on every chapter. Michael E. Brown read an entire draft and gave me support and encouragement. Sonia Robbins provided expert technical and substantive editing help on an early draft. Kathy Deirlein checked all the citations and commented on several chapters. My colleagues at the College of Staten Island not only heard me present, but the following people also gave me their comments, support and encouragement: Judith Kuppersmith, George Rozos, Michael Greenberg and Steven Rosen.

Jeffrey Alexander, Stanley Aronowitz, Daniel C. Bologh, Howard Bologh, Gary Bologh, Terri Brickett, Sondra Farganis, Kathy Ferguson, Richard Harris, Terry Haywoode, Margaret Heide, James L. Marsh, John O'Neill and Isabel Pinedo all read various portions of the manuscript. Guenther Roth and Steven Seidman recommended and provided helpful references to secondary sources. Gisela Hinkle generously helped me with some of the German. Stephen Kalberg offered friendship, support and conversation through years of common struggle with our respective manuscripts.

Finally I would like to thank Sam Whimster for finding something of value in the very rough first draft that was sent to the publisher.

Preface

Weber's thought has meaning to me as a woman belatedly admitted to a man's world. His wealth as a man long a part of that world enriches me. He knows, he has long contemplated and confronted, that important and impressive world of history and politics. He has drawn his own conclusions, has heeded his own images and looked to his own vision as one who has been accustomed to doing so almost as a birthright – as the eldest male son of a political father, born into a home frequented by political figures engaging in political gossip and discussions. As a child he escaped from the emotional dynamics or intellectual boredom of domestic life into a world of books, of history and philosophy written by, for and about men, much as I escaped into a world of books and magazines written by, for and about women – and men who are in an explicit relationship to women.

Weber speaks to me as a guide, one who can lead me into the vastness of a little known world and provide me with paths for making my way through it in much the way that novels of interpersonal drama, books of etiquette and advice columns in women's magazines do for women's world.

As a relative outsider to the world of men, I find the classical social theorists great guides. Their sociological concepts and insights help me to put things in historical, political, economic and cultural perspective and enable me to take a position with regard to my own life and world, enable me to relate to myself and my situation, including the world situation.

Added to these concepts and insights are those of feminists who elucidate the subtle and not so subtle relationships of domination and accommodation, struggles of power and resistance between men and women. These struggles include not just the more blatant kinds of violence and abuse that women experience in great numbers, but the subtle kinds of oppression, particularly internalized oppression, that women including myself know first hand, and that without the challenges of feminism we might never have known consciously, that is with conceptual, theoretical and political awareness.

Karl Marx helps me to understand my experience of alienation; I am not in a position of control over the conditions and social context of my existence – or that of my children – even though today I am in a privileged position compared to much of the world.

But beyond Marx, Max Weber opens up a new world, not Marx's world of impersonal processes and relations between capital and labor with people being the personifications of these. Weber opens up a world of men who struggle for power, men who strive to dominate their world, to give meaning to and find meaning in that world. And so I move into a no-woman's land and learn how meaning has been made and found in it. Now I, too, know about this world.

Of course I do not mean that Weber offers us truth or accuracy in his rendition of the world and its meaning; he offers us his rendition. This rendition takes me into the world and guides me, gives me an understanding, a perspective.

I now have a way to conceive of the differences between East and West: receptive vessel and active agent; Protestantism and Catholicism; Calvinist sects and Lutheran church; individual striving and institutional obedience; traditional authority and modern authority – patriarchal, patrimonial domination and impersonal bureaucratic, rational, legal domination; and of the differences among magic, religion and science and their consequences, including a rationalized and disenchanted world. I now have a way to understand the meaninglessness of and various kinds of flight from a disenchanted world as well as the intellectual attempts at explaining and relieving the experience of undeserved suffering and a way to understand how these attempts are colored by external social-class conditions as well as internal problems of logical consistency and coherence.

I have now entered the larger world – the whole world almost. I have no one to thank more for my entry and introduction to this complex, variegated world than Max Weber. No other theorist offers me ways of understanding so much of the larger world beyond my ken. I can think of no more comprehensive introduction to the world beyond my own experience, a world, nevertheless, that impinges on my own experience, than the writings of Max Weber. However, as a guide to understanding my own world and relating my world to the whole world, Marx seems to promise more.

Marx responds to a cry for liberation from self-alienation that wells up in me from my 1950s childhood in New York City as the daughter of assimilating parents, themselves the children of Jewish immigrants. Marx enables me to find a common identity with others, a position from which to view and enter the world and to challenge and change it. Max Weber, on the other hand, enables me to see differences within the world, particularly the unique and singular difference that is the modern West.

From Marx I learn how most of us are oppressed pawns in a worldwide game of capital and relations of domination, and so we can eschew our unique differences that Weber teaches us to appreciate, and relate in kinship to those all over the globe who share the common condition of oppression. From Weber I learn how different we are from each other, how our differences are as great as our similarities. Although we may all be oppressed pawns and hence share a common identity and even a common fate, we also have different histories and traditions, and the world holds different meanings for us.

I referred above to the paths provided by Weber that I can follow and that can lead me through the men's world. Using these paths I can make my way in and around this world. But the way is disturbing to me. I am learning, with the help of both a self-reflective feminist consciousness and personal friendships with more or less feminist men and women, that I am not simply a no body who enters this world and tries to find a way within it, but I am some body. I am some body on whom gender has been inscribed, a particular body who needs to find a way that is comfortable to me, a way that can accommodate me, that is, my own way. And so I search beyond the paths laid out by Weber, beyond his concepts and polarities, and I scrutinize the paths that he has laid out for us in answer to his own internal quest. I ask, how do these paths move us and toward what? Is this the way I want or need to go? Is this the journey I want or need for my self, for my gendered body and its spirit?

I look to Weber's work for paths not there. I look into the vastness and see the worlds from which I and others come that cannot properly be seen from Weber's paths. I need to bring those worlds into focus. I need to cut a path from this white, middle-class, Western, imperial men's world to those other worlds, or at least to one of the worlds from which I come and which I know – a particular woman's world. Weber's perspective cannot do this for me. With vision of a more expansive world than the one Weber made his way through, vision of a world that escapes even Weber's purview, I confront the restrictiveness of his vision, Weber's lack as a man closed off to the world of women.

In presenting an alternative vision, I do not claim that my sight is better than his. My own scope is much smaller, tiny in comparison with the magnitude of his. Nevertheless, because he has given me a gift of his vision, I can now look beyond it and say, Max Weber, your vision is limited; we live in different bodies, in different times, and we come from different places. Your vision, extensive and expansive as it is, is the vision from your body inscribed with your gender, your place, your time. It may be the vision that enables you to make your way in and through the world; but it also restricts what you can see, what you can experience and what you can know. It also restricts what you can do. It is the kind of action to which your vision leads that I find most painful. I feel too keenly the restrictiveness of your vision and its consequences. And so I struggle against it; I reread your writings and scrutinize your way, in order to carve out a way for myself.

I have needed to detach myself from, resist and oppose you in order to be able to look at you, see your difference and in that way see my difference and find myself. As I say in Part Four, difference and separateness are essential to sociability, and difference and separateness often involve relations of conflict, struggles for liberation from domination and repression. This work represents such a struggle.

This book has been a long time in the making; it is the culmination of my efforts to understand, not just Weber, but my own reaction, as a woman, a thinking, reflecting, feeling human being, to Weber and to a whole way of thinking that rules our world. My aim is to explore and challenge this masculine thinking.

For readers unfamiliar with Max Weber's writings, this work can serve as an introduction to his major ideas. It may be thought of as two books in one. What may be thought of as Book One contains Part One, World of Greatness; Part Two, Modern World; and Part Three, World of Love. Together, these three parts present, analyze and criticize Weber's thinking. What may be thought of as Book Two, comprising Part Four, presents an alternative conception of social life as erotic sociability, an alternative rationality that is grounded in a female aesthetic sensibility, an alternative theoretical perspective that challenges both Marx and Weber, and concludes with an alternative vision of love and greatness.

The terms in my title, love and greatness, parallel those in Herbert Marcuse's title, *Eros and Civilization*. Like his, this work calls for overcoming the repression of the former by the latter.

Chapter 1 suggests an important kinship between Weber's thought and Freud's with respect to the idea(l) of masculinity as renunciation and repression. Part One explores Weber's "world of greatness," with Chapter 2 introducing Max Weber's influence on contemporary political theory (political "realism"), exploring the patriarchal background of Weber's life and suggesting a connection between masculine thinking and political thinking. Chapter 3 claims that the values of conflict, action and greatness that inform Weber's notion of manliness account for the seeming paradox in his life and politics: the championing of both political liberalism and illiberalism. Chapter 4 discloses an association of masculinity with a "heroic ethic" and femininity with the "ethics of the subjugated," also, the historical and patriarchal origins of the masculine political community and the public world. Chapter 5 continues Weber's analysis of the political community, exploring his theoretical and practical perspectives on imperialism and the link between manliness and "liberal imperialism."

Part Two opens with Chapter 6, Weber's critical analysis of both bureaucratic capitalism and ethical socialism: both of them stifle heroic greatness. Chapter 7 probably best captures the spirit of Weber's thinking. It examines Weber's generally admired idea(l) of the political actor and hero. A fear of worthlessness and possible dread of the body seem integral to this idea(l).

Chapter 8 locates the irrationality at the heart of Weber's conception of rational action and shows how this irrationality accounts for the dilemma of modernity and the dilemma of modern "man." Chapter 9 suggests that Weber's sociology of religion re-presents the defining tension of Weber's life and thought: not only a debate with historical materialists (spiritual interests matter) and with ethical socialists and ethically and religiously oriented political activists (an argument that self-interest and desire for wealth and power operate), but a conflict between rationality and ecstasy. For Weber religion represents the nagging and emasculating presence of sublimated desire – a "feminine" desire for love and ecstacy.

Part Three beginning with Chapter 10, recounts the tension Weber perceived between the man of action and the man of love, a tension that is played out in religion and in practical, political and economic life. He shows how religious ethics of brotherly love ultimately repress practical action – economic and political development – while practical action must ultimately repress ethics of brotherly love. Chapter 11 attempts to refute Weber's thesis by recovering from his own historical scholarship the finding that an oath of brotherhood is crucial to the revolutionary development of the occidental city state and the history of the West. His own work reveals how a commitment to some brotherhood – community and equality (but not with women and "others") – has been critical to Western political and economic development. Chapter 12 examines Weber's thesis that adhering to a religious ethic of brotherly love would undermine cultural development. He considers not just art and intellect but the dilemma of science and modernity. Chapter 13 addresses Weber's (proto-feminist) interpretation of the coercion and brutality at the heart of (heterosexual) erotic love – imposition of the stronger will (soul) on the weaker. His work suggests that neither brotherly love nor erotic love can provide the basis for reforming the world.

Part Four opens with Chapter 14 which offers an alternative, erotic love as sociability, to Weber's patriarchal conception of erotic love as coercion. Sociability, Georg Simmel's "play form of human sociation," has implications not only for erotic love but for all of social life. Pursuing the link forged earlier (Chapter 8) between gender and rationality, Chapter 15 focuses on women's world to reveal an alternative female rationality, aesthetic rationality, that is integral to sociability. Chapter 16 provides an alternative perspective that challenges Marx's "utopian" feminine socialism no less than Weber's "utopian" masculine individualism. Chapter 17 opens with Weber's stress on passion. It then addresses the dichotomies, striving and surrender, action and contemplation, individualism and socialism, with which Weber confronts the world. These dichotomies correspond to a division between masculine greatness and feminine love. This division requires a decisive choice. In dissolving these dichotomies, the chapter suggests an alternative vision of social life that overcomes the opposition and transforms Weber's patriarchal conceptions of love and greatness. In this alternative vision grounded in historical, social change, the world orients to greatness, not as patriarchal power and dominance over others, but as creative generativity. A world that fosters human greatness in the form of creative generativity requires human love, not in the patriarchal form of slavish devotion, but in the form of erotic sociability.

LOVE OR GREATNESS

1

Introduction:
Weber, Freud
and masculine thinking

Weber

In some respects, the social and political thought of Max Weber has never been surpassed. As a sociologist, the breadth of his knowledge and the scope of his analyses, his historical and comparative focus, expand our understanding of social life in a way that goes far beyond the more modest scholarship of contemporary sociology. Weber remains a truly foundational scholar whose work continues not only to generate new research and scholarship but stands at the center of contemporary debates about the nature of modernity.[1]

His represents one of the most important voices of modernity and on modernity. However, there is good reason to consider this voice masculine, masculinist and patriarchal: masculine, because it unself-consciously expresses idea(l)s and values that are associated with masculinity; masculinist, because it self-consciously champions these values and denigrates or ignores others considered feminine; patriarchal, because many of its idea(l)s and values assume and require a social order in which women and women's ways continue to be dominated, repressed and defined by subordination to men and men's ways.

From a feminist perspective, it is the last, the patriarchal nature of the thought, that is the most important and most troubling. Weber represents a particularly interesting case of patriarchal thinking because he was also a supporter of women's rights and a critic of patriarchal authoritarianism. That it is possible to support women's rights and still be guilty of patriarchal thought implies that patriarchal thinking includes more than explicit intention or conscious attitude towards women.

This work calls attention to the ways in which certain idealized "masculine" ways of relating and thinking presuppose and reproduce male dominance and female subordination and hence are implicated in maintaining a patriarchal social order. These ways of relating and thinking inform not only our everyday interpersonal relations and attitudes but our global politics and our theorizing. While much feminist work has focused on the world of interpersonal relations,

1

this work follows in the tradition of feminists like Hannah Fenichel Pitkin (1984), Jane Flax (1983), Jessica Benjamin (1988), Jean Bethke Elshtain (1981, 1986) and Nancy Hartsock (1983, 1984) who examine the relationship between patriarchal masculine thinking and social and political thought.

This work explores the issue of masculine, patriarchal thought – idea(l)s and values that recreate an oppressive and repressive social order – through an examination of Weber's conception of manliness, greatness and love in the modern world. As we will see, Weber's conception of manliness and greatness informs the rich complexity of his sociological thought, which ranges from religion, culture, sex and love to politics, economics, rationality and ethics. Weber's social and political thought epitomizes modern patriarchal masculine thinking. His thought assumes and reproduces, wittingly or unwittingly, a social order in which the public, political world of power and greatness represses and oppresses a private, domestic world of caregiving and home-making. Both the public world and the private world are premised on such oppression.

In addition to critically exploring the patriarchal nature of Weber's thought, I also attempt to develop, through responding to key features of his thought, an alternative to Weber's thinking. This dialogue emerges out of a commitment to overcoming the repression and oppression that is inherent in our modern patriarchal ways of being, thinking and seeing.

Weber, himself, used "patriarchy" as a term of opprobrium. He used it to refer to modern social arrangements in which a husband ruled over his wife and a father over his sons.[2] In this modern context he also used it to describe social organizations like the church that were structured according to strict hierarchies based on obedience. He also used the term "patriarchalism" to refer to "the most important type of domination the legitimacy of which rests upon tradition" (1946, p. 296).

He includes in one definition of patriarchalism (ibid.) authority of the father and the husband over members of the household, the rule of the master and patron over serfs and freedmen, of the lord over servants, of the prince over officials, nobles and vassals, of the patrimonial lord and sovereign prince over the "subjects." This is a more inclusive definition than those that limit patriarchy to rule in the household or family. This more expanded definition of patriarchalism as a mode of domination implicates the structuring of a whole social order rather than locating the domination in a social arrangement peculiar to private relationships between men and women, fathers and sons.

Freud

Sigmund Freud focuses on such private relationships in his analysis of masculinity. Freud also analyzes the nature of social life and modern "civilization."

This sociological analysis, however, like Weber's, is informed by his idealization of masculinity and his analysis of the nature and origins of masculinity. His thinking, too, is masculine, masculinist and patriarchal. Moreover, the particular masculine values that Freud champions and his analysis of social life which is informed by those values closely resemble Weber's own values and analysis. Given the great differences between Freud and Weber, this similarity is remarkable and surprising. On the other hand, given the shared masculine and patriarchal culture of their times, it is not so surprising.

Freud provides a theory of masculinity that helps us to identify the masculine nature of Weber's thinking. However, instead of uncritically adopting Freud's theory and applying it, I treat it as itself a symptom as well as a diagnosis of the times. That is, according to this reading of Freud's theory, masculinity presupposes and requires a patriarchal social order premised on the oppression of women and the repression or denial of "feminine desire" by men. Unlike Freud, I do not consider such oppression and repression natural and necessary. Hence I consider masculinity as propounded by both Freud and Weber neither natural nor necessary.

In calling attention to the masculine nature of Weber's thought I am calling into question the oppression of women and the repression of "feminine desire" that such thinking requires and presupposes. The claim that Freud's conception of masculinity presumes (and reproduces) a patriarchal social order derives from Judith Van Herik's indispensable groundbreaking analysis of Freud's theory of gender (1982), Alice Miller's critique of Freud (1984), and Jessica Benjamin's account of the link between gender and domination (1988). This reading of Freud's theory of masculinity helps us better to understand the patriarchal origins and nature of Weber's masculine thinking.

Van Herik shows how, for Freud, masculinity was associated with renunciation, femininity with fulfillment. What men must renounce is wishful illusion – an unrealizable desire. Women on the other hand can have this illusion and their desire fulfilled, but at a cost. The illusion that Freud considered central to the distinction between masculinity and femininity is the illusion of a loving, responsive, protective, consoling "father." Renunciation of this "illusion" produces masculine realism and masculine rationality.

Within patriarchal society, the father represents and embodies power outside the mother–child nexus (Benjamin, 1988).[3] As such, he can confer power and worth on the child by acknowledging and affirming the child as a being like himself. Or he can withhold such recognition. The desire for recognition is a fundamental desire (Benjamin, 1988). In addition to the desire to be recognized as like the powerful figure – able to act in the world and make a difference in that world ("masculine" desire) – the child also desires to surrender to the powerful other who will protect, console, provide and care for the child ("feminine" desire).

3

to recovering the repressed feelings. The major obstacle to psychoanalytic cure for the male patient is the "struggle against his passive or feminine attitude toward another male" (1937, p. 250, cited by Van Herik, 1982, p. 135). Replacing repression with conscious acknowledgement is essential to cure. There are times, Freud explains, when a man must be willing to surrender or submit to another man.

Freud complained of suffering most in analytic work from an oppressive feeling that all of his repeated efforts have been in vain when he is trying to "persuade a woman to abandon her wish for a penis on the ground of its being unrealizable" or "convince a man that a passive attitude to men does not always signify castration and that it is indispensable in many relationships in life" (ibid., p. 136). It is interesting that Freud uses the term "oppression." It is interesting also that his efforts at curing male patients amounted to expanding their repertoire to include a "feminine" attitude, while his efforts at curing female patients amounted to suppressing their desires to adopt a "masculine" attitude.

Just as it is not surprising that he failed in his efforts to persuade women to accept their "castration" and renounce what he interpreted as their desire for a penis, it is not surprising that he failed in his efforts to convince men of the need to acknowledge a desire for feminine passivity in relation to other men. Feminine "passivity" is premised on a lack of power in the public world of men; it is political, social and economic castration.

A male child's desire for a man's love and protection does not have to mean accepting metaphorical castration, except in a patriarchal context. Renunciation of that desire is necessary for retaining one's masculinity, one's power in the world (symbolized by the phallus) only in a patriarchal world. Freud's theory of masculinity as renunciation constitutes an ideology for rationalizing and justifying not just male renunciation of the wish for a maternal father; it is also an ideology for rationalizing and justifying a patriarchal social order.

In contrast to the development of "men" who cannot surrender to each other, preferring to fight to the finish rather than submit, the girl, in Freud's theory, who achieves "normal femininity" gives up her masculinity (active, self-reliant subjectivity, agency, power in the world) for her father's love, a love predicated on her being a passive physical object of her father's affection. Feminine women do not renounce their wish for love from the father. Because they are "castrated" (that is, relatively powerless and unthreatening), they can have their wish for paternal love fulfilled, but at the cost of activity, morality and intellectuality. Freud associated these latter with masculinity. Feminine women cannot develop independent minds or independent moral judgments; they must remain forever dependent on paternal care and protection, on the superior paternal mind and judgment (Van Herik, 1982).

Instead of Freud's belief that "normal femininity" is a result of the female child's discovery of lack – absence of penis – which Freud also calls castration, we can interpret femininity as a response to negative or ambivalent reactions by patriarchal men and women to her attempts at identifying with "the man" (a strong, capable, competent, self-sufficient, independent figure). Unlike the male child, according to Freud, she learns that she can retain or obtain love of the man, but at the cost of identification with him; she must eschew masculinity – active, aggressive, independent behavior. This development is tantamount to social, political, economic "castration."

Van Herik sums up Freud's thinking:

> Submission and its compensatory gratifications restrict intellect and moral-
> ity. When intellectual and moral levels are thus lowered, culture is impov-
> erished. . .The psychical qualities of . . .the feminine man or woman are the
> same: a weak superego, a poorly developed sense of morality, a restricted
> intellect, opposition to cultural advance, insufficient respect for reality,
> *Ananke* [necessity] and *Logos* (p. 192).

Both masculinity and femininity as described and analyzed by Freud presuppose a patriarchal father figure, one who demands either feminine submission to the person of the father or masculine submission to the father's (impersonal) law. Masculinity requires actively identifying with the patriarchal father and internalizing his proscriptions and demands for renunciation. In contrast femininity requires passive submission to the father while receiving fulfillment of the desire for paternal care and protection (Van Herik, 1982, p. 195). Both masculinity and femininity as described and analyzed by Freud are patriarchal conceptions. Both must be considered problematic from a feminist perspective.

Patriarchal civilization

Freud argues that the masculine psychosexual development in which the male child renounces his desire for a loving, protective, consoling father is crucial for the development of civilization. According to Freudian theory, such renunciation results in superior morality (internalized superego out of fear of father), superior intellect (not fooled by illusion nor accepting of dogma, but willing to investigate for oneself a loveless, meaningless reality), personal autonomy and civilization itself. In contrast, feminine submissiveness, which is the price of paternal love by a patriarchal father, restricts intellect and morality. Freud does not entertain the possibility of an alternative morality, intellect, autonomy and civilization that is neither masculine nor feminine but both, a synthesis that transforms both masculinity and femininity, both the public world and the private world.

Freud assumes a division of the world into a masculine public sphere and a feminine private sphere. He then goes on to discuss what follows from this. "Women represent the interests of the family and of sexual life." As such they "come into opposition to civilization and display their retarding and restraining influence." Not only does he claim that "the work of civilization has become increasingly the business of men," but he claims further that it "compels them to carry out instinctual sublimations of which women are little capable" (Freud, [1930] 1961, p. 50). Men are compelled by "civilization" to sublimate their instinctual ("masculine") desires; women not only have their instinctual ("feminine") desires satisfied but are not capable of such sublimations. Beginning from an assumption of a natural patriarchal division of the world into a masculine public world ("civilization") and a feminine private world, he then claims a natural difference between men and women. Here is Freud's description of the nature of men:

> Men are not gentle creatures who want to be loved, and who at the most can defend themselves if they are attacked; they are, on the contrary, creatures among whose instinctual endowments is to be reckoned a powerful share of aggressiveness. As a result, their neighbor is for them not only a potential helper or sexual object, but also someone who tempts them to satisfy their aggressiveness on him, to exploit his capacity for work without compensation, to use him sexually without his consent, to seize his possessions, to humiliate him, to cause him pain, to torture and to kill him. *Homo homini lupus.* Who, in the face of all his experience of life and of history, will have the courage to dispute this assertion? (ibid., p. 58).

The issue, however, is not whether human beings in general or men in particular have the potential for such behavior. The issue is, rather, what are the social conditions and social relations that foster or elicit these behaviors as opposed to other behaviors which also make up the human potential?

Freud's work makes it seem that men are naturally violent and rapacious; women are naturally submissive. The distinction between men and women is given with nature and reproduced by a *natural* and *necessary* (for purposes of civilization) process of becoming a man, a process of repressing and renouncing one's desire for a loving, maternal father, and a natural and necessary process of becoming a woman, repressing and renouncing one's desire to be like the powerful father. According to this interpretation of how men become men and women become women, a loving, maternal fathering relationship ought to contribute to the development of male children able to accept as realistic and "natural" their "feminine desire" to be loved, cared for and nurtured by men. But such a relationship is precluded, according to Freud, by the demands of "civilization" which require that men separate from maternal bonds and enter a world of hostile strangers. A threatening

8

paternal authority figure, who represents the claims of civilization, imposes such demands.

Patriarchal morality

According to Freud, "civilization" itself is a wholly masculine phenomenon attributable exclusively to patriarchal fathering.

> Religion, morality and a social sense. . .were acquired [originally] out of the father-complex: religion and moral restraint through the process of mastering the Oedipus complex itself, and social feeling through the necessity for overcoming the rivalry that then remained between the members of the younger generation (1927, p. 37, cited by Van Herik, 1982, p. 159).

In other words, morality for men within this patriarchal form of life derives from fear of violence: the violent impulses of a son toward his father, the violent impulses of the father toward the son, and the violence of the brothers toward each other. Sociability for men derives from the need of the sons for co-operation and overcoming rivalry. Such morality and sociability involves exercising restraint (control over impulses) and respecting the rights of others to non-interference. "The essence of morality [is] renunciation" (Freud, 1928, p. 177, cited by Van Herik, p. 81). There are no women in this model except as objects of (male) sexual desire.

For masculinity, morality and sociality are equated with renunciation of violence and anti-social impulses out of fear of "the man" and out of need for co-operation with other "men." In other words, violence and anti-social impulses are primary phenomena; morality and sociability are secondary. In contrast, we can formulate feminine morality and sociality as coming from a recognition of mutual dependence and mutual attachment. Morality and sociability take the form of responsiveness to the feelings and needs of others. These are two very different kinds of morality[4] and sociability, both derived from a patriarchal parental relationship.

The son must engage in a constant battle to control his impulses or suffer the humiliation of castration by the father or the retaliation of other men. Furthermore, the son must renounce his earlier wish for maternal, paternal love from the father. Thus, impulse control and renunciation of desire for love from men, recognition of the hostility of men, and the need to control the violence born of that hostility, constitute the masculine morality and "realism" that Freud exalts. I find this kind of morality as problematic as Freud finds the feminine kind of morality and "illusion" premised on personal feelings of sympathy, acknowledgment of personal dependence and expectation of care.

The morality that Freud associates with the superego is a morality whose aim is to restrain or punish erotic, aggressive, destructive and murderous impulses. I call this "patriarchal morality." Freud assumed that murderous or destructive impulses on the part of the male child are a natural response to the oedipal triangle; he did not focus on parents' patriarchal authoritarian attitudes toward and treatment of children and their feelings.

A feminist critique

Alice Miller (1984, 1983) suggests that Freud is blaming the victim when he attributes original guilt to the child in the oedipal drama. She also challenges Freudian drive theory itself (1984). Her work implies that blame belongs with the patriarchal nature of a culture and a family in which the parent (representative of patriarchal power) impresses authority on the children by means of threats, ridicule, humiliation, withdrawal, violence or intimidation. Drive theory is more likely to conceal than to reveal the sexual and narcissistic abuse the patient experienced as a child (Miller, 1984, pp. 6–7). Children must then repress their trauma if there is no sympathetic and supportive person to acknowledge their feelings and support them.

Freud believed that an internalized impersonal superego derives from fear of the father and his threat of castration, a father who is seen as jealous, wrathful, violent and powerful. Such a father is idealized, and the aggression that one feels towards such a figure is turned inward as one's own superego. Alice Miller's work suggests that Freud's belief that such psychodynamics produces manly men and intellectual, moral and cultural development – in short, civilization itself – is a form of rationalizing "poisonous pedagogy." By the latter she means an ideology of childraising premised on the idea that parents can and should use coercion and cruelty to socialize the child, to "discipline" the child, to control and subordinate the child to some "order." In other words poisonous pedagogy exhorts parents to treat their children in a way that is not respectful of children's feelings and rationalizes such "cruel" treatment as being for the child's own good.

Freud can be said to rationalize, as being for their own good and the good of civilization, a patriarchal culture that demands that children honor and obey their parents, especially their fathers, but that does not demand that parents, especially fathers, honor, acknowledge and respect their children's feelings – their "masculine" and "feminine" desires and fears. Alice Miller emphasizes the predicament of the totally dependent child who must repress his (or her) trauma (1984, p. 6). This situation results in children's alienation from their own feelings. This analysis implicates not only our attitudes toward children, but the context within which parenting occurs, the isolated nuclear household which other feminists have referred to as an emotional hothouse.

There is another, related dimension to patriarchal parenting. We can assume that those patriarchal cultures in which politically and economically "castrated" women are subject to patriarchal domination and hence lack of emotional fulfillment in their marriage are likely to induce in women a desire to turn from their husbands toward their sons, provoking guilt on the part of the son and jealous hostility by the father toward his male child.

This aspect of patriarchal culture and family life, therefore, intensifies a patriarchal attitude by the father toward his male children. Where the woman is simultaneously contemptuous of her husband (the situation in Max Weber's home), the son is likely to develop a contempt for the patriarchal, dominating figure and a desire to become a hero who fights the patriarch on behalf of the woman, a desire to replace the father, to become a patriarchal hero who deserves a woman's respect as opposed to the patriarchal tyrant who evokes her contempt.

A patriarchal culture and family structure is responsible, I argue, for the reproduction of patriarchal masculinity and patriarchal femininity, repressed and repressive forms of life. The patriarchal culture of modernity is characterized by a division into a private world of parenting, homemaking and erotic relationships, symbolized by women, and a public world that controls the means of violence, administration and production, all symbolized by men. Within this patriarchal political economy, the private world of personal life and love is dependent upon, shaped by, and subordinate to the public world of power and politics premised on a repressive rationality.

A threatening and hostile world

The father responds with hostility or ambivalence to his male child's "feminine" desire because, I would contend, the latter awakens the father's own "feminine" desires for protection, care, consolation and security which he must deny in order to survive in a hostile world (such as a warfare economy or competitive capitalism). Furthermore, the father feels threatened by the child because the child may actually threaten the father's relationship with his wife.

This attitude of the patriarchal father has its counterpart in that of the patriarchal mother. Her attitude toward her male son and his potential power and privilege which she would like to possess, control or use for her own needs and desires results in a self-protective and defensive attitude by the child. Masculine boys learn to see the world in terms of struggles to protect the phallus – symbol of masculinity and hence symbol of power – a struggle against both patriarchal fathering and patriarchal mothering.

The male child of this historically specific kind of patriarchal parenting can be expected to see the world as a continuing struggle to combat (feminine)

11

temptations that can weaken his resolve and threaten his independence, a continuing struggle to preserve power, position and possession, a struggle for power and dominance, well expressed by Hobbes. Through their attitudes parents teach their male children that this is a hostile world in which one must be ready to protect oneself from menacing others and to control one's own violent and destructive impulses.

By learning to deny their desire for a loving, compassionate, caring father who will acknowledge and respect their feelings, male children become "men." They become capable of facing alone a loveless, hostile reality. In becoming capable of surviving in this kind of world through defensive, protective and aggressive actions, they recreate the kind of threatening and hostile world that they are trying to defend against.

Freud recommends going out into "hostile life," as "education to reality" (1927b, p. 49, cited by Van Herik, 1982, p. 166). This view of reality as "hostile life" is mirrored in Weber's view of social and political reality. Weber and Freud both see the world as a hostile place characterized by conflict and struggles for power. Manliness consists of facing without illusion that loveless, hostile reality. Both see such reality as natural, as founded in the nature of "man." That view continues to prevail in the world today.

A shared masculine outlook can be seen in certain dominant themes and attitudes common to both Freud and Weber. That these common themes and attitudes emerge so powerfully in their writings despite radical differences in their choice of subject matter and approach suggest a confluence of historical and personal factors. These common themes, adumbrated below, include: rationality and disenchantment, illusion and renunciation, commitment to a cause, morality as inner struggle, religion and science, contentment and greatness, heroic individualism and strong leadership.

Disenchantment and masculinity

The "illusory" desire that men must renounce is the desire for a maternal love from fathers that acknowledges the child's feelings (including those of fear, frustration and rage) and offers attention, respect and consolation without a withdrawal of love. Renouncing the desire for this kind of love (what Benjamin calls recognition) (re)produces "manly independence;" it also (re)produces modern (male) rationality and disenchantment. Weber described the process of disenchantment as characteristic of modern life. Disenchantment occurs with the rise of science and the decline of magic and religion. The process begins with the Protestant renunciation of a loving, forgiving God and its replacement with an inscrutable God who predestines individuals for salvation or damnation. The decline of belief in a paternal, loving, forgiving God parallels a rise of belief in science, belief in a nature shorn of metaphysical meaning and characterized by laws of cause and effect. The world simply is; it no longer signifies something.

Disenchantment has its costs — the loss of meaning and charm. People take flight from a meaningless reality into a variety of experiences holding out promise of redemption. Instead of such flight, Weber advocated "facing the fate of the times like a man" and renouncing all illusions, including new religions and ersatz religious experiences — false promises.

Freud, too, advocated renunciation of illusion and facing reality. For Weber, the illusion that had to be renounced was the belief that an ethical and loving world is possible, belief that life in the public world could be lived with and ruled by (an ethic of brotherly) love. For Freud, the illusion that had to be renounced was belief in a loving, protective, consoling father. Renunciation of this illusion produces masculinity. Retention of this illusion produces femininity.

Realism for both Freud and Weber meant acknowledging and facing a loveless reality, realizing that one is "no longer the object of tender care on the part of a beneficent Providence" (Freud, 1927b, p. 49, cited by Van Herik, 1982, p. 166).

Although Freud affirmed the importance of love, he, like Weber, believed that the only place for love is the private sphere of personal relations. But such love does not totally satisfy.[5] There is no place for an ethic of love in the public sphere of politics. To assume otherwise is dangerous. This is the heart of both Freud's and Weber's political realism. Freud castigated the educational system of his day for stressing ethical virtue and not preparing the young for "the aggressiveness of which they are destined to become the objects," (Freud, [1930] 1961, p. 81).

Weber placed great value on action in the public world based on commitment to an impersonal cause and distance from other men. Only this value can make the aggressive struggle for power that characterizes life in the public world acceptable and worthy of a man, of a responsible human being. Freud, too, claims, "The highest mental achievement that is possible in a man [is] that of struggling successfully against an inward passion for the sake of a cause to which he has devoted himself" (Freud, 1914, p. 233, cited by Van Herik, 1982, p. 81). Both Freud and Weber saw the essence of morality as involving a struggle against personal desires or impulses out of commitment to some impersonal cause or ideal.

Religion as feminine

Both Weber and Freud considered religion in general and Christianity in particular to be feminine. Weber and Freud both idealize the prophets of ancient Judaism as heroic figures; for both, Judaism is a more masculine religion than Christianity. It makes ethical demands on its believers that require forcibly suppressing one's impulses and obeying the commands of an omnipotent god who is both revered and feared. There is no intercession by a loving, paternal or maternal figure, nor is there forgiveness and consolation. There is also no magical intervention that can protect one.

According to Freud's analysis the religious person may submit in the feminine mode, as object, to the divine loving Subject, achieving fulfillment at the price of autonomous reason and cultural advance. This is Freud's view of Christianity:

> The Christian religion did not maintain the high level in things of the mind to which Judaism had soared. It was no longer strictly monotheist, it took over numerous symbolic rituals from surrounding peoples, it reestablished the great mother-goddess and found room to introduce many of the divine figures of polytheism only lightly veiled. . .Above all, it did not, like the Aten religion and the Mosaic one which followed it, exclude the entry of superstitious, magical and mystical elements, which were to prove a severe inhibition upon the intellectual [*geistige*] development of the next two thousand years (Freud, 1939, p. 88, cited by Van Herik, 1982, p. 190).

Freud attributed the failure of intellectual development to mental attitudes grounded in feminine desires and illusion and expressed in religious beliefs and practices. This view of intellectual development is reminiscent of Weber's analysis of the uniqueness of Western rationality (Author's Introduction to the *Protestant Ethic and the Spirit of Capitalism*, 1958, pp. 13–31).

Freud argued that, by re-establishing "the great mother-goddess," Christianity brings back the dangers of femininity and the maternal principle which are associated with fulfillment; the world becomes static; the development of culture and intellect is inhibited. Weber held an almost identical view of "feminine" Christian religion (with the exception of Calvinism).

For Freud, intellectual and cultural development required rejection of the nirvana principle with its constitutive wish for peace and contentment. Weber, too, rejected Eastern philosophy and religion with their nirvana principle which, he acknowledged, seems to provide a resolution to human distress, but only at the cost of human action and economic development; it produces passivity toward rather than rational mastery of the world.

Weber believed that renunciation of worldly desire and pursuits that characterizes Buddhism ultimately requires renunciation of all purposeful action. This means renunciation of (practical) life itself. Freud actually identified the nirvana principle with a death instinct. Weber disparaged mere happiness and well-being. For Weber and for Freud happiness and pleasure are associated with contented passivity; greatness with discontented activity. Human contentment and human greatness are incompatible for both Freud and Weber. Fulfillment and contentment result in stasis or regression whereas renunciation of desire for happiness and contentment make possible dynamism and development. Rather than renouncing all worldly desire in order to achieve contentment, as do versions of Eastern and Western religions, Weber and Freud advocated renouncing the desire for contentment, the "illusion" of peace, love and harmony.

Although some religions may be more conducive to furthering civilization (Judaism, ascetic Protestantism), for both Freud and Weber replacing religion with science remained the ideal. Renunciation of (religious) illusion means renouncing not just the feminine attitude that assumes a loving, forgiving, consoling parental figure (Catholic, Hindu, Lutheran) but transcending the ordinary masculine attitude of obedience to a (divine) father's demand for renunciation (Judaism, Calvinist Protestantism) in favor of a scientific (ideal masculine renunciation) attitude of rational mastery toward a post-paternal, disenchanted universe (loveless, meaningless universe devoid of a divine father).

Greatness and heroism

What are the gratifications that come with renunciation of the desire for paternal love? Masculine fulfillment is found in the pride (superiority) that comes from renunciation, from sacrificing wishes to the superego (internal paternal agent) (Van Herik, 1982, pp. 182–3, 192). Hence, the gratification that accompanies renunciation is the gratification of pride, pride in intellect, in morality, in independence of mind and judgment, pride in strength, pride in power and pride in work. With such pride, however, comes a corresponding contempt for the "other."

Despite the masculine renunciation of pleasure in the form of paternal love, there is pleasure that comes with action in and on the world, the pleasure of acting on the world to change it, to impose one's will on it, to achieve human greatness. The ideal man, one who has renounced the illusion of paternal love, gets pleasure only from his renunciation, his realism and the sense of pride and superiority that comes with that renunciation and the turn toward external activity; he finds pleasure and pride in action in the world – his work or vocation. What Freud calls the ego ideal, a "masculine" ideal of mastering reality and deriving pride from that mastery, is a "substitute for a longing for the father" (1923, p. 37, cited by Van Herik, 1982, p. 159). By denying one's longing for the father (masculine renunciation) and substituting the ideal of mastering reality, greatness becomes possible. Hence greatness requires masculinity.

Renunciation of illusion (masculinity) frees one to explore and master a loveless reality. Independence of mind is not possible as long as one lives with the "feminine" illusion of a protective loving father figure, for such an illusion requires submissiveness and perpetuates attitudes of helplessness and dependence. These attitudes in turn preclude the independence of mind that fosters science and mastery of the world. This argument rests on the association of a protective loving father figure with a demand for submissiveness (castration). In other words, for Freud, paternal love is inextricably bound to patriarchal domination and authoritarianism. Therefore, greatness of intellect and civilization, masculine rationality and realism, all require the renunciation of feminine desire for paternal love and with it feminine submissiveness.

For Freud as for Weber, "the qualities of the great man are . . . decisiveness of thought, strength of will, energy of action, and above all, autonomy and independence" (Van Herik, 1982, p. 177). Freud mentions also "divine unconcern which may grow into ruthlessness" (1939, p. 110, cited by Van Herik, 1982, p. 177). Freud compares the qualities of the father of the primal herd with those of Nietzsche's great man: "His intellectual acts were strong and independent even in isolation, and his will needed no reinforcement from others. . .He, at the very beginning of the history of mankind, was the 'superman' whom Nietzsche only expected from the future" (Freud, 1921, p. 123, cited by Van Herik, 1982, p. 189). This is the same primal father who was hated and murdered by the sons.

Freud, like Weber, stressed heroism. Freud found "the origin of the concept of a hero" in a son who "rebels against his father and kills him in some shape or other" (Freud, 1939, quoted in Van Herik, 1982, p. 188). Freud defines three kinds of heroes.

The first is the hero who kills the father figure and liberates "men" from bondage. The second is the hero who responds to the guilt and fear resulting from the murder by reimposing renunciations, restrictions and restraint which aim at resolving the guilt and fear (such as Moses in Judaism). However, the guilt continues to increase as each act of renunciation recalls, unconsciously, the reason for the renunciation – the horrible deed that needs atonement (Van Herik, 1982, pp. 186–7). The accumulation of guilt calls forth a third kind of hero who takes it on himself to atone for the guilt of all – the sacrificial hero (such as Jesus in Christianity), or the hero who establishes some kind of sacrifice – who identifies an object that embodies the sin. Sacrificing the object – a scapegoat – that embodies the sin absolves everyone of guilt and temporarily creates a sense of liberation and rebirth, an escape from the guilt.

Freud and Weber both saw the danger in such heroism and scapegoating. Nevertheless, Weber does hold an image of masculine heroic action as does Freud. Both emphasized independence, autonomy, and self-reliance: "Only very few civilized people are capable of existing without reliance on others or are even capable of coming to an independent opinion. You cannot exaggerate the intensity of people's inner lack of resolution and craving for authority"

(Freud, 1910, p. 146, cited by Van Herik, 1982, p. 87). For Freud, opinion formation does not occur through discussion and interaction; it is not arrived at communally or jointly through a process of dialogue with other(s) and mutual consideration of each other's interests, needs and feelings. For Freud, the ideal man exists "without reliance on others".

Weber, like Freud, placed his hope in heroic individuals – in the lone individual who can take decisive action – one who has killed off the father or the desire for a loving father. Weber's description of the charismatic leader corresponds with Freud's description of the hero – the renunciatory hero who imposes restrictions, restraints and renunciations; the sacrificing hero who offers himself or another as a sacrifice; and the conquering hero who risks his life on behalf of his cause. (These versions of the heroic leader can be contrasted with Rosa Luxemburg's version of leadership.)[6]

Weber placed his hopes for Germany in effective political leadership. He decried the situation in Germany that allowed an incompetent Kaiser to rule while precluding the kind of experience that would enable true leaders to emerge. Weber talked contemptuously of "leaderless democracy," while Freud contended that the danger of modern life

> is most threatening where the bonds of a society are chiefly constituted by the identification of its members with one another, while individuals of the leader type do not acquire the importance that should fall to them in the formation of a group. The present cultural state of America would give us a good opportunity for studying the damage to civilization which is thus to be feared. (Freud, [1930] 1961, pp. 62–3)

That men do not identify with each other as interdependent members of society, but identify instead with the image of a strong man who is dependent on no one – a natural leader – constituted for both Freud and Weber the necessary and essential condition for human (manly) greatness.

If I had to encapsulate all of these ideas into an image it would be that of the strong, stoic, resolutely independent, self-disciplined individual who holds himself erect with self-control, proud of his capacity to distance himself from his body, from personal longings, personal possessions and personal relationships, to resist and renounce the temptations of pleasure in order to serve some impersonal cause – a masculine, ascetic image. The image of devotion to some impersonal cause can be interpreted as rationalizing and justifying self-repression while channeling the aggressive, competitive, jealous, angry feelings that accompany such repression. For Freud and for Weber this image represented not ordinary masculinity but ideal masculinity, an image of manliness and heroic greatness that differs from the image of masculinity as mere aggressiveness or glorification of strength and power.

While Marx, Toennies and others were responding to modernity by idealizing *Gemeinschaft* (traditional community), modeled on a maternal or fraternal image, Weber and Freud idealized the lone individual of *Gesellschaft* (modern society), the man who, without the crutch of religion, metaphysics or illusion, can face a loveless reality, make rational decisions and take rational action – by himself – and bear the consequences manfully, alone and without flinching. This conception of modern, heroic, masculine individualism informs the thinking they share. For both Freud and Weber, the world of greatness is a loveless world. To achieve greatness in the modern public world, one must renounce illusion in the form of desire for a world of love.

This view of life as requiring a choice between "feminine" surrender to love (fulfillment and illusion) and masculine striving for greatness (renunciation and realism) constitutes modern patriarchal thinking.

The modern public world of separate, unattached, competing and contending individuals (as opposed to the public world of patriarchal feudalism characterized by loyalties, attachments and alliances that were simultaneously personal and political, masculine and military) justifies itself as serving the protection and provision of a vulnerable, dependent, depoliticized private world of personal bonds and attachments – sustained by women's labor and women's love. At the same time that the modern public world justifies itself by claiming to be in the service of the private world, the public world subordinates and shapes the private world to its own ends. Hence despite ideology to the contrary, the private world becomes not an end in itself that is served by the public world but a means for furthering the ends of the public world.

Political economy (the political and economic spheres and their mutual dependence) and political economic changes are interpreted in culture, justified in ideology, internalized in consciousness and embodied in personal gendered identities. That is, political economy is embodied, personified and gendered. Political economy reproduces itself through the actions of gendered persons. But people have the capacity for self-reflection, self-change, individual and collective action and social change. Certain historical, social conditions promote such reflection and change.

A political economy of capitalism may have its own impersonal dynamic. That dynamic, however, reproduces itself in and through the psyche of individual and collective actors. The alienated, repressed, gendered nature of our consciousness and psyche has serious consequences not only for the dynamics of political economy and its impersonal relations but for the dynamics of our inner lives and our interpersonal relations. This work is as concerned with the latter as it is with the former. In fact political economy is of interest ultimately only because of its impact on social, emotional and physical life. The divorce of political and economical reality from social and psychological reality reifies and fetishizes "reality", making it appear as a fact and a thing, something solid and immovable out there to which we must pay obeisance or that we can change only through the most violent exertions. Even then most people feel that the effort is futile.

While "reality" appears as a fact and a thing out there, our feelings and desires appear as shadows of reality; sometimes these shadows loom large; sometimes they seem not to be there at all. They seem fleeting and illusory, certainly not "real" and solid in the same way as economic and political reality. Nevertheless, economic and political reality, as Marx has indicated, is no more real than our social relationships; our desires and feelings, which are inseparable from our social relationships, are no more illusory than our economic and political worlds. Psychic reality, like social reality, is no more nor less real than political and economic reality.

Modern political economy produces and assumes not just alienation from external conditions of existence but, as we have seen, alienation from and repression of human feelings and desires. Alienated consciousness becomes a force in its own right. This alienated consciousness manifests itself in the form of gender; it manifests itself *as* gender. Patriarchal masculinity and patriarchal femininity represent different sides of alienated consciousness. Max Weber's social and political thought represents one version of alienated consciousness – modern patriarchal, masculine thinking.

Notes

1 See for example, Habermas, (1984) and Whimster and Lash (1987).
2 That daughters are not mentioned in many accounts of patriarchy may indicate more than just male bias or oversight. It may mean that daughters are ruled directly by mothers and only indirectly by fathers or at moments when fathers feel they must intervene, while sons, who are more independent of their mothers, are ruled more directly by fathers.
3 For both Freud and Benjamin "the father" may take the form of symbolic cultural representations and not necessarily an actual biological or social father that is present in the home.
4 Kohlberg (1971) and Gilligan (1982) represent these two kinds of morality. Kohlberg's model revolves around a version of morality as detachment and restraint; Gilligan claims this is a masculine mode of morality and suggests that there is another model of feminine morality that is based on care and responsibility for others.
5 He seems to believe that "its [sexual love's] importance as a source of feelings of happiness. . .has sensibly diminished." Moreover, it is not only the pressure of civilization but "something in the nature of the function itself which denies us full satisfaction and urges us along other paths." He, himself, is not certain. "This may be wrong; it is hard to decide." Nevertheless, he goes on to provide explanations that strike me as themselves symptoms. I cite one particularly egregious illustration here:

> Another difficulty arises from the circumstance that there is so often associated with the erotic relationship, over and above its own sadistic components, a

quota of plain inclination to aggression. The love-object will not always view these complications with the degree of understanding and tolerance shown by the peasant woman who complained that her husband did not love her any more, since he had not beaten her for a week (Freud, [1930] 1961, p. 53n.).

6 Lorraine Cohen's dissertation (1987) spells out the distinctive elements of Rosa Luxemburg's version of leadership in which the leader both teaches and learns from "the masses," a relationship that is more pedagogical and maternal than authoritarian and patriarchal.

PART ONE

A world
of greatness

2

Strong man

A major thesis of the present work was anticipated by W. E. B. DuBois back in 1890 (as indicated by the fragment recorded in Foner, 1970, "Introduction"): the thesis of the "strong man" who renounces love as a way of being strong, who employs force as a way of "advancing civilization;" the dangerous consequences of this idea(l) and of a state that patterns itself after this idea(l). In his graduation speech at Harvard, DuBois used the theme "Jefferson Davis as a representative of civilization" to develop this thesis. DuBois treated Jefferson Davis as a typical representative of "Teutonic civilization," an embodiment of the idea of the strong man (Foner, 1970, p. 1). According to DuBois:

> The Strong Man and his mighty Right Arm has become the Strong Nation with its armies. Under whatever guise, however, a Jefferson Davis may appear as man, as race, or as nation, his life can only logically mean this: the advance of a part of the world at the expense of the whole; the overweening sense of the "I" and the consequent forgetting of the "Thou" (DuBois, 1970).

DuBois' thesis of the strong man has resonances with Max Weber's ideas of manliness and national greatness. The relationship between I and Thou (a relationship that Martin Buber makes central to his own work) that is repressed by the strong man has been reconceptualized by Jessica Benjamin (1988) as one of mutual recognition. Benjamin argues that the desire for recognition is the fundamental motivating force of social life. She describes how instead of this desire leading to a world of mutual recognition, under conditions of patriarchal society this desire takes two perverse forms: desire to control and dominate, which she links to sadism and I link to the strong man complex, and its complementary form, desire to serve and submit, which she links to masochism and I to the "loving woman" complex.

This gender polarity assumes and (re)produces a patriarchal splitting of public life and private life into symbolic domains with the public world characterized by masculine activity from which feminine maternal activities of nurturance, care, responsiveness to feelings and so on must, in principle, be excluded. Creation of the modern depersonalized masculine public world and the modern depoliticized private sphere makes possible a modern version of the strong man and the loving woman.

23

Political thinking

I became concerned about the corollary of the strong man and his mighty right arm – the strong nation and its army – in the 1970s at a time when American foreign policy under the direction of then secretary of state, Henry Kissinger, seemed to resonate with the political implications I was seeing in Weber's thought. Many years later I discovered through Turner and Factor's book, *Max Weber and the Dispute over Reason and Value*, that in fact there was a definite and strong linkage between Weber's ideas and those of Henry Kissinger.

Hans Morgenthau, major political theorist of international relations, had been a strong influence on Kissinger. Morgenthau, in turn, had been strongly influenced by Weber's ideas. While in Munich preparing for his legal examinations in the 1920s, Morgenthau took a "seminar on Max Weber's politics and social philosophy based on the latter's political writings." Morgenthau relates, "Weber's political thought possessed all the intellectual and moral qualities I had looked for in vain in the contemporary literature inside and outside the universities" (1977, pp. 6–7, quoted by Turner and Factor, 1984, p. 169).

In the view of Turner and Factor, the core of Morgenthau's position is his recapitulation of the distinctive Weberian argument showing the existence of rationally irresolvable conflicts. Morgenthau opposed political liberalism and what he called legalism in foreign policy. He espoused the view that international politics is an unending struggle for survival and power (1977, p. 42, cited by Turner and Factor, 1984, p. 170). For Morgenthau, legalism fails to understand the character of political struggle as a struggle of interests; "legality" can only be a cover for this struggle, a cover that obscures from us and deceives us about the facts of interest. "What is obvious in . . . claims to justice – be it 'just' wage, 'justice' for an ethnic minority, or the 'justice' of a war – is the coincidence of the claim to justice with the self interest of the claimant" (Morgenthau, 1974, p. 164, quoted by Turner and Factor, 1984, p. 171). Morgenthau sees struggles for self-interest as the essential, universal, overriding feature of political life.

Weber himself knew and respected many people genuinely concerned about ethical issues and issues of justice from more than a self-interested perspective. Furthermore, he often defended the underdog and was very sensitive to issues of honor. Nevertheless, his emphasis on "realism" and the need to suspend ethical considerations when dealing with political "realities," the need to subordinate ethical concerns to national interests (reasons of state), his emphasis on struggles for power and greatness, ends up being not very different from Morgenthau's position.

Morgenthau repeats the same argument with respect to liberalism:

Liberalism, as Morgenthau understood it, is the belief that matters of policy are open to rational reconciliation both domestically and between nations. . .Against the "liberal" point of view, Weber and Morgenthau took the reductive view that politics is not "public reason" or about "just government," as it appears to be, but is struggle (Turner and Factor, 1984, p. 172).

This view of politics as struggles for power is the basis of what is called political realism. Weber may be considered the social theorist *par excellence* of contemporary "realism." Jean Bethke Elshtain, a feminist scholar, explains that the sub-discipline of political science called international relations has long been dominated by this tradition of discourse called realism. Two of the classic exemplars of realism are Machiavelli and Hobbes. Elshtain explains that "Realism's hegemony means that alternatives to realism are evaluated *from the standpoint of realism*, cast into a bin labeled 'idealism' which, for the realist, is more or less synonymous with dangerous if well-intentioned naivete" (Elshtain, 1986, p. 104).

Realism presumes a world of sovereign states, each seeking either to enhance or secure its own power. . .Struggle is endemic to the system and force is the court of last resort. It cannot be otherwise for states exist in a condition of anarchy in relation to one another. Wars will and must occur because there is nothing to prevent them (ibid., p. 104).

Elshtain argues that realism exaggerates certain features of the human condition and downgrades or ignores others:

Interpreting realist texts from a vantage point informed by feminist concerns, one is struck by the suppression and denial of female images and female-linked imperatives. Thomas Hobbes, for example, describes a world of hostile monads whose relations are dominated by fear, force and instrumental calculation (ibid., pp. 104–5).

Both exchange theory and contract theory similarly assume a world of monads. Feminists like Hartsock (1984) and Held (1987) challenge those theories by calling attention to the different kind of relationship involved in mothering.

Nancy Hartsock (1984) also shows how eros and power are deeply connected. She sees eros as involving three aspects relevant to politics: relations with or connection to others, the role of sensuality and the body in political

25

life, issues of creativity and generation. In each area, she contends, masculine eroticism which forms part of military and political valor "is defined in such a way that connections with others take only the form of competition for dominance, the importance of the body is systematically denied, and creativity and generation are recast [into] a struggle to cancel death" (Hartsock, 1984, p. 125).[1]

Hartsock points out that, for the ancients,

> the realm of politics, the public realm, both depends on and exists only in opposition to the private realm, that is, the household. One can only be a citizen by being head of a household. . .the realm of freedom and leisure inhabited by citizens depends on the existence of a realm of necessity populated by women, slaves and laborers – but defined in essence by its female nature (Hartsock, 1984, p. 148).

Similarly, we could say that political realism depends on and exists only in opposition to another reality, the reality of women's lives in the private sphere. This thesis suggests that social and political theory presupposes historical relations of domination between public and private life and between masculinity and femininity.

Marianne Weber's biography of her husband bears out the close connections between Weber's social theorizing, his politics and his masculinity. We can understand the idea(l)s of the strong man and the strong state as ones that develop both biographically and historically. I provide below some biographical and historical background to Weber's thought.

Max Weber was subjected to his family's own particular form of patriarchal parenting and developed his own unique responses to it, including his conception of manliness. Martin Green contrasts Weber, "the patriarchal man," with D. H. Lawrence, the "matriarchal man" (not to be confused with a feminist man); one chose "the style of the world of men, the other those of the world of Woman" (1974, p. 102). Green calls Weber "the Brutus of patriarchy, the virtuous rebel" (ibid., p. 67). He, Green, explains the paradox of Weber, "the patriarchal man," supporting the liberation of women by relating how the women's movement appealed "to the reformist wing of the patriarchal mind" (ibid., p. 128).

Weber's biography

By examining Marianne Weber's biographical study we gain a rare glimpse into the psychodynamics of family life traced through three generations as filtered through the female and feminist perspectives of Helene and Marianne

Weber (Max's mother and wife respectively). Because Weber's mother, and possibly Weber himself, believed that Weber resembled in character and personality his maternal grandfather, Fallenstein, I begin with Marianne Weber's description of this forebear:

> He had an abundance of manly strength, a dynamic spirit, a puritanical outlook, and a crusty frankness, coupled with a passionate, easily inflamed temper, which was, however, controlled by chivalry and a childlike softheartedness toward weaker persons, particularly women and children (Weber, 1975, p. 2).

Of course this description is not based on first-hand acquaintance. It is the myth of the grandfather that was passed down and fashioned by members of the family, especially by Helene Weber, Max's mother. This description places Fallenstein's qualities in a somewhat favorable light.

Nevertheless, Fallenstein is described as a stern moralist believing in the maxim "I ought, therefore I can." "Anger frequently made the veins on his forehead stand out. Toward his sons in particular he was a strict demanding father." But "[the] little girls, like all weaker persons, usually found him gentle, yet he also tried to toughen them, using educational methods that today seem barbaric. To cure a headache, for example, he would hold their heads under the cold stream from the water pump early in the morning" (ibid., p. 5). Later we learn that his daughter, Max Weber's mother, was delicate and subject to frequent headaches as a child. Despite the gentler attitude toward the girls we are given many examples of his "barbaric" treatment of them. "Yet they loved their father more than they feared him. . .The sons, however, escaped his rule as soon as they could; three went overseas, and another ran away. Their father never saw them again" (ibid.).

By juxtaposing a reference to Fallenstein as "the old Lutzow corpsman," with his being a "strict moralist," Marianne Weber suggests a connection between his military background and his mode of parenting. In addition to his background as a corpsman, Marianne Weber provides other background on the childhood of this patriarchal figure whose own grandfather had been an assistant principal of a *Gymnasium* and whose father was "the sometime director" of a pedagogical seminary. I assume that these men ran their schools with strict patriarchal discipline. She reports that as the eldest son, born in 1790, Fallenstein "was his parents' darling and bone of contention. He preserved the painful childhood recollection of fleeing from their squabbles. . .His father. . .began drinking, and suddenly deserted his family. He was never heard from again. . .His wife was left in dire poverty with several children." Her son grew up as an orphan living with strangers, "but he overcame all hardships" (ibid., p. 2).

In quoting a description of Fallenstein, "Because of his abundance of strength, everything about him verged on the excessive," Marianne relates that these words apply to her husband, Max Weber, as well (ibid., p. 13). She also describes Fallenstein's father (Max's great-grandfather) as having "an overabundance of undisciplined energy" (ibid., p. 2). Marianne Weber uses the term, "heroic severity" to describe Fallenstein's judgments of his children's "inadequacies," the extreme ethical demands "he thought he could bring to bear on his children's development" (ibid., p. 5). Apparently nobody in Max Weber's family, least of all his mother who loved her father, or Max's grandmother, Fallenstein's wife, thought to denounce Fallenstein's treatment of his young children as cruel and brutal.

Because such treatment is legitimized by a culture that treats children as the property of their fathers, I call it patriarchal parenting. Mothers engage in their own forms of patriarchal parenting no less than fathers. Nevertheless, the relationship between infant and mother (primary caregiver) involves mutual responsiveness. I call that maternal care. Only an interactive relationship of mutual attunement, mutual responsiveness and nurturance enables the infant and young child to develop. Although mothering can include attempts at controlling, as Freud pointed out with respect to the anal stage and the development of sadism, a patriarchal relationship of ruling and controlling will not by itself succeed in the complex task of mothering an infant or toddler.

Helene's mother, Fallenstein's second wife, described her life with Fallenstein as being very unhappy although she "sensed" that he was "a much warmer person than Gervinus. . .For example, he agreed to my going to church. . .and he did not pour cold water over me, as G. did with his wife" (ibid., p. 14). The latter comment reveals the patriarchal treatment that was not uncommon for these wives to receive. Gervinus, to whom Emilie refers, was a famous historian who, with his wife, "a motherly friend" to Helene, lived on the upper floor of the Fallenstein house. After Fallenstein's death Gervinus became the daughters' fatherly friend and teacher, a man they adored. When Helene was 16 he attempted to rape her. It is unclear whether he succeeded. She almost immediately thereafter became engaged to Max Weber, Sr, a man with a sunny disposition more than seven years her senior to whom she confided and to whom she turned for protection and escape. She was apparently traumatized by the incident with Gervinus who continued to harass and upset her emotionally and from whom she fled.

Patriarchal parenting

According to Marianne Weber, Helene Weber communicated to her son, Max, not only a view of sex as sinful (justified only by the procreation of children) but an anxious concern for both his moral and physical development. As a young child he contracted meningitis which affected him for years. There was a danger of his dying or becoming an imbecile. Helene tended him constantly and could not understand any mother entrusting her child to strangers for more than an hour a day. "She regarded trips taken by parents without their children as frivolous 'temptations of God.' She used to carry the 5-year-old boy into the ocean, thinking that this would make him stronger," but his screaming caused the other bathers to demand a stop to the treatment. "Even as a grown man, Max Weber did not forget the terrors of this procedure" (ibid., p. 33).

At home, Helene ran upstairs and downstairs serving her husband and her children. She was up at six in the morning to wash the children's diapers and even when the children were beyond the preschool age she slept only five or six hours a night, although she frequently had an irresistible desire to sleep during the day. Max Sr expected to find happiness, comfort and service at home. However, after thirteen years of a seemingly happy marriage, when Max Jr was 12 years old, a young daughter died. The mother was inconsolable; she wanted to follow her to "eternal rest." The father, Max, Sr, soon left the mother alone in her "life-and-death struggle." He desired inner and outer well-being, a comfortable bourgeois standard of living, social status, and the like. He did not want to suffer (ibid., pp. 34–8).

Marianne Weber reports that although Max Weber's mother, with her delicate constitution, suffered when she was a child from Fallenstein's treatment, she nevertheless adopted her father's principles for her own life and the rearing of her children. Marianne described Helene, Max Weber's mother, as endowed with emotionality, courage, religiosity, energy, ethical passion and selfless kindness. From her father, Helene is reputed to have inherited "an iron will, activity, a heroic moral stance, excitability and fiery dynamism" (ibid., p. 17). Despite Helene's loving devotion to her children, she had no real communication with them at all during the years of their development. Max Weber confided that he held her in secret contempt; he called it his "intellectual arrogance." Marianne explains that "the parents were. . .too closely attached to the authoritarian tradition. . .Firstborn children frequently are the object of excessive moralizing and ill-tempered censure" (ibid., p. 60). His grandmother, Emilie, who lived in Heidelberg and hence did not get to be with him very much, described Max Weber Jr as an "inwardly *vehement* person, and somewhat *reserved*. Yet he has a good mind and also goodwill (that is, if someone else's will has not annoyed him). . .I believe (and I tell you this in confidence) he needs to be treated with a little more *love* so he can break away from himself" (ibid., p. 61).

Marianne Weber observes that Helene "without being aware of it, and in all humility. . .struggled like her father to shape the young souls in her own image. . .She tended to moralize and sometimes rebuked the children in front of strangers – something that her sensitive eldest son greatly

29

resented" (ibid., p. 61). (Alice Miller would see this as a humiliation of the child.)

According to Marianne Weber, the adolescent children adopted attitudes of opposition to their mother in part to escape her attempts to control and change them and in part to escape their feelings of inferiority. Helene was constantly judging herself and others by the highest moral standards. Marianne Weber reports with sympathy for Helene that the latter was unable to make her own children truly happy in their growing years or to communicate with them. Her eldest son in particular (Max Weber) maintained an aloofness which made the relationship even more difficult and painful to the mother (ibid., p. 62).

Max Weber Sr came from a complacent, bourgeois family background; his father was a linen dealer for whom making money was neither an end in itself nor a sign of success, but primarily a means to a comfortable life that was appropriate to one's class. Accordingly the pace of work was slow. This was the "early capitalist" fashion that Max Weber contrasted with the later capitalist spirit, which was influenced by the Protestant ethic. Despite the apparent amiability of family life, the women in particular were under the influence of the Protestant orthodoxy prevalent there and displayed a sterner moralistic attitude than the more flexible men (ibid., p. 25).

To Max Weber Sr any occasion for fighting and action meant an enhancement of life. As a young man and a liberal lawyer, he was caught up in the political excitement of the times. As a 12-year-old boy he had lived through the days of 1848, and their fervor was still burning within him. The excitement of the times revolved around the figure of Bismarck who became Prime Minister. The latter prepared the Prussian state for military expansion, Great Power politics, and German unification under the leadership of Prussia (ibid., p. 27).

Max Weber Sr differed from his wife in never succumbing to self-doubt or introspection, while she "plunged into the depths" every day. "He categorically refused to recognize the serious problems of life." His cheerful openness to the world, his ability and desire to look on the bright side, spared Max Weber Jr the uncomfortable feeling of his own inadequacy, and had a positive affect on the son who was naturally attached to his father. Nevertheless, Weber Sr did not like young people to hold opinions different from his own, and when there were conflicts always felt he was in the right. Unfortunately, "he was too much the traditional, patriarchal paterfamilias, too convinced of his own superiority and his inalienable right to respect and authority. . .the way he let his wife wait on him – drew secret criticism from the children, although they followed his example" (ibid., p. 63). His nephew called him "a real despot," but a person with a rich mind and heart who cared a great deal about the people around him (ibid., p. 49).

I present these elements from Max Weber's biography and family history not to engage in psychoanalytic speculations but to suggest in broad outlines how Weber's life was affected by a patriarchal heritage and environment. That environment could not help but contribute to the shaping of his own thinking, both in his reaction to and his absorption of it. He was raised by a self-sacrificing, overly concerned and controlling, doubt-ridden mother who held up to her children absolute moral standards that they found coercive and impossible to meet, while she herself resented her husband's tyrannical ways but also held him in contempt for his lack of spiritual concerns.

Both parents were extremely demanding and relatively insensitive to their children's feelings. On the part of his mother this is despite and because of great self-sacrificing love and concern for each of her children's "immortal soul." The parents were unable to respond with respect and sympathy to their children's feelings. The parents themselves were products of patriarchal parenting to which they were reacting. We must assume that Weber's inner tensions, conflicts and struggles, his attempts to come to terms with his own experiences, contribute to the unique idea(l)s and perspective that inform his social and political thought. His ideas cannot and should not be attributed in some reductionist or determinist way to his childhood experiences, but the outlook that informs his thinking develops in part as a response to those experiences; also in part as a response to the broader social environment.

Social context

Max Weber Jr grew up in an atmosphere of political excitement. The leaders of the National Liberal Party frequented his house. He daily heard stories about Parliament, the party and Bismarck, who was greatly admired. Even as a 6-year-old boy he was greatly impressed by the outbreak of war in 1870. His wife believed that he was shaped for life by the experience he absorbed:

> the tremendous tension before the decision; the naive belief in the justice of the German cause; the joyful seriousness of a belligerent nation willing to make sacrifices in order to gain the position of a great power; then the overwhelming victory celebration and the proud exultation over the finally achieved unity of the Reich (ibid., p. 40).

He was a withdrawn, reserved youth who precociously and voraciously read philosophy, literature, history and political thought and reflected with great seriousness about historical, philosophical and especially political matters. Although he could not or would not share his feelings, develop close friendships and by his own admission was inept in conversation (ibid., p. 58) he could become passionately and animatedly engaged by political ideas.

The patriarchal context of Weber's background included not just the political values and social structure of Germany, and not just the intimate experiences of family life and religious values, but the everyday life of a young man growing up, including his school and fraternity life. Marianne Weber writes of her husband's college years:

> Fraternity life greatly influenced his inward disposition as well as his outward demeanor. . . .The brothers did not associate with friendly warmth, but were cold as ice toward one another. Friendships were regarded as unmanly. Everyone kept his distance but paid close attention to what the others were doing. There was mutual criticism as well as friction – all decreed by an ideal of manliness that attached the greatest importance to formal bearing. . .Anyone who managed to hold his own within this community felt extremely secure, superior, and blasé toward the rest of the world (ibid., 1975, p. 70).

She writes further that the result of Weber's military training "was a great admiration for the 'machine' as well as a martial and patriotic mentality that made him long for an opportunity someday to take to the field at the head of his company" (ibid., p. 78).

Weber's own predilections were strongly influenced by his experiences in the Germany of his time, experiences that were not unique to him. The ideal of manliness that was current at that time among members of the aristocratic and upper middle classes certainly reflected the political culture of Germany, but that ideal in turn influenced and was reflected in German politics. The emphasis on this version of manliness, the aversion to friendship and warmth as "unmanly," was related to an exaggerated emphasis on personal honor. Marianne quotes Max, "There were no *problems* for us; we were convinced that we could somehow solve everything that arose by means of a duel" (ibid., p. 70).

Talcott Parsons describes pre-Nazi Germany and the importance of the Prussian officers' corps with its connection to the Junker nobility. He refers to the highly distinctive style of life carried on by the officers' corps. This style of life "was in sharp contrast with everything 'bourgeois,'" and its most conspicuous symbol of this difference was the duel and its attendant code of honor. "The most important criterion of eligibility to belong as a social equal was *Satisfaktionsfaehigkeit*, acceptability as an adversary in an 'affair of honor'" (Parsons, 1954, p. 107).

Parsons describes the German civil service which constituted the highest prestige element in the bourgeoisie and which adopted an attitude of social superiority to other bourgeois elements. The devotion to duty characteristic of the civil service was combined with a strong sense of prerogative and authority which would not brook a "democratic" type of control (ibid., p. 109). Parsons also identifies the ideological symbols of this system with Lutheranism for which "This world is dominated by sin, mitigated only by the restraining influence of ordained authority. Society is not and can never be a Kingdom of God on Earth, but is fundamentally a vale of tears" (ibid.). This pattern favors political "realism," but its "benevolent patriarchalism" slips into a harsh authoritarianism, a cynical pursuit of power in defiance of the welfare of the masses of people; and government is considered a grim business, of which war is a very typical and essential part (ibid., pp. 109–10).

The culture at the time was characterized by formality to an extent unknown in America. Furthermore, occupational association and friendship were specifically segregated. American informality would have seemed improper and undignified to most Germans. Relations between men and women involved masculine superiority, with German men dominating and authoritarian, expecting submissiveness and dependency on the part of their wives, particularly in the middle classes. The *Hausfrau* was the antithesis of the "emancipated" woman. Her life, concentrated on the home, on husband and children, with little if any participation in the outside world, in community affairs, or even in cultural life, was more confined than that of the American housewife (ibid., pp. 113–14). Moreover, there was a far lower development in Germany of "romantic love." "The kind of attachment to a woman which we idealize in the romantic pattern, would to most Germans seem possible only to a soft, effeminate type of man, certainly not to the heroic type" (ibid., p. 122).

The relationships of youth were "sentimentalized" in a different pattern: "The Maedchen is more simple, sweet, and submissive, and less glamorous" (ibid., p. 114). It should be noted that Max Weber's mother and wife combined elements of the upper-class "emancipated woman" with those of traditional German womanhood. Similarly, Weber's relationship with his wife combined elements of equality with traditional German patriarchalism.

Along with a sharper segregation of the roles of men and women went a strong tendency to romanticize the relationship of men to one another. On one level, *Bruederschaft*, with its ritual oath and its symbolic use of *Du*, seemed to be invested with a very intense emotional significance. On another, comradeship – the romantic idealization of solidary groups of young men (sometimes with at least an undercurrent of homosexuality) – with soldiers in the field as the prototype, may have been the counterpart to our society's "romanticization of the cross-sex love relationship" (ibid., p. 115).

Parsons engages in some interesting sociological psychoanalyzing in describing the pre-Nazi German culture. He explains that with economic, political and social instability comes psychological insecurity that leads to the formation of wishes or idealized hopes that cannot be realized. These tend to be projected outside creating "irrealism" or "romanticism." The Anglo-Saxon world has a smaller predisposition to romanticism than Germany because Puritanism canalized the orientation to action into active responsibility for translating ideals into reality. Associated with this Anglo-Saxon tradition was an attraction to "utopianism" as well as the romanticism of personal "success" and romantic love. In Germany, he claims, there was a stronger tendency to romanticism, an impression confirmed by the fact that Germany, when "not dominated by a radical political movement, was known as the land of poets, philosophers and dreamers, of religious mysticism, of music" (ibid., p. 121). Neither the romanticism of heterosexual love nor that of personal success, but a romanticism of national glory, military values and the "heroic" ideal of the fighting man, found fertile ground in pre-Nazi Germany (ibid., pp. 122–3). This personal and social background contributed to Weber's conception of manliness.

Manliness and politics

I use the term "manliness" to refer to the association of status honor, gender honor, and self-identity with certain ideals that are supposed to distinguish men from children and from women. I also distinguish manliness from masculinity. The ideals of independence, courage and strength constitute masculinity in the modern Western tradition. Weber recognized that when these ideals of masculinity serve no cause outside of the individual but become ends in themselves, they tend to constitute foolishness rather than manliness. On the other hand, the employment of strength and power in the service of some cause he celebrates as manliness.

The display of strength and power as virtues in themselves he disparages as childish bullying and braggadocio. The emphasis on spirit and inspiration distinguishes manliness from masculinity. That is, some element of charisma is inherent in manliness. Weber explicitly referred to "the inner charismatic qualities that make a leader" and attributes these to commitment to a calling (1946, p. 113). Masculinity (concern for strength, power, courage) as an end in itself expressed in vanity and boastfulness, he devalues and condemns, especially when it appears in the person of a political leader.

For Weber, manliness is mostly identified with politics. He valued the vocation of politics, and in his famous speech on that theme exhorted his audience to respect and espouse politics as a vocation (ibid., pp. 77–128). To achieve this end, he called on the virtues of manliness which he contrasted with attitudes and behavior that are old-womanish. He gave this speech as a way of rallying his compatriots following the defeat of Germany in the First World War, a time when many if not all of those in the audience may have been disgusted with politics.

Weber also used "old women" as a term of denigration years earlier in his response to social policy aimed at protecting the bourgeoisie by suppressing the working class. He referred to the law that punished a striker for putting pressure on those who stayed at work as "a law for *old women*, a protection for cowardice" (cited by Beetham, 1974, pp. 168–9, italics added). Trade unions provided for the working class a "guarantee of a political, *manly*, free independence of outlook" (ibid., p. 169, italics added). Weber's attitude toward the bourgeoisie's fear of too much trade union power and the bourgeoisie's preference for bureaucratic regulation as the solution to social conflict was expressed in a slogan of the time: "Everything for the people, nothing by the people" (ibid., p. 168). Nevertheless, although he supported trade unions he rejected socialism.

Another instance of Weber's use of the feminine as a denigration of men occurs in a letter he wrote to Gertrud Baumer, a leader, along with Marianne Weber, of the conservative branch of the women's movement in Germany. Baumer, a staunch nationalist, opposed pacifism and internationalism, especially in the women's movement. She was later to become a supporter of the Nazis.[2] Weber wrote her, "The pacifism of American 'ladies' (of both sexes) is truly the most deadly cant" (cited by Roth, 1988, p. xxxvi).

Just as he supported trade unions for guaranteeing a political, "manly" independence of outlook, Weber opposed and was sensitive to any form of servility, any hint of subservience, any condition of powerlessness or weakness among men. Servility and subservience were signs of cowardliness, a fear of risking one's life, a willingness to surrender one's independence and honor in the face of threat. He associated such behavior with old women and "ladies." Given his extreme sensitivity to honor, independence of spirit, and integrity, his sensitivity to any suggestion of cowardice, we can see how Weber could be seen to epitomize manliness. His quickness to perceive affronts to his honor and to break off relationships with friends could also be seen as eccentric. Nevertheless we can understand how he could appear as a heroic figure able to inspire younger men[3] and how he could appear as a chivalric figure, a defender of women and feminism (although he rejected socialist feminism and the radical feminism of the time). Weber's liberalism and chivalry in his politics and his personal life can be understood as compatible and consistent with his conception of manliness.

Proving oneself

Weber was a foe of patriarchal relationships not only within the family but within the German state and German industry. He not only despised patriarchal oppression of women, he deplored the "authoritarian mentality . . .which grips the state and the system of industrial relations in present day Germany" (cited by Beetham, 1974, p. 168).

Weber distinguished between greatness and leadership on the one side and patriarchalism and authoritarianism on the other. Weber's contrast between two kinds of discipline helps to illuminate this distinction. Weber makes the comparison between American Protestant sects and the German Protestant church. "Not only did the sects reject all earthly authorities, but the continuous pressure they exerted on the individual *to prove himself* in the possession of distinctive personal qualities, led to the 'inner isolation of the individual' and the 'maximum development of his powers towards the external world' (ibid., pp. 206–7, my italics).

Weber contrasts the religious situation in the United States that promoted individualism, rejection of authority and maximum development of a person's powers with the situation prevailing in Germany. There the church was a "compulsory association" as opposed to the sects in which membership was contingent upon proving oneself. The sects in America, and the voluntary associations to which they gave rise, called forth individualism and independence of spirit in the form of inner discipline. These are the qualities that make for greatness and leadership in Weber's view. The church in Germany in contrast fostered submissiveness and external obedience, conceived as duty and enacted in "officialdom." Weber makes the following analogy: the ethical discipline of the sects which required the individual to "prove himself" (*sic*) was "related to the discipline of the authoritarian church as the rational training and selection of qualities is to command and punishment" (ibid., p. 207). In other words, one promoted inner discipline, the other dutiful obedience.

The struggle to prove oneself and thereby develop one's powers is critical to Weber's conception of manliness and greatness. A formulation of conflict as a means of proving oneself (one's manhood?) and of developing valuable strengths and qualities distinguishes Weber's conflict theory from Hobbes' and Weber's conception of the great leader from authoritarianism. Although Weber's analysis of the implications of conflict differs from that of Hobbes (Weber found conflict stimulating and invigorating), his view of the inherently conflictual nature of social life resembles that of Hobbes. Similarly, although Weber's notion of great leadership is not the same as authoritarianism, his conception of great leadership does not rule out authoritarian or patriarchal consequences.

Weber valued the heroic personality that takes risks and thrives on competitive struggles and conflict. Striving to prove oneself develops strengths and greatness. Hence competitive conflict for Weber was not merely an unavoidable feature of social life or capitalism; it was a desirable feature. Weber's valuing of conflict, struggle and striving, his version of the "strong man," influenced his sociological perspective as well as his political perspective.

Decentering social theory

Although W. E. B. DuBois introduced the thesis of the strong man as the model for the strong state and related the latter to slavery and imperialism, he did not explore the patriarchal origins of "the strong man." Nevertheless, DuBois' work points to this relationship between patriarchy and the strong man. His work also points the way for recentering social theory by showing the centrality of that which is posited as marginal or peripheral, the other that is not treated as a thou: the Third World, developing nations, minority groups, and I would add women.

Anticipating the title of Bell Hooks' black feminist challenge to white feminism, *From Margin to Center*, and anticipating the recent theoretical moves within contemporary social theory, especially feminist theory, DuBois showed how differently the world appears when we move the margin to center. I am referring to his work on Africa in which he shows how the colonization of Africa as well as the slave trade are central to an understanding of European history, economic development and culture.

On reading DuBois (1965), not only does Africa become central to an understanding of the West, but our understanding itself becomes decentered. Our interest is redirected from the development of the West to the brutalization of Africa. After reading DuBois (1965) not only can we no longer see Africa as supplementary or marginal to Western history, we can no longer see the West by itself as central to an understanding of itself, of ourselves. Its pride and its identity, our pride and our identity (as bearers and inheritors of modernity and civilization) have been fractured. We are not even central to ourselves.

We can no longer see ourselves as having an independent identity. We are forced, by his work, to see ourselves in terms of our relationship to Africa. Our imperialism, colonialism, and enslavement of Africans is inseparable from our identity and our "greatness." We can no longer deny the relations of power, violence and brutality that we have concealed from ourselves or justified as necessary for the achievement of greatness. We can no longer avoid a confrontation with our conception of greatness and the consequences of this greatness.

DuBois explains and analyzes the source of modern Western greatness and wealth as follows:

> This wealth was built, in Africa especially, upon diamonds and gold, copper and tin, ivory and mahogany, palm oil and cocoa, seeds extracted and grown, beaten out of the blood-stained bodies of the natives, [and] transported to Europe (DuBois, 1965, p. 23).

Furthermore, he asserts,

> There was no Nazi atrocity – concentration camps, wholesale maiming and murder, defilement of women or ghastly blasphemy of childhood – which the Christian civilization of Europe had not long been practicing

37

against colored folk in all parts of the world in the name of and for the defense of a Superior Race born to rule the world (ibid.).

DuBois draws the connection between such atrocities and the idea(l) of modern greatness and wealth, the idea(l) wealthy gentleman:

a man well bred and of meticulous grooming, of knightly sportsmanship and invincible courage even in the face of death; but one who did not hesitate to use machine guns. . . and to cheat "niggers"; an ideal of sportsmanship which reflected the Golden Rule and yet contradicted it. . .by indulging in lying, murder, theft, rape, deception and degradation (ibid.).

Writing in the same time period as DuBois, Weber was concerned with the fate of the strong, independent man in our modern depersonalized world. He was concerned with whether the image and idea(l) of the strong man could survive as a realistic possibility given the rationalization and modernization of the world. Earlier in his life and career, he was concerned with whether the image and idea(l) of Germany as a great nation state could survive as a realistic possibility without adopting an aggressive, imperialistic but realistic and responsible foreign policy (responsible in the sense of not antagonizing other nations out of realistic concern for consequences). In both instances, the concern is twofold: to prevent emasculation and to strive to attain some ideal.

DuBois shows how our notions of Western civilization and greatness are premised on brutality and debasement; he shows the foreshadowing of Nazism in our historical acts of genocide against natives and rape of other continents. We learn vividly and graphically how central to Western greatness was slavery and the slave trade. Born just a few years after Weber and reflecting on the same world situation as does Weber, DuBois' writing raises for me the question, to what extent are Weber's notions of manly greatness and national greatness related to DuBois' thesis of the strong man?

Furthermore, like W. E. B. DuBois and Karl Marx who decenter modern thought (DuBois does this by making Africa central to our understanding of European wealth and greatness; Marx does this by making the proletariat central to our understanding of capital), I would like to do the same by showing how the idea(l) of the strong man and strong nation assumes and requires the subordination of women and women's life world, how this subordination which appears peripheral to the strong man and the strong nation is *central* to both. Just as we can no longer see the West or capitalism in the same way as we did before reading DuBois or Marx, it is my hope that in the same way we will no longer see modern Western thought as represented by Max Weber in the same way we did before confronting that thought – centered on the idea of the strong man and heroic greatness – from a woman-centered perspective.

Notes

1 Developing a similar theme, Benjamin (1988) describes how the masculine desire for recognition, which is an erotic as well as emotional and cognitive matter, is perverted into desire to control and dominate.
2 Claudia Koontz (1986 and 1987) discusses the support among German women and women's groups for the Nazi regime. She stresses the danger and power of nostalgia for separate masculine and feminine spheres. Richard J. Evans (1976) details the different groups, and the differences among their views, within the feminist movement in Germany 1894–1933.
3 Karl Loewenstein (1966, 1965) describes leaving his first encounter with Max Weber:

> When at last I took my leave. . .I was literally drunk. I was at a turning point in my life. From that moment on, I had taken the oath of fealty to him; I had become his vassal. . .It is a manly face, something elemental, at times actually titanic, emanates from him. . .His volcanic temperament erupts again and again. . .Max Weber was a daemonic personality. Even in routine matters, there was something incalculable, explosive about him. You never knew when the inner volcano would erupt (pp. 94, 98, 101).

3

Conflict, action and greatness

Max Weber's theory of social life is a conflict theory.[1] This theory is intimately linked with the idea(l) of a strong man and heroic greatness in the public world. I argue that Weber's conflict theory and its political implications constitute a one-sided, man-centered perspective, one that denies or represses (or marginalizes) the erotic and the feminine, or that aspect of social life associated with women. This conflict theory of social life engenders the liberal values of individual freedom and greatness, but it also engenders illiberal values of imperialism, nationalism and militarism. For Weber *conflict* is not only inevitable but necessary and desirable because it stimulates *action* and fosters *greatness*.

Conflict

Weber defined conflict as follows: "A social relationship will be referred to as 'conflict' (Kampf) insofar as action is oriented intentionally to carrying out the actor's own will against the resistance of the other party or parties" ([1921-22] 1978, p. 38). Conflict translates into a struggle for power: "Power (macht) is the probability that one actor within a social relationship will be in a position to carry out his own will despite resistance, regardless of the basis on which this probability rests" (ibid., p. 53).

In the inaugural address that Weber gave early in his career, he stressed the theme that "struggle and conflict form a central and permanent feature of social life – struggle between groups, classes, nations, as well as the conflict between differing values" (Beetham, 1974, p. 41). A similar statement from one of Weber's last writings demonstrates the continuity of this theme: "Conflict cannot be excluded from social life. . .'Peace' is nothing more than a change in the form of the conflict" (Weber, [1917] 1949, pp. 26–7). Not only in world politics or domestic politics, but even in the most intimate relations of personal life and the deepest recesses of the human soul, conflict and struggle are endemic. The

40

appearance of peace and contentment is merely the result of repression and domination.

The inevitability of conflict, especially conflict among groups, rules out the ideals of peace and happiness as unrealistic. "For the dreamers of peace and happiness," warned Weber, "there stands written over the door of mankind's unknown future 'surrender all hope'" (cited by Beetham, 1974, p. 42). Weber saw conflict as a "fact of life against which the ideals and values of others should be tested for their realism" (ibid.). Determining actions in accordance with ideals and values that fail to acknowledge the ubiquitous and irremediable character of conflict would leave an actor open to the charge of being unrealistic. Furthermore, with regard to the relationship between social policy and happiness, Weber asserts:

Our aim is. . .to create conditions, not that men may feel happier, but that under the necessity of the unavoidable struggle for existence the best in them – those physical and spiritual characteristics which we want to preserve for the nation – will remain protected (ibid.).

This passage is remarkable not least for its stress on social policy that aims at preserving *for the nation* certain characteristics among its people as opposed to social policy that aims at fostering the general well being or happiness of its people:

Conditions of struggle were to be welcomed because they fostered qualities. . .that Weber regarded as desirable. Indeed, for Weber the highest values could only be developed through conflict – conflict with other individuals, or with other values, or 'struggle against the difficulties which life presents' (ibid.).

Weber's belief in the value of struggle did not extend to a belief that the qualities "selected" are necessarily the most desirable. His concern was to create the social conditions that would enable the most desirable to emerge. Weber was clear that social conditions on their own could just as often favor a social type that is inferior culturally or physically, but, nevertheless, best able to adapt to those conditions.

The nature of the conflict or struggle engendered by a given social structure or social order determines the qualities that will be developed in the individual or group. The struggle for existence may develop actors with a will to power, heroic actors and a dynamic social order or it may develop actors with a will to security, complacent actors and a static social order. These are the alternatives that Weber stressed.

He emphasized the need to analyze "the way in which different institutional and social structures encouraged and selected different types and qualities of person" (cited ibid., p. 102). Weber was concerned about particular qualities that he saw as contributing to social dynamism and national greatness. These qualities he associated with ideal manliness:

> Every type of social order, without exception, must, if one wishes to *evaluate* it, be assessed according to *which type of man* it gives the opportunity to rise to a position of superiority through the operation of the various objective and subjective selective factors. (cited ibid., p. 110, italic in original).

Wilhelm Hennis (1988) criticizes this translation. He proposes, instead, substituting human type (*menschlichen Typus*) for that of type of man or type of person, and proposes "the optimal chances of becoming the dominant type" for "opportunity to rise to a position of superiority." Hennis' translation changes the meaning of the passage from a concern with the kinds of *men* who rise to positions of *leadership* to a concern with the *dominance* of certain *types of human beings*. We can read Weber, as Hennis suggests, as saying that we can *evaluate* a social order on the basis of the human type that it promotes. This means that Weber assumed we all have certain values by which we can judge a type of human being, and hence the social order that promotes it, to be more or less desirable or valuable than another.

The values by which Weber evaluated social orders and types of human beings correspond with his idea(l)s of manliness. Bringing these values to his interpretation of different social orders could not help but color his description of those social orders. It is not that this can be avoided in some ideal notion of value-free cultural interpretation. But we can become conscious of the values that underlie perceptions, actions and relationships, including views of other people and other cultures. Weber believed that social science could show the consequences of certain values and how certain actions were either consistent or inconsistent with particular values. There was an inner tension and contradiction in his own values; that tension and contradiction (repression) is inherent in his conception of manliness.

Marx, too, can be said to believe that a social order can be evaluated on the basis of the human type that it promotes. But for Marx the human being is defined in terms of social relationships. Hence, a concern with the type of human being that is fostered by a given social order leads to a concern with the type of social relationships fostered by that social order. I am interested in the human type that Weber judges to be valuable, the set of social relationships necessary for that human type and the social order that promotes those social relationships and types of human beings.

For Weber, a given social order shapes the nature of the struggle and the conflict that produces a particular type of human being. These struggles and conflicts, in turn, shape the nature of the social order. The repression of conflict produces a stagnant social order; the expression of conflict, through competition and struggles for power, produces a dynamic social order. Conflict, which generates action, makes possible greatness.

Greatness and nations

Weber was concerned with both individual greatness – a great personality, a great leader – and national greatness – a great nation state, a great world power. He declared: "In my view it is not a policy of comfort and ease that we are after, but one of national greatness" (cited ibid., p. 136). Weber wrote of Germany's "duty" to be a power state, its responsibility to future generations, a responsibility to history for the future of world culture (ibid.).

Weber believed that every position, that of a power state as well as that of a parent, involves specific duties and responsibilities. A powerful nation state has different tasks than a "small people."

It is because we are a power state, and thus, in contrast to those "smaller" peoples, can throw our weight into the scales of history – it is because of this that there lies heavy on us this duty and obligation towards the future, to oppose the complete domination of the world by those two powers [Russia and England] (cited ibid., p. 137).

Being a power state, which meant being able to "throw our weight" into the scales of history, Germany had a duty and obligation to oppose the domination of the world by Russia and England. Germany, too, should play a role in the domination of the world. If Germany were to renounce this duty, it might as well have never become a unified nation state:

Were we to renounce this obligation, then the German Reich would become an expensive luxury . . .which we ought to renounce in favour of a small federation of politically powerless cantons. . .and return to cultivate the comfortable cultural values of a small people, values which ought always to have remained the meaning of our existence (cited ibid.).

A small people has different cultural values; its existence has a different meaning, a different set of tasks, than does the existence of a great power state:

It is naive to imagine that a people which is small in terms of numbers or power is any less "valuable" or "important" in the forum of world history. It simply has other tasks and thus other cultural possibilities. . .It is not only a question of the simple civic virtues and the possibility of a more

43

real democracy than is attainable in a great power state; it is also that the more intimate personal values, eternal ones at that, can only flourish in the soil of a community which makes no pretensions to political power. (cited ibid., p. 127).

We see here an irreconcilable conflict between the personal sphere and the political. The values of one require renouncing those of the other. Political power has a corrupting and destructive effect on intimate personal values and civic virtues. Thus a decisive and fruitful choice must be made between intimate eternal personal values and civic virtues on the one side, and political power on the other, a choice between being a smaller people and being a great power state.

This passage could serve as introduction to my thesis, that what Weber calls intimate, eternal, personal values are associated with civic virtues and "a more real democracy." These values and virtues cannot flourish within a state that aspires to political power. The tasks of a politically powerful state, in Weber's view, conflict with intimate personal values, such as love, that are central to the tasks of women's lives. Men who are actors in the public sphere of politics must renounce those values. Weber's solution requires segregating the tasks of women's lives from the tasks of the politically powerful state, a segregation of women's work from men's work and the repressing of the former by the latter.

The repression of the private sphere by the public sphere, of intimate personal values by impersonal political values, of civic virtues and a more real democracy by a state driven by lust for power (re)produces a patriarchal state. By the latter I mean not simply one in which men dominate women but one in which personal values of love and caring, the tasks and virtues assigned to the private world (for which women are mainly responsible), are repressed by politics and the desire for power associated with the public world (for which men are primarily responsible). The tasks and values of the public world come to define masculinity. These tasks and virtues for Weber must be premised on repression of the private world which defines femininity. Greatness requires the repression of love.

For Weber the ends of social policy "could never be merely improving the material position of the working class, but the 'development of those characteristics. . .which make for human greatness.'" Social policy should be aimed at protecting "what seems to us valuable in man: . . .personal responsibility, the deep aspiration for the moral and spiritual goods of mankind." However, for Weber the possession of these qualities were in inverse proportion to "a subjective feeling of happiness" (cited ibid., pp. 43–4). This is a remarkable view of life.

It would seem that the eternal personal values, civic virtues and "a more real democracy" correspond to the "moral and spiritual goods," the protection of which was to be the aim of social policy of the power state. But there is a contradiction between the ends of politics: moral and spiritual goods (domestic and civic virtues that can only be cultivated on the soil of community) and the means of politics: a strong power state. According to Weber's analysis, a great power state does not and cannot promote those virtues. The means preclude the end.

Although acknowledging the value and importance of "small peoples," Weber wanted Germany to have a voice in world affairs, and to be treated, as Beetham phrases it, "in a manner appropriate to her size." It was an affront to German honor to be treated otherwise. Thus, it was a question of honor, Weber wrote, that was at stake in the war, of Germany's claim "to have some share in deciding the future of world affairs" (cited ibid., p. 133).

Weber contrasted two different forms of influence on the part of nations and two different sources of honor. The contrast may be likened to that between influencing by example and influencing by intervention. Small nations have the opportunity of developing democracy, civic virtues, and the values of personal relationships as the source of their honor. As such they serve as exemplary societies, exemplifying the values and virtues from which others can learn and which others can emulate. These domestic or civic virtues may be compared with a female form of life. In both cases actors, out of a sense of powerlessness or mutuality, refrain from imposing their will as a way of directly influencing others. By not having the direct imposing of will as an option, or by renouncing that option, such actors develop the domestic and civic virtues of respect for others, mutual aid and so forth.

Great powers, on the other hand can and do directly influence others as well as history. As a force to be reckoned with, their actions and pronouncements have an immediate effect on the world and the future. Weber clearly favored the role of active agent in the world over that of inwardness. Similarly we can surmise that he valued masculine power over feminine virtues. In any case, he divides the world and its actors into two kinds: stronger and weaker, bigger and smaller, more powerful and less powerful.

Action and power

Marianne Weber, in her biography of her husband, provides some insightful observations about Weber the man. She says, "Conflict as such stimulated him, conveyed life to him" (Weber, 1975, p. 448). When he substituted for an important Berlin attorney, he found particularly satisfying the fact that the work demanded at the same time ingenuity, resoluteness and a fighting instinct. She reports, "He seemed to be a born *fighter and ruler* even more than a born thinker" (ibid., p. 166, italics added). He himself wrote to his mother that of all her children, he believed he had the "strongest innate

45

'martial' instincts" (ibid., p. 571). That his wife describes him as a born ruler is interesting. Weber's political sociology concerns the varieties of rulership, *Herrschaft*, a term which has been translated as both authority and domination.

Marianne Weber describes her husband's disposition as being "unmistakably toward an active rather than contemplative life." He was a strong-willed person who "longed for great responsibilities, for. . .the flood of life and the tempest of action." He envied "the ship's captain who has human lives in his hands hour after hour" (ibid., p. 163). Compare this description of the ship's captain with the following description of the great power state as one which "held in its hands a nerve fibre of historically important events" (cited by Beetham, 1974, p. 137).

Weber seems to have had a sense of the ecstasy of power and action, or perhaps, to be more accurate, the ecstacy of potency, of action that makes an impact on the world, action that makes a difference in the world. Weber did not value action for the sake of action or power in itself as the power to dominate or command, but potency, in the sense of being able significantly to affect the world through one's actions, the power to affect world events and shape the future. Of course having the power to dominate and command makes it possible to make an impact on the world. Hence the former is desired as a means for the latter.

While Weber could appreciate individual and cultural distinctiveness that might have exemplary value, he valued even more individual power – the ship's captain – and national power – the great imperial state. Contrast this view of action and power with Weber's scornful description of the bourgeoisie:

> For decades now they [the bourgeoisie] have been dominated by the spirit of "security": of feeling safe in the protection of authoritarianism, of frightened concern at the riskiness of any change – in short, a cowardly will to impotence (cited ibid., p. 176).

Weber implicitly contrasted a concern for security with a concern for greatness, a will to impotence with a will to power (potency). He identified a will to power with a political spirit. Elsewhere, Weber talked of the bourgeoisie's lack of political spirit. While reviewing a variety of possible constitutional schemes for the German state, he contended: "Far more decisive for the future of Germany is the question: whether the bourgeoisie as a whole will develop a new readiness for political responsibility and a more self-conscious *political spirit*" (cited ibid., p. 53).

One way to understand Weber's unwillingness to advocate a policy aimed at happiness, security and well-being is to think of happiness as self-satisfaction – a static state. Greatness cannot be attained in a static state; it can be attained only through action. Greatness involves a willingness to take risks, to be daring. We may understand the contrast between greatness and happiness further in terms of the distinction between dynamic and static forms of life. Both Weber and feminism may be said to stress movement over stasis, struggle over complacency. For both Weber and feminism the questionable condition of being complacent (self-satisfied) is compounded by its relation to being complaisant, the desire to avoid conflict by trying to please, oblige or comply with the others' wishes. This way of relating often reflects or results in domination by one over the other and hence in relations of subordination, subservience and servility.

Weber's stress on greatness, involving risk-taking and a will to power, differs from the feminist stress on liberation which involves self-change and social transformation. Weber's exaggerated glorification of action and potency may protect against a fear of (and desire for) passivity and vulnerability, a fear of (desire for) receptivity and dependence. The external world, prefigured in the father figure, represents a desired but fearful and threatening other, an other that one cannot allow oneself to trust and to whom one cannot surrender.

Weber's view of social life as conflict among contending wills requires that one must always be alert and on guard. Weber held that conflict "is always present and its influence is often greatest when it is least noticed, i.e., the more its course takes the form of indifferent or complacent passivity or self-deception" (Weber, [1917] 1949, p. 27). Complacency, which fails to notice the existence of an opposing will and fails to be aware of the omnipresence of conflict, leads to passivity rather than active readiness to fight.

This readiness to fight to protect the integrity of the individual I associate with manliness. The readiness to fight to protect the integrity of the state I associate with nationalism. Like Weber, I assume that conflict is always potentially present. As a feminist I am particularly concerned with one insidious form of conflict, the kind that Weber, too, was concerned about, conflict that is hidden or not noticed: repression. Repression means denying (not acknowledging) something that is there. There is psychological repression, there is ideological repression and there is political repression. All of them involve force or the threat of force.

Assuming repression to be an inevitable feature of language, culture, social life and personal identity, including especially gender identity, I conceive of feminism as a continual struggle against repression. This is part of the struggle against oppression. Oppression refers to the imposition of demands and constraints that make life hard to bear. Repression refers to the denial of the feelings, needs, desires which occurs in situations of oppression, situations in which one party has the power to impose his or her will on another. A central feature of feminism has been consciousness raising, a process of becoming aware of repression. The recognition of how the personal is political promotes the struggle to overcome repression as a struggle for liberation. Just as for feminism struggle is conceived as necessary for women's liberation, for Weber struggle is conceived as necessary for political freedom. But for Weber this freedom is defined as freedom to impose one's will on the world. Weber assumes a world in which one's will must be asserted and imposed forcefully. In other words, he assumes a world in which one's will, unless backed by force, will be disregarded.

Tension, conflict, and struggle are important terms in Weber's sociology and politics. The conception of social life as struggle was not uncommon in the Germany of his time. It is also not uncommon today. However, for Weber and perhaps for Germany at the time, the value of conflict and struggle lay in its association with political freedom and power over world events, not in self and social development through liberation from repression which is a value of feminism, psychoanalysis and Marxism. Political freedom for Weber meant freedom to struggle for power. The struggle for power makes possible the attainment of greatness, the ability to impose one's will on the world.

Greatness and leadership

Weber wanted to see a dynamic social order with Germany playing a leading role. He wanted to see Germany engage in the struggle for power. For this political leadership was necessary.

Through the process of political struggle, political leaders are created. "Only those characters are fitted for political leadership who have been selected in the political struggle, since all politics is in its essence 'Kampf'" (cited by Beetham, 1974, p. 110). For Weber, democracy was not a value in itself, a form of collective self-rule or popular sovereignty. It was a method for selecting leaders. Weber wrote in a letter to Robert Michels: "Concepts such as 'the will of the people', the true will of the people, have long since lost any meaning for me; they are fictions" (cited ibid., p. 111).

Weber believed that parliament could provide a training and testing ground for the development of political leaders. It would, he believed, be capable of generating the kind of leadership that could control the bureaucracy. Weber tended to see democratic institutions as technical means separate and distinct from the political ends that they would serve. "Forms of constitution are for me technical means like any other machinery. I'd be just as happy to take the side of the monarch against parliament, if only he were a *politician* or showed signs of becoming one" (cited ibid., p. 102).

Weber deplored collective action and politics, "street politics," claiming that the mass is always subject to emotional and irrational influences. Responsible and realistic politics can best be made by a few cool and clear heads (ibid., p. 112). Beetham astutely observes that:

> The use of the term "mass" itself limits the conception of the people's role in politics to that of objects; it prevents them ever being seen as the potential subjects of political action except in a dangerous capacity (ibid., p. 267).

Beetham recognizes that Weber's liberal, bourgeois values can be found wanting not only from the perspective of socialist values but from the perspective also of bourgeois liberalism, particularly Weber's political values. "His theory of Parliamentary government cannot be called a *democratic* theory, since it did not seek to justify [itself] in terms of recognizably democratic values, such as increasing the influence of the people on the policies pursued by those who governed" (ibid., p. 101).

Beetham reports that Weber contrasted the Russian revolution with previous European revolutions and evaluated the former negatively because of its "lack of great leaders." Everything, he wrote, was simply a "collective product" (ibid., p. 112). Weber disdained such politics. He believed emphatically in individual action and leadership. "Weber's leader is an individualist; the source of his actions lies in himself, in his own personal convictions, and not in his following or associates. . .Someone who was elected to carry out a programme laid down by others was an official, not a leader" (ibid., p. 231).

Liberalism and illiberalism

Some interpreters, like Mommsen, see in Weber's nationalism, his obsession with a powerful Germany, and his advocacy of plebiscitary leadership, a dangerous vision, a vision that could easily culminate in the rise of a nationalistic demagogue and megalomaniac such as Hitler. Others, like Beetham, challenge this interpretation.

For the latter, Weber's nationalism and his emphasis on a powerful Germany is tempered by his commitment to cultural independence and individual freedom. Weber's wartime advocacy of alliances not annexations is the evidence for this view of Weber. Weber had argued that Germany was in a good position to persuade the smaller, vulnerable nations that Germany was interested in protecting them from the imperialistic designs of the other great powers. A policy of alliances with these countries that would give priority to Germany with regard to trade and economic expansion would give Germany a significant sphere of influence. Germany would then be a nation to be reckoned with by the other world powers.

In the more sympathetic view of Weber's politics, his advocacy of alliances to protect the small nations, particularly from Russian imperialism, means that Weber justified his desire for German power by conceiving of it as a means for preserving culture – German culture, of course, but also the culture of other nations that were threatened by absorption from the great powers. This justification of power then serves to limit nationalism and imperialism. Furthermore, this justification could be identified as a liberal value – the preservation of cultures.

Beetham supports this view by pointing out that Weber's rejection of his compatriots' annexationist war aims occurred at a time when Germany was winning the war. Therefore, Weber's position must have been guided by principle, not expedience. For example, Germany had succeeded in moving into Belgium. There was widespread annexationist fever. It seemed that Germany could take over Belgium and other nations as well. Yet Weber opposed such sentiment.

Weber himself justified his position by insisting that the annexationist war aims were "unrealistic." Weber never opposed these war aims as unethical or destructive of culture, even when he admitted the destructive effect of German rule over Brussels, for example. Rather, Weber argued that the annexation of Belgium would turn France and England into mortal enemies of the Reich (Mommsen, 1984, p. 204). He felt that the similar situation with Alsace Lorraine had rendered France permanently hostile and had condemned German diplomacy to eternal failure (ibid.). Weber personally sympathized with Belgium. He was greatly fond of Brussels and aware of the identification of the people there with French culture. He wrote of seeing "the ghostliness of this German rule over that beautiful city, French to the core" (cited ibid., p. 201, n. 37). Weber's personal liberal sympathies tended to coincide with his political "realism."

Thus Weber was able to argue against the extravagant annexationist war aims from a purely "realistic" position. He did not argue on the basis of "soft" ethical or aesthetic values, but on the basis of a "hard" rational appraisal of realistic ends, calculation of alternative means and considerations of possible consequences. Weber's realism or rationality often coincides with liberal political positions and values. Nevertheless he drew no intrinsic connection in his theoretical or political writings between ethics or liberal values on the one side and rationality on the other. In fact he steadfastly maintained the distinction between ethics or values and rationality. He insisted on rational rather than ethical justification for political action. There are two interpretations of Weber's politics. On the one side there is the view of Weber as propounder of German nationalism and strong leadership, willing to subordinate all other values or goals to that of making Germany into a great and powerful nation state. On the other side there is the view of Weber as the pessimistic liberal, the supporter of individualism and liberty in an increasingly bureaucratized age. Beetham sees these values as standing in some tension with each other. Steven Seidman (1985, 1986), too, emphasizes the tension and dualism in Weber's thought between liberal values and illiberal politics.

Manliness: key to the riddle

I contend that what appears as a duality and tension between Weber's liberal domestic politics and his illiberal international politics can be understood as a unified world view contained in a specific conception of manliness, one that idealizes individualism, independence, power and greatness. Weber's emphasis on individualism and independence identify him as a liberal; however, his emphasis on power and greatness make for illiberal politics, especially in the realm of foreign policy. But both sets of values make for manliness. It is neither liberal values nor illiberal ones but manliness that accounts for Weber's politics and for the seeming dualism in his politics. Both sides of Weber can be integrated into or understood in terms of a single, overriding value and fear: the value of manly independence and the fear of servile dependency. This value and fear contribute as well to his support of liberal feminism; neither women nor men should have to live lives of servile dependency. He hated subservience and saw power as the alternative. Furthermore power was inherent in and therefore required for the accomplishment of great deeds. Conflict due to struggles for power and struggles for power due to conflicts of interests and values constitute a major dynamic in Weber's conception of social life and a major reason that many today consider Weber a realist.

Weber held no "illusions" about eliminating domination or radically transforming society. Assuming social life to be based on actions that involve power, conflict and domination, one must strive to be a strong, active, independent power state or individual – a man – or else remain a weak, passive, dependent small state or person – a woman. Weber's complexity and interest can be said to derive from a struggle between "feminine" values of peace, happiness and love and "masculine" values of conflict, action and greatness.

He never attempted to reconcile these. Instead, he advocated the solution of relegating the former to the private sphere and smaller powers and the latter to the public sphere and great powers. A strong man no less than a great power must renounce the "feminine" values of peace, happiness and love. Much of his work takes the form of an implicit defense of this version of separate spheres and an advocacy of masculine values and (manly) action in the public sphere, an argument against "dangerous" and naive pacifists, internationalists, radical feminists and socialists whose values belong in the

51

private sphere. And even there, as we shall see, he argues these values are illusory; the most intimate relations involve actions of conflict and domination – coercion of the soul of the less brutal partner.

Notes

1   Both David Beetham and Wolfgang Mommsen acknowledge the significance of conflict in Weber's social and political thought. This chapter draws heavily on Beetham's work as did the preceding chapter. The following chapter draws on Mommsen's work, as does Chapter 5.

4

Men's world

Weber's values, such as the ones discussed in the preceding chapter – conflict, action and greatness in the public world – may be captured by the term "worldly ethic of heroism" (Weber, 1946, p. 336). This is the ethic of manliness. He contrasted this ethic with other-worldly religious ethics, which he identified with the "ethics of the subjugated." The latter were associated with women and femininity (Weber [1921–2] 1978, pp. 591–2).

The contrast between the "worldly ethic of heroism," the ethic of warrior heroes, and the "ethics of the subjugated" appears in different guises throughout his writings. The opposition between the two constitute a clash between what are often considered, not least by Weber himself, values of masculinity and values of femininity. Weber does not usually address this tension as such. At best it might be seen as peripheral or marginal to his thought. I seek to move this tension from the shadows into the light, from the periphery into the centre. When Weber does address the conflict explicitly he formulates it as one between worldly (primarily political and economic) activity and an ethic of brotherly love. Weber offers a historical analysis of the relationship between religious ethics and political subjugation. In so doing, he implicitly discredits "feminine" religious ethics.

Warrior hero ethics versus ethics of the subjugated

With political subjugation, "The domestication of the masses was assigned to priests by foreign rulers (for the first time systematically by the Persians), and later indigenous rulers followed suit" (ibid.).

Among politically demilitarized peoples under the control of their own priests, such as the Jews, comparatively unwarlike groups of people became, according to Weber, important for the priests' maintenance of their power position. The priesthood "welcomed the characteristic virtues of these classes, viz., simplicity, patient resignation to trouble, humble acceptance of existing authority, and friendly forgiveness and passivity in the face of injustice" (ibid.). Furthermore, "Jewish prophecy, in a realistic recognition of the external political situation, preached resignation to the domination by the great powers, as a fate apparently desired by God" (ibid.).

These virtues of the powerless complemented the special religious virtue, "magnanimous charity (*caritas*)," of the powerful, "since the patriarchal donors desired these virtues of resignation and humble acceptance in those who benefited from their assistance" (ibid.). The priests assigned religious value to "the essentially *feminine* virtues of the ruled" (ibid., p. 592, italics added). Weber self-consciously identifies as feminine the "virtues" of the subjugated: resignation, humble acceptance, and so on.

Weber does indicate that these virtues of the subjugated were virtues to the rulers, to the patriarchal donors of charity, and hence to the priesthood.

Continuing the connection that he makes between religious values, "feminine" virtues and the priesthood, he explains: contributing also to this change in the realm of morality (Nietzsche's "slave revolt"), a change organized by the priests, were the distinctively unwarlike activities of the priests themselves. It is clear that Weber associated "distinctively unwarlike activities" with religious ethics. In addition, he reported, two other historical processes contributed to the same development on a large scale: universal pacification and bureaucratization.[1] Pacification involved the "elimination of all struggles for power in the great world empires." Similarly "the bureaucratization of all political dominion, as in the Roman Empire" had the same effect (ibid.).

Weber identified the virtues of the ruled as "essentially feminine." Many feminists today make the similar claim that femininity both presupposes and reproduces subjugation. Weber further identified subjugation, pacification and bureaucratization along with the instrumental role of the priests as contributing to depoliticization and hence, by implication, to "feminization." All of these factors undermine the political and social interests involved in a "warlike struggle for power" including social class conflict. These developments, with their undermining of political struggle and conflict, tend to promote a rejection of the world and of politics in favor of religious ethics.

Weber treated politics and the religious ethic of brotherly love as absolutely opposed. The former, grounded in worldly interests, involves struggle for power, engagement with the world and an ultimate reliance on violence. The latter involves detachment from and rejection of secular and worldly interests which includes a rejection of violence as means for achieving worldly ends. Weber claimed that it is mistaken to believe that the religious conception of brotherly love derives from a (political) interest in social reform. Rather, the power of the apolitical Christian religion of love and "the increasing importance of all salvation religions and congregational religions from the first and second century of the [Roman] Imperial period" (ibid.) derives from the complete renunciation of such *secular* concerns as social reform. According to Weber, this transformation was carried out by educated strata that had lost interest in politics because they had lost influence or had become disgusted by the politics of the time.

Thus, political repression or depoliticization, the inability or unwillingness to engage in political struggles, is a significant factor in the development of salvation religions, the loss of secular concerns and the development of "feminine" virtues including "Christian love." In contrast, the ability and readiness to engage in overt conflict and warlike struggles for power contributes to and presupposes a worldly outlook, a rejection of salvation religions, and the development of "masculine" virtues (including the renunciation of "Christian love"). The distinction between the two forms of life relates to another distinction that Weber makes between two forms of society: a dynamic conflictual one and a static repressive one. Given that formulation of the difference, it is no wonder that he values the former over the latter, a dynamic society oriented to worldly values over a static one oriented to other-worldly or inner-worldly values.

Weber values a heroic individual who strives to accomplish great deeds in the world by engaging in conflicts and struggles for power, a heroic life which does not shrink from violence and that rejects servility. Weber contrasts religious ethics of brotherly love, which characterize not just apolitical Christianity but mysticism as well, with heroic ethics. "With its 'resist no evil' and with its maxim 'then turn the other cheek,' mysticism is necessarily vulgar and lacking in dignity in the eyes of every self-assured worldly ethic of heroism" (Weber, 1946, p. 336).

Masculinity and political community

Embedded in Max Weber's work is a sociological theory of gender, an explanation of the social conditions responsible for producing cultural notions of masculinity and femininity. We saw above how femininity assumes subjugation, subordination, submissiveness and subservience. We see next how masculinity assumes warfare and membership in a political community.

The public world of politics has historically been a men's world. It has been a source of their power and prestige, their sense of honor and dignity. However, it has also been a source of misogyny, militarism and imperialism.

Drawing on historical and ethnographic material of his time, Max Weber analyzes the historical origins of the political community and its relation to gender. Although Weber's account needs to be reviewed in light of more recent ethnographic research, his work continues to hold interest, not least for the light it sheds on his own thinking about gender and politics.

Here is Weber's definition of the term, "political:" "we generally mean by 'political,' things that have to do with relations of authority within what is. . .a political organization, the state" (Weber, [1921–2] 1978, p. 55). Because political associations have included all kinds of ends and there have been no ends which all political associations have recognized, a political organization, including the state, cannot be defined in terms of the end to which its action points. "Thus it is possible to define the 'political' character of an organization only in terms of the *means* peculiar to it, the use of force." The term, "political" refers to "things which are likely to uphold, to change or overthrow, to hinder or promote, these authority relations" (ibid., p. 55).

For Weber, the political community, which sires the public world, arises with the subordination of a territory, and the conduct of persons within it. The subordination is accomplished by physical force. Every group that has been capable of doing so, such as kinship groups and neighborhood associations, has always, he assures us, resorted to violence in order to protect or defend the interests of its members. However, Weber distinguished between those situations and the existence of an institutionalized political order. The latter is nothing primordial but the product of historical development. He sketched the development, noting, however, that it is not universal.

According to Weber, an early stage in the formation of a political association is the organization of marauding raids by the "most warlike members" of a group. Through the development of military prowess and war as a vocation a coercive apparatus develops that is able to claim obedience. These claims apply to those who are conquered as well as to the militarily unfit within the community from which the warriors emerged. With this political structure a social class with its own distinct status emerges. This social class is also a gender class, as Weber makes clear:

> The bearer of arms acknowledges only those capable of bearing arms as political equals. All others, those untrained in arms and those incapable of bearing arms, are regarded as women and are explicitly designated as such in many primitive languages. Within these consociations of warriors freedom is identical with the right to bear arms (ibid., p. 906).

The "militarily unfit" members of the community as well as the inhabitants of conquered territories are subject to "effective and comprehensive" claims of obedience by the political consociation.

With the development of a warrior group, freedom and manliness become associated with each other, with the "right" to bear arms, with a willingness and ability to employ violence and physical coercion. Thus a distinct warrior mentality becomes associated with manliness. The distinction between being free and being unfree and its correspondence with the distinction between being a man and being a woman arises with a warrior community. By virtue of their not bearing arms, which becomes a right appropriated by the men, women are defined as unfree. Weber repeats the point that those who are not members of the warrior group are regarded as women.

Only those are members [in the consociation of warriors] who have demonstrated prowess in the use of arms and have been taken into the warriors' brotherhood after a novitiate, while he who has not passed the test remains outside as a "woman," among the women and children, who are also joined by those no longer capable of bearing arms. (ibid., p. 906).

In many societies, members of the political fraternity live, until a certain age, in a communistic association apart from wives and household. They live on war booty and on the contribution they levy on non-members, especially on the women by whom the agricultural work is done. The only work, in addition to the conduct of war, regarded as worthy of men is the production and upkeep of the implements of war. Their economic position is based on the continuous plundering of outsiders especially women (ibid., p. 907). Within the space of one page, he repeats the point about living off others, "especially women." Membership in the men's community which is a warrior fraternity, and hence the very status of "man," appears to be linked with separation and differentiation from, as well as domination, exploitation and intimidation of "women."

The men may use religion to intimidate the women and outsiders as do the Duk-Duks in Indonesia. The latter staged masked processions representing dangerous spirits from whom the women and outsiders must flee, or suffer instant death, allowing the "spirits" to plunder the houses (ibid.).

Weber seems to have been taken with the intense male bonding of the warrior community: "the man belongs to the warriors' fraternity with every fiber of his existence," a remarkably subjective judgment for one who has not been there. He follows this statement with another explaining that the members live in communistic association apart from wives and household. I doubt if he would describe the situation of men and women living together as belonging to the household, family, marriage, kin group or community with every fiber of their beings. There is something peculiarly compelling and intense about this all-male community as interpreted by Weber.

It might seem that co-operative arrangements for economic or social purposes would necessitate a political or governmental structure and hence account for the origins of the state. Weber shows that historically this is not the case. He emphasized the historical and military origins of the political community: the subordination of a territory and the conduct of persons within it. He denied that such a political organization is natural and coeval with social life. He gives the example of the free community of nomads, wandering and herding together. In such communities, the only regular, permanent authorities are the elders and the magicians.

Wherever economic needs are developed that cannot be satisfied by the kinship group and household, the institution of village chieftain arises. "But especially under conditions of continuous peace, he is no more than a popular arbiter and his directions are followed as statements of good advice." Further-more, "The total absence of any such chieftain is by no means a rare occurrence in peaceful periods." Instead there is consensual action which is regulated by respect for tradition, fear of blood vengeance and wrath of magical powers (ibid., p. 910). Neither chieftainship nor the social organization of a community according to consensual action (backed by fear of antagonizing the social group to which the hurt party belongs or fear of what I interpret to mean provoking bad spirits – bad feelings – within the group and/or the individual, by offending the spirit of the group) qualified as political organization for Weber.

Thus a political organization, as he defined it,[2] is by no means a natural or essential feature of society. It develops under certain historical social conditions. He emphatically declared that a political organization does not exist when armed defense is a function of the household, neighborhood or some other economically oriented association. In other words if political organiza-tion (social organization based on employment of violence) is not separate from economic organization, it does not qualify as a political community. Given Weber's commitment to the primacy of politics, we can understand why he would reject and despise socialism if the latter expressly subordinates political organization to economic organization, if the state serves primarily or exclusively an administrative function for domestic economic ends.

But for the separation of political organization from economic organization to occur, the political community must be provided for by the economic activity of others. Hence, a political community, membership in which makes one a man, presumes a stratified society in which some members live off the labor of others either in a regularized fashion or through plundering. The ones they live off and plunder are often women. The latest feminist research confirms this aspect of Weber's theory.[3] This stratified society in which warrior men live off the labor of others, primarily domestic women, is also one in which the political organization has power over domestic economic organization, a public world of politics dominates a private world of domestic production. We see here the relationship of patriarchal society to the separation of political-military organization from domestic community.

The men's house

From the sexual division of labour in which tilling of soil and harvesting fell mainly to women, and hunting, tending cattle, wood and metal work-ing and finally and before all, war, were men's activities, arose two types of communalization: house and field work, hunting and fighting. House and field work centers around the woman; she often occupies a dominant social position, not infrequently, he notes, with complete control. While the women's house was originally the workhouse, the socialization of hunting and fighting gives rise to the men's society. It is revealing that Weber makes note of the difference between a men's world in which leadership emerges by proving oneself in a contest with others and a women's world of tradition:

> The socialization of hunting and fighting was carried out under the leadership based on merit or charisma of a chieftain chosen for this purpose. Not his kinship connections but his warlike and other personal qualities are decisive; he is the freely chosen leader with a freely chosen following (Weber, [1923] 1981, p. 39).

Weber is much taken with the contrast between traditional behavior and traditional authority that he associates with women and the household, and striving, competing, heroic action that he associates with men and warfare. This contrast runs through much of his thought and is the principle with which he perceives and divides the world.

Weber reported that wherever peaceful activities are the primary means of making a living, the agent of joint work, the household, is likely to have control over economic objects: fields, pastures, forests and hunting grounds. Whenever maintenance depends on land seized by force, particularly hunting grounds and forests, the polity will have control (Weber, [1921–2] 1978, p. 363). If land is primarily a place to work on and the women do the work of cultivation, then the land and its yield belong to the women's kin group and is inherited through the mother's line. Military equipment is men's property and inherited through the father. If, on the other hand, land is considered male property, "spear land," owned and defended by force, then unarmed persons, especially women, cannot have a share in it.

Nevertheless, he argued that we cannot generalize that the primarily military character of a group points unambiguously to the predominance of the father's house and of "agnatic" family and property attribution. That predominance depends on the type of military organization. If the able-bodied male age groups, those considered to be of military age, live permanently in a "men's house," then the men's absence may establish the household as a "maternal grouping." As a result the woman may achieve a relative domestic independence as has been reported for Sparta (ibid., p. 371).

Weber believed that totemism has its origin in the institution of the men's house ([1923] 1981, p. 41). His theory provides an interesting perspective on Durkheim's gender-blind, apolitical, universalistic theory of totemic religion. By grounding totemic religion in the political institution of the men's house, Weber's historical conflict theory, influenced by feminism, makes explicit what Durkheim's universalistic, functional, sex-biased theory not only leaves implicit but tends to conceal.[4]

According to Weber, members of the men's house conceive of themselves as living in kinship with the spirit of some animal, stone or artefact – the totem. As part of its ritualistic means of affirming totemic kinship, the group exercises ritualistic food prohibitions regarding the totemic animal. Another practice is that of the novitiate. Originally, an individual who does not go through the novitiate of the men's house, which includes submitting to exacting practices such as circumcision and tests of strength (proving one's manhood), remains, as we saw above, a "woman" and does not enjoy the political privileges of men or the economic privileges which go with them.[5]

The members of the totemic community of the men's house constitute a cultural or "peace group" that prohibits fighting among the members and that practices exogamy. Thus one totem stands over against others as a marriage group. With the father absent because he lives in the men's house, what Weber carefully refers to as a "so called matriarchate" may develop. This does not mean that mothers have authority over a household that includes men or that intentionally excludes men (he explicitly challenges the theory that women ever held authority over men), but that in the absence of men, an absence determined by the warrior association, kinship is recognized between the children and the mother or the kindred of the latter. Maternal succession is generally the rule with the children belonging to the mother's clan and being ceremonially alien to the father even when the father lives in domestic communion with his wife and children.

The carryover from the time of a separate men's house includes both maternal succession and a continuing cultic, totemic association among men. Weber attributed to the men's house and its cultic character, the origins of "the so called matriarchate."[6] "Where totemism is absent, we find a patriarchate, or paternal dominance with paternal inheritance" (ibid., p. 41; also p. 37). The military clan maintains its earlier significance long after the men's house has disappeared as an institution. In Athens, for example, it is the group through which the individual holds his citizenship (ibid., pp. 43–4).

The separate men's house disappears with demilitarization and with advances in military technique. With the development of chariot and horseback fighting, the importance of single combat emerges. Now military protection is secured not through the communism of the men's house but through the individual warrior's spear rights to land that enable him to equip himself and join his wife and live with his family (ibid., pp. 40–1).

With the dissolution of the men's house a struggle ensues between an older "maternal system" and a growing tendency to form a patriarchate. As indicated above, the outcome might be decided according to whether land was regarded as the workplace of women, or as the fruit of conquest and subject for military protection. If the main burden of tillage fell on the women, land was inherited by the maternal uncle as guardian of the children. If spear land, the title rested in the military organization; the children were counted as belonging to the father. A further consequence was the exclusion of women from rights in land. Out of an interest in providing economic support for its members, the military group made the allotment of land a function of the paternal clan (ibid., p. 42).

We see here the association of men and masculinity with membership in a political consociation, with a men's house and with totemism. Nevertheless, the development of a separate political consociation and a men's house is not universal, nor presumably is totemism a universal stage in the development of religion, nor, contra Durkheim, is it necessarily an elementary form of religion in general.

An alternative to private property in land (seigniorial property) is the "free community." This form emerges where centralization of work developed on economic rather than political grounds. For example, in the house community of the South Slavs and in the Alps, the head of household is generally elected and generally subject to deposition. The primary condition for this kind of community is pure communism in production (ibid., p. 47). Where there is no separate warrior community, where there is instead communism in production, then there is more likely to be democratic leadership – the head of household elected and subject to deposition.

Origins of seigniorial property

Weber provides a historical analysis of the different ways in which seigniorial property (private land ownership), and the differentiation in wealth that lies at the base of this development, originates (ibid., pp. 51–64):

1 With chieftainship, the clan or military chief can use his prestige or authority to accumulate wealth and privilege. As we saw above, chieftainship, as political rule, tends not to arise within peaceful communities.
2 With the emergence of a professional military class due to development of military technique and military equipment, a differentiation arises between those who can render military service and equip themselves for it and those who cannot with the result that the ordinary peasant was increasingly bound to his economic functions. The upper class could accumulate booty while the non-military men who could not do this became subject to services and taxes.
3 The conquest and subjugation of an enemy people.
4 The voluntary submission of the defenseless to the overlordship of a military leader who offers protection which brings with it the obligation to furnish services or payments.
5 The chieftain with large possessions in human beings and work animals can clear and till land which could then be leased to foreigners, for example

61

to craftsmen who then stand under the protection of the kin or chieftain. Loans are also a means to the accumulation of serfs and of land.

6   The chieftain who develops not out of a military leader but out of a rain maker or medicine man can acquire property by placing a taboo on it. The prince could ally himself with the priest and employ the taboo to secure his personal possessions.

7   The chieftain who originally regulated trade in the interests of the tribe can levy duties as a source of personal income in exchange for the protection he grants to foreign merchants. The chieftain can establish a monopoly of his own in trade and obtain the means of making loans, accumulating land and reducing his own tribesmen to peonage. Or a group of chieftains unite to form a trading settlement which gives rise to a town with a patrician of traders, a privileged stratum whose position rests upon the accumulation of property through trading profits. This development of a town nobility is typical of antiquity and the early middle ages.

8   Seigniorial property may also have fiscal roots in taxation. Control over irrigation required a bureaucratic organization for collecting taxes, payments in kind, which in Egypt for example were stored in warehouses from which the king supported his officials and laborers – the oldest form of official salary. This organization of taxation resulted in the joint liability of the village for the payment of these taxes or obligatory services. With joint liability of the village, the individual peasant was not only bound to the soil but to his village as well. The ruler either farmed out the collection of taxes to adventurers (as in India) or officials (as in China) or he delegated the privilege to soldiers. These three forms of securing money and recruits became the basis of oriental feudalism. A fourth and last method of realizing a royal income is the delegation of functions to chieftains or landed proprietors. This is what happened in Rome in the imperial period.

Seigniorial property seems to rest on chieftainship, which presumes a warrior society and military developments. In other words, an economic organization, private property in land, presupposes a political organization, a warrior-military society.

The typical form of seigniorial development (private property in land), according to Weber, is the patriarchate with vesting of property rights exclusively in an individual head of household from whom no one has a right to demand an accounting. The despotic position is inherited and held for life by the patriarch. This despotism extends over wife, children, slaves, stock and implements. The power of the house father extends to the execution or sale of the wife, and to the sale of the children or to leasing them out to labor. There is no distinction between female slave and wife or between wife and concubine or between acknowledged children and slaves. The former are called *liberi*, in Roman law, only because, unlike slaves, they have a chance sometimes to become heads of families themselves (ibid., pp. 47–8).

Women's status

With economic stratification, the woman comes to be regarded as labor power to be bought as an object of value, as a work animal. The man who cannot buy a wife, serves for her or lives permanently in her house. Marriage by purchase and marriage through service, the one with patriarchal law, the other with maternal law, may exist side by side and even in the same household; neither is a universal institution. The woman, however, always remains under the authority of a man, either in her own house or in that of the man who has bought her. Nevertheless, there is a difference in her status and treatment. The wife obtained by purchase is regularly subject to the absolute patriarchal authority of the man (ibid., pp. 42–3).

This despotic patriarchal system is found in connection with pastoral economy, also in cases where a knighthood fighting as individuals forms the military class, or in connection with ancestor worship. Weber distinguished ancestor worship from worship of the dead which occurs in some societies. Ancestor worship includes worship of the dead but its distinguishing character derives from the combination of worshipping the dead with clan membership (ibid., p. 48). In other words it is a clan-specific ritual for re-inforcing the solidarity of the clan and the clan's system of authority. The clan is originally a military group.

That the military group made the allotment of land a function of the paternal clan had profound consequences for sexual, social and political organization. The disintegration of clan, likewise, had profound consequences. According to Weber, the disintegration of the clan took place as a result of two forces. One was the religious force of prophecy. The prophet seeks to build up his community without regard to clan membership. Among the Jews, the division into clans disappeared probably because the clan, *being originally military in character*, had no roots in the demilitarized Jewish state. The second force was that of political bureaucracy as in Egypt under the New Empire. The royal power feared the clan and encouraged development of the bureaucracy. In China, another bureaucratic empire, the state was not strong enough to break the power of the clan. In contrast, the Egyptian state did not tolerate the existence of clans. One consequence was equality between man and woman and sexual freedom of contract with children receiving the name of their mother (ibid., pp. 45–6).

In addition, the patriarchal house community was modified and broken down and the status of women improved with the introduction of class endogamy, marriage only within one's class. After social stratification appeared, class endogamy arose. In Greek democracy this was carried out in order to keep the property within the citizenship of the city and to monopolize political opportunities for the citizen class by restricting its multiplication (ibid., p. 35).

Class endogamy meant that the upper class married their daughters only to equals and demanded that they receive a status superior to that of female slaves. This development was facilitated by economic changes. As soon as wives ceased to represent primarily labor power, which happened first in upper classes, men ceased to buy them as labor power. A clan who wished to marry off a daughter had to provide her with a dowry sufficient to maintain standards of her class. The dowry provided the woman with the means of limiting the husband's discretion since he had to return the dowry if he divorced her. In time, only an endowed marriage was considered a marriage proper. The woman's clan stipulated that she was to be head wife and only her children could succeed as heirs (ibid., pp. 48–9).

The woman's clan protected the interests of the woman even further. In Rome, it carried through complete economic and personal emancipation of women from men, in establishing the so-called free marriage which could be terminated at will by either party and which gave women complete control over their own property, although they lost all right over the children if the marriage was dissolved (ibid. pp. 49–50).

Wherever the importance of land declines as a possession taken by force or as the basis of maintaining able-bodied men (capable of equipping themselves for war), real estate can be used primarily for economic purposes, especially in the cities, and daughters too can succeed to land.

Weber's history of women's situation stresses the role of militarism which he contrasts with demilitarized bureaucratic societies. For instance, he remarks that nineteenth-century French marriage law was shaped by petty-bourgeois and militaristic considerations in the *Code Napoleon*. In contrast to the situation of women in both England and France, bureaucratic states such as Austria and Russia have minimized sex differences in the joint property law. Furthermore, he observes that this leveling tends to go furthest where militarism has receded most in the ruling classes (Weber, [1921–2] 1978, pp. 371–3). Thus Weber alerts us to the dangers to women's status of a militaristic state, although he also informs us that when men are away at military expeditions, women may gain control over the conditions of their lives.

The political community as state government

Despite Weber's strong endorsement of politics as a vocation and his rejection of socialist anarchism, he does not claim that government or a separate political community is a necessary, natural or essential condition of

64

human community. In many cases, Weber reports, the political action of a community occurs only intermittently and then usually in response to external threat or a sudden internal impulse to violence. Generally, a state of "anarchy" during "normal" peaceful times prevails without reliance on "any kind of coercion either for external or for internal use" (ibid., p. 902).

A separate political community is a historical phenomenon. Only when the *warrior group*, whose economic position is based on continuous plundering, especially of women, is consociated beyond and above the everyday round of life and fitted into a permanent territorial community, a process that occurs only gradually, is a political organization formed with a *specific legitimation for the use of violence.* If the comprehensive political consociation develops a strong enough coercive apparatus, it will suppress private violence in any form. The suppression of violence is directed against forms of private violence that threaten the interests of the *political* community as such (ibid., pp. 907–8). (This interest does not include the suppression of private violence by men toward their wives and children.) Weber gives as an example the French monarchy suppressing the feuds of the royal vassals for the duration of a foreign war conducted by the king. Only subsequently does the coercive apparatus of the political community engender a form of permanent public peace.

The political community monopolizes the legitimate use of violence and becomes transformed into an institution for the protection of rights and public peace (ibid., p. 908). This transformation comes about with the decisive support of economic groups as well as religious authorities. The latter find it easier to control "the masses" under conditions of pacification. The economic groups who are guided by market interests are most interested in pacification. These include the burghers of the towns, those interested in river, road or bridge tolls and in the taxpaying capacity of their tenants and subjects. These interest groups expand with an expanding money economy. Even before the political authority imposed public peace, it was these economic interest groups, who, in the Middle Ages, attempted, in co-operation with the church, to limit feuds and to establish leagues for the maintenance of public peace.

Thus the spread of pacification and the expansion of the market contributes to the monopolization of legitimate violence by a political organization which culminates in the modern concept of the state and its "protection of rights" (ibid., pp. 908–9). Weber fails to emphasize, however, that only members of the political community have such legal and political rights. Women tend to be excluded from both the political community and political rights. Upper-class families may, however, introduce endogamy and the rights of upper-class women to a certain status in marriage. The notion of "rights" presupposes a political community that has a monopoly over the legitimate

65

use of violence (which gives it authority) and on which members can call for protection and enforcement of their interests. As the head of household loses to the state monopoly control over the means of violence, the private power of the patriarchal head of household recedes, according to Weber.

Only members of the political community whose rights to protection by the state are formally recognized share in the subjective feeling of having "rights." Thus membership in a political community, just as membership in a warrior consociation, makes possible a sense of personal power and with it a sense of dignity and honor. (Women and those who are excluded from the political community do not share in this personal feeling of power and prestige.) Nevertheless, there is a difference between the sense of personal power and honor that accrues to those who are independent warrior knights and that associated with members of a political association – the state. In the latter case, each man is subject to the power of the state and does not have the right to employ violence on his own.[7]

A political association which has a monopoly over the legitimate use of violence has the legitimate power to use physical coercion, including the power to dispose over life and death. This power of the political association is a source of its prestige, and the members of the political association share in this prestige. Another source of power prestige derives from the power of the political community in relation to other political communities. Because of this power, the members may pretend to a special prestige which in turn may influence the external conduct of the power structures, particularly the initiation of wars (ibid., p. 910).

Before turning in the next chapter to the relationship between power, prestige and imperialist warmaking, let us review the relationship between masculinity, warfare and politics. The political community originates with a warrior community. The latter draws on and creates the cultural distinction between men and women, masculinity and femininity. The warrior group, the men's house, and the political community create a men's world. The male political community assumes a relationship of power and domination over women. By treating land as spear land, property of the warrior association, warrior men become the proprietors of land. Proprietorship in land and membership in a military political community become mutually conditioning.

Following warfare, proprietorship in land often becomes a condition for membership in the military-political community and membership in the latter a condition for proprietorship in land. These two conditions, private property in land and membership in a military-political community reproduce relations of power and privilege among men. Not surprisingly, this men's world also reproduces the domination and oppression of women.

66

Notes

1 Kathy Ferguson (1984) similarly identifies depoliticization with femininity and modern bureaucratization with the "feminization of the polity."

2 The definition of political organization is a shifting one. In one place he describes its conceptual minimum as forcible maintenance of orderly dominion over a territory and its inhabitants; in another, the monopolization of legitimate violence.

3 Gerda Lerner's research (1986), which takes a historical look at relations between men and women in the West beginning with the earliest known societies, confirms Weber's thesis.

4 Victoria Erickson (1989) uncovers the patriarchal bias in Durkheim's theory of religion. Although Durkheim presents his theory of the essence of religion in universalistic terms, a feminist reading (focusing on gender) reveals that the sacred is gendered masculine and the profane feminine (Durkheim, 1965, pp. 162, 342–4; see Erickson, 1989, pp. 36–7). Moreover, Durkheim also recognizes that this distinction between sacred and profane, resting on force and power, assumes a division of society based on domination and subordination (ibid., pp. 408–9; see also Erickson, 1989, p. 40).

5 Along with the use of violence during these rituals of the novitiate, the men's community forcibly separates the male child from his mother and the women's world while motivating the male child to become a "man," a member of the warrior group "reborn" with a heroic warrior soul. This separation and motivation may involve a humiliation of women (including forcibly restraining mothers from interceding and rescuing their sons from the violent and painful initiation rites) and the consequent humiliation of being like a woman. A ritual humiliation of women may include rape. Victoria Erickson (1989, p. 33) in reviewing Durkheim's *Elementary Forms of the Religious Life*, discovers the apparent gang rape that Durkheim describes as occurring at such times. The description is so man-centered that the rape-like character of the ritual remains unremarked and hence ambiguous.

6 Max Weber takes issue with the socialist theory (of Bebel and Engels which was based on the work of Bachofen) of various evolutionary stages in the institution of marriage, the emergence of prostitution and the "world-historic defeat of women" ([1923] 1981, pp. 28–50).

7 Norbert Elias (1982) describes the difference in personal comportment between independent warrior knights and knights who subjected themselves to the authority of a sovereign in exchange for the privileges that the sovereign could dispense.

5

Imperial greatness

We saw in the last chapter that the men's world of powerful political communities gives rise to a special feeling of prestige – "power prestige." The source of this prestige lies in the power of the political association to dispose over life and death as well as in the power of the political community in relation to other political communities. That men pretend to a special prestige due to the power of their political structure in turn influences the external conduct of the power structure, including the initiation of wars and imperialism. In Weber's view, "claims to prestige have always played into the origin of wars." The realm of "honor" also influences the interrelations of political structures (Weber, [1921–2] 1978, p. 911).

Weber contended that the striving for prestige pertains to all power structures and all political structures. He than distinguished the prestige of power from "mere pride in the excellent qualities" of one's political community such as is the case among the Swiss and the Norwegians. "The prestige of power means in practice the glory of power over other communities; it means the expansion of power" (ibid.). Weber was talking of imperialism. As we have seen, Weber distinguished between small peoples like the Swiss and "big political communities." The latter are the natural exponents of pretensions to the prestige of power (ibid.). Here, Weber qualifies his earlier contention that *all* power structures strive for this kind of prestige.

The striving for "power prestige" occurs over and above the desire for economic benefits that accrue to members of the political community when their political structure enjoys an expansion of power (for example, bureaucrats and officers, for whom an expansion of power means more office positions, more sinecures, and better opportunities for promotion). By generalizing about the prestige of power and treating it as natural to all political structures, especially big political communities, Weber treats as unexceptional Germany's political aspirations and its external conduct including its initiation of war and imperialist attempts to expand its power.

The description of power prestige as "the glory of power over others" together with Weber's reference to political posturing brings to mind an image of male cockiness, somebody who struts around proud of himself, his masculinity, his power, his superiority over others, especially female others. Despite Weber's rational analysis of the role of power prestige in political affairs, he decries as irrational, political posturing and cockiness on the part of political actors. A rational concern for consequences would bring awareness that such behavior only invites resentment, fear and hostility. In Weber's view, all political structures desire to expand their power over others in order to enjoy the prestige that comes with power. If every state desires to expand its power over others, then every state must fear every other state, especially one that makes a show of its power and of its desire for expanding that power.

Thus Weber can describe the response of other nations to Germany's blusterings and behavior as a natural fear of "big political communities." "Every political structure naturally prefers to have weak rather than strong neighbors. Furthermore, as every big political community is a potential aspirant to prestige, it is also a potential threat to all its neighbors; hence, the big political community, simple because it is big and strong, is latently and constantly endangered" (ibid., p. 911). Weber claims that simply being big and strong invites the danger of hostility from others. Therefore if one is big and strong, one must take rational measures to prevent hostile attacks (alliances) and to protect against an attack should one come (military strength).

Weber describes the irony and pathos of a state that desires to be big and powerful, to have the ability to impose its will over others, so that it can join the other big and powerful states only to discover that not only do the other big and powerful states not want to let this upstart join the club, they want to cut him down to size so that they can continue to impose their will without having to be concerned with his. Therefore, like the successful Calvinist, the big political community cannot let itself enjoy its success – its size and strength. It cannot indulge its desire to push its weight around and command deference. It must exercise self-control, remain vigilant, and strive to maintain and expand its power in order to protect against the danger from rivals who want to eliminate the threat to their power that this new power state represents.

Weber assumes a world in which the power and greatness of one is threatening to the power and greatness of the other(s). Power is a zero sum game for Weber because power means ability to impose one's will over the resistance of others. Weber has no conception of power that does not imply conflict or domination; he has no vision of a world in which the power and greatness of one state does not necessarily threaten, but rather promises to enhance, the power and greatness of the other state(s).

Power, prestige and political interests

Those who have vested interests in the political structure tend "systematically" to cultivate a sentiment of prestige associated with that political structure (ibid., p. 912). This sentiment strengthens belief in the might of the political structure, and this belief contributes to political self-assurance and a confident willingness to fight. The sentiment associated with prestige – pride and confidence – makes it possible for the state to call on that sentiment and the related self-assurance for purposes of waging war (ibid., pp. 911–12).

Self-assurance and pride in the power of one's political community contribute to an eagerness to fight born out of a belief in one's own superiority, the anticipated rewards from victory and a desire to maintain that pride. Instilling a sense of pride in one's own superior power or in the superior power of one's political community – cockiness – makes it likely that no slight or insult will be tolerated. A sense of pride in one's superior power brings with it an exaggerated sense of honor. We can see connections here between a cult of masculinity (see Chapter 8) and power politics.

Although capitalist interests as well as power prestige have played a decisive role in political expansion, the relationship may be reversed. Expansion of the territory controlled by a state out of desire to enhance the power and prestige of the state may exert an independent force with regard to domestic economic development.

Germany, for instance, has been made into a unified economic territory, that is one whose inhabitants seek to sell their products primarily in their own market, only through custom frontiers at her borders, which were determined in a purely political manner. Were all custom barriers eliminated, the economically determined market for the Eastern German cereal surplus, poor in gluten, would not be Western Germany but rather England. . . [Similarly] Eastern Germany . . . would be the economic location for strong industries, the economically determined market and hinterland for which would be the whole of Western Russia. Such industries are now cut off by Russian custom barriers and have been moved to Poland (ibid., p. 913).

Weber argues that Germany has been politically united against the economic determinants as such. Weber here refutes certain Marxist theories that stressed trade or commerce (capital) as the determinant of political actions. He stresses that motives other than trade have played their part in every political expansion of the past, including the Crusades. These motives have included an interest in higher royal incomes, in prebends, fiefs, offices and social honors for the vassals, knights, officers, officials, the younger sons of hereditary office holders and so on. Although some kind of economic interest has played a decisive role, trade has not always paved the way for political expansion, and often the causal nexus has been the reverse. Political unification and the pacification of a territory have tended to facilitate the development of trade.

Weber claims that the political sphere and political motives, desire for power and the influence of "power prestige," both of which are associated with masculinity and membership in a political community, must be taken seriously as a force in history. The political sphere is not subservient to the economic. Although he suggests that the relationship between political structures, economic interests, political expansion and trade is not pre-determined in any direction, he does unequivocally assert that "If trade in itself is by no means the decisive factor in political expansion, the economic structure in general does co-determine the extent and manner of political expansion" (ibid., p. 915). The internal dynamics of power politics also contributes to political expansion.

Political interests in maintaining and expanding power have resulted in imperial greatness. Women as well as slaves, cattle and land have been among the original and foremost objects of forceful acquisition by political communities (ibid., p. 916). Violent political subjection has meant that the peasantry of the incorporated was not wiped out but rather made to pay tribute to the conqueror who became the landlord. More recently the forcible enslaving of the inhabitants, or tying them to the soil and exploiting them as plantation labor, has made the acquisition of overseas colonies a very profitable affair for capitalist interest groups: the Spaniards in South America, the English in the Southern States of the Union, and the Dutch in Indonesia (ibid., p. 917). Weber is a realist regarding the preconditions of imperial greatness.

Unmasking interests

In discussing the role of economic interests in imperialism, Weber explains that the acquisition of overseas colonies not only facilitates the monopolization of trade with the colonies, providing profits to overseas traders that are granted monopolies by the state, but political expansion also provides profits for state creditors and suppliers as well. Particularly if the army is not outfitted by the members themselves, expansion through war presents "by far the most profitable occasion" for those groups who provide the monies (the state creditors), the armaments, and so forth. Where the state creditors are a mass of bondholders, profit opportunities are made for bond-issuing banks. "Banks, which finance war loans, and today large sections of heavy industry are *quand même* economically interested in warfare" (ibid., p. 918).

Weber also unmasks the role of other political and economic interests in the conduct of war. He explains the support for the German policy of unconditional submarine warfare. The grenade manufacturers and the agrarians were working for this policy because every extension of the war meant higher earnings for them. Furthermore, many who supported the submarine policy shared a "fear of peace" with those who were the most ardent annexationists. They feared that a peace that failed to achieve the goals that had been trumpeted would have to be paid for with domestic political concessions; "concessions would have to be made in the question of suffrage" (cited by Mommsen, 1984, p. 234). Weber deplored the policies that resulted from self-interest of the ruling classes, the Conservatives and industrial magnates, including the policy of continuing the war regardless of consequences for the nation (ibid.). The ruling classes stressed nationalistic, political pursuits because it was in their particular interests to do so. They were the direct and indirect beneficiaries of such policies as Weber himself clearly reveals.

Weber does not restrict his critique to an unmasking of self-interest. He also indirectly charges his opponents with being unmanly: weak, lacking in courage and strong nerves. Those who embody the manly ideals of strength, courage and fortitude would not support this policy. He accuses those who agitate for submarine warfare of having "weak nerves." It was not mere national feelings that lay behind the widespread submarine agitation, he insists; it was a sense of weakness and desperation on the part of those who were unable to bear the burdens of the war. "People with courage and strong nerves are not the ones that scurried behind the submarine warfare demagoguery, but hysterically weak people who were no longer able to bear the burden of the war" (cited ibid., p. 233). Weber was concerned that the policy would bring the United States into the war. His position, while conforming to liberal sentiments, was influenced not by ethical considerations as much as by rational ones, a consideration of the likely political consequences. Yet, he resorts to techniques of shaming by making reference to images of manliness and failures of manliness in order to win support for his position and rejection of the position he opposes.

Weber opposed the excesses in political posturing (cockiness) and policies both before and during the war because he saw them as unnecessary and irrational vanities that would ultimately hurt Germany's position in the world. They were not in the interests of the nation, but in the interests of a narrow stratum whose interests were not compatible with those of the nation. Although he was a nationalist, Weber opposed the pan-Germans for the same reason. They too placed their own interests above those of the national interest and then hid their interests behind aggressive nationalist rhetoric.

It is not out of character for Weber, who advocated responsible concern for consequences and restraint from unnecessary displays of power or emotion, to denigrate their posturing and characterize their position in terms of a "big-mouth policy." Weber held the pan-Germans responsible for the fact that an understanding with England had not been achieved before the war. The pan-German "hatred of England was above all a hatred of the English constitution. 'For God's sake, no alliance with England that would lead us to parliamentarization!'" Weber felt that a successful colonization program would have required diplomatic agreements with England, something that the pan-Germans would have opposed. The self-interest of the pan-Germans prevented a successful colonization program which was to him obviously in the best interests of the nation.

Economic policy and ethics

Weber's imperialism derived in good part from his analysis of the economic realities of his time. Economic expansion required bringing the still "free" regions of the globe "under the political control of the nation." These regions could then be opened up for the "preferential exploitation of the nation's industrial and commercial interests" (Mommsen, 1984, p. 72). Refraining from imperialism meant withdrawing from the international competition for economic supremacy. It also meant dooming Germany to both a second-rate-nation status and economic inferiority, making the nation vulnerable to political, economic and cultural domination.

Weber argued that domestic social policy depends on successful foreign policy. Imperialism and power politics are justified for economic reasons as well as cultural ones, domestic reasons as well as nationalistic ones: "We need outlets overseas, a widening of job opportunities by the expansion of export markets." For Weber, "that means the outward expansion of Germany's economic sphere of power, and in the long run this is completely dependent upon the outward expansion of political power" (cited ibid., p. 78). The world appeared to Weber to be divided up among the other great powers. If Germany were to be among the great powers, it would have to share in that division. Germany would need its own overseas markets and spheres of influence.

Weber's response to a political economist who opposed German imperialism reveals not just Weber's economic views and their political implications, but also his way of dealing publicly with ethically questionable implications of his own position. The political economist attacked certain trade treaties that would entail long-term risk by encouraging export. This would increase Germany's dependence on overseas markets and would involve deploying German capital in underdeveloped countries. The political economist proposed instead a policy of agricultural autarky, a self-sufficient and independent national economy.

Weber responded by claiming that the latter lacked a "positive ideal of the future," which Mommsen interprets to mean "great-power status." Weber opined, "we cannot carry on a policy of national *comfort* but must seek one of national greatness and therefore take this risk upon our shoulders, provided that we want a national existence different from that of Switzerland" (cited ibid., p. 72). The political economist attacked the ethics of the imperialist position, rejecting the idea of pursuing German greatness and world power "along the 'bombastic' English model, that is, the 'ruthless destruction of foreign rights on all five continents,' by the route of blatant power politics.

He regarded greatness as not worth the striving if it brought 'shame upon you'" (ibid.).

In keeping with his volcanic temperament, as Mommsen aptly describes it, Weber "seized upon. . .the word *shame*. . .and passionately protested: 'We are preaching the gospel of struggle as a national duty, as an economically unavoidable task for the whole as for the individual, and we are not "ashamed" of this struggle, the only road to greatness.'" Weber attributed this struggle to the population increase which he prophesied "will make the struggle for existence, the war of men against men, grow harder and more burdensome in the future" (cited ibid., pp. 72–3). For Weber, the struggle for existence involves a "war of men against men."

In a different economic context, consideration of stock exchange legislation, Weber made an even more emphatic case for the renunciation of ethical judgments in economic matters particularly with regard to the world political economy. "There could be no 'fundamental' solution of economic questions based upon economic or social 'justice' or, more generally, upon any 'ethical' point of view in one country" he argues "as long as the state's *power interests* and those of the national community are themselves contested by other communities in the struggle for political and economic hegemony" (cited ibid., p. 74, italics added).

Weber's view of social life as composed of conflict and struggle directly influenced his views on both domestic politics and international politics. "Just as he approved unreservedly the competition between politicians for power in the area of domestic politics, since it represented a dynamic in, social life," Mommsen infers, "so he also approved the struggle for power between. . .nations . . .and their values as a built-in factor of a dynamic world order" (Mommsen in Wrong, 1970, pp. 189–90). Competition and struggle not only produced a dynamic world order, it also fostered greatness. In Beetham's view, Weber was more interested in Germany's political influence in the world than in Germany's military power *per se*. Like Raymond Aron (in Stammer, 1971, p. 87), I use the term, greatness, rather than power, to describe Weber's political idea(l)s. Political greatness requires the repression of social ethics.

Just as a man must have the power to compel respect and must establish himself as one who cannot and will not be pushed around, so must a nation have the power to resist domination. A nation must establish itself as a power and a force in this world, one that has a will of its own that must be respected and reckoned with. (The assumption is that of a world in which respect is not naturally forthcoming, it must be compelled by power and force.) Germany had to establish itself as one of the great powers in a world in which great power status seemed to require some imperialism.

The more independent powers there are capable of resisting domination, the less will any one of them be able to monopolize power, and the more likely they will be to compete with each other for economic and political control or influence over those who are weaker and, therefore, available to be exploited and "protected." Domination of the weaker makes possible the greatness of the stronger. Weber believed that the struggle for power would end with the division of the globe among the great powers.

Lust for power and rational restraint

For Weber, economic questions had to be considered in the context of the state's national power interests. Those power interests involved the state in a struggle with other states for political and economic hegemony. Marianne Weber writes that Weber expressed the conviction that political economy ought to be guided neither by ideals of finding ways to increase the production of wealth nor by eudemonic ideals such as a fair distribution of goods, nor even by ethical ideals, but by "national" ones (Weber, 1975, p. 308). She says of her husband, his "passion for the national power state evidently sprang from an innate instinct that could not be affected by any reflection" (ibid., p. 125).

His wife's observation suggests that Weber's passion for imperial greatness (which she generally presents in an objective, matter-of-fact manner of which he no doubt would approve) stemmed from a non-rational source and that this passion was not simply a feature of his youth that he later outgrew or renounced. Although Weber's analysis of what could and could not work, as reflected in his critique of the Kaiser's actions for being stupid and ill-considered, tempered his own passion, Weber remained a committed nationalist and imperialist.

By comparing Weber's position with that of a contemporary, Naumann, Marianne Weber succinctly summarizes her husband's perspective: "For Naumann, too, the national power state remained for the time being a means of social reform, while conversely, Weber demanded social and political justice to safeguard the nation-state" (ibid., p. 223). Similarly, she reports of the beginnings of his concern for the working class:

> His new interest in the situation of the working classes, unlike his mother's, was not determined by charitable impulses but primarily by political motives – an interest in making the masses favorably disposed toward the state and wresting them from the clutches of socialism. . .Soon there was also a warm feeling for the mental and spiritual fate [of the laborers] (ibid., pp. 149–50).

But always the fate of the nation, its greatness as a political entity in the world, took precedence over the fate of individuals, groups or classes.

Similarly, economic policy must serve political (national power) interests, rather than purely economic or ethical ones. Whether with respect to an issue like stock market regulation or an issue like trade expansion, Weber consistently analyzes the issue in terms of the effects of alternative policies on Germany's competitive power position in the world. Weber speaks clearly and forcefully about the political and economic implications and ultimate consequences of "seemingly peaceful competition." He contends that the efforts at trade expansion, by "civilized bourgeois-controlled nations," is approaching a point at which *power only* will decide each nation's share in the economic control of the earth." Such control would determine the economic activity that would occur at home and would determine as well the earning potential of the nation's workers (cited by Mommsen, 1984, p. 77, italics in original). Weber seems to have been cautioning against letting appearances deceive; seemingly "civilized bourgeois-controlled nations" will ultimately resort to power and possibly war in order to secure economic advantages. Imperialism benefits not just the capitalists but the workers as well. The period of seemingly peaceful competition must be understood as only a "transitional period."

Weber made this argument in 1897, early in his career, in a treatise on the first navy bill, a bill that would strengthen the German navy. In a lecture that same year Weber again warned that the limits of economic expansion by the appropriation of foreign regions was approaching "with frightening rapidity" and, when that occurs, "it is certain that there will be a bitter struggle for power in place of what appears on the surface to be peaceful progress. And in this mighty struggle, the strongest will be the victor" (cited by Mommsen, 1984, p. 77). Therefore, it is important for the nation to be strong enough to be a victor.

According to Mommsen's interpretation of Weber, it was not just in the interests of privately held capital, but "*in the state's interest* to open the way for its own entrepreneurs and capital to seek profit abroad, especially in economically underdeveloped countries, with political and military means" (ibid., p. 81, italics added). Weber believed that "Eventually, monopolistic structures would replace competitive enterprises. . . Dynamic capitalism would be replaced in the end by a stationary, bureaucratically consolidated economic order." Related to this development and at least as significant in Weber's thought was the belief that ultimately the nations' "economic activities would be restricted to the territory that they controlled politically." Therefore, "it was essential, . . .to win the greatest possible economic elbow room for the nation" (ibid., p. 82).

These political views were expressed by Weber early in his career and no doubt influenced his attitude toward Germany's role in the First World War. But even in his more mature, scholarly writings of *Economy and Society* Weber never renounced the view that "power prestige" and imperialism play a central role in great power politics. Given his assessment of the times, he saw no likelihood in the predictable future of an end to imperialist drives for expansion ([1921–2] 1978, p. 919).

Liberal nationalism, liberal imperialism

With the First World War, Weber's youthful enthusiasm for imperialistic power politics became tempered by more rational and realistic notions of restraint. Unlike those gripped by the annexationist fever that gripped Germany in the wake of its initial military successes, Weber favored a more restrained and responsible imperialism.[1] Weber recognized that military force by itself is not necessarily the best means for achieving political influence. Alliances were a more effective way of achieving that end than the annexation of territory. The smaller nations could be impressed with the advantages of alliances with Germany. Unfortunately, Germany's political ambitions were always being thwarted by a coalition of world powers directed against Germany. Weber believed that this antagonistic coalition was the result of Germany's own political blundering as well as its blustering and posturing. For instance the German occupation of Alsace-Lorraine had turned France into a permanent enemy (Beetham, 1974, p. 139).

Weber wanted an autonomous Poland with military and economic agreements. He rejected the idea of annexations in western Europe, such as the annexation of Belgium. "An expansionist policy in the west would unite all of the western powers against us" (cited by Mommsen, 1984, p. 204). In the east, Weber believed that:

> The Reich should retain the right to maintain fortifications on the eastern borders of Poland. Austria-Hungary should be permitted to have similar privileges to the south. A right to maintain garrisons in Latvia and Lithuania and military railroads would complete the necessary defense measures against Russia. Weber envisaged a trade union with Lithuania, Latvia and Poland that would tie these states economically to the Reich (ibid., pp. 5–6).

Mommsen describes the above as a "liberal approach." Nevertheless, Mommsen points out, "Garrison rights in Lithuania and Latvia, military railroads, a ring of fortifications on Poland's eastern borders – all would have subjected these nations to German military and diplomatic control." In addition, "incorporation in the German . . .tariff union would also have set narrow limits upon the freedom of these nations' internal policies" (ibid., p. 206). Mommsen finds Weber's proposals similar to those of many "liberal imperialists." Like Weber, the latter proposed that Germany became the liberator of the smaller nations in the east and create a new order in eastern Europe characterized by liberal and national state principles "that would act as a buffer against the czarist empire. . .[Also] Germany's new tariff union [among these east European states] would offer ample opportunities for capital investment and a promising market for German commerce" (ibid., p. 207).

Weber's analysis of political, economic and social reality combined with his commitment to manliness resulted in his unique and in some ways peculiar perspective: his liberal versions of nationalism, imperialism and authoritarianism. I distinguish Weber's liberal nationalism from conservative and reactionary nationalism. Weber's liberal nationalism, based on commitment to economic expansion through industrial capitalism which in turn requires external markets and, in Weber's view, imperialism, is characterized by its self-restraint, striving for "no more than is necessary" for guaranteeing Germany's great power status. In contrast to his liberal nationalism, conservative nationalism stood for strengthening Germany by political and economic policies that would strengthen the landowning class and the industrialists. Conservative nationalism represented narrow class interests whereas Weber's liberal nationalism, he believed, represented a broader national interest.

The policies advocated by conservative nationalists were, according to Weber's analysis, self-serving and destructive of the national interest. Although Weber rightfully referred to the interests of the conservative nationalists as reactionary, I distinguish between conservative and what I call reactionary nationalism. Reactionary nationalism expresses itself in anti-Semitism and romantic pan-Germanism. Using nationalist rhetoric to cloak self-interest, as did the "conservative nationalists," reactionary nationalism channels emotions and grievances toward other groups and away from the ruling classes and the political economy. Weber rejected both conservative and reactionary nationalism. He was a liberal nationalist who rationally considered only the national interest – as he conceived it.

Imperialism and culture

Weber contended that German imperialism was necessary not only for economic reasons but also to ensure the independence and world power of German culture. Weber wished to see Germany and its unique culture take its place as a great imperial power. He did not want to see German culture subordinated to or suppressed by the cultures of other power states. According to Weber, the "*laws* of this world . . . [include] the possibility and *unavoidability* of wars for power for the foreseeable future." In this world, "the preservation of national culture is linked necessarily to power politics" (cited ibid., p. 65 italics added).

Weber later justified the First World War in terms of the protection of German culture. "It would be shameful if we lacked the courage to ensure that neither Russian barbarism, English monotony, nor French grandiloquence rule the world. That is why this war is being fought" (cited ibid., p. 208). It is interesting to note not just Weber's depictions of the other cultures, but his use of words like "shameful" and "courage." It is as though he had to dare or goad people into doing what is good or right. Or is it that he must resort to such devices because he cannot justify the action rationally on its own merits, that he cannot rely solely on reason to justify greatness over comfort?

In this statement, Weber clearly asserted that it was worth killing and being killed to protect the world from English monotony. German culture must take its rightful place alongside Russian, English and French culture in ruling the world. Weber accepted the necessity of political dominance and rule; to assume that the "rule of men over men" can be abolished was unrealistic and naive. Thus Weber did not moralize against world *domination* by England, France and Russia, but against domination *by England, France, and Russia*. He wanted Germany to take its place among the ruling cultures rather than be subordinate to, or have the world subordinate to, those other foreign and less worthy cultures.

Weber claimed that there was a link between the prestige of culture and the prestige of power. "Every victorious war promoted the prestige of culture," but "whether it does the development of culture any good is another matter. . .Certainly not unequivocally (Germany after 1870) nor according to empirically palpable signs: pure art and literature of a German nature did not arise from the political centre of Germany." As we saw earlier, he recognised the conflict between human values and power politics: "Not only simple, middle-class virtues, and genuine democracy . . . but far more intimate and lasting values can only bloom on the territory of communities which renounce political power" (cited by Raymond Aron in Stammer, 1971, pp. 87–8). Nevertheless, Weber never suggested renouncing political power; on the contrary, he took the opposite position. Furthermore, as we saw above, he justified his political imperialism in terms of the protection and defense of German culture.

Weber, late in his life, acknowledged the danger to culture from militarism: "Even those artistically inclined: such a true German as Gottfried Keller could never have become so original and individual in the midst of an army camp such as our state is inevitably becoming" (1921, cited ibid., p. 88). Although disgusted with the Kaiser's military policy that was making the state into an army camp, Weber never renounced his own version of power politics.

The excerpt above contains a provocative reference to the "blooming" of "more intimate and lasting values." His use of a flower metaphor indicates something desirable, beautiful, fragile and precious, as does his use of the word, intimate. His reference to intimate and lasting values represents an altogether different set of values from those he had been advocating so staunchly and passionately all his life. Although, as we saw earlier, he acknowledged the importance of these more intimate values, not just for personal life but for the culture as a whole, he never worked out a relationship between these values and political values. To do so would have required renouncing his whole orientation to life and politics, his *Weltanschauung*. The best he could do was to relegate intimate and civic values to the private sphere and small powers and political values of greatness to the public sphere and great powers. (We will return to this issue of the relationship between intimate values and politics again in Parts 3 and 4.)

Raymond Aron (ibid., p. 88) contrasts Weber's position with that of Treitschke. The latter found small states somewhat ridiculous but Weber is glad that a Germanism exists outside the Germany which has become a "national power-state," because then intimate values and art can flourish within a German culture outside of Germany proper.

Cynicism: socialism and pacifism

Weber argued that socialist societies would be no less likely to have imperialist ambitions.

> They would seek to buy as cheaply as possible indispensable goods not produced on their own territory. . .from others that have natural monopolies and would seek to exploit them. It is probable that force would be used where it would lead easily to favorable conditions of exchange; the weaker party would thereby be obliged to pay tribute, if not formally then at least actually (Weber, [1921–2] 1978, p. 919).

Thus Weber claims that "capitalist imperialism" would be found as well among state socialist societies.

Weber's analysis presupposes and (re)produces a cynicism regarding the motives of nation states. This cynicism is identical with political realism, an assessment of the interests of nation states in power and economic benefits regardless of whether these states are socialist (condemning exploitation and propounding international co-operation) or capitalist (affirming freedom and equality). He holds no "illusions" about the motives of either socialist or capitalist states. The nation's power prestige and economic interests are determining principles of social action.

His cynicism or "realism" regarding the motives of power states applies to his views about the mass of citizens as well. He describes societies in which the citizens lived economically off war.

War brought soldiers' pay and, in case of a victory, tribute from the subjects. This tribute was actually distributed among the full citizens in the hardly veiled form of attendance-fees at popular assemblies, court hearings, and public festivities. Here, every full citizen could directly grasp the interest in imperialist policy and power.

He contrasts that situation with today where the benefits from imperialist policies are not so directly comprehensible to the masses. "For under the present economic order, the tribute to 'creditor nations' assumes the forms of interest payments on debts or of capital profits transferred from abroad to the propertied strata of the 'creditor nation'" (ibid., p. 920).

He treated these "tributes" in a matter-of-fact way and realistically appraised their importance. He implied that abolishing existing imperialist policies would adversely affect the labor market, employment and purchasing power and hence would be against the interests of labor. Weber challenged the "socialist" concern for the interests of labor by showing how the socialist position against "capitalist imperialism" would not be in the best interests of labor.

Weber observed that in spite of the objective benefits that accrue to labor from an imperialist policy, "labor in creditor nations is of a strongly pacifist mind. . .shows no interest in the continuation and compulsory collection of such tributes from foreign debtor communities that are in arrears. Nor does labor show an interest in forcibly participating in the exploitation of foreign colonial territories." Weber attributes this irrational position to labor's "immediate class situation" which does not *directly* benefit from such tributes and exploitation. Furthermore, "Those entitled to tribute belong to the opponent class, who dominate the community" (ibid). Weber implied that if labor were to see that it benefited from imperialism, then it, too, would be supportive of imperialism and of imperialist wars. He had no interest in envisioning an alternative world in which all would benefit from international co-operation and mutual aid.

Weber recognized that there are also rational economic reasons for pacifist sympathy among the masses rather than imperialist warmaking. Despite the fact that increased job and income opportunities result from production for war, the temporary period of enhanced business activity and especially the speculation to which the latter gives rise may result in economic recession later. Also significant was the fact that capital is withdrawn from alternative uses making it more difficult to satisfy demands in other fields. Moreover the ruling strata usually transfer to the masses the financing of the war.

Despite these economic reasons for pacifism on the part of the masses, Weber claimed: "Experience shows that the pacifist interests of petty bourgeois and proletarian strata very often and very easily fail" (ibid., p. 921). This is because of the susceptibility of the masses to manipulation and because war is often thought to lead to increased opportunities. Because their interests may not be so directly threatened, the masses may not feel that a war is such a great risk. In contrast, a lost war *directly* threatens the interests of the monarch, the ruling stratum, the propertied bourgeoisie, republican power holders and groups having vested interests in a republican constitution (fear of a victorious general).

"The 'masses,' in contrast to other interest-groups, subjectively risk a smaller stake in the game." In contrast to other groups with concrete interests that could be threatened, "the 'masses' as such . . . have nothing concrete to lose but their lives. The valuation and effect of this danger strongly fluctuates in their own minds. On the whole, it can easily be reduced to zero through emotional influence" (ibid.).

Compare Weber's "the masses have nothing. . .to lose but their lives" with Marx's "the workers have nothing to lose but their chains." Weber implied that their lives are not as valued by the masses as is property by its owners. Marx assumed here that a degraded life is not worth living; there is nothing for workers to lose if they die other than their chains. While Weber was cynical, and Marx idealistic, both placed little value on mere life.

Neither of these theorists assumed that the masses or the working class might find value in perpetuating and nurturing life and in enhancing and sharing life experiences even under the most adverse conditions. Weber and Marx have taken this attitude because they did not consider the re-creation of human life a primary, central value. They considered production and politics not reproduction and re-creation as primary and central. They thought of the masses or the workers as "real men," whose life activity, unlike that of "real women," does not focus on re-creating life. Neither Weber nor Marx in their political theories gave much recognition to the importance of children (as opposed to an abstraction like future generations or progeny) in giving meaning and value to life or in guiding and constraining political action and political policy for either class.

Weber did not necessarily devalue workers' lives nor did he advocate their manipulation; he merely acknowledged their susceptibility to manipulation. He did suggest, however, that property owners and power holders are more concerned over risking their property and power than are the propertyless and powerless masses – men – over risking their lives. Weber may have been right. It is interesting that property, power and the prestige of power can be more valued than life itself. To what extent that value is due to a concern for one's progeny as opposed to a concern for one's own (national) greatness remains unexplored.

Weber's analysis and assessment of the likelihood of imperialist policies and wars being either supported or opposed by various groups according to their interests could lead to a pessimistic cynicism, but Weber's cynicism was not pessimistic. Weber adopted the same attitude that he did toward the rationalization and intellectualization, the disenchantment, that characterizes the modern world: one must face the fate of the times like a man. People must accept as a challenge the reality of their world, the fact that they live in a period of great power politics, a period of capitalist imperialism. He did not consider working to change that reality. He liked the challenge. Given the reality of a world composed of competing and contending nation states, political actors must rise to the challenge, enter the fray and with a "cool head" and a passionate heart determine the best posture and policies that will serve the interests of their nation state.

Internationalism

Weber's analysis of the economic and political realities of the time make his liberal imperialism seem eminently rational and responsible. However, it was also possible at the time to recognize those realities and rise above them, not just morally in judgment, but politically in practice. Sandi Cooper (1980) documents the development from the 1880s until the First World War of regional, national and international organizations devoted to liberal internationalism (as distinct from socialist internationalism), a co-operative and collective international system for maintaining peace.

Cooper recounts the tensions, dilemmas and divisions within the liberal international peace movements over issues of existing political and economic injustices and the question of peace without justice. Nevertheless, the existence of liberal and socialist internationalism shows that a critical analysis of a historical reality and its "rules of the game" can give rise to policies aimed at transforming that reality and its rules, rather than trying to succeed within the constraints of that reality. Success within that given reality requires accepting the rules of the game with its inevitable outcome: victors and victims.

Mommsen considers that, from the perspective of today, Weber's imperialist beliefs are the most historically bound aspect of Weber's political thought. "Today we are more inclined to agree with Ernst Troeltsch, who in 1915. . .fought bravely against German imperialism and pleaded for reconciliation among the world's great cultural nations" (Mommsen, 1984, p. 80). I am more interested in the underlying assumptions in Weber's thinking than in assessing its validity today. Weber's political analysis was based on certain assumptions about social life that make his thinking not only of historical and political interest but of sociological interest. Weber assumed that struggles for dominance are the key factor for understanding social life in general and political life in particular. I argue not that this is an incorrect assumption, but that it reflects a partial view. Treating a partial view as the whole produces a distorted picture of reality that becomes a self-fulfilling prophecy.

World policy over domestic policy

Mommsen treats Weber's views as a reflection of the dominant thinking of his times, which he, Mommsen, believes was based on improper priorities. He explains that the eyes of the ruling classes "were deflected from German constitutional and social problems at home to questions of German world policy. They neglected the reordering of their own house for Zanzibar, Samoa, Tsingtau and Morocco. This is why German policy would fail in the end and lead Germany into a world catastrophe" (ibid., p. 89). While I do not wish to speculate on the accuracy of Mommsen's analysis of the failure of German policy, I do wish to highlight his stress on *domestic* policy and the reordering of one's *own house*.

The tension between focusing on world policy and struggles for power and focusing on internal problems and domestic policy parallels the tension between what may be called a will to power (world dominance) and a will to sociability (interpersonal pleasures and well-being). The issue as I see it is not simply one of giving priority to world policy over domestic policy, but of giving priority to conflict and struggles for dominance as opposed to conflict resolution and community building, priority to "masculine" values over "feminine" virtues, to politics and power over communal life and human welfare.

Weber argued that the latter depends ultimately on the former, and therefore the latter must be subordinated to the former. One could argue, however, that the former, politics and power, has no meaning or value in itself (a view that Weber shares) but gets its value or meaning from serving the interests of the latter, domestic life and social well-being. Hence, one could conclude that politics and power must serve and thus be subordinated to domestic interests. One would then weigh the potential gains and losses from any given political policy in terms of human welfare. One might then ask if the situation is so desperate, the likelihood of the world domination of "English monotony" so threatening, that Germany must kill and be killed to prevent it? Instead of an either–or choice between political power and domestic welfare, an automatic prioritizing of one over the other, it is necessary to consider both and the particular relationship and tensions between them at any given time.

Weber did recognize the relationship in one respect. Modern warfare depends on the commitment and loyalty of the masses. Therefore, social policy must be devised with an eye to assuring their loyalty. The attitude of the masses toward those in power will be influenced by how well they, the masses, fare under the leadership of those in power. They judge the worthiness of the struggle and of those in power in terms of their welfare; is the struggle justified in terms of its relation to their lives?

The view of international relations as struggles for power blinds us to the reality that other nations, too, have domestic interests to which they must be responsive. These domestic interests may conflict with the interest in national struggles for power and greatness. The strength of those domestic interests could constrain international power struggles and predispose the nation states to a different, less belligerent way of relating to each other, one more in keeping with international co-operation. Weber, on the other hand, believed that the interests of the masses coincide with those of the power politicians because a powerful nation state redounds to the economic benefit of the workers. Furthermore, the masses can be easily manipulated (Weber, [1921–2] 1978, p. 921). He had no vision of a different relationship between domestic and foreign policy, no vision of an alternative world in which power and greatness do not entail domination and imperialism.

Weber was not interested in such alternatives because for him peace meant the repression of conflict through subjugation – political castration. He desired "masculine" conflict and action and seemed to fear "feminine" peace and inaction. The peace that Weber feared was not the absence of war, *per se* (he was not a warmonger); it was the absence of struggles for power. Weber believed that where there is conflict, action, struggle, there is dynamism, development and, hence, greatness. Where there is no conflict and struggle, there is subjugation, impotence, lack of greatness. There is either the life of heroic "men," struggles for power, or the life of subjugated "women," peace and stagnation.

The sociological grounds of Weber's politics

Weber's politics was grounded in his analysis of social and political reality, an analysis influenced as we have seen by his commitment to certain values of manliness as well as by his class position, his biography and his knowledge of history. Weber's politics presumed and (re)produced his conception of and commitment to a manly form of life. Weber advocated this manly form of life both for the individual and for the nation, a form of life which was more in keeping with bourgeois capitalism and imperialism than either monopoly capitalism or socialism. In other words, Weber's self-conscious support of capitalism derived from an analysis of social reality that is informed not so much by commitment to values of liberalism, as by commitment to values of manliness. These values presume and produce a masculine perspective that is not unique to Weber. This perspective dominates international political thought and as Weber intimated is not limited to capitalist societies.

Weber's adherence to the principle that struggles for power and dominance are basic to social life and necessary for social dynamism resulted in political positions that appear to be opposed to each other: liberalism and imperialism. Although they appear to be opposed to each other, they were united in Weber's thought by a shared grounding in a commitment to independence, autonomy and greatness through competition and conflict. The belief that struggles for power are essential to social dynamism and the development of greatness accounts for Weber's brand of nationalism and imperialism as well as his advocacy of capitalism.

In bourgeois capitalism struggles for power take the form of economic competition which produces a dynamic economic system. Because it fosters and channels the struggle for power, competitive capitalism produces among entrepreneurs the kind of individual initiative and boldness that are the characteristics of individual greatness and leadership. Furthermore, and most decisive for Weber, the future of Germany depended on the kind of economic development that only competitive capitalism could provide. A politically strong entrepreneurial capitalist class was superior to continued rule by a declining feudal agrarian class, the Junkers, whose interests were clearly detrimental to the national interest. Capitalism was also superior to socialism.

Beetham suggests that the view of Weber as an ardent nationalist, as well as the view of him as a committed liberal, must be complemented by a view of him as a pronounced anti-socialist. Although opposed to socialism, Weber was not, as I have indicated above, unsympathetic to the proletariat. On the contrary, he desired to see the proletariat gain political power and engage in conflict and struggle, joining with the capitalists against the Junkers, but in a "politically responsible" way – in Parliament. In this way they would gain political maturity and therefore the capacity for political leadership.

Weber identified political maturity with readiness "to place the long-term economic, political and *power* interests of the nation above all other considerations" (cited by Mommsen, 1984, p. 88, italics in original). We get an illuminating insight into his notion of political leadership in his assessment of the German working class. The class lacked "the great *power* instincts of a class called to political leadership. . .No spark of the Catilinarian energy of *action*, and no breath of the powerful *national* fervor" (cited ibid., italics in original).

Weber believed that the proletariat needed to recognize, in addition to its own class interests, its common interests with the capitalists, a common interest in a great power state. The common interest – nationalism – had to take precedence over the particular interest of the proletariat as a class. Revolutionary socialists, in Weber's view, took the politically irresponsible position of placing class interest above the national interest. Weber's anti-socialism (Beetham's point) as well as his imperialism and nationalism (Mommsen's point), I conclude, were all grounded in his commitment to the idea(l)s of manly, heroic action – the kind of action that makes possible imperial greatness.

Weber hated the idea of Germany's becoming either a bureaucratic socialist society or a bureaucratic capitalist welfare state dominated by industrial magnates, *rentiers* and bureaucrats.[2] He hated the idea of Germany becoming a society that would foster civic values rather than imperial ones, feminine virtues rather than masculine ones, economic and domestic well-being over the political greatness of a man's world.

Notes

1 Ilse Dronberger (1971) explains Weber's political views on the war and on the period immediately following Germany's defeat while also presenting the political context of his views.

2 Weber opposed any policy that "encouraged German bourgeois capital away from international economic conquests to the path of creating rentier life styles" (cited by Mommsen, 1984, p. 98). Weber, like Marx, believed that German politics required a decisive choice between supporting bourgeois progress or unconsciously propping up feudal reaction. For this reason, Weber opposed the anti-entailment laws of 1904 and 1917 which enabled the bourgeoisie to own landed property that would bring with it titles of nobility and the status of *rentier*. These laws would have the effect of encouraging the bourgeoisie to identify with the reactionary Junker aristocracy. German capital needed to be involved in the economic "conquests" on the economic battlefield. If "an interest mentality replaced economic daring, Germany's economic position would be endangered" (ibid.). Weber rejected the "static, security-conscious, economically conservative mentality characteristic of interest-income capitalism" (ibid., p. 99). Investment in land, as would be encouraged with the anti-entailment laws, is not a productive use of capital. Marx would agree.

PART TWO

The modern world

6

Modern bureaucrat

We turn now from a concern with manliness and politics to a concern with the nature of modern society and modern "man."[1] Weber considered the fate of modern man to be linked to the bureaucratic nature of modern society – capitalist or socialist. In both capitalism and socialism that fate hinges on a conflict between means and ends with means – such as capital and bureaucracy – coming to replace ends – ultimate values. Similarly, a bureaucratic mentality comes to replace a heroic warrior mentality.

Weber's major concern was the effects of bureaucracy on heroic individualism. That is why he rejected socialism. Nevertheless, he raised still another issue regarding socialism. Overlooked or denied by the proponents of socialism was the issue of conflict and coercion. Weber used his analysis of the inevitability of conflict and coercion within socialism to refute and discredit the idea of socialism as an ethical form of life that overcomes domination, oppression and economic conflict. This leaves socialism as differing from capitalism only in terms of its being a more comprehensive, centralized bureaucracy. In other words, whether under capitalism or socialism, most men will become bureaucrats. (That women too may become bureaucrats is irrelevant; Weber is concerned about the loss of manly heroic action.) Only a competitive capitalist society allows room for some men (and presumably some women) to become heroic individuals – successful entrepreneurs. And only a world that is divided into competing nation states allows room for some men (and presumably some women) to become heroic political leaders.

Weber analyzed modern society in terms of its own internal dynamics. Although a form of social life that offers the most freedom from the constraints of tradition, including patriarchal and patrimonial authority, modern life introduces new, impersonal constraints that threaten again to reduce if not eliminate individual freedom of action. The greatest threat in this regard is bureaucratization which offers the most technically efficient and rational mode of administrative control. Nevertheless, Weber acknowledged and stressed that impersonal bureaucratic domination offers greater personal freedom, freedom from personal domination, than patrimonial, feudal modes of domination in which loyalty and obedience is owed to the person.

Weber's analysis of bureaucracy uncovers a dynamic that for Weber appeared to be the dilemma of modernity: a conflict between formal, bureaucratic means and substantive ethical values as ends. The conflict between formal and substantive rationalities, between formal rules (including rational, methodical, technical means) and human values (ends), represents what Marxists might call the contradictions of capitalism. But Weber's analysis does not exempt socialist societies.

Given the basic value by which he judges society, personal freedom of action, a society that threatens to promote society-wide bureaucratization is therefore one to be avoided and resisted. Weber was concerned not just about an outside danger of bureaucratization – socialism – but about the danger from the internal dynamics of modern capitalist society, itself, a society that was inevitably becoming increasingly bureaucratized.

The abstract conflict between ends (human values, ethics or substantive rationality) and means (instrumental, technical or formal rationality) takes concrete form within the major spheres of modern capitalism – bureaucratic administration, the economy and law as well as democracy. In each case, the means come to obstruct the ends.[2]

For instance the most rational form of capitalistic enterprise is the bureaucratic which despite its formal rationality, tends to cause a "paralysis of private economic initiative," (Weber, [1921-2] 1978 p. LVIII) thereby restricting rationalization of the economy. Although it starts out as a rationalization of economic enterprise, bureaucracy ends up obstructing further rationalization of the enterprise and of the economy. Another conflict between means and ends (substantive values) occurs when economic rationality conflicts with the substantive values of job security and workplace democracy (ibid., pp. 137–8).

Weber accepted the inevitable conflict between substantive human values, including ethical values and formal, technical and instrumental rationality. He held no illusions about creating an ethically rationalized world in which human values would rule, and contended that it is not possible to regulate relations between banks and debtors ethically, for no personal bond exists – to try to do so would stifle formal rationality which is what happened in China (Weber, 1946, p. 331). In other words, if formal economic relations were subjected to the rule of human values and personal ethics, as in traditional societies, then economic development would be stifled. On the other hand, modern society runs the risk of ossification from the other end – an emphasis on formalized rules and procedures.

What is Weber's solution to the problem of bureaucratic organization: conflict between formal means and substantive ends? For Weber, the solution came at the level of the individual who can negotiate between means and ends, between formal rationality and human values. Weber looked to the heroic individual, a strong political leader, who can take charge of the state bureaucracy and master it, subordinating bureaucratic rules and methods to substantive, political ends. Weber looked to a political leader to take decisive action and choose between ends and means based on a weighing of consequences. Only a political leader able to control the bureaucracy and act out of commitment to some substantive cause – such as imperial greatness – can rescue the nation from the ossification of bureaucratic rationalization and bring dynamism to a society. Only such a leader is able to bear the burden of making decisions that may mean sacrificing ethics and employing violence.

In the economic realm, although technical economic rationality must prevail over human values, individual leaders, entrepreneurial captains of industry, can take heroic actions and prevent ossification of the economy – but only so long as the economy is not socialized and controlled by a centralized bureaucracy.

In the political realm, the ethic of responsibility resolves the dilemma. The responsible leader considers both means and ends. Political ends may require resorting to violence as means, and certainly involves some system of domination. Being rational and realistic means acknowledging that the former is occasionally necessary and the latter is an inevitable fact of social life.

Weber accepted the tension and conflict between ends and means as a necessary concomitant of modernity. He also accepted as inevitable the conclusion of this conflict: the ultimate irrationality of modernity, the replacement of human values (ends) with technical bureaucratic means. His recognition of this irrationality, his intellectual integrity and courage in confronting and exposing it, his outspoken opposition to particular instances of the irrationality while acceding to the general irrationality as unavoidable, without evasion or self-deception and without reacting emotionally and irrationally or escaping into utopian illusions, establishes Weber as a modern realist *par excellence*.

Only with respect to the political sphere did the substantive irrationality of modern society arouse in Weber a passionate response and attempt to overcome it. Otherwise he was cynical about radical change and resigned to the inevitable domination of human values by technical, capitalistic, bureaucratic rationality – the inevitability of means becoming ends. With the exception of the political system which he saw to be in dire need of reforming so as to produce political leaders, he treated modern society as peculiarly, inevitably and necessarily irrational at the same time that it was the most rational form of society possible. He therefore opposed as naive, self-deluding and destructive the desires and attempts of others to transform modern society so as to overcome its ethical irrationality.

Although he recognized the ways in which modern society was irrational, he also showed that this irrationality was the product of the very rationality that distinguishes the modern world from all others. Weber saw the technical rationality of means as responsible for the unique freedom, dynamism, and productivity of modern life. He saw that modern rationality as well as modern irrationality was due to the transformation of means – such as bureaucracy – into self-perpetuating ends.

Weber's concern for political leadership and national greatness took precedence over all other issues. Yet Weber realized that the technical and bureaucratic rationality of modern social organizations works against commitment to values, idea(l)s and causes that give meaning to life. A rationality of means reduces all actors to bureaucrats, "cogs" in a machine, each desiring only to become a larger cog. Hence Weber turned to the possibility of charismatic, patriarchal leaders who could infuse a rationality of values or ends into social and political life, who could reinvigorate an effete public life. I call Weber's conception of charismatic leadership "patriarchal," because it means taking charge and ruling or commanding (in the name of something that people feel they must obey) as opposed to leadership that is more maternal in principle – either of an exemplary type, leading by example or suggestion; or of a representative type, leading by representing or carrying out the wishes of those whom one represents; or of a pedagogical type, leading by teaching and learning from (being responsive to) those whom one teaches.

Weber saw no modern choice other than capitalist bureaucratization tempered by patriarchal leaders. This stand led him to reject socialism or anything like a feminist solution.

Weber's rejection of socialism rested on three theoretical premises: a Hobbesian view that social life is based on struggles for power and conflicts over self-interest, hence the need for either market regulation or autocratic, bureaucratic control; a view of work as self-sacrifice which requires external inducements or threats, particularly threats to the welfare and security of one's dependents; a view that the economic rationalization of production requires a market and a profit motive, and that ethical interests in social welfare and rights to a job would prevent the technical rationalization of production. In other words, technical rationality of the economy would be stifled if ethical rationality prevails.

Whereas the capitalist stress on means may involve a conflict with ends, a socialist stress on ends may involve a conflict with means. Weber offers the following examples:

1 A planned economy oriented to the satisfaction of wants must weaken the incentive to labor if there is no risk of lack of support. It would be impossible to allow a worker's dependents to suffer the full consequence of his lack of efficiency in production. In a rational market economy this is an important incentive (Weber, [1921–2] 1978, p. 110).

2 Where a planned economy is radically carried out, it must accept the inevitable reduction in practical, technical calculations which would result from the elimination of money and capital accounting. He refers to this as a fundamental and unavoidable element of irrationality. Hence, socialism does not avoid the social problems due to the conflict between formal,

technical calculating rationality and substantive, ethical, human–value rationality (ibid., p. 111).
3 With an economy planned in terms of substantive ends, individuals would be administered by autocratic determination from above in which they had no voice. "But once any right of co–determination were granted to the population, this would immediately make possible the fighting out of interest conflicts." Without autocratic domination and without the regulation of the market, "violent power struggles" would ensue (ibid., pp. 202 3).
4 Socialism would require "a still higher degree of formal bureaucratization than capitalism. If this should prove not to be possible, it would demonstrate . . .another of those fundamental elements of irrationality – a conflict between formal and substantive rationality" (ibid., p. 225).

Beyond his rejection of socialism as planned economy, Weber denied as inconceivable or impossible the broader intent, portent and content of the whole concept of socialism: that individuals would recognize their individual interests as social and social interests as individual ones; that they would collectively define and determine the social interest as the satisfaction or enhancement of individual interests; and that they would define and determine their individual interests as the satisfaction or enhancement of the collective interest. In other words, socialism means that the development and enhancement of social life would be based on and require the development and enhancement of individual life and vice-versa.

Such a recognition or orientation would not eliminate conflict, nor would it presuppose the elimination of conflict. Conflicts of opinion over the best means for realizing individual and collective interests and over the definition of collective interest could still occur. But conflict based on an essential division within society – conflict between the interests of capital and the interests of labor – could not occur. Any and all conflict would take place within a transcendent yet immanent interest in the social whole: social life.

Society is both transcendent over the individual and immanent in the individual, just as the individual is able to transcend the society and yet remain immanent in it. The individuals would recognize themselves as particular, unique personifications of the society, as inherently social individuals, while recognizing that society is possible only through the individuals who comprise it. The individual would be committed to the community and the community to the individual. The community would recognize the fulfilment of each individual's needs and interests as valuable and essential to itself, and the individual would recognize the needs and interests of the collectivity as valuable and essential to the individual.

In contrast to this idea(l) of socialism, Weber considered a socialist society to be as follows:

The decision-making, of course, would lie in the hands of the central authority, and the functions of the individual engaged in the production of goods would be limited to the performance of "technical" services; that is, to "labor" in the sense of the term employed here. This would be true so long as the individuals were being administered "dictatorially," that is, by autocratic determination from above in which they had no voice (ibid., p. 202).

I take this to mean, especially in light of what follows, that in socialist society, as in capitalist society, those engaged in production would be restricted to the mere carrying out of bureaucratic technical functions rather than involved in determining collectively on the basis of individual and collective interests what those functions might be, how they might be carried out, and how they might be allocated. However, Weber did consider another version of socialism based on co-determination, but he had a different idea of what that would be like than the ideal sketched above:

Once any right of "co-determination" were granted to the population, this would immediately make possible, also in a formal sense, the fighting out of interest conflicts centering on the manner of decision-making and, above all, on the question of how much should be saved (i.e., put aside from current production). But this is not the decisive point (ibid., pp. 202–3).

Before examining the "decisive point," I want to consider Weber's explanation for the fighting out of interest conflicts. The fight over the method of decision-making refers to the awareness that no method is completely neutral, some groups or individuals stand to benefit, others to lose. If the method is one of majority rule, for example, then the minority suffers. The other source of conflict involves the question of surplus: how much labor is needed to produce what the community considers necessary to meet the needs and desires of the community, and how much additional labor (saving or surplus) is needed to produce additional values over and above those that are considered necessary? And how will it be determined which additional values are most needed or desired? These questions suggest a conflict of interest over the amount of time to be used in producing necessary consumer goods and the amount of time to be used in producing the means of production (heavy industry); and also a conflict over the amount of time to be used in producing necessaries for consumption and the amount of time to be used in producing goods for exchange (in order to obtain capital that can be used to import other goods).

If we identify the interest in consumer goods and in reduction of labour time with the individual, and the interest in heavy industry and production of surplus value for exchange with the collective interest, these conflicts could be seen as a conflict between the community and the individual, between those who purportedly orient to the interests of the community as a whole, for example the party, and those who purportedly orient to their own individual interests, the workers/consumers. But this view presumes that the social and the individual are divided as if the workers/consumers had no interest in developing heavy industry or in obtaining needed imports through exchange. On the contrary, it could be argued that differences in interests and needs regarding the issue of "surplus" does not preclude reconciliation.

The quotation above left off at the point where Weber stated that the decisive point is not the substance of the conflict. He continued:

> What is decisive is that in socialism, too, the individual will under these conditions ask first whether to him, personally, the rations allotted and the work assigned, as compared with other possibilities, appear to conform with his own interests. This is the criterion by which he would orient his behavior, and violent power struggles would be the normal result (ibid., p. 203).

Assuming that there were no central authority making autocratic determination from above, violent power struggles would occur. These would be the result of the inevitable fact that in socialism, just as in capitalism, individual self-interest would be the first concern and the criterion by which individuals would orient their behavior. Weber did not see the possibility of individuals identifying their own self-interest with the communal interest and therefore voluntarily subordinating some of their interests some of the time. He did not imagine a society in which an interest, both transcendent and immanent, could voluntarily take precedence over individual and separate interests, such that each would willingly sacrifice some particular interests as a way of "proving" commitment to a mutual interest that would encompass and transcend particular interests.

Weber insisted that all kinds of conflicts of interest would prevail and be the normal phenomena of life as much as or more so, he implies, than under capitalism:

> Struggles over the alteration or maintenance of rations once alloted – as, for instance, over ration supplements for heavy labor; appropriations or expropriations of particular jobs, sought after because of extra remuneration of pleasant working conditions; work cessations, such as in strikes or lock-outs; restrictions of production to enforce changes in the conditions of work in particular branches; boycots and the forcible dismissal of unpopular supervisors – in short, appropriation processes of all kinds and interest struggles would also then be the normal phenomena of life (ibid.)

He saw socialism as no different from capitalism with respect to the pursuit of self-interest and the conflicts that would result from that. The differences between socialism and capitalism would not extend to this "fundamental factor." "The *structure* of interests and the relevant situation would be different, and there would be other *means* of pursuing interests, but this fundamental factor would remain just as relevant as before" (ibid.).

The fundamental factor, of course, is conflict over interests. Self-interest in opposition to the interests of others would underlie all action. Certain individuals and groups would have advantages in those struggles then as now:

> that advantages would be enjoyed on the one hand by the workers engaged in the most essential services, on the other hand by those who were physically strongest, would simply reflect the existing situation. But however that might be, it would be the interests of the individual, possibly organized in terms of the similar interests of many individuals as opposed to those of others, which would underlie all action (ibid.).

All action would be based on the fundamental factor of pursuit of individual interests as opposed to the interests of others. Weber does consider the latter possibility:

> It is of course true that economic action which is oriented on purely ideological grounds to the interests of others does exist. But it is even more certain that the mass of men do not act in this way, and it is an induction from experience that they cannot do so and never will (ibid.).

Thus conclude Weber's comments on the matter: some actors will have an interest in giving to others based on commitment to some ideology, but most will have a material or practical orientation to their own self-interest. The only alternative to egoism is altruism based on commitment to abstract ideology. He does not conceive nor perceive the possibility of an immanent and transcendent interest that is neither an egoistic interest nor an altruistic one but a recognition that each requires the other.

Feminist philosophers have addressed this issue and come to very different conclusions than Weber. They reject both egoism and altruism as such and suggest a model that has elements of both, despite the apparent opposition between them.

If the men that Weber describes are motivated by their competitive desire to secure advantages for themselves or their interests, it would be irrational and weak to succumb to feelings of love and compassion when acting within the real world of conflicts of interest, coercion and violence. For the less brutal, more vulnerable actor will end up being taken advantage of and coerced. Some feminists, too, claim that it is futile to try to alter relationships between men and women in a world that is based on male-appropriated advantages. Since it is assumed that men will not renounce those advantages, the only solution is to renounce heterosexual relationships and turn to all-female relationships and all-female organizations.

The feminist assumption is that non-coercive relationships and organizational forms are possible and that women are capable of creating them. Feminism aims for relationships and forms of social life that self-consciously attempt to foster individual self-realization, the development of individual capacities and interests in the context of commitment to caring, loving, communal relationships. Feminists want women to discover and express their desires and interests and to strive for and receive recognition. This vision presumes, however, that the expression of desires and interests of one will not be perceived as a threat to the desires and interests of other(s). According to Weber, such a presumption is naive. For him, community is based on the sharing of interests in common. As soon as there are different interests within the community, the community as such is threatened.

There is no guarantee that interests will not conflict and that some will not be threatened by others. Given the potential conflict, some will strive to achieve advantage over others with the result that the more powerful will prevail and attempt to secure their advantage. Such security is accomplished by mobilizing the means of violence in support of the appropriated advantage, by institutionalizing the rights to that position and securing those rights legally. These appropriated advantages are then backed by the political community's capacity to employ violence on behalf of legally established rights.

According to Weber's model, a feminist solution is doomed to fail by reproducing the same kind of social world to which it is a reaction. It is doomed to fail just as is socialism. The aim of ridding social life of conflict, coercion and violence is a naive, utopian one. At best, women and the disadvantaged can hope that through struggle and conflict they can achieve positions of dominance over others or use whatever power and influence they can muster through struggles and conflict to mitigate against the worst abuses of power and coercion.

Feminists who are committed to overcoming male domination must become like men, and not only not shrink from pursuing their interests but strive to secure advantages for themselves. They must acquire access to the means of violence (state power) in order to appropriate for themselves advantages over others. The world cannot be otherwise. This is the kind of realistic, liberal feminism that Weber might support. The only alternative would be to accept and submit to the conditions of subservience, an alternative that Weber, with his keen sensitivity to any kind of servility, would find abhorrent. On the other hand, Weber also believed in chivalry.

Weber's thesis ends up with a duality of strength and weakness, power and powerlessness in which either one or the other prevails. Relationships and social life are ultimately based on coercion and domination; this is as true for the most intimate relationships as for the most impersonal relationships of economic activity, whether socialist or capitalist.

In Weber's rejection of socialism and, by analogy, any version of radical feminism, he argues again and again that modern social life is based not on mutual desire, recognition and trust but on the pursuit of individual interest, the appropriation of advantages and the threat of violence. In such a world, trust, vulnerability and renunciation of violence are self-deluding, foolhardy and self-destructive. In the pursuit of interests each will take advantage of the vulnerability of the other and try to secure that advantage. This view of social life becomes a self-fulfilling prophecy. Given this view of the world no actors would knowingly suspend their own interests, renounce violence and trust other(s).

Max Weber's conflict theory of social life is a masculine one that perpetuates public distrust, domination and the possibility of violence at the same time that it advocates individual integrity, responsibility and chivalry. That masculine conflict theory limits modern choice to bureaucratized capitalism with patriarchal, heroic leaders. By the same token, it rules out alternatives like feminism as well as socialism.

Notes

1   I place quotation marks around the word "man" to indicate the problematic nature of its status as a generic term for both men and women. As we will see, modern "man" is gendered, and the gender is masculine. That is why I adopt the term, modern "man."
2   Bologh (in Glassman and Murvar, 1984) traces the basic tensions between formal and substantive rationality in all these spheres as laid out by Weber.

7

Modern hero

Weber's analysis of modern bureaucratic society led him to stress the need for a political leader who can control the bureaucracy and redirect it in accordance with some substantive good or, even more preferable, some notion of greatness. It is important to note that Weber does not talk about transforming bureaucracy itself by politicizing and democratizing it, enabling all its members to participate directly or indirectly in making policy. Rather, he turns to a hero, a political leader who can take charge and move the bureaucracy on behalf of some idea, value or cause.

Weber considered his view to be grounded in a realistic acceptance of modern life. Transforming bureaucracy into a democratic political community would undermine efficiency, technical rationality and consequently the effectiveness of the leader. For Weber, bureaucracy was essential to efficient administration. He distinguished administration from politics, just as he distinguished the official from the politician. Weber's primary concern was effective political leadership. He considered a rationalized administrative bureaucratic staff essential to a modern political leader.

We have already seen how Weber's politics were grounded in his assumptions about the nature of social life. Given his view of social life, one is left with two choices: masculine will to power or feminine acceptance of powerlessness. One either adopts a feminine attitude of passivity in which "life is permitted to run on as an event in nature" or one adopts a masculine emphasis on decisive action in which life is "consciously guided by a series of ultimate decisions." I think it is fair to conclude that the latter heroic form of life constituted an ultimate value for Weber.

Weber's dualistic conception of human life as either masculine or feminine informed his sociological and his political analyses. However, Weber's view was more subtle and complex than this simple dualism suggests. He distinguished between two versions of masculinity, one that is more unassailable than the other. The strong version I will refer to as Weber's conception of manliness. Weber's conception of manliness is distinguished from ordinary masculinity, the weak form, by the former's emphasis on restraint which derives from a sense of responsibility.

Restraint

The strong version of manliness makes for the modern hero. This version of manly greatness requires restraint, rationality and responsibility as opposed to the weak version of masculinity which involves behavior that is impulsive, foolish and irresponsible. The emphasis on restraint and responsibility takes the form of a politics of moderation which often leads to liberal political positions. His emphasis on rationality and realism, however, leads to nationalism and imperialism. Given Weber's view of reality only certain attitudes, values and positions appear rational while others must appear foolish.

Weber justified all his political positions as rational and realistic. He never included ethics or morality in his justification for one position over another. Similarly he denounced other positions for being stupid, foolish or short-sighted rather than for being unethical or unjust. The separation of rationality from ethics corresponds with his version of manliness. Although an *appeal* to others based on ethics is feminine, a commitment to ethics in one's own actions can be heroic or foolish depending on one's perspective. It can be considered heroic from a subjective perspective because it imposes demands on the actor which require striving and self-denial to achieve; it can be considered foolish from an objective perspective because it exposes the actor to danger from the unethical behavior of others.

The psychiatric ethic

Weber distinguished between hero ethics and average ethics. In the course of debunking and discrediting what he called a psychiatric ethic, Weber reveals the importance he ascribed to placing extreme external demands on oneself regardless of the hardship or sacrifice that may entail. It is precisely the hardship or sacrifice that one must endure or experience that makes for a hero ethic. Weber reveals also his contempt for and resistance to the idea of living according to the value of mere well-being, allowing oneself to be guided by one's feelings and desires as opposed to being guided by an ideal that requires sacrifice and renunciation. Just as he denounced with anger and contempt the political ideal of peace and contentment for the nation,[1] he reacted just as sharply and negatively to the idea of mental and emotional well-being (inner peace and contentment) as a personal or social ideal.

Weber sarcastically disparaged the views of the radical anarchist psycho-analyst, Otto Gross, for espousing "an ethics which believes that it can discredit some 'norms' by proving that their observance is not 'beneficial' to the dear nerves" (Weber, 1975, p. 377). His use of the term "dear nerves" resonates with masculine contempt. Contrast his usage here with his reference to people with courage and strong nerves, who are able to bear the burdens of war and not "scurry" behind demagogery. When it suited his purposes, he valorized "strong nerves" and disparaged "hysterically weak people;" other times he disparaged any concern for "the nerves" as itself a form of weakness.

Weber's disdain for the psychiatric ethic, as he called it, and his contempt for those who espouse it are discernible in the following analysis of two kinds of ethics and, by implication, two kinds of people.

> One can divide all "ethics," regardless of their material contents, into two major groups according to whether they make basic demands on a person to which he can generally *not* live up except for the great high points of his life, which point the way as guideposts in his *striving* in infinity ("hero ethics"), or whether they are modest enough to accept his everyday "nature" as a maximal requirement ("average ethics"). It seems to me that only the first category, the "hero ethics," can be called "idealism" (cited ibid., p. 378).

Weber pointed to a passage in which Gross talks of the "*sacrifices* that the 'adaptation' (. . .the suppression of 'desires' for the sake of adhering to the norms) *costs*" and reported, disdainfully, "these 'sacrifices' are sacrifices of *health*," a concern that the "precious nerves might be injured" (cited ibid., p. 378). This passionate rejection of the psychiatric ethic is made by a man who suffered for *years* from severe incapacitating emotional distress which he himself referred to as an illness. He reported reading and respecting the important contribution made by Freud's work. Nevertheless, he claimed that he himself did not learn anything new from a technique that requires one to "know oneself," to bring back some "dirty impulse I have 'repressed' and 'forgotten.' For I make the *en bloc* admission. . .that nothing 'human' is and was alien to me. Basically, then, I am certainly not learning anything new" (cited ibid., p. 379). We see here, in the guise of adopting an all-embracing acceptance of any and all human impulses, a resistance to the idea of exploring one's own particular feelings and desires.

Weber made explicit his ultimate values regarding human life, values that center on a conception of "hero ethics" that make demands on a person to which he can *not* live up except in the great high points of his life. The striving that is required by such an ethic involves struggles and conflict. It is precisely this striving in infinity that Weber admired.[2] Struggle and conflict are features of inner life, not just of politics. Here, too, heroism is possible. (This description of hero ethics bears a striking resemblance to the description of his mother's life. In fact Marianne Weber refers to Helene Weber's everyday life of continual inner struggle, her fight against a despairing sense of her own absolute inadequacy and her continued reliance on absolute standards of morality, as heroic, not misguided and unfortunate.) For Weber, an ethical ideal was necessarily one that was difficult to achieve, one that required struggle against impulses toward pleasure or self-indulgence, especially if that struggle required constant striving and even if it required repression and illness. A concern for "hygiene" should not be represented as an ethical ideal.

Despite his respect for hero ethics, Weber rejected striving toward self-perfection or self-embodiment of an ideal. He resisted the attitude that "venerated the highest meaning of existence in the *earthly* embodiment of the divine and that considered formed beauty, the *kalokagathia* ["the combination of goodness with beauty – the Greek ideal of education" (Harry Zohn, editor of Marianne Weber's biography)] of the Greeks, the highest norm of human development" (ibid., p. 457).

Weber rejected the aim of trying to embody some idea(l); he preferred an ideal that one did not strive to embody in oneself but one that required striving for tangible achievements in the world. Neither making life itself into an art form nor treating an act as an occasion for manifesting some idea(l) constituted the kind of manly heroic action that Weber championed. The distinction between embodying as immanent in one's life some value and striving to achieve some external goal corresponds to the distinction that Weber makes between action that he calls value rational – attempting to realize in action some ultimate value – and purposive rational action with its means–end orientation. The distinction corresponds as well to that between an exemplary hero and an emissary hero as well as to the distinction between great power politics and the civic virtues of a small people. It also corresponds to a distinction between ethics and rationality, living according to some principle and living to achieve some external goal.

Living according to some ethic that one tries to manifest in all one's actions represents a form of immanent, absolute value rationality which Weber rejected for himself. It is not the kind of heroic ethic that he championed: it does not result in world mastery. He advocated instead purposive rational action. The former value he considered incompatible with life in the practical world, particularly politics to which he felt a calling. Success in the practical world requires rational consideration of means and ends. He believed in worldly success as opposed to an innerworldly sense of satisfaction that one has acted rightly. Practical action in the world should be judged according to criteria of rationality not ethics.

The ethics of politics

Weber himself respected ethically oriented individuals, including ethical socialists, as responsible human beings (because they exercised restraint), but felt that as political actors they were foolish and irresponsible and should stay out of politics. Weber questioned whether the same ethic can govern "erotic, business, familial and official relations; for the relation to one's wife, to the greengrocer, the son, the competitor, the friend, the defendant" (Weber, 1946, pp. 118–19). He asserted that "we are placed into various life-spheres, each of which is governed by different laws" (ibid., p. 123). For instance, "the decisive means for politics is violence" (ibid., p. 121). Therefore, politics involves a tension between means and ends. "No ethics in the world," he contends, "can dodge the fact that in numerous instances the attainment of 'good' ends [often requires] . . . morally dubious means or at least dangerous ones – and . . . the possibility or even the probability of evil ramifications" (ibid.). The belief that "from good comes only good, but from evil only evil follows" is belied by the whole course of world history as well as by everyday experience. In politics, especially, often the opposite is true. "Anyone who fails to see this is, indeed, a political infant" (ibid., pp. 122, 123). He concludes, "Whoever wants to engage in politics at all. . .lets himself in for the diabolic forces lurking in all violence" (ibid., p. 125).

Weber puts the question: what relations do ethics and politics have? His answer is that one may adopt either an ethic of responsibility or an ethic of ultimate ends. The ethic of reponsibility requires that one give an account of the foreseeable results of one's action. An ethic of ultimate ends requires that one disregard the foreseeable consequences of one's actions and focus instead on making certain that one's conduct is ethically exemplary (ibid., p. 120). An ethic of responsibility endangers one's soul while an ethic of ultimate ends endangers one's goal (ibid., p. 126).

Just as Weber's strong version of responsible, realistic manliness turns out to correspond with both liberalism and imperialism, his weak version of masculinity corresponds with his perception of radicalism of both the left and the right. Weber justifies his opposition to various forms of radicalism by claiming that radicalism is excessive as opposed to restrained; emotional as opposed to rational; naive, romantic and unrealistic and a shortsighted reaction to the immediate situation as opposed to sophisticated, rational and realistic action based on concern for long-term consequences.

When radicals on the left drew strength towards the end of the First World War and succeeded in establishing a revolutionary socialist government, Weber excoriated their conduct as *irresponsible*, unconcerned about consequences. It was unthinkable that they could weaken national unity at a time when the only hope for a decent peace settlement depended on the victors believing Germany to be united in its resolve to repel any foreign military or political intervention. Weber's position earned him the scorn of all those on the left.

A second principle of politics was *restraint*, avoidance of emotional or violent excess. Not only did he have nothing but contempt for what he considered mobs of the street and their leaders, such as Rosa Luxemburg, he also condemned reaction on the right. When the forces of reaction succeeded in repressing a revolutionary government established at the end of the war and murdering the leader of the socialist government, Weber assailed such conduct and excess. The latter position evoked protests, demonstrations and denunciations of him and his views by the right-wing students who had regained a position of strength.

A third principle of politics was *chivalry*: protection of the weaker. Although Weber differed with the socialists and opposed their politics, he nevertheless spoke up on behalf of vulnerable individuals, socialists and anarchists, who were being brought up on charges. By speaking the language of the military, and contending that the accused were foolish but not dangerous, he managed to sway the court.

Central to his thinking was the view that the exercise of power must be restricted not by ethics but by chivalry and consideration of long-term consequences. Weber rejected absolute domination – patriarchalism, authoritarianism and political repression – as stifling the manly values of struggle and striving and the cultural virtues of dynamism and development. Furthermore, since conflict is never eliminated, only driven underground, a heavy-handed repressive, authoritarian approach is ultimately counter-productive. It provokes reactions that threaten the social order.

Of Bismarck's policy of employing the police to destroy unions on the basis of anti-socialist laws, Weber complained that this had driven "the only possible bearers of the workers' objective interests. . . into the most extreme and partisan radicalism" (cited by Mommsen, p. 102). This radicalism in turn provokes a reactionary response that threatens the national interest.

In a strongly worded statement supporting unionism Weber opposed "patriarchal welfare policy." His rejection of the latter reveals his commitment to manliness.

> We reject, partly in principle and partly as inadequate, the point of view of master rule or patriarchalism, the bonds of welfare institutions and those who would treat the worker as an object for bureaucratic regulation, and insurance legislation that merely creates dependency. We affirm the equal participation of the workers in the collective determination of working conditions, and to this end we also affirm the strengthening of their organizations, which spearhead this effort (cited ibid., p. 120).

Although Weber championed struggle and conflict, he did not support a policy in which the strong emasculate the weak. The strong must exercise self-control or what he often calls chivalry. He supported strengthening the workers through unionism so that they might struggle on behalf of their interests, but not so that they might become strong enough to overpower the stronger and create a different form of life, socialism. Society should remain a playing field if not a battle ground of competing interests. Similarly, he opposed capital hegemony. "We resist, without compromise, the conditions of capital hegemony, with government cooperation." The reason: "because we want to live in a land of citizens, not of subjects" (cited ibid.).

Weber saw social life as composed of struggle and conflict. However, he had no notion of dialectical transcendence (*Aufhebung*), no notion of synthesis that emerges out of opposition and negation. He always posited mutually exclusive categories and ultimate, "either–or" choices or compromises, without offering any transcendent possibility of radical transformation of the opposing forces or values. The already existing one-sided and opposed virtues, positions or categories become strengthened through conflict, but they do not become radically transformed or transcended.

Weber consistently stood for a notion of honor that means restraint in victory and dignity in defeat: no indulgence in gloating; no wallowing in guilt or self-pity. He insisted that political actions should not be evaluated on the basis of moral judgments. Following the war he passionately denounced "searching like old women for the 'guilty one' after the war – in a situation in which the structure of society produced the war" (Weber, 1946, p. 118). There are two interesting elements in this statement: "searching like old women," and "the structure of society produced the war."

It would seem that a responsible position prior to the war would have been a position committed to changing that structure. But that presumes a rejection of war and the vision of a different world order. For Weber, acting responsibly meant acting rationally and realistically. A realistic perspective recognizes and accepts realities. A realistic approach does not include, for Weber, attempting to transform those realities. Rather, a rational and responsible approach requires assessing the various possibilities for attaining success within the parameters set by the given realities.

Associating old women with searching for the guilty one suggests that women who are unable to stand up for themselves and fight must rely on ethics as a way of restraining and manipulating the behavior of others. A man takes action and then accepts the consequences. He advises: "Everyone with a *manly and controlled attitude* would tell the enemy, 'We lost the war. You have won it. That is now all over'" (ibid., p. 118, italics added). Neither moral justification nor moral denunciation, neither self-righteousness nor self-mortification, are appropriate in Weber's view. Instead, "responsibility towards the *future* which above all burdens the victor" should be the sole concern (ibid.). Because the victor is in a position to impose a settlement, the victor is responsible for the future. However, neither side has ethical responsibility for the war itself.

Weber stressed that only objective considerations should enter into the deliberations following the war. He contrasted an objective approach with a subjective one that concerns itself with ethics. "Only through objectivity and chivalry and above all only through dignity" is it possible to allow the war at its end to be buried at least morally. "But never is it possible through an 'ethic,' which in truth signifies a lack of dignity on both sides" (ibid.). The only subjective attitude that is consistent with manliness and dignity is that of chivalry. The introduction of an "ethic," that is, raising the issue of moral guilt, is undignified; it is the refuge of old women. Politics must concern itself with political consequences not with moral intentions or ethical consequences. To determine political action on the basis of an "ethic" as opposed to rational assessment of alternatives for achieving political success is to doom political action to impotence and failure.

Regarding Germany's conduct leading up to the First World War, Weber emphatically rejected ethical criticism. "Our policy before the war was stupid, not ethically objectionable. The latter charge is completely wrong. I stick to this" (cited by Mommsen, 1984, p. 294). Similarly, in adopting a moderate war aims policy when others held annexationist ambitions, Weber did not charge that the latter was ethically objectionable but politically foolish. It was much wiser to strive for alliances and protectorates than outright annexations.

Weber expected political behavior to adhere to a political ethic: reasons of state take precedence over all. One must act rationally on behalf of this value even if that means, as it often must, suspending ethical considerations. Thus with regard to Germany's conduct of the war, he charges that it was stupid not morally unjustified. The leadership had tempted destiny with politically and militarily foolish acts. These mistakes had returned to haunt Germany. Nevertheless, the nation had to accept responsibility for them. "It was cowardly and dishonorable to complain about this in retrospect. It was necessary to bear the consequences manfully and *silently*" (Mommsen, 1984, p. 294, italics in original).

We have encountered the emphasis on manly self-restraint before. Elsewhere Weber denigrated "the German [who] must turn Realpolitik into a slogan, which he then embraces with all the ardor of feminine emotion" (cited ibid., p. 43). This is just one of a number of passages where Weber distinguished between a masculine, sober, controlled demeanor and feminine emotional, expressive behavior which he clearly disparaged. The latter is associated with weakness, an inability to take strong action. We encounter still again the association of manliness, self-restraint and silence in Weber's discussion regarding the separation of facts from values within the university. At the time only some values could be heard because "certain value-questions which are of decisive political significance are permanently banned from university discussion." Because it is not possible to have "unrestrained freedom of discussion of fundamental questions from all value-positions," it is "only in accord with. . .dignity. . .*to be silent* as well about such value-problems as he is allowed to treat" (Weber, [1917] 1949, p. 8, italics in original). Weber coupled being silent and having dignity with a manly and controlled attitude. Dignity requires keeping one's feelings to oneself. Heroism requires individual self-restraint. It requires that the individual take a stand. It does not require collective struggle to transform the social structure.

Weber's notion of heroic greatness did not include a social movement in which collective actions are taken on the basis of some kind of collective deliberation rather than as the result of a leader taking command. Weber recognized only individual or unitary greatness as opposed to collaborative or multipartite greatness.

Political hero

The heroic actor may be likened to a *Mensch* (a responsible human being). A *Mensch* recognizes his or her power to affect others and uses that power responsibly – with a concern for consequences. Being a *Mensch* also means accepting responsibility for those consequences even if they turn out differently than anticipated. Weber's version of the *Mensch* resembles his version of the patriarch. Like the patriarch, the *Mensch* accepts with pride his possession of power and strives to live up to the privilege by acting in the name of something outside of his own physical being.

The patriarch acts in the name of the household on behalf of all its members just as the hero acts in the name of his cause. The decisive characteristic of patriarchalism according to Weber "is the belief of the members that domination. . .must definitely be exercised as a joint right in the interest of all members and is thus not freely appropriated by the incumbent" (Weber, [1921–2] 1978, p. 231). Nevertheless, "the patriarch's authority," although exercised in the interest of all members, "carries strict obligations to obedience . . . within his own household."

However, according to Weber's account, the patriarch has no machinery to enforce his orders; he is largely dependent upon the willingness of the members to comply. Weber contrasts this situation with that of patrimonialism in which the ruler has an administrative staff to enforce his rule. Under patriarchalism, "the administrative functions are performed on behalf of the group as a whole. Appropriation by the master personally is a phenomenon of patrimonialism" (ibid., p. 234). For Weber, the heroic leader, too, does not use force to gain compliance from his following, but unlike the patriarch whose authority is vested in him by tradition the heroic leader must win a following by displays of superiority.

Whereas belief in the hero's authority derives from the hero proving himself successful, belief in the patriarch's authority "is based on personal relations that are perceived as natural." The woman is dependent, he believes, because of the "normal superiority of the physical and intellectual energies of the male" (ibid., p. 1,0007). It is startling to come across this passage by a man who was the husband of a leading feminist of the time. Despite Weber's assertion that the patriarch, as opposed to the patrimonial ruler, has no machinery for enforcing his orders, Weber recognized that patriarchalism views household authority as the power of disposition over property. In other words, the power of the patriarch resides not in natural superiority but in his control over property which is granted to him by tradition and upheld by the community.

That women and children are considered property, and expected to comply with the master's orders as long as he himself abides by tradition, Weber recounted but did not subject to critical scrutiny. What accounts for a tradition that makes women and children into property? That the community that upholds the property rights of the patriarch is a political community composed of men who control the means of violence Weber likewise failed to subject to critical comment.

Although authority is grounded in tradition, it must be exercised on behalf of all members of the household who in turn comply voluntarily with the master's orders as long as those orders can be justified as being in accordance with tradition. The modern hero exercises authority on behalf of some cause to which he wins followers who comply with his orders voluntarily as long as those orders can be justified as serving the good of the cause and as long as the cause itself is not discredited. There is much similarity between Weber's description of the partriarch and his description of the hero. Both patriarch and hero exercise power over others, yet do so "responsibly" which means with restraint. Whereas concern for tradition restrains the patriarch, concern for the cause restrains the hero.

Weber explored the relationship of actor to power in his more mature, thoughtful analysis of politics as a vocation composed at the end of the First World War. He claimed that knowledge of the tragic possibility that untoward consequences may follow from one's acts is interwoven with all action, but "especially with political action." Weber stressed the individual nature of the actor. The actor independently determines action that affects the lives of others and then has to live with the consequences. An alternative anti-patriarchal version of political action includes responsiveness and responsibility of each to the other(s) in the determination of action, such that responsibility for the action and the bearing of the consequences is shared if at all possible by all parties to the action. There is no actor who intentionally and wilfully determines policy independently of those who are affected by that policy.

For Weber, political action "comprises any kind of *independent* leadership in action. . .[even] the policy of a prudent wife who seeks to guide her husband" (Weber, 1946, p. 77, italics in original). Weber's definition of political action assumes an *independent* actor; it involves also the guidance of others' actions. Political action presumably excludes mutual influence and mutual dependence.

Weber narrowed his focus on politics to the leadership of a political association. What distinguishes politics in this more restricted sense is the "specific *means* peculiar to. . .every political association, namely the use of physical force" (ibid. p. 78). Thus a consideration of political action brings us face to face with the issue of power and force in social relations.

Weber made a distinction between an official and a politician. The official "will not engage in politics . . .He shall not do precisely what the politician, the leader as well as his following, must always and necessarily do, namely, *fight*" (ibid., p. 95, italics in original). That the politician who is also a leader must fight implies conflicting differences or interests among political actors who feel passionately about those interests (ideal or material). It also implies that the conflict cannot be resolved by other means.

Weber elaborated the description of the political actor as distinct from the civil servant:

> To take a stand, to be passionate – *ira et studium* – is the politician's element, and above all the element of the political *leader*. His conduct is subject to quite a different, indeed, exactly the opposite, principle of responsibility from that of the civil servant. (ibid., italics in original)

The principle of responsibility that distinguishes the servant produces its own kind of honor, but not greatness.

> The honor of the civil servant is vested in his ability to execute conscientiously the order of the superior authorities. . .This holds even if the order appears wrong to him and if, despite the civil servant's remonstrances, the authority insists on the order. (ibid.).

Weber avoided the issue of orders that demand criminal acts. Following Weber's analysis of the distinction between politician and civil servant, we may infer that the honor of a wife as wife or mother as mother derives from serving her husband or family regardless of her husband or family's political actions. Weber implied that one must choose either to fight or to serve another who fights. Fighting is part of striving and struggling for a cause against external obstacles.

The honor of the civil servant contrasts with that of the political leader. "The honor of the political leader, of the leading statesman, however, lies precisely in an exclusive *personal* responsibility for what he does, a responsibility he cannot and must not reject or transfer" (ibid.). Weber implied that those who serve an external authority can and should remonstrate with that authority over orders that appear to them wrong; however, if servants have no choice but to serve, then there is no reason to consider consequences or alternatives. If one's honor attaches to serving without any personal judgment, then one learns not to take any interest in those matters. One leaves judgment to those whom one serves.

Civil servants, officials and bureaucrats take no personal responsibility for the nature, content or consequences of their actions; they take responsibility only for carrying out orders or for serving the other. Because the meaning and

111

consequences of the action make no difference to the actor, we may conceive of such action as serving in the abstract without regard for the end which their acts ultimately serve.

Followers can be distinguished from servants because the former knowingly and willingly accept the cause of the leader, whereas servants devote themselves to an office or person without concern for the ends or cause that the office or person represents and that their action ultimately promotes. The distinction between politicians, followers and civil servants lends itself to a distinction between men and two different kinds of women.

A "man" serves some cause for which he is willing to fight; a "woman" serves the man. The distinction between leader, follower and servant corresponds with two different kinds of women in two different kinds of patriarchal relationships. One kind devotes herself as a follower to a man, the hero; she shares his passions or ideas, the heroic cause to which he devotes himself and for which she admires him, and respects his ability (the modern romanticized relationship of the white middle classes). The other devotes herself as a servant to a man, the head of household; she serves him out of personal loyalty and duty to him as his wife (the traditional white, middle- and working-class, patriarchal marriage relationship).

The difference between the honor of the civil *servant* which comes from serving and that of the politician which comes from personal responsibility accounts for why "It is in the nature of officials of high moral standing to be poor politicians" (ibid.). By analogy that would be true of the second kind of woman, who is also a servant, and of mothers as well. It also accounts for why men like Freud considered women to be morally inferior beings.

Weber acknowledged that the division of the political world into leaders and followers involves domination and repression of the followers' souls. He stated, "the plebiscitarian leadership of parties entails the 'soullessness' of the following, their intellectual proletarianization, one might say. In order to be a useful apparatus. . .the following of such a [plebiscitarian] leader must obey him blindly. . .This is simply the price paid for guidance by leaders" (ibid., p. 113). This intellectual proletarianization and soullessness constitutes the unfortunate consequences of modern mass society. It is the price to be paid for leadership. We will see in Chapter 13 how this brutality to the soul is the price to be paid also by the weaker party in a relationship of erotic love.

For Weber, a revolutionary social movement would not be much different in this respect. Here, too, we find "depersonalization and routinization, in short, the psychic proletarianization, in the interests of discipline" (ibid., p. 125). Contrast his realistic acceptance of the condition of proletarianization to be endured by the followers with his romantic idealization of heroic leadership. Marianne Weber describes her husband's view of the military leader, Ludendorff, at a time when accusations and condemnations were being hurled at the latter: "The ethics of a great military leader should not be measured by yardsticks other than those appropriate to them; a general must have confidence and daring. If he loses, he must not be judged only on the basis of success. The dignity of heroic greatness must not be encroached upon" (Weber, 1975, p. 651). While the souls of the followers are coerced, the hero's dignity must not be encroached upon.

Later, when Weber learned the extent of Ludendorff's responsibility for the policy toward the Poles and Czechs, he changed his view of Ludendorff but his reasoning remained consistent: a military leader should be judged by one set of criteria, a political leader by another set. "A general must subordinate himself to the responsible statesman" (ibid.). Civil servants and followers should be judged by still different criteria, all of which differ from the criteria that should be used with regard to personal life and personal relations.

For a long time Weber "believed in Ludendorff's personal dignity and greatness despite everything" (ibid.). He wrote to Ludendorff and then met with him in order to convince the latter to give himself up, a "heroic and chivalrous act" that would save the honor of the nation and cause the enemy great difficulties. Weber was not just disappointed but dismayed when Ludendorff refused, placing his personal welfare over the honor of the nation. This story reveals as much or more about Weber as it does about Ludendorff. It reveals the unrealistic, irrational romanticism that underlay Weber's conception of the rational, realistic hero. In Weber's view the responsible leader not only lived for his impersonal cause, he lived only for his cause.

Weber conceived of dehumanization, the coercion of the soul, as inevitable in relations between a leader and his following, a stronger personality and a weaker personality. Weber divided the social world into stronger and weaker, leader and follower. From this division come self-sacrifice and loss of the soul on the one side (the weaker ones, followers and losers), and chivalry and paternal protection on the other (the stronger ones, leaders and victors). In exchange for giving up one's soul, one gains paternal protection and provision as well as closeness to and participation in human greatness.

I compare Weber's view of the hero with the view held by another prominent figure of the time with whom he was acquainted and who had attracted his own small but influential following, the poet Stefan George. As we might imagine, Weber rejected the poet as a leader of "men." Nevertheless it is quite interesting to see how much they shared in their respective versions of the hero. It is even more interesting to see how they diverged; the divergence reveals the subtleties – the qualifications and modifications – of Weber's thinking. The Stefan George "faith" required "subordination to the authority of the hero, and for a woman, subordination to a man." There should be a "fundamental subordination of a smaller person to a greater one, and by the latter he [George] meant a person distinguished by greater *cultural* achievements" (ibid., p. 457, italics in original). For Weber, in contrast, the hero was not one who embodies some cultural ideal but one who strives to

113

achieve in the world some external ideal. Consequently, subordination should not be to the person of the hero but to the cause that the hero advocates and pursues. Should the hero prove unsuccessful in his endeavours the followers may leave him.

Weber rejected crude hero worship. Although he believed in the necessity for the masses to submit to a leader, he also believed that the leader must be recognized as a fallible human being. His leadership is justified only as long as he can prove himself by his deeds and accomplishments. If his actions fail, the followers reject him. Furthermore, as a finite human being, the leader or hero can reasonably be expected to be a leader or hero in only a limited sphere of life. He cannot be expected to be an authority on all aspects of life.

In this way Weber reconciled his commitment to heroism and leadership with his commitment to individual autonomy. The elevation of a human being to the position of an authority on all existence represented to Weber a "deification of a living creature." Since Weber believed in the "absolute value of intellectual and moral autonomy, he denied the necessity of new forms of *personal* dominion and *personal* service" that the George cult represented (ibid.). Marianne Weber informs us that Max did acknowledge "service and *absolute devotion* to a *cause*, an ideal, but not to an earthly, finite human being and its limited aims, no matter how outstanding and venerable that person might be" (ibid., italics added).

George's conception of human greatness was a masculine heroic one. His talks with Weber about what apparently the latter and his wife considered "beautiful and profound things" included remarks about "the blessings of war for a heroic humanity and the meanness of struggle in peacetime, about our enervation through the increasing pacification of the world" (ibid., p. 463). Weber's own views of heroic warriors were not uncommon in the Germany of his time.

Weber enumerated three pre-eminent qualities decisive for the politician as distinct from the official: passion, a feeling of responsibility, and a sense of proportion. Making the analogy with social action of any kind to the extent that power is inherent in any social act, we may expect these qualities to be important for any social actor, but particularly so for the person who is a leader and therefore in a position to exercise power more so than most.

Passion refers to "devotion to a 'cause,' to the god or demon who is its overlord" (Weber, 1946, p. 115). With the idea of passionate devotion to a cause, we arrive at what distinguishes "man as man." "For nothing is worthy of man as man unless he can pursue it with passionate devotion" (ibid., p. 135). Weber seems to be using the word "man" in the universal sense of human being. Nevertheless, passionate devotion to an impersonal cause is associated with manliness not womanliness. Weber's definition of what is worthy of man as man if interpreted to mean human being implies that woman as woman does not live up to her capacity for being fully human;

she is less than human to the extent that she does not devote herself to some abstract cause.

Women in contrast to men have tended to devote themselves to concrete persons rather than abstract causes: husband, family, friends, community, even strangers, the elderly, the very young, the infirm, the ill; concrete persons. Only because women have devoted themselves to persons have men been able to devote themselves to a cause. Weber, and a whole patriarchal tradition, has been able to construct "man" only by taking advantage of the existence of "woman" whose form of life Weber then decries as not worthy of man as man.

Weber did recognize that *nature* has made life infinitely easier for men than for women. Nature has made men devote themselves to external pursuits and goals where they can see the success of their doings and dealings. Nature has made women, as mothers, sisters and daughters (Weber significantly leaves out wives from this list), devote themselves to others; women "freely undertake to care for us [men] as a matter of course," thereby demonstrating a "feeling of being part of us [men]" and providing inward enrichment for others – men. In so doing they suffer from never knowing what their devotion has meant nor how their ministrations have affected others – men. Men for their part have been given [by nature] an unfair advantage, he acknowledges. None the less, men suffer from an impoverishment of inner life which is the price they have to pay for their privileged nature. (Weber, 1975, p. 161). Weber never came closer than this to suggesting that men's lives, including the lives of heroic men, may be less than fully human, nor that men's unfair advantage may be due to something other than nature.

Returning to Weber's description of the qualities of the political actor, we find that passionate devotion to a 'cause' is not enough. It is necessary also that there be "responsibility to this cause as the guiding star of action. And for this, a sense of proportion is needed. . . Hence his *distance* to things and men" (Weber, 1946, italics in original). Distance from things and men makes possible a sense of proportion which in turn makes possible responsible action. For Weber, an ethic of responsibility referred to responsibility to the cause not to the welfare of other people, hence the need for distance. In today's world, women entering the world of business are similarly cautioned to beware "the compassion trap." The responsible actor in Weber's view is accountable to others for his actions but only with respect to the cause that those actions purport to serve.

This ethic of responsibility enables the actor to accept the ethically compromising dimensions of his action. One justifies the violence of the means (including sacrifice of self or others) by reference to the end it serves. However, the end, too, like the means, is treated as something that could be otherwise, something that is not absolute. One must be willing to reconsider the end based on a consideration of consequences. The key element is choice.

Choice makes it possible for the individual to take responsibility for his or her actions.

Weber replaced the illusion than an ethical world is possible with the reality that no end and no means – action – is ever absolutely free of violence or coercion. Nevertheless, despite the ethically imperfect nature of our actions, we can enjoy our freedom to choose; we can choose rationally to whatever extent that is possible; and we can accept the responsibility for our choice as part of what it means to be human.

Notice that a responsible decision about action is an individual decision to be made by examining alternatives and consequences, by searching one's soul, not by communing or conversing with others who are affected by one's actions. The end that justifies action is an individual's own personally held end; it is not an end arrived at in common with others. The end is not life itself whose meaning derives from social relations. Where the meaning of life comes not from social relations the individual must create that meaning for himself. From this assumption, Weber's conclusion follows.

Given the existence of violence and the struggles for power that characterize human life, conflict and its consequences must be borne manfully as an inevitable feature of social life. Each contender fights for his or her own values and uses whatever means seem most appropriate. The winners refrain from humiliating the losers; the losers accept the situation knowing they did their best; and a settlement is arrived at with chivalric restraint and a view to the future, knowing that humiliation of the losers, now, will come back to haunt the victors in the future.

Personality

Distance, proportion and responsibility reciprocally determine each other. Weber speaks explicitly about a strong personality. "The 'strength' of a political 'personality' means, in the first place, the possession of these qualities of passion, responsibility and proportion" (ibid., p. 116). Without distance from men and things, none of these would be possible.

Such distancing requires self-discipline. Without self-discipline there would be no distance; without distance, no sense of proportion; without a sense of proportion, no responsibility. The only aspect of political action that would be left is passion. Passion without a sense of proportion makes for irresponsible action.

In order to avoid irresponsible passion, the characteristic of a weak personality, a political actor (a "man") must develop detachment "in every sense of the word." He must distance himself from people and things. He must discipline himself daily and hourly to overcoming a vulgar vanity, self-intoxication with power. Because the politician works with the striving for power as an unavoidable means, the instinct for power belongs to his normal qualities. However, the "sin" of political action "begins where this striving for power ceases to be *objective* and becomes purely personal self-intoxication, instead of exclusively entering the service of 'the cause'" (ibid.).

In other words, the political actor must not succumb to his desire for power as an end in itself, a form of self-love or vanity. He must discipline that desire by subordinating it to some external objective thing – a cause. He does not understand self-mastery that comes from self-understanding and self-love. Rather, he sees the need for some external master – the cause – as a way of subordinating the self. He fears (surrender to) the self and (to) self-love. He sees the self that is not disciplined in this way as ultimately self-destructive or impotent.

Weber referred to "the inner collapse" of those power politicians who worship power and who are the typical representatives of the attitude of vanity, of self-intoxication with power. They are not strong or potent. From the inner collapse of these individuals, "we can see what inner weakness and impotence hides behind this boastful. . .gesture" (ibid., pp. 116–17). Serving a cause contrasts with the boastful gesture. Serving a cause gives inner strength to the action; it disciplines the actor. Weber's analysis of the inner weakness of the actor who struts and shows off his power reveals a fear. Without an external cause and the self-discipline that serving it requires, the actor succumbs to his own vanity, inner weakness and impotence. Without a cause, the actor is damned; he is condemned to burn in his own passions, his vain impotent love of himself. For Weber, there are only two choices for a man: worthless self-love, what Weber might call deification of the creature, or the worthy love of a cause. Weber's image of the hero conceals self-loathing and fear of weakness and impotence that comes with succumbing to self-love, to love of things or of other people.

Manly devotion to a cause makes for objective action. Without devotion to a cause, "it is absolutely true that the curse of the creature's worthlessness overshadows even the externally strongest political successes" (ibid.). Notice the unconditional "absolutely true." One must have a cause or else suffer the curse of the creature's worthlessness. This is a total devaluation of the body and in fact of human life itself, particularly women's life if women are more likely than men to lack devotion to a cause. Weber's hero must discipline himself "daily and hourly" to deny his own human feelings and body. In some respects this description resembles the kind of cruel upbringing to which Weber's patriarchal grandfather subjected Weber's mother. It also resembles the kind of self-denial, out of devotion to a spiritual ideal, practiced by Weber's maternal grandmother and emulated by Weber's mother.[3]

The desire to elevate one's life, to be more than a mere functionary carrying out assigned tasks and doing what is necessary, the desire to give meaning to life over and above mere physical existence and survival is an essential feature of being human. Even the functionary elevates his activity by conceiving of "duty" as transcending private interests. This desire for a meaningful life becomes particularly salient, according to Weber, the more human life seems reduced to that of carrying out tasks, the formal rationality of the functionary. The more that formal rationality is developed, the greater is the desire for some substantive value that can provide meaning. In a rationalized and secular world, this desire becomes not a search for God but for "personality" and "personal experience," with the latter constituting the former.

Weber observed that "People belabor themselves in trying to 'experience' life – for that befits a personality, conscious of its rank and station" (ibid., p. 137). However, this is a delusion. For "experience" devoid of some ideal that can give meaning to it is, Weber claimed, mere sensation. Weber offered a different source of personality than that of personal experience. He chastens us: "Ladies and gentlemen. In the field of science only he who is devoted *solely* to the work at hand has 'personality.' And this holds not only for the field of science; we know of no great artist who has ever done anything but serve his work and only his work" (ibid., italics in original). The same is true for politics. Instead of trying to make one's life into a work of art, one must devote oneself to something outside of oneself.

What raises mundane work to a level worthy of a man is the idea. Enthusiasm alone, although necessary, cannot yield results. "Some idea has to occur to someone's mind, and it has to be a correct idea, if one is to accomplish anything worthwhile. And such intuition cannot be forced. It has nothing to do with any cold calculation" (ibid., p. 135). However, work and calculation are necessary too. "The idea is not a substitute for work; and work, in turn, cannot substitute for or compel an idea, just as little as enthusiasm can. Both, enthusiasm and work, and above all both of them *jointly*, can entice the idea" (ibid., p. 136, italics in original).

The importance of an idea is not unique to science. Even the often despised and derided merchant or big industrialist "without 'business imagination,' that is, without ideas or ideal intuitions, will for all his life remain a man who would better have remained a clerk or a technical official. He will never be truly creative in organization" (ibid.). For Weber to be creative meant to transcend being a creature, that which is created, and aspire to being like a God, a creator. To remain merely a creature is to be a lowly being in Weber's scheme of things.

What elevates the human above the creature is precisely the capacity for creating as distinct from reproducing and staying alive which presumably any creature can do. That is why man the creator has a heroic ring while woman the procreator remains despised, even while she is idealized as mother. Like Mother Nature, herself, who remains despised even while she is idealized, woman the procreator possesses no ideas that can consciously and intentionally transform and transcend the self-reproducing world of nature in accordance with her own vision.

118

Creativity and imagination are linked to passion and enthusiasm by mediation of the "idea." This linkage characterizes inspired work whether it be that
of the merchant, the scientist or the artist. Yet, there is always risk that no
idea will occur. "He may be an excellent worker and yet never have had any
valuable idea of his own" (ibid.). In this case, Weber reflects, the person
would better have remained a technician. Yet work without any idea or
inspiration is precisely work that is not worthy of a man. "Whether we have
. . .inspiration depends upon destinies that are hidden from us, and besides
upon 'gifts'" (ibid.). Implicit then is the differentiation of humankind into
those with such "gifts" and those without them.

Weber implied that the world naturally divides into those who are worthy of
the title "man" and those who are not, and this worth can be thought of only as
a grace, for it is not something that the individual can achieve by means of will.
Hard work and enthusiasm which an individual could muster are insufficient.
Weber seems to have believed in a secular version of Calvinist grace, where
those who are unworthy are doomed not to hell but to second-class status in
the world while those who are graced must devote themselves to their idea in
order to be blessed with personality and saved from the hell of a rationalized,
routinized, servile existence.

Max Weber's mother also noted and took issue with her son's tendency to
divide the world into two kinds of people. "Max and I proceed from very
different points of view, since I cannot share his theory that some people
exist only to work for others and mechanically earn their daily bread" (Weber,
1975, p. 95). This difference in point of view also distinguishes Weber from
Marx and from feminism. Helene Weber "was unable to [support the idea] of
a culture which as a matter of course demands the sacrificing of the masses
for its purposes" (ibid.). But Max continued to divide humanity.

Weber begins with and arrives at a notion of manliness that distinguishes a
man from those human beings who are not worthy of the name. Although we
began with the political leader as the prototype of the social actor for Weber,
we see that "a man's value does not depend on whether or not he has leadership
qualities" (ibid., p. 150). Rather, it is inspiration and passionate devotion to a
work that distinguishes "man" and determines his personality and his value
or worth. As we saw above, in his address to "ladies and gentlemen," Weber
includes women in membership in the elect, but only if they are graced
with the gift of inspiration and combine this gift with passionate devotion
and work.

If the rest of humankind, men and women, must engage in work that is
not worthy of man as man, does this make them less than men, less than
fully human? Should these people be considered women as is the case for
all unarmed people, men and women, within warrior societies, and should
they accept their second-class status as natural or unavoidable, the necessary
consequence of innate differences? Or should they treat their subordinate status

119

as the necessary price for the benefits of a modern rationalized society? Should they decry the repression and dehumanization that is the price to be paid and strive to overcome it or should they bear it heroically as a sacrifice or naturally as a fact of nature?

All of these questions come down to one: Is the two-tiered nature of society a historical product of social arrangements that could be otherwise, or is it the product of natural differences among people? Weber's ambivalence comes out in his answer. On the one hand, established, routinized societies – bureaucratic and traditional – are historical modes of domination that reproduce two classes of people and a two-tiered social structure. On the other hand, there is a natural order composed of two kinds of people, those who are gifted and those who are not. The social structure can select certain gifts as the ones needed for survival or success and thus can select certain people who are graced with those gifts to rise to the top while others remain below.

Given the nature of social life as inherently conflictual in Weber's view, there is a natural inevitability that all social orders will end up repressing some for the benefit of others. His response: a modern society that does not limit by birth access to superior positions but selects through competition and struggle those who lead and those who follow, those who are superordinate and those who are subordinate, creates a dynamic and therefore desirable social order that is the product of both history and nature. For a successful modern society, those who are not gifted should remain technicians or functionaries, wives or mothers, servants devoting themselves to the needs and decisions of those who have the ideas and can achieve great things. They should not take on positions of power and influence where they will remain impotent and uncreative, uninspired and uninspiring, producing a stagnant and undynamic society.

Weber had no vision of social life empowering and nurturing individual and communal creativity. He divided social life into those who are naturally creative and those who are mere creatures of nature, implying a division between a ruling, creative mind and a subordinate, laboring body. Such a division constitutes a well-ordered society and human being. Unfortunately, as we see in Weber's own life and in a common view of the social order, sometimes the laboring body becomes insubordinate, preventing the workings of this well-ordered system and creating social disorder. Weber did not dwell on the vision of a mutually responsive as opposed to a repressive relationship between mind and body, ruling and following.

From his conception of two kinds of persons we can derive Weber's conception of human relationships and human society. Human relationships when they are not composed of conflict are composed of one person serving another who in turn serves an idea. We meet with this image again and again in Weber's sociology and in the real world. The description resembles that of the charismatic leader and his followers, the patriarch and his household, the capitalist and his workers. Only modern bureaucracy seems to challenge this patriarchal world of human relationships. In bureaucracy the actors serve only an impersonal office, and they serve without passion and without idea(l)s. That is why Weber despairs of the absence of heroes in modern rationalized bureaucratic Germany. Nevertheless, modern rational society produces modern rational man.

Notes

1 Weber regarded as frivolous the comments of German intellectuals who denounced the German "world spirit," its ambitions for world power, as "the national congenital sickness" and who dared to suggest "peace and contentment as a future ideal" (Mommsen, 1984, p. 98). Weber disdained this ideal, claiming that it "could only be the ideal of a group that lived on trust funds and interest payments" (cited ibid.). Weber implies that only people who are economically secure and provided for can afford such an ideal. Given the nature of social life and the reality of struggle for economic dominance, it is irresponsible to suggest such an ideal.

2 See Steven Kent's article (1983) on Weber, Nietzsche and Goethe where he stresses this aspect of Weber's thought, the stress on striving as a value in itself.

3 I make these references to Weber's mother's life because of the theory that people re-enact in different ways the unresolved conflicts that they have experienced in their childhood, and because of Alice Miller's theory of the effects on the next generation of these unresolved conflicts and of the effects of "poisonous pedagogy" or what I would call the ideology of patriarchal parenting.

8

Modern "man"

For Weber, modern man is rational man.[1] This chapter lays out the dilemma at the heart of modern man and modern society, a dilemma contained in Webster's dual conception of rational action.[2] By tracing the connections between rational action and masculinity, we see how the dilemma at the heart of rational action (the relationship between means and ends) creates not only the dilemma of modern society (formal, bureaucratic, capitalist, calculating rationality subordinating substantive, ethical, human values and ends – a loss of meaning in life) but the dilemma of modern man: the cult of masculinity dominating the man of culture.

We see how the dilemma of modern man derives from the divorce between individual and community, a divorce that constitutes the ultimate dilemma of ethics, according to Weber. The dilemma of rationality can be found in the very formulation of rational action, one that presupposes a separate, autonomous, independent individual, an individual who has no compelling ties to a community of other human beings.

Weber saw the threat to heroic individualism posed by modern rational bureaucratic society. Yet he also recognized that modern, rational society makes possible the free, rational individual. He distinguished modern life by its freedom from the constraints of tradition. He identified this freedom with rationality. Traditional and emotional modes of action, the only alternatives to rational action according to Weber's schema, are not free because they are not the outcome of conscious deliberation and choice. An emphasis on rational action constitutes the distinctive character of modern man.

Rational action means the ability to choose consciously between alternatives according to some measure or criterion that others can understand, some objective measure or set of criteria that is external to the subjective feelings of the actor, one that in principle can be understood and utilized by others. In this way the actor can give a reason for choosing one action over another and have that reason justify the action to others. For Weber, rationality sets aside emotion, convention, tradition and custom in order to consider and choose among all possible alternatives and their consequences in terms of objectively calculable (quantifiable) criteria like cost and gain – instrumental rationality – or in terms of some objective (non-calculable, non-quantifiable) value or principle – value rationality.

For Weber, the capacity for living according to ideals and values elevates the human being above other merely physical forms of life. A life that is devoid of all values is ultimately meaningless and irrational. (Even the rationalization of the economy occurred under the auspices of a value, the Protestant ethic, according to Weber's account.) Yet there is no rational way to choose among values, to determine the relative merits of one over another; values are incommensurable. It was Weber's deeply held belief that "the various value spheres of the world stand in irreconcilable conflict with each other" (Weber, 1946, p. 147).

Furthermore, not just value spheres but "The ultimately possible attitudes toward life are irreconcilable and hence their struggle can never be brought to a final conclusion. Thus it is necessary to make a decisive choice" (ibid., p. 152). It is also necessary to be ready to fight on behalf of one's ultimate values (the ones that one lives one's life by and that give meaning to one's life). This means one must be prepared to defend, through the use of violence, one's human form of life (as opposed to mere physical survival). Every value implies its opposite. "The individual has to decide which is God for him and which is the devil. And so it goes throughout all the orders of life" (ibid., p. 148).

He uses the metaphor of polytheism for these struggles. He contended that Christian ethics had blinded us to these struggles, but now after a thousand years "Our [modern] civilization destines us to realize more clearly these struggles again" (ibid., p. 149). Modern life is characterized by conflict. Weber brings in metaphors of gods, devils and demons to convey his view of the irrational and absolute nature of values and the irreconcilable conflict among them. Nevertheless, as other commentators have observed, it is not clear that the ultimately possible attitudes toward life are irreconcilable. Perhaps that is why Weber resorts to these metaphors.

Reliance on these metaphors as a substitute for analysis may signal a weakness or gap in his analysis. On the other hand, his association of ultimate values with gods effectively conveys his view that values cannot be rationally chosen. They are treated as obligations or duties. "In our terminology, value-rational action always involves 'commands' or 'demands' which, in the actor's opinion, are binding on him." These demands are "unconditional" (Weber, 1978, p. 25).

Weber's conception of rational action was a dualistic one. By this I mean not only that there are two forms of rational action but that they are mutually exclusive. Action can be rational in the sense of orienting to some end or goal that is external to the action itself – choosing the most effective or efficient means for achieving some external goal. This is instrumental rationality. In the context of bureaucracy this can mean choosing and institutionalizing as formal rules those procedures deemed most effective or efficient for achieving the goals of the institution. This is formal rationality. Or action can be rational in the sense of orienting to some ethic, principle or value that is realized in the action itself: "the meaning of the action does not lie in the achievement of a result ulterior to it, but in carrying out the specific type of action for its own sake" (ibid.). This is value rationality.

Weber deplored the reduction of human life to merely acting according to formal rules, the life of the functionary or bureaucrat. He also deplored the meaninglessness of a life of pure expedience that would value material survival above all else, the life of a creature devoid of ideals.

Nevertheless, value rationality, living according to some ethical principle or ideal, is a limited rationality that severely limits the freedom of the individual – making as it does "unconditional demands." Moreover, the limited nature of the rationality includes an inability to consider consequences; the meaning and value of the action – which holds an imperative control over the actor – lies in the action itself, not in external consequences.

Formal (instrumental) rationality assumes a division not only between means and ends but between ruling and following, between determining values or ends (ruling) and carrying out rules or procedures (following), a division that presumes and produces a division of labor: between those who rule by making decisions regarding the ends or values to be pursued and who make demands in the name of those values or ends, and those who carry out the decisions and follow the procedures or techniques for realizing those values or ends (bureaucrats, technicians, officials, specialists); and between both of these and those who are subject to the procedures and practices – clients, customers, the public. Like the well-ordered society and well-ordered life, the division within rationality resembles the division between ruling mind and laboring body. This is true not only for the division between formal and substantive rationality but between value and instrumental rationality, as can be seen from Weber's use of words like "commanding," "demanding," "binding" and "unconditional."

There is another feature of value rationality that is pertinent to our understanding of the dilemma (irrationality) of modern rational life. Values may come into irreconcilable conflict with opposing values, which means that the conflict cannot be resolved by reason. Therefore commitment to a value requires power and force as means for protecting, enforcing or imposing that value. However, "force and the threat of force unavoidably breed more force" (Weber, 1946, p. 334). The individual who starts out oriented to some value must end up orienting to power, to resisting, accommodating, opposing, increasing or imposing power as a means for protecting, ensuring or realizing his or her value.

The individual who desires to live according to some value in a world of irreconcilable conflict among values cannot do so without recourse to force. However, a reliance on force, a willingness to consider the employment of means which are justified by the ends which they serve, transforms value-rational action – that is to say, action that has intrinsic meaning and value – into instrumental action – its opposite. The instrumental use of force breeds more force and produces a world of violence and coercion, an ethically irrational world, one that does not conform to ethical values. In an ethically irrational world one cannot afford to live according to some ultimate value without concern for consequences. To do so is to risk one's life and one's value. One must renounce commitment to an absolute value and be willing to employ force or power to defend that value. But this in turn tends to result in the means subordinating or replacing the end.

Given a world of irreconcilable values, action that has meaning and value in itself degenerates into expedience, the use of force. On the institutional level, commitment to some end or goal degenerates into commitment to formal procedures, just as striving for human wealth degenerates into striving for capital. In each of these instances the means come to dominate, subordinate and repress, in short, undermine, values, ideals and ethics. More accurately, this conception of rational action presumes and (re)produces a separation between ends, values, ideals, ethics, and means, methods, techniques, procedures, with priority given to means, methods, techniques, and procedures.

Weber showed this to be the case with the Protestant ethic. According to his analysis the emphasis on worldly success as a means of serving God and proving one's grace produces the instrumentally rational world of capitalism which in turn undermines the religious values and ethics of Protestantism.

Instrumentally rational action tends to subvert and undermine all ultimate values and ethics. Actors who begin with a commitment to some value, but who employ instrumental means such as economic success, power and force, end by producing an ethically irrational world that values only economic success, power and force. Once power and force are valued as necessary and essential because of a presumed opposing value that must be defended against or repelled (every god presumes its devil), these morally suspect methods end up taking precedence over the intrinsic values that they are supposed to serve. Value rationality then turns into its opposite and suffers extinction. The undermining of value rationality begins with the assumption of opposing, irreconcilable values.

The cult of masculinity

An actor who rationally determines his or her action according to some ultimate value that gives meaning to the action and to one's life requires the ability to stand up for that value. This in turn requires a willingness to use force and violence because, as we have seen, irreconcilable conflict among values remains an ever-present possibility, according to Weber. Therefore, the traditional masculine virtue of taking pride in physical strength as a value in

125

itself, the *cult of masculinity*, can justify itself, as Weber claims it must, by claiming that power is necessary for the realization and protection of values or, as Weber argues on the national level, the realization and protection of culture. The cult of masculinity refers to practices and beliefs that exalt physical strength, force and power as ends in themselves.

Instead of acknowledging the tragedy and failure inherent in having to use force and violence in order to sustain certain values, the cult of masculinity denies the ethically irrational and morally questionable nature of the means that it values. The cult of masculinity implies pride in strength, pride in being able to stand up for oneself, and pride in not allowing any doubts to surface and weaken resolve. The cult of masculinity means not questioning or even recognizing the conflict between means and end. Rather, the willingness to use force becomes valued as an end in itself, an indicator of moral worth, a way of proving oneself, of showing that one is willing to risk bodily harm, that something else is more important than mere physical existence. However, in the cult of masculinity, the something else is less important than the act of proving oneself. Max Weber explicitly rejected and opposed such mindless displays of power and braggadocio, the valuing of power as an end in itself.

Weber recognized that often the original end or value that called forth the need for force as a means becomes replaced by the means itself. The cult of masculinity means refusing to re-examine the original end in terms of its ultimate value and in terms of its relationship to the means, but merely accepting both the end and the means without question or reflection. In this way, the actor avoids confronting the contradiction between means and end; he avoids confronting the dangers of uncertainty, weakening of conviction and irresoluteness that recognition of and reflection on the contradiction can bring forth. A lack of determination, paralysis, and/or cowardliness with regard to taking any action at all might result from such reflection, and all contradict the values of masculinity. Weber rejected such masculine cowardice. He believed in confronting the contradiction and taking moral responsibility on oneself. In this way one can distinguish masculinity from manliness.

Value-rational action tends to degenerate into instrumentally rational action which corresponds with the cult of masculinity, a male chauvinism that values physical strength and bravado as an end in itself. This traditional version of masculinity becomes supplemented in the modern capitalist world with the instrumental use of monetary calculations for determining the most effective, most efficient means for realizing one's material self-interest. Instrumental, purposeful, calculating rationality, determining the least costly, most beneficial means for achieving some end, implies reliance on precise measurement, comparison and quantitative calculation of costs and benefits with a jettisoning of all non-quantifiable qualitative considerations. Such a mode of determining action leads to confidence because one can show or prove quantitatively that one mode of action is better than another, and one can therefore act decisively, untroubled by the differences, doubts and inner conflicts that questions of qualitative value can introduce. Instrumental, calculating rationality brings with it qualities considered masculine: smart and decisive self-determination or free, confident, aggressive action.

Each of Weber's two types of rational action turns out to be irrational by requiring in practice what it denies or opposes in principle. Value-rational action requires violence and force as means for sustaining itself in the face of opposing values. These means must therefore be valued. The original value becomes subordinated to the means, and the means become the end. Thus value-rational action is overturned and replaced by its opposite. With this, value-rational action ends up producing a subjectively irrational, unprincipled life, a life without intrinsic meaning or value – that which it expressly opposes.

Not only value rationality ends up being self-repudiating. Instrumental rational action concerns itself with calculating the relative costs and benefits of alternative means and ends. Yet these ends must ultimately justify themselves in terms of some value. But values cannot be decided upon through rational calculation of costs and benefits; they are adopted on the basis of irrational faith. Hence instrumental rationality requires that which it opposes as irrational. Furthermore, in its commitment to survival and success, instrumental rationality cannot answer the question "survival or success for what?" Without any ultimate value to give it meaning, the pursuit of worldly success proves meaningless and irrational.

Yet instrumental rationality makes for a life of freedom, the possibility of self-determination. Instrumental rationality replaces unthinking acceptance of tradition or convention. Value rationality makes for a life of dignity; it elevates human life above that of mere physical survival and material self-interest. Thus both seem to be desirable. However, as Weber pointed out, the two conflict with each other. Particularly in modern society, the institutionalization of instrumental rationality as formal (bureaucratic and technical) rationality tends to triumph over substantive (value and ethical) rationality. The freedom of individuals and organizations to pursue their own self-determined ends (the essence of human dignity and rationality) leads to the decline of human dignity and rationality (bureaucratization and the cult of masculinity).

In valuing rationality as the basis of human freedom, Weber was led to the paradoxical position of arguing for the necessity of force, the very antithesis of human freedom and reason. Similarly, although his deepest values are those of the man of culture, of high-minded ideals and principles, his analysis led him to the conclusion of the inevitability of the mass "man," the "man" of expediency, the "man" who lives and acts according to formal rules and material self-interest.

Hence, Weber presents us with the paradox and dilemma of modern life. The dilemma of modern life arises with the decline of (religious) ethics (their

127

subordination to the "ethics" and rationality of the various life spheres such as politics and economics) and the rise of bureaucratic rules and organization, wealth and power, as ends in themselves. Life becomes meaningless and disenchanted. Ultimate values retreat from public life. Instrumental rationality oriented toward success in the form of wealth and power becomes irrational without some ultimate value to authorize it. The fate of the times is characterized by a loss of meaning, a competition among the value spheres with an irreconcilable conflict among them and their respective values.

However, an examination of the various value spheres and the conflict among them reveals that the conflicts reduce to one between the "masculine" values of the public political and economic world – power, wealth and self-interest – and the "feminine" values of the private domestic world – peace, pleasure and human welfare, a conflict between greatness and love.[3]

Modern life and internal conflicts

Each of these divisions, public and private, undergoes a further division based on a conflict between individuality and community. The division between public and private produces an internally divided public world and an internally divided private world. In the public world, the conflict is between individualistic capitalism and nationalism on one side and communal socialism and internationalism on the other. (By communal socialism I mean an orientation that stresses the well-being of the whole such that individual interests do not dominate over the interests of the collectivity.) In the private world, the conflict is between being a "tool," an active, instrumental, self-assertive, success-driven, ascetic *agent* and being a "vessel," a passive, contemplative, self-abnegating, love-driven *being in (comm)unity* with other(s) or Other (Fig. 8.1).[4]

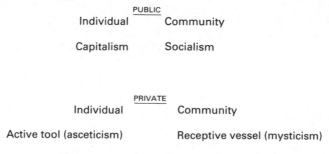

PUBLIC

Individual	Community
Capitalism	Socialism

PRIVATE

Individual	Community
Active tool (asceticism)	Receptive vessel (mysticism)

Figure 8.1 The modern divided world

One way to understand the divisions and how they come about is to recall Weber's discussion of the political community and its origins. A political community has its origins in a warrior group that distinguishes itself as a separate group from the original community. In so doing it destroys the sense of (comm)unity between members of the warrior group and the rest of the community (Fig. 8.2). The self-removed group lives off the community either by appropriating for itself the community's products in the form of booty and plunder, or by ruling and forcing the now oppressed community (composed predominantly of women or those deemed "women") to offer up the products of their labor in the form of tribute (Fig. 8.3). This group introduces its own rituals of re-creating the individual and the group (initiation rites, rites of rebirth and so forth). These rituals are borrowed and adapted from rituals of re-creation employed by the original community.

POLITICAL COMMUNITY   DOMESTIC COMMUNITY

Warfare, plundering   (Re)production

Re-creation of self and group   Re-creation of self and community
(heroic warrior soul and   (psychological state of ecstasy, orgiastic
heroic warrior community)   rituals, etc.)

Figure 8.2   Division of original integrated community

(Re)production, consumption, re-creation

Figure 8.3   Domination and appropriation

This division into a political community of ruling, warfare and re-creation and a household community of production, reproduction and re-creation undergoes further division when production for exchange (a market economy) supplants production for consumption (a self-sufficient household community) and the firm separates from the household. We now have a public world composed of an impersonal political community and an impersonal market community and a private world of personal community composed of household, domestic labor and consumption. In exchange for financial support the political community make political concessions to merchants who profit from the market economy (Fig. 8.4). The public world comprises warfare, political rule and (re)production and circulation of wealth and the private world comprises domestic (re)production, consumption and (re)creation of individual and community (Fig. 8.5).

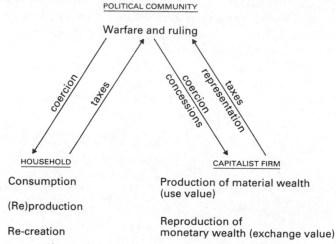

Figure 8.4 Separation of firm from household

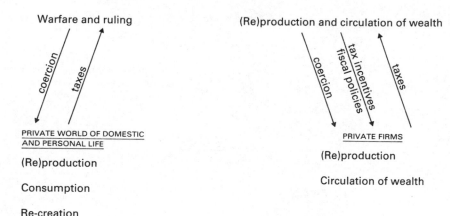

Figure 8.5 Public world of state and economy

Each of these worlds, public and private, are further divided. One side represents a stress on individual; the other side a stress on community. In the public world this division is represented by (masculine) capitalism of rugged individualism (manly renunciation of love and dependence) on the one side and (feminine) socialism of a welfare state (maternal principles of care) on the other. In the private sphere one side expresses itself in an ethic of individual success that Weber associates with rationality and self-discipline. The other side expresses itself in an ethic of love and community (Fig. 8.6).

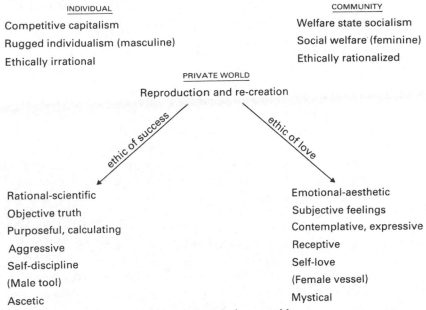

PUBLIC WORLD

Warmaking, ruling, (re)production and circulation of wealth

INDIVIDUAL	COMMUNITY
Competitive capitalism	Welfare state socialism
Rugged individualism (masculine)	Social welfare (feminine)
Ethically irrational	Ethically rationalized

PRIVATE WORLD

Reproduction and re-creation

ethic of success   *ethic of love*

Rational-scientific	Emotional-aesthetic
Objective truth	Subjective feelings
Purposeful, calculating	Contemplative, expressive
Aggressive	Receptive
Self-discipline	Self-love
(Male tool)	(Female vessel)
Ascetic	Mystical

Figure 8.6   Modern world

Weber seems to perceive the world in terms of these divisions and these conflicts. He conceives of an unresolvable tension, which the modern man must confront, between the value of encouraging and rewarding individual greatness, talent or accomplishment which serves the interest of encouraging and fostering the superior individual, and the value of reducing inequalities and social divisions that can arise from the unequal distribution of talents and rewards, in the interest of a sense of community. He claims that the ethical problem in most social–political issues is of this type (Weber, 1949, p. 15).

Weber's pessimism can be understood as directed at those social conditions (bureaucracy on the one side, religious ethics on the other, for example) which undermine the possibility of a manly life. These social conditions are emasculating in that they produce a weak and ineffectual social actor unable to provide the type of action – decisive, heroic action – that is necessary for achieving greatness. The dilemma of modernity turns out to be a dilemma of manliness, the dilemma of a rationalized world.

Acceptance of Weber's version of rationality commits us to a pessimistic view of the world and of modern man. The pessimism stems from the impossibility of a rational life and a rational world, the impossibility and irrationality of a life and a world committed to human freedom and dignity, the impossibility and irrationality of a life and world committed to reason. Such a commitment must, given the ethically irrational nature of the world and the bureaucratic context of individual action, degenerate into some version of the cult of masculinity or else emasculation. These are the possibilities for modern man. The only hope lies in the exceptional man – the charismatic hero.

Reflection

However, there are problems in Weber's formulation of rational action. I have already mentioned the individualistic nature of Weber's idea(l) of rational action. Weber's conception of rational action does not include any notion of dialogue or dialectical development. Although he values freedom from the constraints of tradition or emotion, he does not consider dialogue, mutual recognition or self-reflection to be central to freedom or reason. For Weber, rational action is realizing or enacting one's individually held values or striving to achieve one's individually chosen goals.

Weber limits rational action to choosing among alternatives, rather than reflecting on the social conditions that make those choices and alternatives meaningful and valuable. An actor who does not simply choose from among ends and means but reflects on the conditions that make those means and ends conceivable and meaningful engages in a kind of contemplative action. Deliberating and calculating differ from contemplating and reflecting. Deliberating and calculating tacitly assume taken-for-granted, unambiguous and unproblematic ends and means. Contemplation and reflection tacitly assume that all ends and means are questionable and worth reconsidering.

Why does Weber limit rationality to deliberating, calculating and choosing? Why does he disregard the possibility of reflection, contemplation, self-change, social change? Why does he develop the typology of action he does, and especially the typology of rational versus non-rational (traditional) and irrational (affective) action?[5] To what is Weber's typology a response; of what is it a denial?

It seems to me that Weber's typology is a denial of community and body, embeddedness and embodiedness, perhaps a matter of fear and loathing. He cannot acknowledge communal embeddedness and human embodiment because he wants to preserve his notion of the free, self-determined individual. Weber believes in self-determined action, the actor who is the free author of his acts. For Weber, freedom of this sort is a necessary condition for rational action.

In an alternative feminist view, only those who are able to recognize and analyze the conditions of unfreedom are capable of rational action. Freedom is not the condition but the object of rational action. A rational actor would be one who does not assume independence from others but rather one who engages the social relations and constraints that both enhance and limit human possibilities.

Hence this alternative rational actor would be one who recognizes that reason is neither abstract nor disembodied; that one's actions are constrained by needs, emotions and traditions, by the body, by social relations and by community. Instead of rationality based on self-discipline, self-control and repression, rationality, here, is based on recognizing, responding to and reflecting on needs and feelings, attachments and relationships that give meaning and value to action and life.

I contend that rational action must include reflection and contemplation, not just calculation and deliberation. Weber would reject this version of rational action. Reflection and contemplation, responsiveness to that which is other and those who are other, represent distractions that threaten to obstruct decisive action and to disrupt unity of purpose.

An actor who can self-consciously analyze his or her own unfreedom (the historical origins and social constraints that ground individual action) and can choose between accepting that unfreedom or challenging it is a rational actor. A community that is committed to reflection on its own conditions of unfreedom, a community that is committed to reconsidering its own most basic social arrangements, is a rational community.

Dualism

Running through Weber's work is a dualism of rationality and love, individuality and community. He focuses most of his attention on rationality. Instrumental rationality assumes separate, independent, autonomous individuals who pursue their own self-determined interests – a version of egocentric individualism. Similarly, value rationality assumes separate individuals who adhere to individually determined values – a version of committed individualism. Whether the values are accepted as absolute or are consciously chosen or created, at center in Weber's conception of rational action remains the separate, autonomous, independent individual. Love (attachments, community, ecstasy) remains the undertheorized other in Weber's work, that which creates tension with a world of (autonomous individual) rationality or that which provides an escape from the meaninglessness of a world of rationality.

Weber's way of coming to terms with the tension is by separating the two into separate spheres, a public world of rationality and a private world of brotherly love and erotic love.

Instrumental rationality involves objective, quantitative, materialistic calculation. The character type involves confidence, egocentrism and insensitivity. Value rationality involves a sense of conviction, self-righteousness and ultimately a willingness to fight and reject opposing values. The associated character type includes the qualities of pride, assertiveness and forcefulness.

As we can see, these qualities and character types derived from Weber's individualistic notion of dualistic rationality resemble those of modern "man."

The realms of politics and economics as currently constituted require and (re)produce two forms of rationality that create two sides of modern masculine identity: the strong, forceful, committed, ethical individual (value rationality) and the calculating, self-interested, aggressive individual (instrumental rationality). Political rationality, for instance, may take the form of instrumental rationality, the stereotype of the "politician" who is interested only in promoting his own self-interest and who supports whoever or whatever interests can help him. Or political rationality may take the form of value rationality, the image of the statesman who stands for and negotiates for the good of the state, however he might define that, rather than his own personal self-interests. However, value rationality in the political sphere tends to degenerate into the valuing of power as an end in itself and to devolve into instrumental rationality on behalf of the state which makes for what is called *Realpolitik*.

The conflict between instrumental, formal rationality (technical means, methods and procedures) and value, substantive rationality (ethical ends, principles, ideals), from which instrumental, formal rationality emerges as dominant, creates the dilemma of modernity as Weber conceives it.[6] This conflict also creates the dilemma of manliness. The political leader who combines convictions (value rationality that is not absolute) with a consideration of consequences and alternatives (instrumental rationality) epitomizes the ideal of manliness. However, formal instrumental rationality (a valuing of money, power, technique) leads to the repression of substantive value rationality (ideals, ethics, principles) and hence to the impossibility of heroic manliness.

The conflict between value rationality and instrumental rationality and the conflicts internal to each mode of rationality produces an internally conflicted actor, one who is unable to take decisive action except by one-sidedly emphasizing one aspect of rationality – instrumental, worldly action that is burdened by ethical guilt, a connection with violence – while denying or excluding the other – a rationality of living according to values and ethics. An internally conflicted individual finds himself unable to act. Weber himself suffered for many years from an inability to live up to the image of the free, rational, decisive actor; he was often unable to make any decisions at all. I think it fair to attribute such paralysis of action to an internal conflict.

Internal conflict

Weber's work can be interpreted as driven in part by this internal conflict and his need to come to terms with it. The internal conflict that I find running through his work is the conflict between the independent, rational actor capable of greatness, on the one side, and that which must be sacrificed in order to achieve this ideal – human values and ethics of love – on the other, a conflict inherent in an ideal of greatness that requires the repression of love.[7] I do not mean that Weber was incapable of loving or being loved. On the contrary; he was a loving man in many respects. I mean that the kind of rational action he advocated required suspending considerations of love. The Protestant ethic embodies such a conflict which it resolves by repressing brotherliness.[8]

Weber's mother also embodied a somewhat different conflict, but one that is decisive for understanding her son. Weber's mother held up to her children and herself absolute moral standards (an ideal of greatness). Her love was expressed as a love for the well-being of their souls which required that they live up to those standards. But this kind of love is demanding and intolerant – qualities that are antithetical to love. Weber's mother's love was an internally conflicted and hence repressive kind of love that was inseparable from her commitment to religious idea(l)s. Marianne Weber reports that Helene Weber was unable to make her children happy. The inability to make her children happy was inseparable from her inability to be happy, her need to struggle against impulse, self-indulgence, self-love, "undeserved" love, a struggle to prove herself worthy.

Weber's inner conflict reflects, I believe, an inability to come to terms with his feelings about (his mother's) love or to come up with an alternative notion of love. He could not denounce even to himself his mother's love and the cruelty inherent in it. To do so would have meant denouncing his mother's whole life, all that gave meaning to her life, her way of coming to terms with the horrors of her early years, the patriarchal parenting to which she was subject. To denounce his mother's love – to acknowledge its cruelty – would have been to denounce (destroy) his mother's life and the patriarchal world that created it. Instead of reflecting on his mother's version of love and morality and the internal conflict it presumed and reproduced, Weber renounced both (his desire for) her love and her morality.

Neither his mother's love and morality nor his father's unheroic complacent attitude (which his mother found contemptible) satisfied Weber. Nevertheless, he saw the conflict between their orientations to life as requiring a decisive and fateful choice on his part. Marianne Weber reports that her husband became conscious as a young man that he had to choose between his parents and that his choice was less an emotional matter than a moral decision, one that would be "decisive for the future of his soul and the formation of his personality" (Weber, 1975, p. 84). Mitzman believes that Weber's refusal to chose between his father and his mother was reflected in his conception of a rigid separation between value spheres (Mitzman, 1971, pp. 60–1). The conflict between the moral faculty and the sensual faculty was to be mediated by an autonomous, rational, and responsible will that could make a conscious choice. Freud's division of the psyche into the superego, id and an ego capable of rational choice and reflection mirrors Weber's own conception.

As early as a letter of 1887, Weber elaborated on three faculties of judgment which existed, he argued, separate and independent of each other: a sensual faculty that distinguishes between the pleasurable and the unpleasurable, a rational faculty that deals with how things come to be the way they are, and a moral faculty that concerns right and wrong (ibid.).

As late as 1918, in a speech delivered to students on the theme of science as a vocation, Weber was still insisting on the sharp separation between the three faculties now conceived as value spheres: truth, beauty and goodness (Weber, 1946, p. 148). However, "these are only the most elementary cases of the struggle that the gods of the various orders and values are engaged in." The struggle takes other forms as well. "I do not know how one might wish to decide the value of French and German culture; for here, too, different gods struggle with one another, now and for all times to come" (ibid.). He made this statement at the end of the First World War!

Weber may never have come to terms with his inner conflict; he continually felt the need to justify his rejection of his mother by repeatedly and compulsively showing how an absolute commitment to a religious ethic is stifling, repressive and self-destructive. On the other hand, he also had the need to reject his father's unheroic bourgeois patriarchal complacency. He did this in his analysis of bureaucratic, materialistic society – its inability to foster heroism. Weber embraced "realism," an acknowledgement and acceptance of the unloving character of rational action and rational society (whether instrumental rationality as in his father's case or absolute-value rationality as in his mother's case.) He rejected anything else as unrealistic and politically infantile. He had to reject the infant in himself, the desire for a loving world (what Freud would call feminine illusion), and replace it with a (manly) politically "realistic" and "rational" attitude.

Notes

1 I use the term "man" in its gendered sense, not as a synonym for a universal human being.
2 Others have noted "the tensions between formal and substantive rationality" and have talked about the "anguishing dilemma of form and substance" (Bendix, 1960, p. 485). Stephen Kalberg (1980) describes the complexities in Weber's use of the term "rationality," which encompasses more than the dual conception of rational action that is discussed here. Formal and substantive rationality are not identical with but based on instrumental and value rationality.
3 Brubaker and Mitzman have also argued that the conflict among values and value spheres that Weber considers infinite in number is in fact limited, but they have different breakdowns of the value spheres. They do not conceive of

the conflict in terms of masculinity and femininity, public and private, individual and community.

Brubaker reduces the conflict to that between the spheres of economics and politics characterized by instrumental rationality and the other spheres characterized by value rationality. I see this as a conflict between instrumental rationality and value rationality. This conflict finds concrete expression in the antagonism between the religious ethic of brotherliness and the necessity for instrumentally rational conduct in the economic and political spheres (Brubaker, 1984, p. 77).

Mitzman (1971, p. 190) admits four gods to Weber's value pantheon: "the god of Luther – bureaucratic traditionalism; the god of Calvin – ascetic rationalization; the god of Tolstoy – mystical immanence; and the god of Nietzsche and George – aristocratic aestheticism and worldly heroism. . .Weber pits ascetic rationalization [Calvin], against bureaucratic traditionalism [Luther]." Weber attributes independence of character and initiative in action (masculinity) to the former and authoritarian subservience and obedience (femininity) to the latter (Weber, 1946, pp. 302–22, and 1978, p. 575). Mitzman concludes (p. 191): "to the extent that Weber finds the world created by ascetic rationalization drained of meaning, he [lumps] together the gods of Calvin and Luther" (doing one's duty in the world and striving for personal success) against mystical immanence (acosmic brotherly love) and aristocratic virtue (heroic greatness).

4 The conflict between asceticism and mysticism can be reformulated as a conflict between a public world of instrumental rationality and a private world of love and feeling. As Mitzman indicates (1971, p. 218) asceticism is antagonistic to non-rational forces of life: eroticism, art, and so on, which are associated with the private sphere. Asceticism requires the repression of these non-rational forces. Asceticism is compatible with economic and political rationalism, the public sphere.

Mysticism is antagonistic to political and economic goal oriented activity, the public world, but substitutive for the non-rational force of life, such as art and eroticism, the private sphere.

5 Alan Sica (1988) details Weber's "compulsive dependence on the rationality–irrationality dichotomy, a bipolar conceptualization which apparently held for him some great private meaning, and which became, one might argue, an incantation" (p. 194).

6 Bologh (1984) elaborates on this dilemma of modernity.

7 For an alternative account of Weber's inner conflict and his emotional breakdown, see Randall Collins' more orthodox Freudian analysis (1986). Edward B. Portis (1986) provides still another interpretation.

8 Jeffrey Alexander (1987) describes how treating self as a tool of God lays the foundation for and justifies treating others as a tool.

9

Modern God

Given Weber's commitment to realism and rationality, his rejection of illusion, his advocacy of science and politics, and his emphasis on conflict, heroic greatness, and worldly action, how are we to make sense of his focusing so much of his effort on the study of religion? Weber explained his work on religion as an interest in the effects of religious ethics on worldly activity, particularly economic activity. Most commentators assume that the motivating force is a desire to refute vulgar historical materialists. Hennis' thesis that Weber was interested in the kind of person that a given civilization makes possible expands the explanation.

Weber's debate with historical materialism and his interest in human types may be only a part of what motivated him. Weber looked at the relationship between religious ethics and economic vitality not just as a way of challenging historical materialism but also as a way of challenging the idea(l) of an ethical economy and an ethical society, what he called an ethically rationalized economy or society. He was engaged in proving the impracticality of such an idea and the unrealistic nature of such an ideal. His studies on the world religions are rife with the struggles for power and conflicts over interests. He shows how these prevail at all times in all different circumstances, among all strata and status groups, including religious virtuosos. In other words, the idea(l) of an ethically rationalized society that prevailed in traditional society did not produce a world of love and harmony devoid of conflict and struggles for power. Weber also focused on the negative (as well as positive) effects of peace and unity as contrasted with rivalry and conflict. The latter represent "strong and independent forces. . .[that can serve] to shatter traditional fetters" (Weber, [1916] 1951, p. 62).

It is not the intention here to review and analyze Weber's studies of world religions. Instead the focus is on the nature and significance of sacred values. Why did the issue of religious ethics and sacred values have so much salience to him? Why should he have devoted so much time and energy to the study of religious ethics and sacred values in order to prove their deleterious effects on the various spheres of life, particularly practical activity in the public world, rather than simply dismissing them as anachronistic or irrelevant? After all, the economy had already undergone rationalization. And politics was in little danger of succumbing to religious guidance.

I submit that the sociology of religion plunges us directly into the central dynamic of Weber's thought: the tension between love and greatness. In his political and economic sociology, Weber can be read as arguing that considerations of love must be excluded from practical life if any kind of worldly greatness is to be achieved. An ethic of love not only makes an individual and a nation vulnerable to the will of others, as he was wont to argue in his political writings, it also obstructs dynamism and development, striving and struggle on the level of both the individual and the society. Weber repeated this theme time and again.

Nevertheless, the desire for love keeps reasserting itself. And Weber must keep banishing it; love must be relegated to a separate and subordinate sphere: the private world. Religion represents the voice of the private sphere gone public. As such it mediates between the private and the public spheres. Thus religion, especially in its most extreme variant like Buddhism, which stresses acosmic love, represents the radical alternative to practical and political realism. The latter, Weber believed, must prevail in the public world.

The nagging presence

The continuing presence of religion within a world that Weber describes as an ongoing struggle for power and advantage represents the other side of social life, the side that Weber in his writings keeps trying to vanquish. In confronting religion, Weber is confronting a challenge to his realism. Religion represents the other, the nagging presence, that keeps tugging at him and which he keeps resisting and defeating in a never-ending battle to retain his identity, his manliness. Weber is not engaged in a struggle with religion, but with what religion represents.

Unlike other political realists who successfully banish from the public sphere all considerations of love in relations with a political other, Weber is not simply indifferent to the appeals of love in the guise of religion; he does not simply shrug off the appeals of love. Rather he engages in a continual struggle, a battle against the desire for love, a continual battle to deny that desire.

Running through Weber's sociology of religion is a tension between ecstasy and rationality that parallels the tension between love and greatness. Weber tends to see religion as developing away from a primitive original stress on magic and ecstasy to a modern, more sophisticated stress on ethics and rationality. Yet this is not simply a matter of progressive evolutionary development.[1] The difference between these two kinds of religions, Weber argues, is not a result of historical, *evolutionary* development. Nor, I would add, is it simply a matter of unique historical factors, as Weber claims. It is also a matter of on-going tension, conflict and repression with different religions expressing and resolving this tension in different ways.

139

Religions that Weber considers masculine, such as Confucianism and Calvinism (Puritanism), are those that stress sober rationality. Religions such as Lutheran pietism and Hinduism, which he considers feminine, stress erotically tinged devotion and more acute ecstatic states. There is an on-going struggle to suppress the latter within the more masculine religions.

Weber generally circles around the relationship of eros to religion. His sociology of religion as a whole reveals an integral relationship between eros, love, ecstasy and religion, a relationship that Weber notices but the significance of which he avoids confronting directly – the importance of eros and love in human life. He keeps wanting to rope it off in the corner, in the margins of life, leaving it to the private sphere. Yet, in studying religious ethics, he confronts it.

Weber never considered eros as a dimension of life that could or should influence the nature of public life and heroic greatness. He could only see it as a force distracting men from their duty or reinvigorating them for the struggle. Erotic love, especially outside of marriage, represented an escape from a routinized, rationalized, disenchanted, lifeless world. But erotic love remains marginal to that rationalized world.

The tension between the modern rationalization of the world and the continuing presence of religion corresponds to a tension in Weber's thinking and psyche between desire and rationality. In his political and economic sociology, rationality and realism prevail; love is the absent presence. But in his sociology of religion the tension between the two (rationality and love) becomes explicit. Religions stressing ethical rationality over erotic ecstasy are more likely to contribute to rational world mastery and hence to promote achievements and greatness of a worldly nature. Erotic ecstasy, in contrast, merely promotes a psychological state in the individual with no positive, practical outcome in the world. This is Weber's thesis. The tension between a "masculine" desire for rational control and a "feminine" desire for erotic surrender helps us to understand Weber's sociology.

Ideal types and dualism

For Weber these two different kinds of religion represented not just ideal types, but polar opposites, mutually exclusive categories and mutually exclusive forms of life. They are mutually exclusive because one threatens the other. Eros, ecstasy and emotion represent the threat of losing control: loss of mastery, loss of rationality, loss of manliness. (We have seen that Weber disparagingly identified emotionality with femininity.)

For Weber, one side takes privilege over the other. Rationality is the privileged side; ecstasy is the other that threatens rationality. Nowhere does Weber suggest that rationality is equally a dangerous threat to ecstasy. He does not treat ecstasy as a serious value, only as a serious threat. For Weber, the desire for erotic surrender to ecstasy represents a danger to rational control, a regressive force that threatens to drag rationality down, back into a dark past from which it has struggled to disengage and emerge as a separate and independent thing unto itself. Rationality represents a more recent and progressive force ushering in the modern world.

The dichotomous categories (magical religion, ethical religion; ecstatic religion, sober religion; emotional religion, rational religion; mystical religion, ascetic religion) can be seen not as mutually exclusive — which is how Weber presents them – but as different aspects of a whole, different moments within a movement toward mutual recognition that overcomes the antithetical relationship between them and results in a new self-consciousness. I am not talking here of a movement within consciousness alone – a movement toward greater self-understanding; I am talking also of a movement toward mutual recognition on the part of the bearers of these different attitudes and orientations to the world.[2]

In setting up ideal types as mutually exclusive categories, Weber implicitly created an asymmetrical relationship in which one category appears to be of greater value than the other. Not only is greater value implied, but dominance as well; one side defines itself by the exclusion and repression of the other. The excluded other is then formulated as an absence or lack. We can see this with regard to the categories: man, woman; black, white; as well as the categories Weber used to distinguish among types of religion. The excluded, implicitly devalued other(s) – in the case of Weber's sociology of religion this includes the magical, ecstatic, emotional and mystical – are characterized by an absence – of the ethical, sober, rational, ascetic. The latter, in contrast, are characterized not by lack but by discipline, renunciation, resistance. The privileged set must continually struggle to keep "the other" in its place: outside, excluded, peripheral, secondary, supplementary, subordinate, quiescent and ineffectual.

One could argue that Weber's corpus of work presupposes and reproduces the dualism of personal ethics (religion) and political ethics, a private, domestic world of feminine values and virtues and a public political world of masculine values and virtues. However, the relationship between religion, ecstasy and ethics and politics, rationality and domination is more complex than a reduction to a dualism between femininity and masculinity. Weber's *attitude*, however, does not seem complex or ambiguous. He did not express ambivalence. He emphatically insisted, time and again, that ethics must not interfere in political or economic decision-making. Nevertheless, he seems to have had a compulsion to keep returning to the issue under the guise of different interests (socialism, political realism, rationality, conflicts among values and value spheres, heroism, religion and so on). Despite his desire to banish ethics and love to the private sphere, they keep reappearing – most

141

explicitly in relation to religion. As indicated above, religion represents a sphere that mediates between the public and private and hence brings values of the private sphere into the public.

The complexity of Weber's thought is reflected in his writings on religion and ethics. Although he would like to rest content with the view that religious ethics are reducible to idealizing the virtues of domestic life and the oppressed, he cannot. Such a view would correspond to a historical materialist approach. Weber contends that in addition to the effects of such external historical material conditions on religion, there is an internal dynamic to religion as well, a concern with sacred values and psychological states. Weber recognizes an intrinsic appeal to religion centering on what he calls sacred values.

Sacred values

Sacred values referred originally to things of this world, health, long life, prosperity, and so forth. In addition, the earliest religions were concerned with the experience of ecstasy. Weber contrasts religions that promote ecstasy with those that promote rationality. He treats these as antinomies. The former are associated with love and femininity; the latter, with greatness and masculinity. Nevertheless, Weber recognizes that ecstatic emotional (feminine) states are valued because of the extraordinary powers that they induce. But these powers along with the experience of ecstasy must be denied in the name of masculine, rational, heroic greatness.

The sacred value that the devout have pursued has always been a psychological state in the *here and now*. This psychological state of ecstasy comprises a more or less sublimated experience of erotic love. Different groups pursued somewhat different forms of this experience. Here is how Weber describes the kinds of psychological states that counted as sacred values:

> The Buddhist monk, certain to enter Nirvana, seeks the sentiment of a *cosmic love*; the devout Hindu seeks either Bhakti (fervent *love* in the possession of God) or apathetic *ecstasy*. The Chlyst with his radjeny, as well as the dancing Dervish, strives for *orgiastic ecstasy*. Others seek to be *possessed by God* and to possess God, to be a *bridegroom* of the Virgin Mary, or to be the *bride* of the Savior. The Jesuit's *cult of the heart* of Jesus, quietistic edification, the pietists' *tender love* for the child Jesus and its "running sore," the *sexual and semi-sexual orgies* at the wooing of Krishna, the sophisticated cultic dinners of the Vallabhacharis, the gnostic *onanist* cult activities, the various forms of the *unio mystica*, and the contemplative *submersion in the All-One* (1946, p. 278, italics added).

142

In addition to these, he mentions still another, the Puritans' sacred object: "The puritan *certitudo salutis*, the permanent state of grace that rests in the feeling of 'having proved oneself,' was psychologically the only concrete object among the sacred values of this ascetic religion" (ibid.).

In each instance, Weber describes the psychological state as one of erotic intensity of one form or another, often interpreted as an expression of love for a divine Other or an experience of love by a divine Other. Even the orgies were not simply orgies of food, drink, song, dance or sex. The aim was a psychological state that transcended sensual indulgence.

> Rationalized religions have. . .sublimated the orgy into the "sacrament."
> . . .Yet even after such a sublimation of orgy into sacrament has occurred, the fact remains, of course, that for the devout the sacred value, first and above all, has been a psychological state in the *here and now*. . .The two highest conceptions of sublimated religious doctrines of salvation are "rebirth" and "redemption" (ibid., pp. 278–9).

Despite the overriding and underlying erotic element at the core of these different "sacred values" or psychological states, "the kind of empirical state of bliss or experience of rebirth that is sought after as the supreme value by a religion has obviously and necessarily varied according to the character of the stratum which was foremost in adopting it" (ibid., p. 279). Here we move on to differences in religious ethics and their relationship to economic activity. Weber recounts the differences among social strata, chivalrous warrior class, peasants, business classes, intellectuals, for instance, that predispose them to expound different values. Intellectuals have been the exponents of a theoretical rationalism; the business classes (merchants and artisans) have been exponents of a more practical sort of rationalism. Rationalism of either sort, he tells us, has exerted a great influence upon the religious attitude (ibid., pp. 279–80).

Intellectuals have sublimated the possession of sacred values into a belief in redemption. The belief in redemption is a response toward something experienced as senseless, usually some form of undeserved suffering. Intellectuals ask of religion that the senselessness of life – specifically undeserved suffering – be made meaningful, the world order, a meaningful cosmos. Other strata, such as political officials, ask of religion very different things.

Political officials, for example, are suspicious of individual pursuits of salvation and of free formation of communities. These are feared as sources of emancipation from domestication at the hands of the state. Weber informs us in a number of places that emotional, ecstatic religions can encourage revolutionary sentiment and action. Nevertheless, he considers such religions unmanly. The state, he reports, feared the rise of revolutionary movements of the lower classes out of the emotional excitement connected with orgiastic phenomena (Weber, 1981, p. 32).

Similarly, priests of institutionalized religions have an interest in maintaining their position of authority and power and have, therefore, considered highly suspect and in need of institutional regulation and control the quest of individuals or free communities for salvation by means of contemplation, orgies or asceticism. The institutionalization of religion with specialized offices and priests produces a separation of the "private sphere" from the "official sphere" (Weber, 1946, p. 295).

As noted, intellectuals have sublimated the possession of sacred values into a belief in "redemption." This idea is very old if one understands it as liberation from distress, hunger, drought, sickness and ultimately from suffering and death. "'From what' and 'for what' one wished to be redeemed and, let us not forget, 'could be' redeemed, depended upon one's image of the world." For example, "one could wish to be saved from political and social servitude. . .from the eternal and senseless play of human passions and desires" (ibid., p. 280).

Behind such beliefs "always lies a stand towards something in the actual world which is experienced as specifically 'senseless.' Thus, the demand has been implied: that the world order. . .is, could, and should somehow be a meaningful 'cosmos'" (ibid., p. 281). Weber contrasts the effects on religion and sacred values of strata who are active in practical life from those, like intellectuals, who are not. Weber separates intellectual life, especially with an emphasis on contemplation, from practical life. Yet another view might have it that contemplation and intellectual life can and should be integrated with practical life. Among those he mentions as active in practical life are "chivalrous warrior heroes." He contrasts peasants with knights in their respective and distinctive attitudes. "Orgiastic and ecstatic states of 'possession,' produced by means of toxics or by the dance, are strange to the status honor of knights because they are considered undignified. Among the peasants, however, such states have taken the place that 'mysticism' holds among the intellectuals" (ibid., p. 283).

Returning to his main thesis, he claims that wherever the sacred values of a virtuoso religion have borne a contemplative or orgiastic–ecstatic character, there "has been no bridge between religion and the practical action of the workaday world." But this also means that "a deep abyss separates the way of life of the laymen [*sic*] from that of the community of virtuosos" (ibid., p. 289). Weber implies that contemplative or ecstatic religious activity remains aloof from practical, worldly activity. When religious virtuosos reach into the masses for economic support, the religion undergoes change; laypeople reshape it in terms of their own needs. Weber shows how religions of virtuosos become transformed in the direction of a savior religion; the religions become transformed by lay followers' need for magic (in a world determined by non-rational, non-calculable forces of nature) and for belief in a savior. The laymen, who are involved in practical life, continue to orient to values of this life, including prosperity.

That capitalism developed in the West along with and under the impetus of Protestantism, does not mean that *laymen* in the East did not have the psychological orientation requisite for economic development. The caste and clan system enforced by magical, religious taboos obstructed economic development, according to Weber. But the caste and clan systems were political and economic arrangements as much as or more than they were religious systems. A radical change in political and economic arrangements could occur first, with changes in religious beliefs, practices and taboos following. It is the social, political, historical context that influences the relationship between religious practices and practical, worldly activity, as Weber shows in rich detail.

The life situation of some strata under certain conditions, notably intellectuals of a literary as opposed to practical sort who have lost political influence or interest in politics, predisposes them to a life that more or less values contemplation. The life situation of other strata under certain social conditions, notably merchants, traders and artisans at a period of sudden and great expansion of trade and opportunities for wealth, predisposes them to a life that more or less values practical activity in the world. The nature of sacred values is influenced by the life situation of strata that are the bearers of those values. But that relationship is not solely determinate, according to Weber. The converse also holds. A religion contains its own distinctive sacred values which influence the attitudes and practical orientations of the religious virtuosos (ibid., p. 290). Sacred values are not simply erotic in nature and interpreted according to life situation; they are also spiritual.

Spirits and gods

There is an intrinsic relationship between sacred values and spirit, the spirit of an individual and the spirit of a culture. In early religions the ecstatic state as sacred value is interpreted as spiritual possession. This state is seen as a means for influencing the spirits. As such it is a precondition for producing certain effects in healing, meteorology, divination, telepathy, and so forth. The earliest religions involve a belief in spirits, forces that inhere in and are responsible for the powers of special objects, animals or persons. Spirit endows the latter with its distinctive power.

Spirit comes to refer to a number of different but related phenomena. We refer to spirit when we talk about raising somebody's spirit or the fact that somebody is in low spirits. We speak of inspiring as giving spirit to another. In this sense spirit strengthens and enables people to carry out some action; it is a power. To be inspired is to be empowered, to be inspiring is to empower others. Certain experiences can affect one's spirit. One's interactions with others, one's success or failure at some task, can raise or lower one's spirit. Conversely, these experiences may be attributed to the state of one's spirit. Being in good or bad spirits may contribute to the success or failure of an endeavor or encounter. Thus being able to influence spirit is an important and valuable power. Religious rituals focus on the spirit as an extraordinary or sacred power. Religious rituals both inspire the participants and produce ecstasy. Those who conduct the rituals and produce the ecstatic experience are able to control or influence the spirit.

The experience of ecstasy (*ex-stasis*) is one in which one is taken outside of one's self, one's ordinary state of being. An extraordinary spirit takes over one's body and controls one's actions; one is able to do things one could not ordinarily do. This extraordinary power has been designated by such terms as "mana," "orenda," "maga" (from which derives our word, "magic"). Weber uses the term "charisma" to refer to such extraordinary powers. From this word, we get the word "charm" as in a magic charm, as in somebody living a charmed life, and as in somebody being charming, having the capacity to enchant.

For most people ecstasy is accessible only on occasion. It occurs in a social form, the *orgy*, which is the primordial form of religious association! Because of the routine demands of living, most people can experience ecstasy only occasionally as intoxication. Ecstasy may be induced by such means as alcohol and especially music, which originally served orgiastic purposes (Weber, [1921–2] 1978, p. 401). The ability to induce an ecstatic state in oneself or others, to lose possession of oneself, to be taken over by an extraordinary spirit, is a special power that confers special status. The powers of such persons may include those of divination, hence they should be consulted and their powers and the powers of the spirits invoked before any important undertaking or decision.

The distinction between mundane powers and charismatic ones, matter and spirit, makes possible magical rituals (magical "religions"). The assumption that behind real things and events there is something spiritual of which real events are only the symptoms means an effort must be made to influence the spiritual power through actions that address themselves to a spirit or soul. This development depends upon the power of professional necromancers within the community (ibid., p. 404). Thus the power and self-interest of the religious virtuosos – the necromancers – influences the development of magical religion and its impact on mundane activity.

The belief in spirits eventually becomes transformed into a belief in anthropomorphic gods. The difference between a spirit and a god involves a difference between immanence and transcendence. In the former case, the spirit of the fire is identical with the fire itself; it is immanent in the fire.

We may engage in certain actions to evoke or invoke the spirit of the fire. However, in the latter case, the anthropomorphic god of the fire is separate from the fire; he transcends it. He controls the fire but is not one with the fire.

From warrior gods to ethical gods

Every function originally had its god. The worship of earth deities such as Mother Earth presumes the relative importance of agriculture. Every permanent political association had a special god who guaranteed the success of the political action of the group. Political and military conquest entailed the victory of the stronger god (ibid., p. 413). Worshippers of the weaker or unsuccessful god would stop attending the temple of that god and start attending the temple of the victorious god. The heavenly gods represent a heroes' paradise beyond the earth. "The inferiority of earth divinities to celestial personal gods who reside in the clouds or on the mountains is frequently determined by the development of a knightly culture" (ibid., p. 410) and the subordination of a peaceful, agricultural culture. Thus earth deities persist along with celestial gods.

Just as the warrior community can dominate the unarmed (re)productive community, the celestial gods of the former can dominate the earth deities of the latter. Warmaking differs from the making of all other things, and the god of warmaking differs from all other deities. The making of things, even the making of a person, involves working with nature. While warmaking does involve (re)making the person into a warrior, which can involve working on and with nature, this work is preparatory to the activity of warmaking itself. Warmaking involves no (re)productive work: it involves fighting and looting or fighting and conquering.

Just as warmaking differs from the making of all other things, the god of war differs from all other deities. Warmaking does not simply renounce (re)productive work; it takes control over the (re)productive work of others. The god of war is a transcendent god, not an immanent spirit. Just as warmaking is a male and hence masculine activity; the god of war is a male god whose traits are therefore masculine.

It was the ancient warrior god of the Israeli confederacy that became the local god of the city of Jerusalem. The rise of local gods (gods of particular localities) is associated not only with permanent settlement but with the founding of a city as a separate political association. Consequently, the full development of the local god is not found in India or the Far East, for example. Instead, the idea of an immanent divine force remained paramount there. From the city states, local deities spread to confederacies such as those of the Israelites (ibid., pp. 414–15). As a consequence of prophetic preaching, the deeds of other nations that were affecting Israel's vital interests came to be regarded as wrought by its god, Yahweh. The entire history of the Hebrew nation came to be interpreted as consisting of the deeds of Yahweh who took on the universalistic traits of transcendental omnipotence and inscrutability (ibid., pp. 418–19).

The process of anthropomorphization occurs as gods are conceived by analogy to earthly rulers. Those beings that are worshipped as divine and entreated religiously may be termed "gods," in contrast to "demons" or spirits which are magically coerced or charmed (ibid., pp. 422–4). The primordial ways of influencing supernatural power were (for immanent spirits) to control them through magic, or (for transcendent gods) to make oneself agreeable to them by gratifying their egotistic wishes (ibid., p. 432). With the transformation of the belief in spirits into a belief in gods, and the control of spirits into the worship of gods, the notion developed that transgression against the will of God is an ethical sin punished by concrete ills. Prophecy is decisive in moving the mass of the population from magical practices to an ethical rationalization of life (ibid., p. 437).

Weber explains the rise of ethical religions as due to new needs in the community. He claims that increased ethical demands were made upon the gods by men, and by inversion upon men by the gods, parallel with four developments: the increasing power of orderly judicial determination which occurs with the development of large and pacified polities; the increasing regulation of ever-new types of human relationships by conventional rules; the dependence of "men" on these rules in their interactions; and the growth in social and economic importance of the reliability of the given word, such as among partners in an exchange transaction (ibid., p. 430). In other words, a complex, stratified, social order with varying kinds of social tensions and class conflict calls forth the need for new methods of social control; no longer is social control located in the immediate relationships and traditions of a personal community.

Weber contrasts the belief in ethical gods of pacified urban groups with the unreceptivity of a military caste to the belief in an ethically concerned, yet impartial, wise and kindly "providence" (ibid., p. 431). He comments on the deep sociological distance separating a warrior class from every kind of religious or purely ethical rationalism. Nevertheless, the ethical god derives from the god of war, the god of a political association, the god of "men." This masculine god later becomes feminized – a god of love – as the polity becomes disarmed, pacified and domesticated. We can surmise that before the rise of a transcendent ethical god, ethics were immanent in social relations. Only with the rise of impersonal exchange relations did the need for an ethical god arise.

The prophet was essential to the rise of an ethical god. Weber distinguishes between the prophet and the lawgiver although he claims that the transition is fluid. Lawgivers were generally called to their office when social tensions were evident. This was apt to occur with special frequency when there was economic differentiation of the warrior class as a result of growing monetary wealth of one part and the debt enslavement of another. An additional factor was the rise of a wealthy commercial class which was challenging the old warrior nobility. Hence, class conflicts called for the talents of a lawgiver. It was the task of the lawgiver to resolve the conflicts between status groups and to produce a new sacred law of eternal validity, for which he had to secure divine approbation. Moses would be classified as such a lawgiver (ibid., pp. 442–3).

The prescriptions of the oldest sacred legislation of the Hebrews presuppose a money economy and hence sharp conflicts of interests within the confederacy. Moses found a compromise solution for these conflicts – the debt release of the sabbatical year – and he organized the Israelite confederacy with an integral national god (ibid.).

Prophets were not necessarily lawgivers, although "a distinctive concern with social reform is characteristic of Israelite prophets." The latter "hurled their 'woe unto you' against those who oppressed and enslaved the poor, those who joined field to field, and those who deflected justice by bribes. These were the typical actions leading to class stratification." These actions were "intensified by the development of the city-state (*polis*). Jerusalem . . . had been organized into a city-state by the time of these later prophets" (ibid., p. 443). Weber explains Hebrew prophecy's concern for social reform as a "means to an end. Their primary concern was with foreign politics, chiefly because it constituted the theatre of their god's activity" (ibid.).

Weber identified himself with these Hebrew prophets. He emphasizes that the Israelite prophets were concerned with social and other types of injustices that violated the Mosaic code "primarily in order to explain god's [*sic*] wrath, and not in order to institute a program of social reform" (ibid.). If God's wrath occurs in the theatre of foreign politics, then Weber is interpreting the prophets' concern with social reform and domestic ethics to be merely a means for avoiding devastation in foreign politics. Weber may be interpreting the motivation of the prophets as being more like his own motivation than is warranted by the evidence. The prophets' concern was that the individuals who made up the community follow the divine precepts and live an ethical life. This was seen as essential to the social well-being of the community. Violating these precepts was likely to incur the wrath of God and the devastation of the community. Weber does not consider the direct and immanent relationship between social ethics and social well-being. Social well-being, in his view, depends on foreign politics. Social reform is important only to the extent that it has bearing on foreign politics, such as the willingness of the masses to fight in foreign wars.

Weber distinguishes between the ethical teacher and the ethical prophet. Ethical prophecy involves emotional preaching (ibid., p. 445). Ethical prophecy developed with the conception of a personal, transcendental and ethical

149

god. The personal, transcendental and ethical god is a Near Eastern concept. It corresponds closely to that of an all-powerful mundane king with his rational bureaucratic regimes. Weber assumes a causal connection between the concept of an all-powerful mundane king and a personal transcendent ethical god (ibid., p. 448). The transition from a priesthood serving a polity into a priesthood serving a religious congregation was associated with the rise of great world empires of the Near East, especially Persia, and the destruction of political associations and the disarming of the population.

Members of the priesthood of the vanquished political association were assigned certain political powers and were rendered secure in their positions because the religious congregation was regarded as a valuable instrument for pacifying the conquered, just as the neighborhood association was turned into a compulsory community for the protection of financial interests of the conquerors. The members of the community were held jointly responsible for the payment of tribute (or taxes) to the rulers. By virtue of decrees promulgated by the Persian kings, Judaism evolved into such a religious community under royal protection (ibid., pp. 454–5).

Weber contrasts the warrior class with the middle classes, claiming that the religious need of the middle and lower bourgeoisie expresses itself less in the form of heroic myths than in more sentimental legend. Weber attributes this difference to the peaceableness and the greater emphasis on domestic and family life of the middle class, in contrast to the ruling strata. Middle-class religion is therefore transformed in the direction of domesticity (ibid., pp. 487–8). Salvation religions like Christianity tend to glorify the non-military and even anti-military virtues (ibid., p. 490). Socially privileged groups become involved in salvation religion when demilitarization has set in and when they have lost either the possibility of political activity or the interest in it. Consequently, salvation religions usually emerge when the ruling strata, noble or middle class, have lost their political power to a bureaucratic militaristic unitary state. The withdrawal of the ruling strata from politics favors the development of a salvation religion (ibid., p. 503).

The "need for salvation is remote and alien to warriors, bureaucrats and the plutocracy" (ibid., p. 486). Furthermore, salvation religion changes its character when it reaches into the disprivileged social strata. That move involves the emergence of a savior or emphasis on the concept of a savior (ibid., p. 487).

The Near Eastern salvation religions were the consequence of the educated strata's enforced or voluntary loss of political influence and participation. The intellectual seeks to endow his life with a pervasive meaning and thus to find unity with himself, with his fellow men, and with the cosmos. It is the intellectual who conceives of the "world" as a problem of meaning. As intellectualism suppresses belief in magic, the world's processes become disenchanted, lose their magical significance, and henceforth simply "are" and "happen" but no longer signify anything (ibid., p. 506).

150

The conflict between the way the world is and the way it ought to be if it were to be a meaningful cosmos, the conflict between the desire to endow one's life with meaning and the meaninglessness of the world, creates a problem for intellectuals, a tension between them and reality. Their response may be world-fleeing romanticism; it may be more contemplative or more actively ascetic; it may seek primarily individual salvation or collective revolutionary transformation of the world in the direction of a more ethical state (ibid.).

Salvation and ecstasy

The idea of salvation is related to the experience of ecstasy through charisma. The various methods for breaking down organic inhibitions were important in producing ecstasy. As indicated above, these include, in addition to alcohol or other drugs, music, dance and sexuality. However these acute ecstasies are transitory and leave few positive traces on everyday behavior. A much more enduring possession of the charismatic condition is promised by milder forms of euphoria, either mystical illumination or active ethical conversion. They produce, unlike the acute ecstasies, a meaningful relation to the world (ibid., p. 535).

The experience of acute orgiastic ecstasy can become transformed by sublimation into a milder but more permanent "possession." This milder form of charisma (a charmed life), protection from harm, possession of a powerful spirit able to ward off evil spirits, may take the form of feeling the presence of this spirit or god, or of knowing God, gnosticism. God's presence may be conceived of as love or approval. The milder form of euphoria that is induced and interpreted as God's presence may take the form of feeling oneself loved or protected by the god or of feeling love or gratitude toward the god. This mild euphoria or love, translated as the love of a personal deity or savior, includes sublimated erotic devotion to the deity and the subjective experience of feeling love from the deity.

Prophets of ethical salvation oppose ecstatic orgiastic intoxication because the latter stands in the way of the systematic ethical rationalizing of life that they require. The goal in both orgiastic practices and methodically planned procedures of sanctification is the same. In Weber's view it is the incarnation within the individual of a supernatural being and therefore of a god – in other words, self-deification. An alternative conception is that the goal in both is the ecstatic experience associated with sublimated erotic love or with actual erotic orgies that have symbolic and spiritual meaning. Wherever there is a belief in a transcendental god, the goal can no longer be self-deification (an immanent experience of sublimated love or ecstasy) and becomes instead the acquisition of qualities demanded by God. I interpret this to mean that the goal can no longer be the experience of ecstasy and

151

spiritualized (sublimated) erotic love, but rather avoiding the wrath and winning the favor of a patriarchal god that demands obedience to his will. In Weber's terms, "The aim is no longer to possess god [*sic*], for this cannot be done, but either to become his instrument or to be spiritually suffused by him. . .[The latter is] closer to self-deification" (ibid., p. 536), or what I call spiritualized erotic love.

The concept of a transcendental, absolutely omnipotent god arose in Asia Minor and "was imposed" upon the Occident.[3] One result of this was that for the Occident self-deification or mystical, ecstatic possession of God was not possible because this was considered a blasphemous deification of a mere created thing – idolatry. Salvation could be accomplished only by some sort of active conduct in the world (ibid., p. 552).

The social stratification of Roman society was important in influencing the negative attitude of Christianity toward ecstasy. A ruling military stratum, an office nobility, that distances itself from the ruled and stresses (self)discipline and (self)control must despise as unmanly the loss of (self)control and restraint that is integral to the ecstatic experience. Weber contrasts the Greeks with the Romans in this regard.

The Greeks set a positive value on ecstasy, both the acute orgiastic type of divine intoxication and the milder form of euphoria induced primarily by rhythms and music, as engendering an awareness of the uniquely divine. The ruling stratum lived with this mild form of ecstasy from their very childhood (ibid., p. 554). The social structure of Greece lacked a stratum that paralleled the office nobility in Rome (ibid.). Relations of social control in Greece differed from those in Rome. There was less need for social distance and reserve.

Social relations between Greek citizens and those who were not citizens, slaves, women, strangers, were more personal, "simpler and less feudal" (ibid.). In contrast the control of Rome over a large population by means of the authority of office, meant that the social relations between the ruling class and the subordinate classes were impersonal and mediated by the rationality of office (ibid.).

Weber's work suggests that there is more receptivity to a breakdown of inhibitions (emotional ecstasy) among people who do not have to maintain impersonal social control and social distance. The Romans with their noble bearing, characterized by maintenance of reserve and social distance, regarded dancing and music as unseemly and unworthy of a (noble) "man's" sense of honor. Therefore, Rome remained uncreative in these arts. Rome's world-conquering, military-official nobility rejected every type of ecstasy. Christian communities found this contempt for ecstatic procedures to be characteristic of all religions possible on essentially Roman territory. The Christian community of Rome adopted the Roman attitude of contempt for ecstasy (ibid).

Middle-class religiosity, sublimated eroticism and women

Nevertheless, emotionally and erotically tinged practices tend to develop within middle-class religions of salvation. Weber notes that there is a striking similarity to contemplative mysticism that characterizes all religions of faith oriented to salvation which are found among peaceful groups. However, that is not true of ancient Islam nor of the religion of Yahweh. In both of these the primordial trust of the warrior in the tremendous power of his own god was still dominant (ibid., p. 568) Faith in these religions took the form of simple allegiance to the god or to the prophet.

> Faithfulness is rewarded and disloyalty punished by the god. This personal relation to the god takes on other qualities when the carriers of salvation religion become peaceful groups, and more particularly when they become members of the middle classes. Only then can faith as an instrument of salvation take on the emotionally tinged character and assume the lineaments of love for the god or the savior. . .God now appears as a gracious master or father of a household (ibid., p. 570).

Weber implies that peaceful middle-class life gives rise to the idealization of love as opposed to war. The idealization of love includes valuing a certain emotional, erotic state that can be likened to ecstasy. Like the other ecstatic form of salvation religion, mysticism, the emphasis on an emotional state of being contrasts with an emphasis on action in the world. When a salvation religion that stresses ethical probation through action in the world is taken up by peaceful middle-class groups the religion is likely to become transformed.

"The emotional content of religions of faith may be deepened whenever the followers of these religions substitute the view that they are children of god for the ascetic view that they are merely his instruments" (ibid., p. 571). The effect is an anti-rational one on the conduct of life, particularly when the relation to the god or the savior is one of passionate devotion and consequently whenever the religion has a latent or manifest tinge of eroticism. Weber cites as the most striking illustration the Hindu religiosity of love in which devotion to Krishna, and more especially to the Krishna child, is raised to a state of erotically tinged devotion. He reports that this process takes place through four levels of contemplation, all of them different versions of love: servant love, friendship love, filial or parental love, and, at the highest level, a piety tinged with definite eroticism, after the fashion of the love of Krishna's mistresses for him (ibid.).

The dispriviledged strata require belief in a savior and emotional, sublimated forms of erotic, devotional practices that produce a feeling of euphoria. They seem to desire a sublimated release from inhibitions which may serve as a release from suffering. Among the nobility the euphoria of heroic action and the status, power and authority that result may substitute for the euphoria of erotic devotion or orgiastic intoxication of the dispriviled. Nevertheless, there are differences among different ruling strata such as the Romans and the Greeks, just as there are differences among the dispriviled, differences attributable in good part to differences in the particular social relations and economic activity of the various groups.

Religions of the dispriviled strata, in contrast to the aristocratic cults of the martial nobility, are characterized by a tendency to allot equality to women. "The greater or lesser, active or passive participation (or exclusion) of women from the religious cults is everywhere a function of the degree of the group's relative pacification or militarization (present or past)" (ibid., pp. 488–9). There is a great receptivity by women to all religious prophecy except that which is exclusively military or political in orientation. Every political and military type of prophecy is directed exclusively to men (ibid., p. 489). The association of manliness with military activity was not based solely on excluding women. It was based also on plundering women. "The cult of a *warlike spirit* is frequently put into the direct service of controlling and lawfully plundering the households of women by the male inhabitants of the warrior house" (ibid., italics added).

Under the impact of a warrior society the belief and rituals of rebirth originally associated with the cyclical and seasonal nature of agriculture become appropriated and transformed into initiation rites for young boys as a way of acquiring a new soul – the soul of a heroic warrior. The boy must die to his old peaceful but subordinate life – among the women and children – and be reborn as a "man," a warrior, capable of intimidating, subduing, ruling and killing as well as taking the risk of being killed or hated, rather than allow himself to be ruled – like a woman, child or slave.

Weber explains that wherever an ascetic training of warriors involving the rebirth of a heroic soul is or has been dominant, woman is regarded as lacking the higher heroic soul and is consequently assigned a secondary religious status. This obtains in most aristocratic or distinctively militaristic cultic communities (ibid.). Thus aristocratic and militaristic societies that foster the development of a heroic soul through religious cultic activity have serious negative consequences for women. These cultic activities produce a distinctive, exclusive religious status that is reserved only for men. This results in an attitude of superiority and contempt for women. We may speculate about the effects of these cultic communities on the relationship between men and women since women are not seen as worthy objects of emotional attachment. In fact they may be seen as inferior beings to be used and abused by men, and/or beings who can be treated as prizes to serve the greater glory of the hero.

In contrast, salvation religions tended to glorify the non-military and even anti-military virtues (ibid., p. 490). In the Occident, pristine Christianity as well as the later pneumatic (charismatic) and pacifist sects of eastern and western Europe, derived a great deal of their missionizing power from the circumstance that they attracted women and gave them equal status. In Greece, too, the cult of Dionysos at first gave to women an unusual degree of emancipation from convention. The greatest competitor to Christianity, according to Weber, was the religion of Mithra, an extremely masculine cult that excluded women. This accounts for the superiority of Christianity in its missionary enterprises over its most important competitor (ibid.). During a period of universal peace (when domestic relations become valued), the adherents of Mithra had to seek out for their women a substitute in other mysteries, such as those of Cybele. "This had the effect of destroying, even within single families, the unity and universality of the religious community, thereby providing a striking contrast to Christianity" (ibid.).

Ethical rationality and prophecy

The civic strata of artisans, traders, entrepreneurs and so forth have an elective affinity for special types of religions that correspond with a way of life detached from dependence on nature and based on economic calculations and mastery. This form of life lends itself to an ethical and rational regulation of life.

The emergence of ethical rationalism usually requires prophecy. There are two types of prophecy: exemplary and emissary. The former involves exemplary living as a way of displaying the path to salvation. It usually involves a contemplative and apathetic-ecstatic life. The emissary type of prophecy makes demands on people in the name of a god. These demands are of an ethical nature and often involve active asceticism, the means for proving oneself to be God's tool. This contrasts with contemplative surrender to God, which is the supreme value of religions influenced by strata of genteel intellectuals. Weber conceives of striving (to prove oneself) and surrender (to another) as antinomies – polar opposites.

Emissary prophecy generally assumes a conception of God as a supra-mundane, personal, wrathful, forgiving, loving, demanding, punishing Lord of Creation. In short, a patriarchal god. In contrast the supreme being of an exemplary prophecy is an impersonal being, a static state that is accessible only by means of contemplation. The conception of an active god, held by emissary prophecy, has dominated the Iranian and Middle Eastern religions and those Occidental religions which are derived from them. The conception of a supreme and static being, held by exemplary prophecy, has come to dominate Indian and Chinese religiosity. These differences, explainable in terms of historical, social and political differences, are themselves a matter of sublimation; the supreme being of exemplary prophecy, an impersonal state of being, is a sublimation of primitive conceptions of animistic immanent spirits;

155

the supreme being of emissary prophecy, an ethical, personal, transcendent god, is a sublimation of later conceptions of heroic, transcendent deities, which originate in warrior-dominated societies.

In the development of occidental religion, transcendent gods of warrior heroes struggle against immanent spirits of the peaceful agricultural masses; rationalized ethical religion against the magical ecstatic rituals and (their interpretation in) myths – "superstition" of the folk or masses. Again we see the repression at work, the struggle.

Conclusion: masculine, feminine and feminist religion

Despite the complexities and varieties of religious orientations that he describes, running through Weber's analysis is a duality, the duality between an active heroic form of life and a contemplative, receptive form of life, between being an agent and being a vessel, between mastering and changing the world and perpetuating and reproducing the world as it is. In short, a duality of love and greatness that in the West is associated with masculinity and femininity.

We have seen how under certain historically specific conditions the psychological state of ecstasy becomes sublimated into a concern about being ethical as a way of experiencing a modified form of ecstasy – God's love or grace. In this regard Weber seems to recognize the power of a primary desire for ecstasy and erotic love underlying even the most rational, ethical, ascetic religions. However, he does not inquire into the significance of this desire as a primary force at the heart of ethical religion – and, I might suggest, at the heart of social life. He tends, instead, to treat it as other – an alternative to rational, ascetic action. He ends up treating the two: ethical, rational, ascetic religion and ecstatic, erotic, contemplative religion as mutually exclusive despite a recognition of their common origin and the fluidity of the distinction between them. Weber recognizes the repressed other – magic, emotion, eros, the desire for ecstasy – at the core of ethical religion. However, he stops short of seeing the relationship as one of repression; he never inquires into the significance of that relationship; he never "contemplates" an alternative relationship.

The original division within religion appears to have been between "female" earth deities (spirits), reflecting an agricultural society, and "male" heavenly deities (patriarchal gods and goddesses), reflecting a warrior society. As we have seen, warrior societies devalue and denigrate women and non-warriors as lacking a heroic soul. Often men and women participated in different cults, reflecting and (re)producing different cultures, a feminine culture and a masculine culture. With demilitarization, pacification and the growing importance of domestic life, the masculine warrior deity is transformed into a loving and loved father evoking sentiments of sublimated erotic devotion and "feminine" virtues.

156

Weber analyzes the origins and practical consequences of different kinds of religious ethics: the ethic of obedience to worldly authority (Lutheranism) or of adaptation to the world (Confucianism), the ethic of brotherly love (Christianity), the ethic of ecstatic mysticism (Hinduism), and the ethic of heroic asceticism (Calvinism). He particularly contrasts religions of immanence, such as the contemplative mysticism of Buddhism, with religions of transcendence such as the active ascetism of Protestant Calvinism. He treats the contrast as one of oppositions: one an attitude of passivity toward the world, an escape into private life; the other an orientation of world mastery.

The relationship between private and public, domestic and political, love and greatness, feminine and masculine is mediated by religion. A distinctively public world of political and economic activity originates out of warfare, as do masculinity, heroic deities and transcendent gods (as distinct from the world of the folk who must work with the irrational forces of nature and who believe in magical immanent spirits and chthonic deities). As depoliticization and demilitarization set in along with the establishment of an imperial bureaucratic state, the development of a personal, transcendental, universal, ethical god emerges and mediates the relationship between private and public.

A relationship to a patriarchal, transcendent, omnipotent, personal, ethical god as opposed to an impersonal divine force that is immanent in the world, produces a world in which individuals need to prove themselves through ethical action in the world. Ethical salvation religion of this kind requires disciplining one's will and desires by subordinating them to a higher desire and a higher will, a desire to live according to the demands and commands of a patriarchal god's will. The aim is to achieve salvation in this world or in another future world and to avoid the patriarchal god's wrath. But the aim also includes the attainment of a psychological state in the here and now, a state of grace, of feeling possessed by the god's love. Achieving the aim requires ethical action in the world, living according to the commandments of the patriarchal god as a means of proving oneself.

A salvation religion that does not sublimate love through a relationship to a patriarchal, transcendent, omnipotent, personal, demanding, wrathful god, but rather treats the divine itself and divine love as immanent, devalues action in the world. There is no need to prove oneself to achieve divine love; there is no desire motivating action in the world. Knowing that one's desire is fulfilled, a knowledge that comes with contemplation, results in a passive attitude toward the world. This passive state of fulfilled desire – oneness with divine love – is nirvana. Because the divine love with which one is infused is also immanent in all things, in all the world, one can feel and know oneself to be one with all things as one comes to feel and know oneself to be one with divine love. Feeling at one with the world does not lead to action and striving. This is Weber's argument against such feminine mystical, contemplative religion.

157

However, despite ideology to the contrary, one can never preserve such a state of oneness and fulfillment of desire for love. We are embodied beings. As such, material needs and differences, including embodied erotic desire, emerge ever anew. There will always be some irritant or stimuli – internal or external – that provokes discontent, struggle, striving – action. Thus, even mystical religion requires efforts aimed at securing the necessities for sustaining life as well as continual struggle against desire and against the distractions of the world.

Weber employs ideal types to distinguish between religions that result in what he considers rational action in the world and those that result in contemplation and the achievement of a psychological, emotional state. Although he recognizes that the distinction between ethical, ascetic religion and ecstatic, contemplative religion is a fluid one, based on consequences for action, he distinguishes between masculine religions of rational world mastery or world adjustment and feminine religions of world flight or contemplation. However, the "feminine" religions may be understood as masculine reactions against a masculine world of politics, a reaction by intellectuals who Weber suggests are removed from or disgusted by the political world and who endeavor to endow their lives with meaning.

An alternative to both masculine and "feminine" religions can be found in those "magical" practices that inspire and empower: aesthetic, mimetic and erotic practices that create a psychological state that enables people to withstand and transcend their suffering and to find pleasure in the world and power in themselves.[4] Spiritual feminists have been working on practices that inspire and empower people, enabling them to overcome their suffering. However, feminists recognize that the suffering derives from social arrangements that are disempowering and demoralizing. Feminist "magic" consists in empowering and inspiring women to resist and overcome those social arrangements (Starhawk, 1982). Such practices do not result in passivity toward the world but action, often collective and political action, in the world.

Weber's sociology of religion can be read as a narrative tracing the tension between a subordinated community made up primarily of women and children, and later of other subjugated peoples, and a political community of ruling men. Before the formation of a separate political community, we can assume that the magical rituals and practices of the community were intregrated into the everyday lives and communal occasions of the whole community; they do not constitute something separate called religion.

The practices and rituals of that original, undivided community continue to live on after a political community has separated out and come to dominate what is now, in contradistinction to the political community, the personal community. The political community continues to struggle against the personal community which both resists and accommodates to the former. Transcendent gods continue to struggle against immanent spirits; rationalized ethical religion against magical ecstatic rituals and their interpretation in myths – "superstition" – of the personal community, the folk or masses.[5]

The personal community becomes a "feminized" oppressed community. In order to maintain control, the political community acknowledges and uses the priests of the personal community. In this way, some of the magical, ecstatic rituals and myths of the personal community become transformed into a separate institution – religion – that serves the spiritual needs of the personal community as well as the material interests of the political community. But the tension between rational control and ecstatic and magical practices remains, the attempt to suppress, control or rationalize these practices of the masses requires constant struggle.

For Weber, the God that is responsible for modern rational, ascetic action, for the vocational ethic of modern life, is the God of Luther and Calvin. The God of Luther and Calvin is the rational God of modern society, a society in which economic and practical rationality must forever struggle with the desire for (a world of) love. Weber analyzes the conflict between love and practical activity in the modern world.

Notes

1 This is the way Schluchter (1981) tends to interpret Weber's work. Schluchter interprets Weber's work as a developmental history which is not quite the same as evolutionary theory. Guenther Roth in his introduction (1981) places Schluchter's interpretation in the context of neo-evolutionary theories that are current in Germany.

2 Edward Said (1979) and Marnia Lazreg (1988) have each in their own way called attention to the dangers of treating another group or religion as radically other. Each of them has called for the need to recognize the other as sharing the same basic humanity. Lazreg, especially, is aware of the critique of the Euro-centered grand narrative tradition with its setting up of a universal subject such as humanity. She is also aware, however, that the emphasis on difference ends up creating the very kinds of dualisms that the critique was trying to overcome.

3 From some passages in Marianne Weber's biography of her husband, I interpret this phrase, "was imposed on the Occident" to refer to "'Semiticization,' that is, the defeat of the Aryan culture" (Weber 1975, p. 47). Compare this line and the following, both from the biography, "The ancient culture was ruined by the renewed penetration of Semitic influences – among other things, the Christianization of the Occident" (ibid.). In the biography, Marianne Weber presents this as the thrust of an essay Max wrote before his sixteenth birthday. I do not take this essay as an indication of any anti-Semitism in the mature Max. He was a friend and supporter of Jewish intellectuals. I think that his phrase, "was imposed on the Occident," implies a view that a patriarchal religion (domination of the sons by an ethically demanding, all-powerful father figure) that emasculates warrior heroes, Aryans, was imposed on the Aryans by a Semitic people. His early view, if it was retained, was retained as an anti-patriarchal, anti-Christian view that resents the feminization of warrior heroes who now must subordinate

and subject themselves to an all-powerful, demanding and ethical God. Only in the sense that the Semites introduce ("impose") a patriarchal, ultimately feminizing religion which he, like Freud, rejects could his mature view be considered anti-Semitic; but there is no evidence of prejudice toward Semitic people themselves any more than toward Christians.

4 This section draws on Victoria Erickson's (1989) discussion of the relationship between magic, folk religion and feminist spirituality.

5 Weber reports that the Romans who rejected ecstasy, like the dance, rendered the Greek word for ecstasy into Latin: *superstitio* (1978, p. 554).

PART THREE

A world of love

10

Brotherly love and practical action

The essential tension and conflict of modern life may be characterized as one between an ethic of impersonal relations and one of personal relations. Ferdinand Toennies associated the former with *Gesellschaft* (society) and the latter with *Gemeinschaft* (community). He explicitly linked gender with society; *Gemeinschaft* is associated with a feminine maternal world, *Gesellschaft* with a masculine world. Mitzman reports that in the earlier part of Weber's life, he, Weber, had viewed *Gemeinschaft* in terms of patriarchy conceived of as the arbitrary power of the patriarchal overlord. Weber's "realism" prevented him from romanticizing traditional society. Mitzman sees Weber as later reconceiving *Gemeinschaft* as society based on the bonds of brotherhood (Mitzman, 1971, p. 303), softening somewhat his (Weber's) initial distaste for traditional society.

According to Mitzman, Weber considered the desire of the sons to free themselves from patriarchal power to be an important factor undermining traditionalism. For Weber, as for Freud, patriarchy involved a relationship among men: fathers and sons. The sons struggle for liberation from the patriarch; they do not join with women in a joint struggle against patriarchy. Patriarchy is conceived primarily as the domination of the sons, not the domination of wives and daughters.

Weber's ambivalence toward *Gemeinschaft* derived from his perception of it as both a personal relationship among a band of equal brothers and an authoritarian personal relationship between a despotic patriarch and his family. Mitzman sees Weber as coming to appreciate in his later writings the ethos of brotherhood within traditional society. Mitzman implies that this move represents a salubrious change in Weber's attitude toward the values of love and personal relations over against those of power and politics. Despite this change, it is important to note that Weber's ambivalence toward "traditional" society derived from his awareness that personal relations can be even more coercive and destructive of human freedom than impersonal ones, that domination in and through personal relations can be worse than domination in and through impersonal relations.

Modern bureaucracy is a social organization of impersonal relations. It involves impersonal domination which means that the domination is limited only to official relations that are spelled out by terms of the contract (stipulated or assumed). Bureaucratic domination of this type allows for a degree of individual personal freedom that is unknown and unthinkable in traditional feudal societies.

Man of love, man of action

An alternative to *Gesellschaft* that seems to have held great interest for Weber and other intellectuals of his time was Slavic mysticism. A member of the Weber circle wrote that he could recall no Sunday afternoon at which Dostoevsky was not mentioned, and Weber himself had talked of writing a book on Tolstoy. Weber perceived a relationship between Slavic mysticism and Toennies' concept of *Gemeinschaft* (ibid.). Slavic mysticism presented the man of love as the ideal. In reading the novels of Tolstoy and Dostoevsky, Weber observed that the welter of events and passions that at first confronts the reader represents the meaningless surface of life, while the meaningful aspect of human life resides not in all the actions and events but beneath it all in an "amorphous, unformed love relationship" which Baudelaire calls the "sacred prostitution of the soul" – love for one's fellow man, whoever he might be. According to these novels, it is such amorphous love that leads to the "gates of the eternal, the timeless, the divine" (cited ibid., p. 196).

The "man of love" is not one who enjoys erotic love but rather "amorphous love," or what Weber calls brotherly love, the love of any and all without distinction, hence the sacred prostitution of the soul. Weber referred to the substratum of characteristic figures in the Russian novels who represent this ideal as "the spiritual antipodes of the men of action whose doings occur on the stage of the world" (cited ibid.). Weber used the polarity of *Gemeinschaft–Gesellschaft* to represent not just the opposite poles of personal relations and impersonal relations but the opposite poles of mysticism and Calvinism, "men" of love and "men" of action. He said that *Gesellschaft* is a form of human relationship that strips away the "human." The other form of human relationship, acosmic love, is always *Gemeinschaft*, "on the purely human basis of 'brotherliness'" (cited ibid., p. 197).

Mitzman draws from Weber's interpretations of Russian literature the centrality of the terms "outer" and "inner," "external" and "internal." The inner search for meaning is associated with mysticism. External practical action in the world (action oriented to survival and worldly success) which is ultimately as meaningless as the creature itself who strives to survive and succeed, is associated with Calvinist asceticism. The latter stresses action in the world, not as meaningful in itself, but as a service to God. Weber conceived of the man of love and the man of action as polar opposites. Marianne Weber reports that Max identified with being a man of action.

However, the following scrap of conversation between Max and Marianne is revealing.

Max asked Marianne if she could think of herself as a mystic. She replied in the negative and then asked the same of him. He responded, "It could even be that I *am* one. . .I am. . .not really *quite* securely at home anywhere. It is as though I could (and wanted) to pull myself back from everything, and completely" (cited ibid., p. 218). Apparently, despite his powerful rhetoric on behalf of greatness through action in the world and his negative attitude toward withdrawal from the world, he, himself must eventually have entertained some doubts about the value of heroic action in the world as an end in itself. At least he must have recognized a strong desire on his part to surrender his desire for conflict, action and greatness. He seems here to have been aware that his desire for these things covered over some lack, some emptiness, some sense of not being securely at home *anywhere*, which means of course that he was not at home or at peace with himself. We will see in Chapter 15 the significance of the fact that an orientation to making a home in the world defines women's work in the private sphere.

Mitzman refers also to Weber's "lifetime of wavering between scholarship and politics" (ibid., p. 65).[1] The polarities that Weber set up between those who devote themselves to the inner life of contemplation, illumination and (acosmic) love (women, intellectuals and mystics) and those devoted to the outer life of practical action, accomplishment and success (men and Calvinist ascetics), between the brotherliness (or motherliness in Toennies original account) of *Gemeinschaft* and the lovelessness of *Gesellschaft*, seem to pit action and success in the world against love and withdrawal from the world. Weber compared erotic love to mysticism; one can be substituted for the other, he claimed. Both are forms of ecstasy offering an escape from the deathlike and ultimately meaningless life of *Gesellschaft*, the disenchanted, rationalized, modern world. However, erotic love also competes with mystical love, which the latter rejects as a form of self-love.

Women, love, mysticism fall on one side; men, action, accomplishment on the other side. This polarity is not the same as the one he posed between the ethics of warrior heroes and the ethics of the subjugated. Nevertheless, the association of men with action brings to mind the image of heroic warriors; just as the association of women with love brings to mind the image of vulnerable dependency. The man of love seems womanly; the woman of action, manly. These images suggest that a woman is a woman when she loves; a man is a man when he takes action.

Perhaps this association helps to explain Weber's emphasis on the word "brotherly." Weber used the term "brotherly love" when he could just as readily have used "love." I believe that the emphasis on brotherliness serves to obliterate a connection with womanliness and motherliness that might otherwise come to mind. The emphasis on "brotherliness" serves to eliminate another association as well – the association of love with eros and desire. By using the term "brotherly love," Weber could treat love as a possible alternative to "action." Otherwise, the idea of love would be too threatening; it could not serve as a possible alternative for a man. Love had no place in a man's world; love belonged in the private world of women, not the public world of men. Manly actors do not yearn for love. They must be above sentiment and desire. Only camaraderie and loyalty, simple reciprocity and mutual protection, could define manly relationships. The term "brotherliness" could convey this meaning better than the term "love," with all its womanly, sentimental and unmanly associations.

Hence to the loveless, impersonal world of *Gesellschaft*, the only alternative that Weber considered as a basis for (re)organizing social life or relationships was that of brotherly love. If we substitute the word "motherly" for the word "brotherly" the analysis would be entirely different. A form of life based on a model of motherly love would have little appeal to a "man of action."[2] The domestic life of motherly love has little of the wildness, daring and passion that characterizes a life of action. Domestic life seems tame; motherly love could be seen as an attempt to domesticate or reign in the child's spirit, especially a patriarchal motherly love characterized by "poisonous pedagogy" intended to control the child and his or her spirit rather than learning from and nurturing that spirit.

Brotherly love, likewise, seems to preclude passion, wildness, daring. It, too, makes for a safe, secure, protected life. However, brotherly love, unlike motherly love, may imply the camaraderie of a band of brothers who face the world together, supporting and protecting each other. They may form a band to unite against obstacles or threat from outside; they might be united against the patriarchal father or against an external enemy. Hence brotherly love and brotherly loyalty do not preclude violence, risk and excitement as patriarchal maternal love seems to. Nevertheless the universalistic religious ethic of brotherly love does preclude violence.

I review below Weber's serious consideration of the religious ethic of brotherly love as a possibility for transforming the world. Needless to say, his analysis is not favorable. Brotherly love, despite the powerful works on its behalf by the Russian novelists, cannot compete with heroic action. As we will see below, the ultimate failure of brotherly love as an ethic for organizing social life is that it is stifling. It stifles the development of all value spheres, from economics and politics to aesthetics, science and all culture.

An ethic of impersonal relations

The ethic of personal relations involves treating the relationship and the members to the relationship as intrinsically and inherently valuable. An ethic of impersonal relations involves treating the relationship and the members to the relationship as having extrinsic or instrumental value only. An ethic of impersonal relations, whether of the political sphere, the economic sphere or the public world in general, becomes salient at a particular time and place in history.

At first, Weber recounts, social life had been divided into in-group morality and out-group morality. Then salvation religion raised to a universal ethic the rule of reciprocity that had governed the relations among "brothers." This ethic of brotherly love involved tension with the impersonal world of social, political and commercial relations.

The Protestant ethic with its suspiciousness and indifference toward others (due to belief in predestination and an inscrutable, transcendent God) then created and legitimized an ethic of impersonal relations. According to this ethic, one did not treat others with love, either particularistic or universalistic love, but treated others as one treated the rest of the world including oneself – as a means for doing God's work – and evaluated and valued them accordingly. Ethics now meant serving God through work in one's vocation; it no longer meant treating others with brotherly love.

One took the same demanding, uncompromising, unsympathetic attitude toward others as one took toward oneself. And, even more important, one did not treat the sufferings, ill-fortune or selfishness of others as human problems or failings, but as a matter of God's inscrutable will, perhaps an indicator of damnation.

For Puritanism, with its "groundless and particularized grace," salvation was not something attainable in principle by everyone. Therefore, as Weber acknowledged, "In truth, this standpoint of unbrotherliness was no longer a genuine 'religion of salvation'" (1946, pp. 332–3). The ethic of personal relations, brotherly love, was replaced by an ethic of impersonal relations, success in one's work. Instead of holding out the promise of salvation to those who were suffering, which is what a salvation religion offers, Puritanism divided the world into those who are predestined for salvation and those who are not. The individual, through his or her own efforts, could not attain salvation. Thus we arrive at the paradox that salvation religion, which originated out of concern for ethical irrationality (suffering and injustice) including especially the lack of love in the world, ends up affirming ethical irrationality, taking an unbrotherly, unloving stance, and excluding much of humanity from any possibility of salvation.

Weber was keenly sensitive to the tensions and conflicts of a world based on a secularized Protestant ethic of impersonal relations. I associate the latter ethic with the public world that traditionally has been the domain of men and the alternative ethic of personal relations with the private world that traditionally has been the domain of women. Weber did not make the association of impersonal ethic with men and the public world and personal ethic with women and the private world. In fact it was not women, but men with access to the public sphere, religious men and socialists, who were often the ones to articulate and represent the ethic of compassion and concern for the "disprivileged."[3] It was they who were likely to express outrage at a world indifferent to human need and human suffering, a world that permits and produces exploitation. It is the views (not the values) of such men that Weber intended to refute.

Because of his recognition of the tensions and conflicts inherent in the impersonal modern world, Weber considered the critique of the impersonal world that "strips away the human." His work focuses on the critique that is grounded in the religious ethic of brotherly love. I consider the religious ethic of brotherly love to be a patriarchal, albeit "feminine" in Weber's terms, ethic. I do so not because the religious ethic is enunciated by men, nor because of its reference to "brothers," but because it divides body from spirit, treating the former as if it did not "matter," or as something inferior and disruptive of rational order. This division presumes a servant class ("women") who care for bodies and respond to bodies while a master class ("men") can devote themselves to higher things. The ethic of brotherly love turns out to be an ethic of impersonal relations of love, an ethic of impersonal love, a contradiction in terms, I contend.

Max Weber considered the possibility of a world rationalized on the basis of the religious ethic of brotherly love. In this way, he attempted to address the critique made of the unethical nature of a modern world that is rationalized not in accordance with an ethic of love, but with an ethic of success. Nevertheless, both the vocational ethic of success and the religious ethic of brotherly love as described by Weber are impersonal ethics. I distinguish an impersonal ethic of love from a personal ethic of love. It might be more accurate to designate these respectively as an ethic of impersonal disembodied love and an ethic of personal, erotic love.

By "ethic of impersonal love," I mean an ethic of responsibility for those who are less fortunate or as Weber has described its origins in religion, a love for one's fellow sufferer. According to this ethic, each actor ministers to the other's suffering regardless of his or her own personal feelings of sympathy, antipathy or indifference. Each disregards or denies his or her own feelings and relates to the other solely in accordance with an abstract principle. By "personal ethic of erotic love" or "ethic of personal love," I mean an ethic of mutual responsiveness that requires mutual responsiveness to the needs, desires and feelings of both self and other. Neither the other's feelings nor one's own are disregarded.

The possibility of an ethic of personal love (mutual responsiveness among persons) that is made into a universal ethic (mutual responsiveness of each to the other) is never explored by Weber as a possibility for rationalizing the world. In Weber's schema, an ethic of personal love is by definition irrational.

If it is personal, requiring responsiveness to the particularity of the other, then it cannot be universalistic or rational. Action cannot be deduced from it, as from an abstract universalistic principle, and applied in a logical way to a particular case as can an impersonal ethic of brotherliness, reciprocity and mutual obligations.

In considering the possibility of a world that is substantively rationalized according to a religious (what I consider patriarchal) ethic of brotherly love, Weber questions the effect that such an ethic would have on practical economic and political activity. In addition, he analyzes the relationship between the religious ethic and such seemingly non-practical spheres of life as aesthetic activity, intellectual activity, culture and erotic love. He concludes that a world rationalized according to an ethic of brotherly love would be a world that represses economic development, political life, art, culture and intellectual development. I review first Weber's analysis of the relationship between an ethic of brotherly love and practical economic and political action; I then turn to Weber's analysis of the other spheres of life and their relationship to brotherly love.

The economy

Weber declares, "The tension between brotherly religion and the world has been most obvious in the economic sphere" (1946, p. 331). The most rational economic system is a market economy based on quantitative calculation in terms of money. Money prices, however, are created from the "interest struggles of men." Also "Money is the most abstract and 'impersonal' element that exists in human life. . . The more rational, and *thus impersonal*, capitalism becomes. . .the less accessible it is to any imaginable relationship with a religious ethic of brotherliness" (ibid., italics added). Because a market economy is based on impersonal calculations and struggles of interest, it precludes the carrying out of an ethic of brotherly love. When economic relations were personal ones, even as between master and slave, it was possible to regulate ethically those relations precisely because they were personal relations. "But it is not possible to regulate. . .the relations between the shifting holders of mortgages and the shifting debtors of the banks that issue these mortgages; for in this case, no personal bonds of any sort exist." If one nevertheless tried to regulate economic relations, "the results would be the same as those we have come to know from China, namely, stifling formal rationality. For in China, formal rationality and substantive rationality were in conflict" (ibid.).

Thus rationalizing the world in accordance with an ethic of brotherly love would stifle the development of economic rationality. From the one side we saw that economic rationality precludes ethical considerations for the person of the other and hence threatens ethical life. From the other side we learn that ethical concerns for the person preclude formal rationality and hence stifle economic development.

Instead of trying to regulate economic life ethically, which requires stifling it, religions of brotherly love may attempt to escape from the tension between love and the economic world "in a principled and *inward* manner." That is, they may attempt to "rationalize" their subjective attitude toward the world. There have been only two consistent ways for doing this. One way has been the Puritan vocational ethic which "rationalized" all work as the serving of God's will and the proving of one's state of grace, and which devalued everything of the world as creatural and depraved. The other is mysticism.

Mystical salvation religions, too, warn against attachment to money and goods. They reject all worldly endeavors and pursue instead spiritual unity with God or the universe. Unlike Puritanism, mystical religions do not conceive of worldly activity as a way of proving religious grace. However, the renunciation of economic activity and dependence on gifts, alms or the bountifulness of nature cannot in practice be a universal solution. Gifts and alms presuppose the labor of others which provides enough of a surplus to be shared with those who do not labor. Similarly, nature unattended does not provide enough to sustain the lives of great numbers of people. Thus mystical religion's solution to the tension between economic activity and brotherly love presupposes an unbrotherly division of the world into those who can live in a state of spiritual bliss and those who must attend to the worldly economic activity on which the former depends. Both Puritanism and mysticism end up being self-contradictory. Both the Puritan solution and the mystical solution end up dividing the world into two kinds of people, a spiritual elite and the remainder of humanity.

Thus Weber implies that it is impossible to overcome the tension between brotherly love and economic rationality. Either economic action will undermine brotherliness or else an ethic of brotherliness will repress economic rationality. He explains the latter point not just with respect to what happened with China but also when he considers the possibility of socialism.

Politics

The brotherly ethic of salvation religions has also come into tension with the political orders of the world. This problem did not exist for magical religions nor for the religions of functional deities which included gods of war. The gods of locality, tribe and polity were only concerned with the interest of their respective associations. The problem arose with universalistic religions with a unified God of the entire world. And "the problem arose in full strength only when this God was a God of 'love'" (Weber, 1946, p. 333). According to Weber, it is "absolutely essential for every political association to appeal to the naked violence of coercive means in the face of outsiders as well as in the face of internal enemies" (ibid., p. 334). Hence by definition, a political state cannot rest on a universalistic ethic of brotherly love.

Weber relates another source of tension between religion and politics. Politics and war in particular, he suggests, may serve the same needs and retain the same essential features as religion. War creates pathos and sentiment of community – an unconditionally devoted and sacrificial community among combatants – and releases an active mass compassion and love for those who are in need (ibid., p. 335). Here Weber provides the only indication of acknowledging that the desire for community, for the sentiment of community, may be an ultimate value in political life (and especially warfare). The sentiment of community – a "devoted and sacrificial community" – is precisely the sentiment of love. Weber does not perceive that a self-conscious acknowledgment of love or community as an ultimate value in politics could overcome the conflict between politics and an ethic of love.

Weber continues his analysis by focusing on the "consecrated meaning" that death has for the warrior, a feeling and belief that one is dying for something, that one's death has meaning, and in fact an exalted meaning. This is a feeling and belief that is unique only to war. "Only those who perish 'in their callings' are in the same situation as the soldier who faces death on the battlefield" (ibid.). Weber goes on to describe the possibility of such death ("its location within a series of meaningful and consecrated events") as providing the ultimate support for the "autonomous dignity of the polity resting on force" (ibid.). In other words the sense of devotion to the community that is expressed in the willingness to die for the group, a willingness that is made more real by the possibility of warfare that is implicit in any political community, provides the ultimate foundation for the dignity of a polity that rests on force.

Weber does not consider how a self-conscious awareness of love and community as the ultimate warrant of political activity would make for an internal tension within politics, between its ultimate grounds, its ultimate end, and its ultimate reliance on force, its means. Rather, Weber, like the political community generally, externalizes the tension by treating it as a tension between politics as one sphere of life and religion as another. He explains how religion which in principle denies violence must reject the political community that is involved in warfare, either actually or potentially, as a glorification of fratricide. He does not acknowledge the tension between love and violence as internal to the political community.

Weber makes the astute observation that the "extraordinary quality of brotherliness of war, and of death in war, is shared with sacred charisma and the experience of the communion with God" (ibid., p. 336). Nevertheless, because the religious community must deny the possibility of any internal violence (because it must orient only to brotherly love) and because the

171

warrior political community must in principle deny love and community as its *telos* (because it must orient exclusively to conflict and struggles for power), each must reject and exclude the other as its opposite, its opposing other. The internal tension becomes externalized. As with the tension between ethical salvation religions and economic activity, the only two consistent solutions to the tension are those of Puritanism and mysticism.

Puritanism interprets God's will to mean that the "fixed and revealed . . . commandments should be imposed upon the creatural world by the means of this world, namely, violence." In this way, the religion "resist[s] the obligation of brotherliness in the interest of God's 'cause'" (ibid.). Puritanism can externalize violence because it rejects the creatural aspects of life including the violence and "ethical barbarism" of the "creatural world." On the other hand, mysticism which also aspires to the spiritual life and a spiritual world adopts the maxim, "turn the other cheek." Adherence to this maxim means that mysticism cannot even protect itself against threat to its very existence from the external violence of others. Thus, Puritanism accepts the use of violence and ends up eschewing brotherliness, while mysticism which espouses only brotherliness ends up succumbing to external violence.

Weber, too, sees the conflict as an external one between religion and politics. He does not acknowledge that politics, with its glorification of power, is based on love which is inherent in the very notion of a political community willing to risk death on behalf of the community. Although politics, as described by Weber, presupposes love, it denies or represses this presupposition in its conscious practices.

Weber recapitulates the self-understanding of both religion and politics – their understanding of themselves as precluding the values or "rationality" of the other. He does so in order to clarify the values of each so that the inevitable tension and conflict between them can be brought into relief (but not relieved). He does not provide a new self-conscious understanding of the internal relations between them. He does not show how each presupposes but denies the other. He does recognize how the two spheres of life both presuppose community. But in politics the orientation to love and community remains mute or negated, while in religion the orientation to love and community is central and explicit. Nevertheless, the situation of warfare – the ultimate warrant for the political sphere – reveals the ultimate grounds of politics in love and community. But because the orientation to love and community exists in two different forms – implicit but denied in politics, explicit and affirmed in religion, the two come into competition with each other instead of forming a unity. The brotherliness experienced among combatants then "raises the competition between [the two] to its extreme height" (ibid.).

If each recognized its internal relation to the other; if politics recognized community, compassion and love as internal to itself; and love recognized politics, power and the imposition of will as internal to itself; then each would be transformed. Instead of an external(ized) conflict between them, each would acknowledge and have to come to terms with both sides of itself. It could no longer be claimed that rational political action excluded relations of love, caring, compassion, nor could it be claimed that loving community excluded relations of coercion, power, domination.

If both were to consciously orient to the fact that each is internal to the other, that politics – power or the imposing of will – is internal to love, and that love – compassion and community – is internal to politics, then our conceptions of love and politics, the private sphere and the public sphere, would be changed. Instead of an external(ized) relationship between them, we would recognize an internal relationship between them. Such recognition would make for self-conscious actors and would obviate romanticized (one-sided) conceptions of community, personal relations and love as well as illusory (one-sided) conceptions of the state, politics and power.

By not acknowledging the other as internal to itself, by denying that which is essential to itself, each sphere of life ends up being self-contradictory. Puritanism, despite, and because of, its asceticism and devaluation of worldly values, ends up affirming and accumulating worldly value. Although it purports to be a salvation religion that is an answer to the ethical irrationality of the world, it ends up denying salvation to those who are most in need of it, and (re)producing ethical irrationality. Mysticism withdraws from the "pragma of violence which no political action can escape" (ibid.). It ends up withdrawing from social life and condemning any and all desire-driven, purposive-rational action. But condemnation contradicts acosmic love. Similarly, by reducing life to meditation or contemplation (renunciation of desire and purposive action), the body is denied even while it is presupposed (only a living body can meditate).

Because violence or the potential use of force underlies all political action and hence all political relations and because all social action may be understood as political action (affecting the power relations between people), denial or repression of this knowledge, this side of itself, of human life and human action, results in contradictions for mysticism. The mystic assumes that human action and human relationships may be voided of any and all violence. By rejecting and denying violence within itself, mysticism externalizes violence and then withdraws from that external world – the world of violence and politics. "Mysticism ultimately condemn[s] the social world to absolute meaninglessness." The mystical "acosmism" may increase to the point "where it rejects purposive-rational action *per se*." The actor's own conduct is therefore "condemned as irrational in its effects" (ibid., p. 339).

Weber recognizes that "all rational action somehow comes to stand in tension with the ethic of brotherliness, and carries within itself a profound tension" (ibid.). Conversely, one could say that the ethic of (brotherly) love carries within itself a tension with rational action. This tension between

173

(brotherly) love and rational action (human greatness) seems to underlie and animate much of Weber's sociology.

Weber, however, insists on externalizing this tension (projecting it?) and assuming that there is no possible resolution of the tension except to separate the two from each other or else for the two to cease treating themselves as absolute. Either those who adhere to an ethic of brotherly love should stay out of politics and business, or they must cease treating that ethic as absolute. If they insist on absolutizing the ethic, they must withdraw from political and economic action, from all purposive rational activity. The latter is by definition tied to desire for worldly things which interferes with brotherly love. Thus purposive rational action must be rejected as unspiritual, "estranged from God." Only if they are willing to suspend the ethic of brotherly love can they participate in politics or engage in rational, purposive action. But if they are willing to suspend the ethic, then the pragma of political action will effectively silence that ethic altogether.

Weber, as we have seen, is less willing to demand the same of those who are involved in political or economic activity. He does not suggest that they must be willing to relativize their "rational" action, to suspend their interest in power or profits out of a sense of love. However, he does say that political actors must supplement their ethic of responsibility (rational consideration of consequences) with some ultimate values. This solution may be adequate with regard to free self-determined individual action but not with regard to institutional activity. We have seen how formal rationality of rationalized institutions undermines human values (Chapter 6). Brotherly love as an ultimate value must be suppressed within the spheres of the economy and politics.

Although an individual, out of commitment to some ultimate value, may take a stand and refuse to conform to the demands of "rational" action, defined in terms of achieving economic or political success, a rationalized economy or nation state is one that institutionalizes means for achieving success. These cannot be suspended out of commitment to human values like love. The individual may save his own soul, but political or economic institutions have no soul, only political and economic success. No institution and no responsible leader of an institution is going to act in a way that is contrary to the interests of the institution, the institution's own reason for being, its own definition of success.

Despite Weber's valuing of the actor who can consider the realities of the situation in terms of a rational consideration of ends, means and secondary consequences, and who can consider also the dictates of conscience and weigh both kinds of considerations, Weber recognizes that the character of the individual is influenced by the kinds of qualities necessary for survival or success in the world in which s/he finds herself or himself. Therefore there is reason to believe that the modern world is not likely to create political or economic actors who distance themselves from and suspend the definitions of success that define political and economic action, actors who are able to consider suspending a commitment to individual and institutional success, out of a concern for human values.

Conclusions

On the individual level, Weber recognized the possibility and necessity of internalizing the tension between love and politics, love and economic activity, love and rational action, but with a stress on the second half of each pair. However, this solution does not address the problem of institutionalization. That is, "rational" action is institutionalized in the (rational-legal, bureaucratic) state and in the "rational" capitalist economy. Following from Weber's own analysis, we may conclude that *recognition* of the irrational foundations of such "rational" institutional forms must be explicitly acknowledged and institutionalized in the form of an institutionalized ethic of love along with an ethic of success. Or, rather, the ethic of success must be broadened to include the well-being of all those involved in or affected by the institution.

I take it that Schluchter (1981) is making a similar argument, and that Habermas (1981) is too. That is, the need to be able to suspend "rationality" in the name of love must be institutionalized as a possibility. However, neither Schluchter nor Habermas use the term love. They prefer to emphasize rationality, but a more encompassing notion of rationality than that used by Weber, an ethical rationality, a form of rationality that overcomes the irrationality that Weber attributes to modern institutionalized "rationality."

Weber describes the "rationalized" institutional, impersonal, public world as needing to be infused with human spirit, needing to be made more human, more like the manly man that Weber describes, able to weigh both the demands of conscience (human values like love) and the success of the institution (its survival, power, wealth and status). Weber's solution fails to address this need. Instead he advocates facing in a manly way the "fate of the times," the "rationalization and intellectualization", the "disenchantment" of the world. Although he recognizes the need to bring the two considerations – love and reason – together on the level of the individual, an ethic of responsibility (rationality) supplemented with an ethic of ultimate ends (brotherly love), he does not believe it possible to institutionalize the two together.

Politics ultimately precludes brotherly love. Either one value is institutionalized or the other is. There is politics with its institutional orientation to power and there is religion with its institutional orientation to brotherly love. Each precludes the other. Only the individual (a heroic individual, not the ordinary individual) can transcend the opposition between them by weighing and considering each and determining when to comply with which. For institutions

175

to be truly "rational" in the same way that the individual can be, institutional decisions and actions must be informed by considerations of both "rationality" (in the narrow sense) and love. By institutionalizing both dimensions of human life – rationality and love – we arrive at a transformed, more comprehensive rationality. In addition, the nature of public, institutional life changes. We may best characterize this change as one from "bureaucracy" to "community."

Institutionalization means that formal procedures are established that determine the mode of action to follow in any given case. If we are to avoid absolutization, the aim must be to transform impersonal institutions by infusing them with the rationality of love, compassion, and aesthetic pleasure; to counterbalance the one-sided concern with quantitative, measurable outcomes and "objective" impersonal considerations with a concern for qualitative, singular effects and "subjective" personalized considerations; to make institutional actors responsible for both kinds of considerations and accountable to their institutional "community" in terms of both.

For Weber, such a non-absolutist form of institution was inconceivable; the state and by implication all institutions have their own absolute end, their own absolute "reason" for being. "The state's absolute end is to safeguard (or to change) the external and internal distribution of power" (Weber, 1946, p. 334). This means that "In the final analysis, in spite of all 'social welfare policies,' the whole course of the state's inner political functions, of justice and administration, is. . .regulated by the objective pragmatism of 'reasons of state'" (ibid.). Furthermore, Weber insists that we acknowledge that "the state asserts: 'You *shall* help right to triumph by the use of *force*, otherwise you too may be responsible for injustice." However, "according to the inescapable pragmatism of all action . . . force and the threat of force unavoidably breed more force." This means that "reasons of state" "follow their own external and internal laws. The very success of force, or of the threat of force, depends ultimately upon power relations and not on ethical 'right'" (ibid.). Weber saw the pragmatism of force generally precluding a non-absolutist form of society and form of life in which love and "rationality" may both be reasons for actions and both be weighed and considered.

Because of the pragmatism of force, rationality requires that "reasons of state" orient absolutely to power relations and the possibility of force. Here we see the masculine nature and appeal of Weber's "realism" and cynicism regarding the infusion of love or ethics into politics. One must always orient to the possibility of violence. For the same reason, all other political actors must do the same. If all actors do the same, it is foolhardy to take a chance and orient to the appeal of community and allow one's vulnerable state to be taken advantage of.

Nevertheless, revolutionary changes may sometimes occur if "the pragmatism of force, calling forth more force and leading merely to changes in personnel, or at best to changes in methods of ruling by force, is not recognized as a

176

permanent quality of the creaturely" (ibid., p. 340). Implicit in this statement is the view that ultimately the pragmatism of force, because it *is* a permanent quality of the creaturely, reasserts itself and "rational" institutional action will take its characteristic, unbrotherly form. Only when people (under the sway of some illusion) fail to recognize the pragmatism of force as a permanent quality of human life can a revolutionary change in institutions occur. Only during a revolutionary period, which is by definition temporary and anti-institutional in character, is it possible to transform radically a political, social or economic order. However, once transformed the newly institutionalized forms will be subject to the same pragmatism. To prove his point, Weber offers the example of divine "natural law" which was to serve as foundation for the new revolutionary society. Presumably, what happened in the case of natural law would happen in the case of brotherly love. The introduction of natural law constituted revolutionary change. Nevertheless, the old pragmatism ultimately reasserted itself in the new form of positivist law. The pragmatism of power (defined as the ability to realize one's will despite the resistance of an opposing will) undermined natural law. Unlike Marx, Weber does not believe that the interest and power of capital undermined the possibility of a revolutionary form of life, that the elimination of capital would make possible a revolutionary form of life. In Weber's cynical or "realistic" view, even under socialism the pragmatism of power will undermine any ethic of brotherly love.

If love cannot be institutionalized together with rationality, then love cannot really co-exist along with rational action on the level of individual political action either, despite Weber's homage to the "mature man." An individual must be realistic and recognize force as a resource in social action and human relations. Recognizing this "reality" means that one must always act out of concern for power and force rather than love. Love must be banished from the political sphere and relegated exclusively to the private sphere. Nevertheless, Weber's *General Economic History* reveals that brotherly love has been the basis of successful revolutionary political communities; in fact it was the basis of the revolutionary city state.

Notes

1 Edward Bryan Portis (1986) sees the conflict between scholarship and politics as central to Weber's emotional disturbance. Portis sees the conflict as irreconcilable.
2 Virginia Held (1987) explores an image of society founded on principles of mothering rather than on contractual relations.
3 Weber's use of this term has always struck me as peculiar. It is interesting that we have no positive construction to refer to people who may be at an unfair advantage not just in the competitive struggle in the economy but in life. What would a positive construction be: the oppressed? the exploited? And why does Weber prefer the term "dispriviledged"?

11

Brotherly love and revolution

Despite Weber's ruling assumption that social life must be understood in terms of conflict and struggles for power, Weber's own research presents sufficient evidence for the claim that social life can also be understood in terms of community and struggles for liberation.

Weber does go to great pains to show how an orientation toward brotherly love is unrealistic for the public, political world. Yet we find in Weber's historical writings that a sense of community among men who share an oath of brotherhood is crucial to the history of the West and the development of the city. For Weber, of course, a brotherhood of warriors was central to the political community. Here, I trace the significance of brotherhood committed not to war but to peaceable community, albeit a community that is exclusive and repressive of women.

Along with and related to this commitment to communal brotherliness, Weber's research reveals another motive force in history, the struggle for liberation from arbitrary control and the attempt to replace the latter with relations of equality. I consider this important because Weber's description of power as the ability to realize one's will over the will of others implicitly suggests that the struggle for power derives from a desire to dominate, to impose one's will over the resistance of others, not just a desire for liberation from domination or a desire to live in equality with one's "fellows." In other words, desire for the power to influence and control seems central to Weber's understanding of social and political history.

I document below with reference to his *General Economic History* my counter-claim to Weber that commitment to communal brotherliness and struggles for liberation and relations of equality are just as central to an understanding of social life and political history. In other words I use Weber's own historical account to refute his theory of history. Social and political life, I contend, is a continual movement back and forth between struggles for power, status and self-interest *and* struggles for liberation, equality and community. Furthermore, the latter struggles do make a difference in history; they are not merely ineffectual struggles that are doomed to repeat the past and be replaced by the same old forces of domination. Rather, successful struggles can and do create new social orders that eliminate old sources of domination and oppression even though new forces of inequality and unbrotherliness may emerge.

This movement for liberation and community on the political level parallels the one on the individual level. The latter may be understood as a struggle for independence, autonomy and mastery *and* a struggle for relationships, attachment and surrender.

Brotherhood and community as a revolutionary force

Weber reveals the importance of brotherhood as a political force in his analysis of the Western city. "The earliest references to cities as political units designate rather their revolutionary character. The occidental city arose through the establishment of a fraternity." The key feature seems to be a brotherhood in arms for mutual aid and protection, not domination and exploitation. The brotherhood usurps political power from those who held it and were external to the brotherhood (Weber, [1923] 1981, p. 319). We must assume, he claims, the same background for the origin of every ancient city. "The *polis* is always the product of. . .a confraternity or synoecism, not always an actual settlement in proximity but a definite oath of brotherhood which signified that a common ritualistic meal is established and a ritualistic union formed" (ibid., p. 320).

There are two elements that made possible the origin and existence of the city, and both are lacking in the East. One is self-equipment for war and the other is religious brotherhood. Religious brotherhood, although a necessary condition and one that Weber stressed heavily, was not a sufficient one. The religious brotherhood had to have enough military strength to establish and defend itself as an independent political body.

> Whether the military organization is based on the principle of self-equipment or on that of equipment by a military overlord who furnishes horses, arms and provisions, is a distinction quite as fundamental for social history as is the question whether the means of economic production are the property of the worker or of a capitalistic entrepreneur (ibid.).

Control over the means of independence, economic and political, are crucial to social history. However, the economic and the political overlap. In the East the economic conditions that led to irrigation and the great empires that arose on the basis of water regulation meant that the development of the city was prevented by the fact that the army of the prince is older than the city. "That the king . . . expressed his power in the form of a military monopoly is the basis of the distinction between the military organization of Asia and that of the west" (ibid., p. 321).

In the West it was only in the modern era that the military organization involved the separation of the soldier from the paraphernalia of war. Earlier, the fighting men were those who were economically able to equip themselves for war. The city of antiquity, like the medieval city, is composed of families leading an aristocratic existence, those of knightly birth; the remaining population is bound to obedience. The possibility for political independence was precluded in the East due to the nature of military organization.

Grounds of community and community as grounds

The possibility of political independence requires another condition before it can be realized: the possibility of community. The second obstacle which prevented the development of the city in the Orient was the restricted notion of community and brotherhood that existed there. In India, no sense of sacred brotherhood or community could be formed across caste lines. The caste taboos prevented it. In the West, however, two factors – economic and religious – conditioned the breakdown of clan taboos. In the East, crafts and manufacture were monopolized by various castes and contained within the village. Production was for the consumption needs of the village, and the social, political and religious organization of the village shaped the social, political and religious organization of craft and manufacture.

In the West, crafts and manufacture took up an independent existence in the town without the restriction of clan and caste taboos. For this to happen certain economic preconditions were necessary. The development of towns in the West viewed from an economic viewpoint was attributable, according to Weber, to speculative ventures of the princes. The latter wished to acquire taxable dependents and therefore founded towns and markets, as settlements of people who bought and sold. The emperors especially granted privileges to the towns, giving rise to the principle "town air makes free" (ibid., p. 132). The residents of these towns became independent of any village and of the blood and clan groupings of the village.

That the princes could set up towns as settlements for trade required a transition from manorial, household or village craft production to production for a clientele and a market. The latter required that a circle of consumers with purchasing power to absorb the output be available. This was made possible by the consumptive requirements of the Occident, which Weber attributes to differences of climate, and a change in the economic and political status of the peasants whose increased productivity due to intensive tilling was not appropriated by the lord who was tied to his military duties. "This fact made possible the first great development of the handicrafts" (ibid., p. 132).

The occidental city with its concentration of crafts and trade, composed of runaway serfs and slaves as well as nobles and merchants, saw a relative recession in the importance of blood groupings, particularly of the clan. "The urban dweller finds a substitute for blood groupings in both occupational organizations, which in the Occident as everywhere had a cultic significance, although no longer associated with taboos, and in freely created religious associations" (Weber, [1922] 1964, pp. 96–7).

The obstacles in the Orient to the development of the city as political community included the absence of a self-equipped military, the absence of a market economy and the absence of a ritually guaranteed and sanctified community that cuts across clan lines and breaks down caste taboos.

"In India the castes were not in a position to form ritualistic communities and hence a city" (Weber, [1923] 1981, p. 322). This is because the castes were ceremonially alien to one another. The Western city of both antiquity and the Middle Ages offers a contrast with the situation of the East. Weber attributes the development of cities to religious developments in the West; on the other side, he attributes religious developments in the West to the existence of cities. He claims that the congregational type of religion was a consequence of the relative recession in the importance of blood groupings, particularly of the clan, within the occidental city. He writes:

> early Christianity was an urban religion. It is highly unlikely that an organized congregational religion, such as early Christianity became, could have developed as it did apart from the community life of a city (notably in the sense found in the Occident). For early Christianity presupposed as already extant certain conceptions, viz., the transcendence of taboo barriers between clans, the concept of office, and the concept of the community as an institution. . .an organized corporate entity serving specific realistic functions. To be sure, Christianity, on its part, strengthened these conceptions, and greatly facilitated the renewed reception of them by the growing European cities during the Middle Ages (Weber, [1922] 1964, pp. 84–5).

In the *General Economic History*, Weber attributes the breakdown in clan ties to Western religion (Judaism, Christianity) and the cities; in his *Sociology of Religion*, he attributes Western religion to the existence of cities and the breakdown in clan ties. The relationship between religion and urban life is not one of simple causality, the causality runs both ways; the relationship is one of mutual interaction.

Nevertheless, according to Weber's own account, cities were the result of a revolutionary movement to secure political independence by a community of men who were militarily capable and who took an oath of brotherhood or formed a spiritual community. The East and the West differed in terms of the possibility for creating an independent political community. This possibility depended on material factors of military, political and economic developments and non-material factors of religious and communal life.

The East was hampered by the military and political organization of the king which was related to an irrigation economy. The West developed from a forestry economy based on the principle that he who clears the land and works it gets to own it with the consequences that those individuals who had enough men (slaves) and implements to clear the land could then lease the land and live off the payments. The political economy of the East perpetuated clan ties and caste taboos while that of the West broke them down. But both East and West were based on religious or magical, spiritual communities or brotherhoods. In the East the exclusive nature of these clan communities and caste taboos prevented the emergence of an independent political community. In the West, the inclusive nature of a universalistic religious community facilitated the breakdown of clan ties and the emergence of a political community.

Weber held that in modern times a universalistic religious community based on an ethic of brotherly love prevents economic, political, and cultural development. But here we see that at an earlier period in history, it was precisely such a community that made possible the economic and political development of the Western city according to Weber's own account.

Furthermore, only in antiquity did the city rest on a militarily offensive orientation; in the Middle Ages, due to both military limitations and economic developments, it rested on a defensive orientation. It is not true that political history is the struggle for power or control over others; it is also the struggle for liberation from the power and control of others, a struggle for political independence. The two are not always identical. It is also not true that history is a struggle for political, economic and social dominance; it is also, as I show next, a struggle for social, political and economic equality within community.

We find repeated time and again in Weber's *General Economic History* a movement on the part of subordinate groups to reduce or eliminate external control. Weber documents such movements occurring when economic, political or military power or indispensability make success possible.

Economic equality

In addition to reducing or eliminating political domination, history is rife with movements for economic equality. The medieval guild, for example, is a free association that as a group bought and distributed certain raw materials, such as iron and wool, "to safeguard the equality of the members" (Weber, [1923] 1981, p. 118). Guild policy is livelihood policy. This means that the individual guild members were to obtain the traditional standard of living and be made secure in it – an analogue of the "living wage." The guild endeavored by every conceivable means to provide equality of opportunity for all the "brothers" of the guild (ibid., p. 138).

One method employed by the guilds was to limit free competition by fixing the number of workers, especially apprentices, a member might employ. Also, if a shortage arose any guild member might demand that his "brothers" in the guild provide him with raw material at its cost to them. Price cutting was also forbidden.

Weber similarly describes the struggles of miners for political and economic equality. Through struggles, the mine workers succeed in becoming the mine owner – a co-operative association of the workers that divided the income in the same way in which peasants divided their holdings, that is, with the strictest maintenance of equality. Over time, due to external pressures, the need to hire additional workers who are not accorded membership in the co-operative, and the selling of shares to non-workers on retirement, this equality again breaks down (ibid., pp. 187–9).

Weber describes the successful struggles of various economic groups – guilds, mines, traders and so forth – to attain, sustain and maintain relations of economic equality and liberation from external control. He also describes the dissolution of such attempts as internal differentiation emerges, conditioned by new unanticipated developments.

The power and independence of the cities were eventually swept away by larger, more inclusive political units. In antiquity the freedom of the cities was swept away by a bureaucratically organized world empire. The fate of the city in the modern era was different. Here again its autonomy was progressively taken away. The cities came under the power of competing national states in a condition of perpetual struggle for power in peace or war. The separate states had to compete for mobile capital. The latter dictated to them the conditions under which it would assist them to power. Out of this alliance of the state with capital, dictated by necessity, arose the national citizen class, the bourgeoisie in the modern sense of the world.

A movement to establish a political community on the basis of mutual commitment, a sacred bond of reciprocity and mutual protection among individuals (men) regardless of any actual ties of blood, kinship or contiguity as the basis for regulating relations – a religious brotherhood – represents a revolutionary political movement. This revolutionary form of political life contrasts with political life in which external authority formulates the regulations or dominates individuals (men) on the basis of its own interests; it differs also from a form of life in which some individuals compete and contend with each other for the power to rule over other individuals. Hence, by this revolutionary form of life Weber himself presents a model for a larger, more inclusive notion of community as a basis of political life.

However, Weber's history reveals that as changes occur over time, the same institutions that were established to ensure equality may serve to perpetuate the new inequalities that are bound to arise. Furthermore institutions that emerge as ways to ensure equality and protect livelihood and welfare may stifle the kind of development that could occur if people had an incentive for competing with each other. Therefore a community that is self-consciously committed to communal development with relations of mutual protection and reciprocity must make provisions for limited competition and for continual re-evaluation of its institutions based on commitment to the spirit and principle of community.

In other words, the formal letter of the law, the formal institutions that are established according to procedures intended to ensure equality or limit inequality, must be open to change or modification based on the spirit of the law and responsiveness to diversity, to new movements for development, for equality or equity. Concerns for development, for reciprocity, equity and respect for diversity must be made explicit and on-going concerns of a political community committed to revolutionary principles.

A free and independent individual or community that must determine its own (re)production and carry out (re)productive labor itself, including human nurturance, comes to recognize its own diverse and often conflicting needs, interests, desires, impulses and so on and must confront and deal with them. A free, self-determining actor (community or individual) that must itself carry out the actions it decides on, an actor that neither represses others nor is repressed by others, cannot conceive of itself as a unitary being. It must recognize its own internal divisions; it must be responsive to its many competing interests and impulses and must strive self-consciously to realize them, to prioritize them, to reconcile them, or maybe to sacrifice some of them. Such recognition, responsiveness, reconciliation and self-consciousness is what we mean when we speak of a liberated and liberating full community or human being as opposed to a repressed or repressive community or human being.

However, when we think of community as a band of brothers, we exclude women from that community. Like the model of the individual who devotes himself to a single, unitary cause, the model of a unitary community or brotherhood as opposed to an inclusive and pluralistic community of men, women and children requires continuous control, discipline and repression. Only a community or individual that controls others, one that produces and reproduces by controlling or living off the labor of others (like women, slaves, "wage-slaves," foreigners) without engaging in that labor itself, that is, only a repressive community or individual that presupposes coercion and reliance on force or violence can conceive of itself as a unitary community (a band of brothers) or a unitary being (a master).

To envision community as a brotherhood of men makes sexual reproduction, heterosexual relations and childraising seem unimportant and unproblematic; women and children are simply assumed to be there, passively, outside the community of brothers. The relations with women and children may be a matter for the community of men to determine, or it may be a matter for the brothers to determine individually, but women and children as active subjects or speakers for themselves with opinions, needs, feelings and interests that might make a difference have no place in a community of brothers.

Although committed to freeing itself and defending itself from relations of domination and inequality, a brotherhood of men actually perpetuates relations of domination and exploitation with women and all those who do not qualify for membership in the community. What happens when a community defines itself not as a brotherhood of men but as a community of men and women? Immediately, heterosexual relations and reproduction of the human community (including human nurturance) come to the fore as issues to be considered, not taken for granted. The issue of difference and cultural diversity emerges, challenging the idea(l) of a unitary community. Is it possible for an ethic of brotherly love to produce a community committed to overcoming domination and inequality with women and "others," a community committed not to instrumental values of wealth and power but to cultural values of art, intellect, science and culture in general?

12

Brotherly love and culture

As we have seen, Weber considered the possibility of revolutionizing society in accordance with an ethic of brotherly love. Not only would such an ethic undermine practical activity in the economic and political spheres, he contended, but the ethic would also obstruct the development of art, intellect, science and all cultural values. Unlike the spheres of political and economic activity, these other spheres represent intrinsic values that are meaningful ends in themselves. Therefore, we might expect them to conform to an ethic of brotherly love which stresses intrinsic rather than extrinsic value in human relations.

Art and ethics

Weber relates that only ethical salvation religions of brotherly love conflict with these "non-rational" spheres of life: magical religions do not. In fact, magical religions are intimately related to the aesthetic sphere. They offer opportunities for artistic creation and for stylizing through traditionalism, in idols and icons, for instance. Stereotyping of forms which have proved successful in influencing spirits and bring about the desired effects creates stylization as opposed to naturalism. Music, too, is formalized with stereotyped tone relations that were developed as a means of ecstasy. The magically proved dance step was also developed as a source of rhythm and as an ecstasy technique.

Weber suggests that art, as a carrier of magical effects, functions as a this–worldly salvation from the routines of everyday life, especially from the increasing pressures of rationalism. As such, the religious ethic of brotherliness devalues art and treats it with suspicion. All sublimated religions of salvation (sublimated into a spiritual love relation with God) have focused upon the meaning alone, not upon the form, of the things and actions relevant for salvation. Salvation religions have devalued form as contingent, as something creaturely and distracting from meaning. This causes conflict with art only if art becomes a cosmos of independent values or magical effects which exist in their own right.

Art must have meaning only in terms of religion, not as a value in itself. Otherwise, it becomes an irresponsible indulgence, a secret lovelessness

(Weber, 1946, p. 342) because it draws attention away from the relationship with God or with acosmic brotherly love as the only absolute value. By setting itself up as something valuable or meaningful in itself, art and the ecstatic experience of art competes with and devalues the religious ethic. Thus, Weber claims that aesthetic activity stands in a dynamic tension with the religious ethic of brotherliness. The latter, if it can, must repress art as an autonomous domain of value and subordinate it to serving the ends of the religious ethic.

Weber draws out the conflict between mystical salvation religions with their acosmic brotherliness and art.

> The mystic believes. . . .in the experience of exploding all forms, and hopes by this to be absorbed into the "All-oneness" which lies beyond any kind of determination and form. For him the psychological affinity of profoundly shaking experiences in art and religion can only be a symptom of the diabolical nature of art. (ibid.)

If the religious experience is the only authentic absolute value, and if the profoundly shaking experience that characterizes it provides the evidence or criterion for such a claim, then the similar experience provided by art appears as a deception, as something that claims to be as meaningful as religion. From the perspective of religion that sets up the spiritual experience of oneness with the divine and the acosmic brotherliness that accompanies such an experience as the ultimate and only absolute value, the competing experiences provided by art must seem diabolical. "Especially music, can appear. . .as an irresponsible *Ersatz* for primary religious experience. . .Art becomes an 'idolatry,' a competing power, and a deceptive bedazzlement" (ibid., pp. 342–3).

Sublimated religious ecstasy produces a feeling of love. "From being 'moved' and edified to feeling direct communion with God, ecstasies have always inclined men towards the flowing out into an objectless acosmism of love" (ibid., p. 330). Thus spiritual ecstasy inclines one to an ethic of brotherly love, but as we shall see the ecstasy of erotic love does the same. So for that matter does the experience of ecstasy from any source. From ecstasy radiates goodwill and love. Religion rejects sources of ecstasy other than itself as false and transient because they derive from worldly activities or relationships.

Worldly activities and relationships are inherently unstable and unreliable; they cannot provide a permanent state of ecstasy. However, a spiritual relationship, because there is no material and hence changeable object involved, can offer a permanent sense of ecstasy and salvation. Salvation is the transcendence of a suffering that is due precisely to the instability and unreliability of the material world. Therefore, the only true and lasting form of ecstasy and salvation is spiritual unity with the divine or the cosmos, a subjective

187

experience. Spiritual ecstasy does not depend on any concrete object or other but is an entirely subjective state.

Because all other sources of ecstasy succumb to the transience of material things, ultimately no other sources of ecstasy can provide true salvation. Material things and relationships and their transient nature produce the pain and suffering that was the reason salvation was desired in the first place. Purely spiritual ecstasy can provide enduring salvation, but at the cost of subordinating to itself all worldly interests and attachments. The absence of worldly interests is integral to the experience of ecstasy. Spiritual salvation can give rise to the ethic of brotherly love by making the latter into a condition of salvation. Religion must reject or repress all other forms of ecstasy as false and deceptive temptations that lead away from the only true, enduring salvation.

Ethical religion rejects all naive surrender to the most intensive ways of experiencing existence, artistic and, as we shall see, erotic. All experience must be mediated by religious ethics: all activity or inactivity must serve ethical ends. No activity can be an end in itself. This renunciation of intense experience might then free energies for rational achievement, ethical as well as purely intellectual. However, the "self-conscious tension of religion is greatest and most principled where religion faces the sphere of intellectual knowledge" (ibid., p. 350).

Intellectualism

As with art, there was originally an intimate relationship between religion and rational intellectualism. This relationship was particularly true of religion that relies less on magic or contemplative mysticism and more on doctrine. For then it needs rational apologetics. Religion becomes closely tied to, in fact a source of, intellectual development, just as it was originally a source of artistic development. From the development of scriptural religion and doctrine emerged lay thinkers, and from lay thinkers emerged prophets, mystics, skeptics and philosophers all of whom were hostile to or independent of priests and priestly religion.

Religion rejects any *intellectual* search for knowledge about the meaning of the world. Religion claims that religious knowledge is entirely different and separate from intellectual knowledge. Religion claims to unlock the meaning of the world not by means of the intellect but by virtue of a charisma of illumination. Such charisma is imparted only to those who free themselves from the empty abstractions of the intellect which are irrelevant for salvation. "Religion, therefore, frequently considers purely empirical research, including that of natural science, as more reconcilable to religious interests than it does philosophy. This is the case above all in ascetic Protestantism"

188

(ibid.). Intellectual or philosophical attempts to grasp the meaning of the world or to gain intuitive knowledge are a product of the very rationalism that intellectualism creates. In other words intellectualism creates the very problem – rationalism of the world and the loss of meaning – that it then attempts to resolve. Just as religion creates intellectualism as its own nemesis, which it then tries to repudiate, so intellectualism creates rationalism as its own nemesis, which it then tries to repudiate.

Intellectual rationalism ends up with an intellectual quest for escape from rationalism, a quest for meaning or salvation from an unmeaningful, causal, empirical, scientific universe. The tension between religion and intellectual knowledge comes to the fore wherever rational, empirical knowledge has transformed the world into a causal mechanism. The rationalism of empirical science reveals a world in which conditions of life are the result of empirical factors and not the manifestation of some metaphysical meaning. Any attempt to provide such meaning must be relegated to the irrational realm as science more and more reveals the interplay of causal factors devoid of metaphysical meaning.

All religions have demanded that "the course of the world be somehow *meaningful*, at least in so far as it touches upon [human] interests" (ibid., p. 353). This demand has taken the form of a postulate of just compensation for the unequal distribution of individual happiness in the world (ibid., p. 353). However, "rational thought" that addresses this problem shows the course of the world to be little concerned with the postulate of compensation. "The ethically unmotivated inequality in the distribution of happiness and misery. . .has remained irrational; and so has the brute fact that suffering exists" (ibid., p. 354). Religion turns to the idea of sin to explain suffering as punishment or discipline. But that raises the question of the origin of sin. "A world created for the committing of sin must appear still less ethically perfect than a world condemned to suffering" (ibid.).

Therefore, the need for meaning, to which religion responds, conflicts with "rational thought," with science and with the intellect. "There is absolutely no 'unbroken' religion," Weber asserts, "working as a vital force which is not compelled at some point to demand. . .the 'sacrifice of the intellect'" (ibid., p. 352).

Science creates a cosmos of natural causality which is unable to answer with certainty the question of its own ultimate presuppositions, the ultimate meaning of science as of all of life. Nevertheless, in the name of intellectual integrity, science claims to represent the only possible form of a reasoned view of the world. Hence intellectualism produces a dilemma: it disenchants the world which results in a need for meaning; it cannot provide such meaning; but it must reject any other source of meaning. The kind of meaning which rationalism rejects provides the justification for brotherly love. Intellectual life conflicts with the ethic of brotherly love, also, because the former creates an

189

aristocracy based on the possession of rational culture independent of the personal ethical qualities of the individual. "The aristocracy of intellect is hence an unbrotherly aristocracy. Worldly man has regarded this possession of culture as the highest good" (ibid., p. 355).

Given the absolute imperfection of the world, that is, the ineradicable nature of suffering and sin as part of the world, which "rational thought" reveals, the intellect must face the meaning or meaninglessness of life and the world, the futility of worldly things. Furthermore, "the fact that death and ruin. . .overtake good people and good works, as well as evil ones, could appear to be a depreciation of precisely the supreme values of this world" (ibid., p. 354). This is so especially once the idea is conceived of a perpetual duration of time. This idea arises with the idea of an eternal God and an eternal order. The intellect responds by hallowing values, particularly the most highly cherished ones, as timelessly valid and by orienting to the realization of these timeless values in culture. Because they are considered timelessly valid, the realization of these values becomes meaningful and significant. That is, although worldly things including good people and good works are overtaken by death and ruin, values and their embodiment in culture can endure indefinitely. This emphasis on the significance of cultural values, however, turns out to conflict with the ethic of brotherly love.

Cultural values

Weber seems to develop his analysis to prove that if one wants to be an ethical absolutist, one would have to concede that ethical guilt adheres to all worldly activity. Cultural activity is no different from political and economic activity in this regard. Ethical guilt is integral to them all. He goes on to build the case by showing how cultural values, as ends in themselves, are burdened by the ethical guilt that adheres to politics and economic activity as well. In other words, culture is not some pure realm unlike the corrupt political and economic spheres of life.

Intellectual rationalism in its search for meaning turns to the realization of values in the form of "culture." However, ethical religion indicts precisely the cultural values which usually rank highest. The cultivation of these values requires modes of existence, education and aesthetic development which make for insuperable status differences that interfere with brotherly love. Thus "these values have borne the stigma of a deadly sin, of an unavoidable and specific burden of guilt." This means that "the ultimate values which this world offered have seemed burdened with the greatest guilt" (ibid.).

Weber explains that education and aesthetic cultivation are the most intimate and the most insuperable of all status differences. They create the deepest divisions among people and peoples. These differences produce feelings of pride and shame, attraction and repulsion, esteem and contempt. Thus all culture, all conduct in a civilized world, all of structured life, bears some ethical guilt. "Religious guilt could now appear. . .as an integral part of all culture" (ibid.).

Weber takes the analysis further: "Wherever the external order of the social community has turned into the culture community of the state it *obviously could be maintained only by brutal force*, which was concerned with justice only nominally and occasionally and in any case only so far as reasons of state have permitted. Furthermore, "This force has inevitably bred new deeds of violence against external and internal enemies; in addition it has bred dishonest pretexts for such deeds" (ibid., p. 355), italics added).

Just as cultural values are burdened by ethical guilt, the state, too, is burdened by ethical guilt. For Weber, the state can maintain itself only by brutal force. Weber is a "realist;" he does not romanticize the state as something that exists for the promotion of justice. At best, the state exists to maintain and protect itself as a cultural community although, as Weber admits, cultural communities and cultural values do not seem to flourish in military states. Nevertheless, in the modern world social communities have become the cultural communities of the state. In other words "culture" in today's world exists as part of nation states.

All worldly culture bears a guilty relationship not only to the state, but to economic activity. "Culture" requires material support which is best provided in the context of a rationalized economy. However, the absence of love is attached to such an economy at its root (ibid.). Weber seems to be saying that it is a delusion to believe that one can escape from the ethical guilt of political and economic life by devoting oneself to "culture."

In addition to the burden of ethical guilt, the valuing of culture involves an internal inconsistency. On the one hand culture is presumed to be the one value that gives meaning to life, the one value that is enduring. However, the cultivation of culture lends itself to a belief in the senselessness of death and hence the senselessness of life (ibid., p. 356). In contrast, the peasant, the feudal landlord and the warrior hero could die "satiated with life" having experienced the fulfillment of a life cycle, the substance of which appeared unambiguous. Death, then, would make some sense as the completion of a life.

But those who devote themselves to culture rather than just living out the natural cycle of life, to acquiring or creating cultural values, cannot do this. They can become "weary of life" but not "satiated with life" in the sense indicated. This is because there is little likelihood that an individual could absorb either culture as a whole or the essential in culture. Moreover there exists no definitive criterion for judging the latter. There is no guarantee that the individual will feel that his or her selection of cultural values will have reached a meaningful end at the time of death. This attitude differs from that of ethical religion for which life has a God-ordained ethical meaning to which individuals must give themselves. Devoting one's life to "culture" does not

191

avoid the problem of ethical guilt nor does it overcome the problem of the senselessness of death, the inability to feel fulfilled or satiated with life in the modern world.

Weber makes the case that it is impossible to live a life of brotherly love and still live in this world. One would have to withdraw from this world as much as possible, and certainly renounce all worldly activity, if one wants to adhere to the ethic. Weber wants to burst the bubble of ethical self-righteousness through which the moral critics of political and economic activity see the world.

His implicit defense of "rational" political and economic activity is not that the critics are wrong; nor that they are right and politics and economics need to be transformed; nor that they are right and no ethical actor ought to participate in such activity. He defends "rational" politics and economics by arguing that all worldly activity, all cultural values, share the same ethical guilt if they are to be measured by the same religious ethic of brotherly love. In this way, he forces the critic to face up to the essential and unavoidable absence of love that inheres in all worldly activity. His reasoning forces the reader to conclude that if one adheres to an ethic of brotherly love one must, if one is going to live in the world at all, live with the burden of ethical guilt and not deceive oneself that it is possible to do otherwise. Politics and economics are no different in this regard than any other worldly activity.

Not only does a religious ethic of brotherly love conflict with the worldly spheres of culture, intellectualism, science, art, politics and economics, according to Weber's analysis, but the ethic itself ends up conflicting with itself. That is, the attempts to live a life of brotherly love must entail some lovelessness. The charisma of mystical religion, for example, is not accessible to everybody; hence mystical salvation means aristocracy. For those who must live a workaday life, there is little room for the cultivation of brotherliness, unless it is among the strata who are economically carefree.

Religions attempt to reconcile an unloving world with an all-loving God. The existence of radical evil in a created world and the admission of sin, together with the eternity of hell's punishments for "one of God's own and finite creatures," simply does not correspond to divine love. For this kind of religion, "only a renunciation of benevolence is consistent" (ibid., p. 359) as we saw was the case with the Protestant ethic, or a renunciation of omniscience as was the case with Zoroastrian dualism. With Protestantism, the answer to undeserved suffering, the belief in an ethical god who requires of people an ethic of brotherly love as a condition of salvation, ends up in a renunciation of brotherly love.

Weber's analysis shows the untenability of a religious ethic of brotherly love as a principle for organizing the world. It simply cannot be maintained. The attempt to impose it would mean stifling and repressing human development, not only economic and political development, but aesthetic, intellectual, cultural and scientific development as well. Such repression, itself, conflicts with brotherly love. Weber's rigorous and extensive analysis of the theoretical and practical impossibility of an ethic of brotherly love constitutes a thorough-going critique of all this-worldly as well as inner-worldly and other-worldly beliefs in salvation. Weber's analysis results in cynicism. His analysis here parallels his analysis of the inherently irrational nature of modern rational society. In both cases we are left with cynicism: a rationalized world must be substantively irrational (meaningless); a world of brotherly love must be repressive and hence unbrotherly or loveless.

This cynicism translates into inner strength; one cannot be seduced by false promises or visions. One learns not to look outside oneself for salvation. One learns to give up illusions and become realistic, to develop the inner strength and resolve with which to face an essentially meaningless, ethically irrational, loveless world and life. Only in personal life and personal relations can brotherly love survive. However, the personal relationship of erotic love, Weber will argue, is ethically compromised.

Max Weber is not alone in these views. As we know, Sigmund Freud held similar ones (Chapter 1). For Weber as for Freud, facing up to reality means facing up to a loveless world, a world in which there is no maternal father, protection, security, love. The world of men is and must be a world without love.

By rejecting the illusion of any kind of salvation, cultural as well as religious, social as well as personal, Weber's analysis represents a reasoned justification for rejecting any and all movements that are grounded in the "illusion" that an essentially different kind of world is possible. Weber talks about the need for measuring up to the demands of the day, facing the lovelessness and disenchantment of the world, doing one's self-defined duty, following the daemons of one's own soul.

"To the person who cannot bear the fate of the times like a man" (*Wer dies Schicksal der Zeit nicht männlich ertragen kann*),[1] Weber counsels, "return [to] the arms of the old churches [which] are opened widely and compassionately." The fate of the times, Weber states, is characterized by the "disenchantment of the world." "Precisely the ultimate and most sublime values have retreated from public life either into the . . . realm of mystic life or into the brotherliness of direct and personal relations" (ibid., p. 155).

With the German defeat in the war and with it the retreat of sublime values from public life, Weber, himself, confronted a loss of meaning. He was able to bear up under this loss by devoting himself to his work and his personal relations. Weber's usage, retreat of sublime values from public life, gives one pause. The sublime values that had given meaning to Weber's life and presumably to the lives of any and all "men" were the values of achieving greatness for the nation through political and military exploits and decisive heroic action. Without these "ultimate values" how is one to live a manly life?

193

A gender-sensitive interpretation suggests that it is difficult to be a "man" in today's world. Those who seek meaning in life can find it only in mysticism, personal relations or the old churches. None of these constitute a "man's" way of relating to the world. Mysticism, church religions and personal human relations are more appropriate for women than for men. What is a manly response to the fate of the times, the disenchantment of the world, the loss of sublime values in public life? Not flight from this reality but facing it by meeting the "demands of the day" in human relations as in one's vocation, resigning oneself to doing one's duty at home and at work, an acceptance of defeat. The nation had risked its all for world greatness, had made mistakes, had suffered incompetent leadership, and had lost. Now, one must accept the fate as a man and return to the rationalized, everyday life of practical activity. This solution is much easier when one feels a calling, when one "finds and obeys the demon who holds the fibers of his very life" (ibid., p. 156). When the possibilities of greatness have receded from public life, a man must fall back on finding meaning in a vocation.[2]

In the end, one can only look inward to oneself for guidance, an essentially individualistic ethic, a profound belief in the power of the individual to find meaning for himself. What makes a manly life possible is some idea or cause, some calling or vocation, that can substitute for illusion, and at the time Weber was writing, that could substitute for the "ultimate and sublime" values of public life.

We have seen the grounds for Weber's rejection of an ethic of brotherly love as the basis for rationalizing the world; it represses human and cultural development and conflicts with the realities of the material world and material existence. It represents an illusion of salvation, not a possible reality. The ethic of "brotherly" love fails as a means for ethically rationalizing the world. It cannot be consistently carried out without becoming self-contradictory and hence irrational. In the end it promotes repression instead of love; it is stifling rather than life-giving. Only renunciation of the principle of love as the basis for acting in the world can free one from a repressive, stifling and ultimately impossible standard.

There is another possibility for finding meaning in life and for overcoming the ethical irrationality of the world. That is the possibility of erotic love. The next chapters explore the possibility of drawing on erotic love as a model for "rationalizing" the world.

Notes

1 I am grateful to Gisela Hinkle for providing me with the German version of this passage together with her translation.
2 Jeffrey Alexander provides an interesting and similar analysis in Whimster and Lash (1987).

13

Erotic love as coercion[1]

Weber's generally overlooked discussion of erotic love relationships is brief, embedded in his examination of the "religious rejections of the world and their directions" in the essay by that name (Weber, 1946, pp. 323–59). Nevertheless, the discussion is suggestive and provocative. Although he describes the joy and meaningfulness of erotic love in a disenchanted, rationalized world, he also describes erotic love in terms of conflict, coercion and brutality. His analysis resembles the analysis made by some modern-day radical feminists of all heterosexual relationships.

History of erotic love

Weber briefly traces the evolution of eroticism from preclassical Greece to the rationalized world of modern society. Of the attitudes of preclassical Greece he says: "To the unrestrained feelings of a warriordom the possession of and the fight for women has ranked about equally with the fight for treasure and the conquest of power. . .The tragedians [of preclassical Hellenism] knew sexual love as a genuine power of destiny" (ibid., p. 345). To this society, sexual love was not only a value but one that could inspire "heroic" wars of conquest. In contrast, the classical period of Greece conceived of erotic matters in a relatively and unusually sober manner and did not treat the erotic experience with *women* as the power of destiny or a life-fate. "To the exclusively masculine character of this epoch of 'democracy' the treatment of erotic experience with women as 'life-fate,'" Weber concludes "would have appeared as almost sophomoric and sentimental" (ibid.). Instead, the "comrade," the boy, was the object of erotic interest. This fact stood in the center of Hellenic culture (ibid.).

Under conditions of feudal society, with its stress on knightly (manly) honor, the value of the erotic sensation became accentuated. The symbols of knightly vassalship were carried over into the erotically sublimated sexual relation. The troubadour love of the Christian Middle Ages was an erotic service of vassals. It involved the probation of the man, not before his equals, but in the face of the erotic interest of the "lady." The conception of the "lady" was related to her judging functions. The masculinist culture of Hellenism, in contrast, had precluded such a conception of "the lady;" the culture was premised on the exclusion of women from political and cultural life and power (ibid., p. 346).

The feminist historian Joan Kelly refers to the contrast between "democratic" classical Greece with its repression of women and feudal Europe in which some women at least had greater economic and political power and freedom. Both Weber and Kelly suggest that the attitude toward erotic love reflects as well as contributes to the position of women in a given society and culture. Weber's comments about the Renaissance also support Kelly's thesis that the Renaissance was not a renaissance for women. According to Kelly's research women may actually have lost status and power during the Renaissance. Although traditional masculinist historiography has evaluated classical Greece and the Renaissance as periods of human progress and cultural flowering, for women these seem to have been periods of social, cultural and political regression and repression. Weber anticipated Kelly's thesis about the Renaissance in his historical analysis of eroticism. "Despite the great differences between the conventions of Antiquity and the Renaissance, the latter were essentially masculine and agonistic; in this respect, they were closely related to antiquity (ibid., p. 346).

According to Weber the value of eroticism was enhanced during the transition from the conventions of the Renaissance to the increasingly non-military *intellectualism* of salon culture. "Salon culture rested upon the conviction that inter-sexual conversation is valuable as a creative power." This creative power emerges, in Weber's view, as men strive to prove themselves before a woman. "The overt or latent erotic sensation and the agonistic probation of the cavalier before the lady became an indispensible means of stimulating this [inter-sexual] conversation" (ibid.).

The last accentuation of the erotic sphere occurred with the development of modern intellectualist culture, particularly with the evolution of the vocational specialist type of man. "Under [the] tension between the erotic sphere and rational everyday life, specifically extra-marital sexual life. . .could appear as the only tie. . .with the natural fountain of all life" (ibid.). The erotic love sensation offers this worldly salvation from rationalization.

The rationalization of everyday life that accompanies the development of Puritan salvation ethics ultimately undermines the religious ethic, leaving only a rationalized life-world. Demystification and disenchantment, together with the pressures of rationalism to eliminate or resist any and all impulses that do not readily assimilate to rationalism, give rise to a new desire for salvation. The desire to escape from the over-rationalization of the world is experienced as a desire for meaningfulness and joy in life. Rationalism gives rise to the desire for some ultimate purpose or source of joy that could transcend rationalism. With the loss of religiosity, undermined by the very development that was spawned by religion, alternative non-religious sources of salvation take on great appeal.

One such source of salvation from instrumental, formal, technical, and intellectual forms of rationality is the erotic sphere which Weber describes as providing a joyful triumph over rationality. "The erotic relation seems to offer the unsurpassable peak of the fulfillment of the request for love in the direct fusion of the souls of one to the other. This boundless giving of oneself is as radical as possible in its opposition to all functionality, rationality, and generality" (ibid., p. 347). It is the antithesis of instrumental rationality, utilitarianism and formal rationality, the antithesis of bureaucratic rationality that treats each person as merely another case for the application of a general rule. The lover "knows himself to be freed from the cold skeleton hands of rational orders, just as completely as from the banality of everyday routine" (ibid.).

The joyous triumph over rationality corresponds with the equally radical rejection of any kind of other worldly or supra-worldly salvation. A principled ethic of religious brotherhood is radically opposed to this inner-worldly salvation of erotic love. There are only two forms of salvation that appear genuine to the patriarchal religious ethic of brotherhood. One is devotion to a supra-mundane God which entails devotion to an ethically rational order of God. The other is the mystical bursting of individuation which requires renunciation of the body. Erotic love offers a salvation that leads away from both.

The Puritan takes the same attitude toward erotic love as toward the mystic "having" of godliness, the ecstatic experience of possessing and being possessed by a divine spirit. Puritanism, which views the individual as the instrument of God, rejects such mystical experience as a form of self-indulgence. Although Puritanism compares erotic love to mysticism and rejects both as self-indulgent, erotic love differs from and is rejected by mysticism as well.

The experience of being vibrantly alive in one's love for another person compares with the mystic's bursting of individuation but differs in that the mystic experience involves no human other. The bursting of individuation refers to the feeling of detachment from one's own body and the achievement of mental emptiness. Bodily sensations and mental content make for individuation; they distinguish one self from another. The seeming absence of bodily sensation and mental content achieved through various techniques makes for the mystical experience of individual self-transcendence and hence unity with the cosmos.

Erotic love, in contrast, elevates the sexual aspect of a relationship between particular, embodied individuals into something more than mere physical sensation; it endows the other and the relationship to the other with (sublime) meaning that transcends mere instrumental practical interest. Eroticism then is substitutive for the mystic's union with God and for the mystic's transcendence over mere physical and practical interests. However, from the perspective of mysticism, just as from the perspective of rational salvation ethics, eroticism

197

appears as a "slipping from the mystic realm of God into the realm of the All-Too-Human." (ibid., p. 348). As such the experience of erotic love is opposed in principle by both immanent and transcendent forms of religious salvation with their ethics of brotherly love.

Erotic love conflicts with brotherly love because it is exclusive, particularistic and self-indulgent as opposed to the inclusive universalism and self-abnegation of brotherly love. The passionate character of eroticism appears to the rational, religious ethic of brotherhood as a loss of self-control and as the loss of an orientation to the rationality and wisdom of norms willed by God. To the rational ascetic, the sublimated sexuality of eroticism is idolatry of the worst kind. According to the religious ethic, it is given to man to live according to the rational (functional, instrumental) purposes laid down by the divine order and only according to them. All elements of passion are considered residues of the Fall (ibid., p. 349).

A principled ethic of brotherly love conflicts with the amoral nature of love. Because "no consummated erotic communion will know itself to be founded in any way other than through a mysterious *destination* for one another," which the lovers interpret as fate in the highest sense of the word, it thereby legitimizes itself in an entirely amoral sense (ibid., p. 348). There is no moral or ethical reason for the attachment. It is fate that brings them together. The two souls were "meant" for each other. Because it is founded on amoral, irrational fate (a "fortuitous flaring up of passion" from the perspective of salvation religion) and not on ethical reason, the relationship is essentially an ethically irrational one, "the most complete denial of all brotherly love and of *bondage* to God" (ibid., italics added). Yet erotic love has a close connection with goodness in general. "The euphoria of the happy lover is felt to be 'goodness,' it has a friendly urge to poeticize all the world. . .in a naive enthusiasm for the diffusion of happiness" (ibid.).

Weber here touches on a dimension of erotic love that has implications for ethical conduct. The happiness of a happy lover produces a "naive" enthusiasm for the diffusion of happiness. Yet the religious ethic of brotherly love not only tends to discount this aspect of erotic love, it meets it with "cool mockery." The goodness and good feeling toward the world that accompanies erotic love is seen as merely a mood, a subjective state, rather than a rational commitment founded in an enduring state and an enduring desire, the desire for and state of oneness with the divine. The subjective mood derives from human desires, bodily sensations and human relationships that are unstable and unreliable. The passionate lover changes; the desired other changes: and with these changes, the subjective mood of good feeling and the goodness that it generates similarly changes. The experience cannot be counted on as a reliable on-going source for good actions toward the world and others.

Erotic love is exclusive. It does not attach itself to any and everybody, except in its desire to spread happiness as a consequence of a particular attachment. In contrast, brotherly love must include all others in principle. Erotic love is subjective in the highest imaginable sense; it rests on the lover's own personal unique sensibilities. Brotherly love is objective; it rests on an impersonal objective principle independent of individual sensibility. Because of the intensity of the lover's experience, because of the immediacy of the possessed reality, because the consciousness of the lover rests upon his or her own sensibility, and because of the nature of communion, the experience is not communicable. Because it is "absolutely incommunicable" it represents a counter-pole to all religiously oriented brotherliness which in principle is something taught and hence communicable.

Brutality, conflict and coercion in erotic love

The greatest indictment of erotic love from the perspective of an ethic of brotherly love concerns the essentially and inherently "unbrotherly" nature of the relationship. Weber interprets erotic feelings as individual desire and sees the latter as compromising love. Weber describes the relationship of erotic love as involving brutality, conflict, and coercion. He presents this other side of erotic love as the way erotic love looks from the perspective of a religious ethic of brotherly love. From that perspective, "the erotic relation must remain attached, in a certain sophisticated measure to brutality" (ibid., p. 348).

Weber asserts: "Veiled and sublimated brutality. . .[has] inevitably accompanied sexual love" (ibid., p. 355). Note the use of "inevitably." He also states: "The more sublimated it [the erotic love relationship] is, the more brutal" (ibid., p. 348). This notion of a veiled and sublimated brutality, not to be confused with physical violence, links Weber's analysis of erotic love relationships with the analysis of heterosexual "love" relationships made by some contemporary feminists.

By sublimated brutality, I assume Weber means brutality that is elevated from the base, material level of physical violence to a higher level of spiritual violence. By sublimated erotic love, I assume similarly that he means erotic desire that is raised from the base, material level of sexual lust to a higher level of idealization or symbolization in which the other is desired and appreciated as embodying (symbolizing) some idea or ideas that are valued and that represent the good – hence as embodying some ideal(s). Thus, base, material lust is made sublime and the other is idealized. The other ceases to be a mere sexual object and becomes the embodiment of some good.

Nevertheless, Weber sees the relationship as brutal and coercive: "unavoidably, it is considered to be a relation of conflict." The conflict is not a contingent matter: "This conflict is not only, or even predominantly, jealousy and the will to possession, excluding third ones." Rather, he explains, "It is far

199

more the most intimate coercion of the soul of the less brutal partner" (ibid.). In addition to "conflict," "coercion" and "brutality," Weber introduces the idea of the soul. A relationship of lust may be depicted as one of physical violence, but a relationship of erotic love is described as one of spiritual violence, "the most intimate coercion of the soul." The similarity to a radical feminist analysis of the psychological oppression of women by men begins to reveal itself. The relationship between brutality and sublimation involves the paradox that "this coercion exists because it is never noticed by the partners themselves. Pretending to be the most humane devotion, it is a sophisticated enjoyment of oneself in the other" (ibid.).

A principled ethic of brotherly love does not involve any enjoyment of oneself in the other. Rather, the actor acts out of moral commitment only and not out of desire for personal pleasure, except, perhaps, for the pleasure or salvation that comes from carrying out God's will. There is no personal desire that is expressed and hence imposed on the other.

Acts of brotherly love must express a desire to serve or please the other. Such acts express not one's own personal desires, but an impersonal ethic motivated by desire to please God or to do good. Thus a relationship with the other becomes an occasion for demonstrating one's commitment to God or to an abstract moral principle. The relationship is desired not because it is pleasing or meaningful to the self, but because it is pleasing to God. This contrasts with the erotic love relationship which is desired because the relationship is physically and emotionally pleasing to the self. Erotic love is an expression of one's own pleasure, one's own desire.

The ethical problem associated with enjoying oneself in the other relates to treating the other as a means for one's own enjoyment and not as an end. Treating the other as a means to one's pleasure involves imposing one's will or desire on the other. For example, the other's presence may be intensely pleasurable. Expressing an intense desire for the other's presence may be matched by the other's desire to please. But in that case, the "less brutal," that is to say, less imposing, more accommodating, partner will have been coerced. According to Weber, "This coercion exists because it is never noticed by the partners themselves" (ibid.).

On first reading it may seem odd and untenable to contend that coercion can exist without either partner noticing it and because neither partner notices it. Coercion implies the use or threat of force to gain compliance because it is assumed that the other would not voluntarily comply. Is Weber changing the meaning of coercion? Can the expression of desire be judged as coercive if in fact the other voluntarily complies out of a desire to please? Weber's judgment of coercion may not be as far-fetched as it appears on first reading, particularly in light of recent feminist thought.

Take the case of a stereotypical heterosexual relationship. The one who desires to please will see her action as voluntary. She will not necessarily see

200

the action as compliance, but may identify the other's wishes as her own. In this way she denies that she has a soul with any self-defined desires of its own other than the desire to please. The particular content of the act is defined by the other. Hence precisely because neither she nor he realize that she is denying her own soul, the love is a "coercion of the soul."

Feminists have made this analysis because it is women who are expected to surrender to the other out of a desire to please. Men are expected to express their desires by making demands or expressing their preferences and expecting women to comply out of desire to please them. Like Weber, feminists have begun to expose the brutality to the soul that occurs within traditional heterosexual relationships. Weber points out that the coercion exists because the partners do not notice it. This suggests that if the woman or the man were aware of the coercive aspect of the relationship, then the coercion would cease. People who believe themselves to be devoted to each other presumably would not want to coerce each other. But Weber may mean that the desire to please the other precludes the ability to see the other as coercive or to resist demands and desires expressed by the other. For Weber, the inability to resist the will of the other signals domination or repressed conflict.

How can we account for a relationship in which one party expresses his or her own desire and the other party expresses desire only to please the first? We must see such a relationship as socially, historically and politically grounded as well as psychologically grounded. The image of the self-denying, self-sacrificing woman who serves her husband out of love or duty is a historical one associated with the bourgeois marriage.

Feminist political theory has identified a relationship between the liberal political state, the bourgeois marriage contract and female sexual desire. Coltheart (1986) reminds us of the assumptions about human nature and desire that are internal to the liberal political philosophy that shaped the modern liberal state. For Hobbes, the primary human motivation was acquisitive desire (possessive individualism) and the primary restraint was fear (C.B. MacPherson, 1962; Coltheart, 1986, p. 113). Thus the assumption of acquisitive desire legitimizes the restraining power of the Leviathan. With the Leviathan and the securing of a civil society, men's desires are restrained and limited by the law while women's desires are denied altogether; women become objects of men's acquisitive desire (Coltheart, 1986, p. 114).[2]

Locke's contract theory of government was built on Hobbes' "facts." Locke's contract was a contract for the protection of property owners. Workers were included as proprietors of their labor power, but women remained at one remove from the public agreement to be governed. Women's status was dependent on a sexual contract in which a "naturally" superior, active and sexually aggressive male makes an initiative, or offers a contract, to which a "naturally" subordinate, passive woman "consents" (Pateman, 1980, p. 164).

201

In this scenario, women's sexual desire is denied: "the sexual contract based on Hobbesian desire and Lockeian consent. . .produces the female eunuch," a woman who must deny her own sexual desire (Coltheart, 1986, p. 121). She is not an active desiring subject, but a passive object of another's desire who may "consent" to a man's initiative or offer and who may covertly or overtly encourage a man's interest.

Feminists have identified a transformation in the representation of female sexual desire from the seventeenth century, in which women's sexual passions were viewed as large and problematic, to the early eighteenth century when "revised sexual ideology deprived the virginal daughters of the respectable middle class of passion and desire" (Fox Keller, 1985, p. 63). "By the nineteenth century the fearful devourer, with her insatiable lust, had given way to the 'angel in the house' – a chaste, desexualized and harmless dependent" (ibid., p. 62).

Just as Marx looked at the exchange between workers and capital and showed how the consequences of that exchange relationship included the domination of the worker by a whole world ruled and mystified by capital, feminists have looked at the exchange between women and men represented by the sexual contract and have shown how the consequences of that contract include the domination and suppression of active female desire by a whole world ruled and mystified by male desire.

Women have expressed their knowledge of the oppressive "contract" of marriage, but this was never seriously accepted as political while the intellectual agenda was drafted by men for whom only the public world is political (Coltheart, 1986, p. 117). With the challenge to male domination and female social, political and economic dependence came not only a challenge to the sexual contract itself, but a challenge to redefine and reclaim female sexual desire.[3] To challenge Hobbes' and Freud's masculine conception of desire involves not only a revolution in personal sexual and gender identity but a revolutionary challenge to the foundations of liberal political society. (I explore this challenge in the chapters that follow, especially Chapter 17.)

If the public world were not premised on active acquisitive desire and its restraint what would public life and the desire that motivates it look like? If masculine desire no longer defined itself in terms of repudiating maternal nurturance and renouncing "feminine" passive desire, both of which are then relegated to women (creating what Weber perceives as a coercive relationship) what would masculine desire look like? If the sexual contract changes what would feminine desire look like? If citizenship and its ethics were no longer defined in terms of the transcendence of feminine concerns (Lloyd, 1986) what would citizenship and its ethics look like?

Weber does not inquire into or seek to challenge the gender division of desire. He does not ask what a non-coercive erotic love relationship would be like. In Weber's view, if there were no coercion, there would be overt conflict which would, then, preclude erotic love. Thus sublimated conflict and coercion are integral to the erotic love relationship. Some feminists would agree with respect to heterosexual relationships; therefore, they advocate separatism. Other feminists would not agree.

If, as Weber claims, the partners do not notice the coercion, why is it an issue, particularly a feminist issue? If one partner, such as the woman, gives in to the desires of the other out of a desire to please the other, why should this be cause for concern? Why should this aspect of the relationship be denounced by those adhering to an ethic of brotherly love as well as by feminists? The ethic of brotherly love would denounce it on principle: that it is a form of coercion and as such it is unacceptable; it contradicts the premise of brotherly love and of erotic love itself. Love, whether it be spiritual brotherly love or sexual erotic love, means a "boundless giving of oneself" to the other. To the extent that one is demanding, or imposing one's will or desire on the other, it is not a giving but the opposite.

Philosophically and religiously one may see this dimension and reject it. But on the practical level of the concrete relationship, why should men or women make an issue of it? If the partner willingly gives in to the desires of the other, willingly sacrifices for the other, considers it a pleasure and/or a privilege to do so, why should that be challenged rather than admired? Is the philosophical, religious and feminist position advocating narcissism, or asceticism? Should women or men resist or refuse the demands, desires, will of their mates on principle? Is narcissism – responding only to one's own desires – or asceticism – denying any and all desires, one's own as well as other's – as a moral duty necessary for the honor of womanhood? Does this not spell the end of erotic love?

We arrive at a paradoxical conclusion. To impose desire on another or to express one's own desire contradicts the essence of love as a giving. However, to refuse the desires of the other is similarly to contradict the essence of love as giving. Love based on desire seems to be a philosophically untenable form of love, a contradiction in terms. Religion responds by challenging the basis of erotic love in sexual desire. It argues that only love without desire is a true giving. Not sexual love but love for God or for the good would motivate such giving. Without desire there would be no coercion.

Similarly the desire to acquiesce to the other, to please the other, that is motivated by sexual love is not true giving; in spite of its self-sacrificing character, it is self-serving. Only love or giving that is founded in a relationship with God or the good is free of the self-contradictory aspects that characterize erotic love. Only such principled brotherly love, as opposed to spontaneous or impulsive expressions of love, is authentic, devoid of coercion, brutality, conflict or unbrotherly self-indulgence.

Weber's analysis of the conflict between erotic love and brotherly love suggests that the former, despite its pretensions and protestations to the contrary, is not and cannot be true love, free from the above defects. Feminist critiques of heterosexual love relationships make a similar claim, but not on the basis of abstract philosophical or religious reasoning. They base their critique on the concrete consequences that befall women who find themselves in such relationships. They cite the one-sided nature of those relationships that, despite protestations of devotion, somehow end up with women doing the serving, giving, acquiescing, often without men's awareness that this is the case. Even in relationships not characterized by the dependence of women on men, as witnessed by the New Left movements of the 1960s, women were expected to be subservient. When women of the New Left initially raised the issue of the inequity in the relationship between men and women within the movement, the men responded with derision. They humiliated, ignored, rejected or patronized the women who dared to call attention to the issue.

Other women whose consciousness was raised by the women's movement encountered similar resistance on the part of their husbands and lovers when they called attention to inequities in their relationships, or when they tried to express their own desires, interests, needs, opinions which were not shared by their men. Women now found that although they had willingly given to their men, and acquiesced to their wishes, their men were not so willing to do the same despite their protestations of love. That discovery led to a feminist analysis of heterosexual relations that resembles the philosophical, religious critique of erotic love presented above and referred to by Max Weber.

The "less brutal" partner in an erotic love relationship resembles the person who acts out of a religiously motivated commitment to brotherly love. There, too, the actor denies her own desires; she subordinates and devotes her soul to God. Love for God that requires a denial of one's own desires and love for the other that likewise requires a denial of one's own desires are both coercive to the soul. In the former case, the reward is in knowing that one has God's grace or salvation, whereas in the latter case the reward is in knowing that one has the other's favor or good will. Or, rather than speak in terms of rewards, we may speak in terms of the mystical merging of one's soul with God or with the other such that one does not experience having any separate desires of one's own.

Coercion to the soul of the less brutal partner is inherent in erotic love relationships wherever the less brutal partner denies any desires of her own. By not acknowledging any separate desires, one denies having a separate self with its own soul. Since each desires to please the other, if it were acknowledged that one's actions or desires were an imposition that displeased the other, then they could be withdrawn and coercion would not exist. Only by not acknowledging one's own desires, which might conflict with the desires or actions of the other, is it possible and in fact unavoidable, as Weber claims, for an erotic *love* relationship to be coercive.

If an erotic love relationship is premised on the desire to please and be pleased, and if the less brutal partner is by definition the one who shrinks from expressing and therefore imposing her own desires or pleasures, then the less brutal partner will be left only with the desire to please. Furthermore, if the less brutal partner expresses no desires of her own for the other to serve, then the more brutal one, the one who is willing to express his desires, will be left only with the desire to be pleased by the other, as there can be no possibility of pleasing the other in any other way. He can only please the other by expressing pleasure at the other's serving of himself and his desires. One's pleasure with the other becomes, under such conditions, the pleasure one would feel at a docile and devoted pet who tries to serve and please.

Thus the inherent coerciveness that Weber attributes to erotic love relationships requires as a condition of its possibility, one partner who desires only to please and who denies all other possible desires of her own, especially those that conflict with the desires of the other, and one partner who desires only to be pleased by the other, and who denies himself the pleasure of pleasing the other. We may call this patriarchal desire and the relationship a patriarchal one. It is the relationship of the ideal typical bourgeois sexual contract. If the only desire the female partner expresses is the desire to please the other, then there is no desire of hers that he can serve. He can, however, strive to be worthy of that devotion by devoting himself to some worthy cause or by accomplishing some worthy task or by achieving some kind of success. Nevertheless, brutality to the soul is not precluded by such an arrangement, only legitimized.

Weber seems to assume that the erotic love relation would not be possible if the parties were not blinded to the coercion that occurs. If they recognized the coercion, overt conflict might replace covert domination. Some feminists argue the same. According to Weber, not only in world politics or domestic politics, but even in the most intimate relations of personal life and the deepest recesses of the human soul, conflict and struggle are endemic. Even among "mutually loving persons," there is an inner struggle for "subjective values" and, instead of external compulsion, an inner control "in the form of erotic or charitable devotion" (Weber, [1917] 1949, p. 27). Devotion for Weber means the voluntary subordination of oneself (one's soul) to another out of erotic desire or charitable concern for the other.

For Weber, interpersonal and intrapersonal struggle over competing values is an inevitable feature of human life. Either the stronger succeeds in winning the weaker to its side (voluntary compliance) with surrender of the weaker one's values or soul, or the stronger overwhelms the weaker with superior force, or the two agree to compromise. The last occurs when there is relative equality. However, compromise may not be possible; the conflict may be irreconcilable. Because overt conflict is not the rule, the model of devotion with its coercion to the soul is also the model of modern social life.

This model of erotic love presumes a patriarchal arrangement in which the stronger party accepts and expects the devotion of the weaker one and the weaker one accepts and expects guidance by the stronger. Modern society is modeled on the erotic love relationship that Weber describes. Instead of surrender of the soul out of devotion to the person of another, modern society requires surrender of the soul to the boss or political leader, proletarianization of the soul, as Weber calls it.

If the basic premise of an erotic love relationship is mutual desire, that means that both have desires, idea(l)s and wills (souls) of their own. Each is elated by the recognition and affirmation of the other. However, if one partner exclusively identifies her own desires, idea(l)s, subjective values or pleasures with those of the other, she denies having any desires or pleasures of her own. Such self-denial transforms a relationship of mutual desire and recognition into something close to its opposite, a repressive and coercive relationship. One who has desires of her own but does not acknowledge or express them is one who is repressed and therefore not capable of being recognized. If she complies with the desires of the other without expressing any desires or will of her own, then her own spirit is suppressed and coerced. The one who does not deny or suppress his own desires becomes coercive by virtue of the other's inability to express her own desires or resist those of the other.

"Weber often said that a wife *must* resist her husband, or else she is partly guilty of his brutality towards her" (Green, 1974, p. 122). Some feminist thinkers have been arguing the same and distinguishing between altruism, which may be likened to "feminine" passive desire, egoism, which may be likened to "masculine" acquisitive desire, and a third mode of relating that is both and neither. They have been inquiring into the conditions and presuppositions of the feminine ethic of self-sacrifice (Tormey, 1973–4; Blum *et al.*, 1973–4; Held, 1973–4; Straumanis, 1984).

The inability to express one's own desires is itself a product of a coercive relationship. The way in which the depiction of women changed from sexually aggressive, dangerous, lusty beings to the "angel in the house" involved political and economic changes with consequent psychological changes. Neither version of women is "natural."

Coercion implies that the unexpressive partner does have desires and a will of her own that differ from those of the expressive partner. If, in fact, one partner had no will or desires of her own but were merely an instrument of the other, then we could not speak of coercion. If Weber is correct that the soul of the "less brutal" partner gets coerced, and if it tends to be women's souls that get coerced, then men must constitute the more brutal sex. Many feminists object to this biological reductionism. They attribute to social factors both the problem and the resistance of men to the acknowledgment of the problem. Men do not want to give up privileges to which they are accustomed, especially when such privileges are identified with being a man. It is a source of pride, an affirmation of their worth, to be served by a woman. It is an affront to their dignity and their manliness to have that expectation called into question. Furthermore, the unwillingness automatically to serve the man also calls into question the woman's love for the man. If she truly loved him, she would be happy to give to him, to serve him, to please him.

If, then, a greater propensity for brutality is not inherent in the male sex but a matter of social conditioning, the question still remains whether a relationship of erotic love can be free of the coercive aspect noted by Weber. Or is it an inescapable feature of erotic love? Is desire inherently a coercive element in a relationship, as Weber, following the religious argument, seems to suggest? If male dominance is an essential feature of masculinity as defined by our culture, then self-consciousness of masculinity, a self-conscious critique of masculinity as male dominance, should make it theoretically possible to transform male identity and eliminate the coercion deriving from male privilege. But if coercion is inherent in the expression of desire itself, the imposition of one's will on another, then the problem is not even theoretically resolvable except through a self-disciplined renunciation of erotic love, a learning to discipline sexual desire as opposed to elevating it into erotic love.

The question comes down to whether the expression of desire is identical to the imposition of desire. If I express my desire, am I imposing my desire? The answer is not as clear cut as it might seem. One might say that there are various ways of expressing desire which theoretically ought not to involve any coercion. Yet to express oneself to another is to impose oneself, and to impose oneself is a form of coercion. We can use the analogy with communication and speech. Any time I attempt to speak or express myself, verbally or otherwise, I am imposing on another. My verbal sounds, physical gestures, bodily movements assault the senses of the other. The other has not invited my speech act, and if she has, then in so doing she has imposed on me, assaulted my senses.

Cultures implicitly recognize in the various interaction rituals and patterns of etiquette the offensive character of self-expression. These include autonomous bodily expressions such as sounds, smells, movements, and intentionally determined expressions such as verbal ones, gestures and so on. The greater the familiarity allowed, the less are self-effacing rituals required. Familiarity implies exposure to those aspects of the other that are generally not acceptable in public because they are considered an unwelcome expression of the particularity of the individual.

The etiquette necessary for negotiating everyday life includes apologetic phrases like, "Excuse me," "Pardon me," and so on. Such phrases may precede the initiation of communication particularly between non-intimates. Similarly they may follow unintended, involuntary bodily acts like sneezes, coughs, belches, flatulence, accidental poking, jostling, stepping on a foot. Any expression of self in the company of another constitutes a form of imposition or possible offense. So no communication can occur without self-expression, and consequently no communication can take place without imposition. That may be why some religions require vows of silence as a humbling device for entrants into monasteries or retreats. Others allow only expressions of worship or communication necessary for carrying out one's service to God. In both cases, the self must be humbled and subordinated to the divine; the expression of self is a failure to do so and hence an offense against God.

Religions have developed ways for dealing with self-expression: self-denial or, in Weber's view, treating the self as vessel of the divine or as God's tool. The latter case gives us the functional or crusading orientation to life whereas the former gives us mystical contemplation of the holy with its flight from the world. In both forms of salvation religion, active asceticism and world-renouncing mysticism, self-expression in general, not just as it occurs in erotic love, is seen as a form of hubris, a self-righteous or self-indulgent, offensive imposing of self on the world. Religion articulates this problem of coercion without offering a way of reconciling desire with ethical relations. It solves the problem by sublimating all particular desires into the general desire for God or the divine. However, this sublimation requires repressing all particular desires.

The struggle to deny all desires results in a continual "heroic" struggle against one's self and against the temptations of the world and other people. In contrast, the everyday life of sociability offers an alternative solution to the problem of imposition and coercion.

Notes

1   This chapter is based on an essay that first appeared in Whimster and Lash (1987) *Max Weber, Rationality and Modernity* (Allen & Unwin).
2   In the state of nature each individual sought to acquire the objects of his desire by force and lived in fear of the violence of others. There is a conflict between the laws of nature (justice, equity, modesty, mercy and in sum, doing to others as we would be done to) and our natural Passions. Only terror of some Power can cause the former to be observed instead of relying on one's own strength and art against other men (Hobbes, 1968, pp. 223–4). This conception of human nature however excludes the traits culturally attributed to females – sociability, nurturance, concern for dependent and helpless persons (Flax, 1983). Human beings are driven by a perpetual and restless desire of power after power that ceases only in Death (Hobbes, 1968). The state of nature is a war of each against all. The Leviathon may be likened to a good patriarchal father who controls and channels the passions of his sons, creating the possibility of civil society, morality and culture; the preservation of life, peace and security are

guaranteed by obedience to his will (Law) and renunciation of the absolute right to gratify any passion (Flax, 1983, p. 264). The similarity with Freud's thinking is striking.

3 Influenced by Lacan and Derrida much French feminism has been concerned with this issue. But the sexuality debates in the United States as well as feminist psychoanalytic and sociological theory (Benjamin, 1988) also address the issue of female sexual desire that is not a mere response to or identification with male desire.

PART FOUR

An alternative world

14

Erotic love as sociability: an alternative reality

The problem of coercion that Weber discovers in relationships of erotic love is inherent in any form of social life. Hence, all cultures must have some way of reconciling the offensive, imposing, coercive character of self-expression with the need and desire for social contact and social attachment. Such reconciliation constitutes the essence of sociability. This chapter develops a feminist model of erotic love as sociability that contrasts with Weber's patriarchal model of erotic love as coercion.

By sociability I mean a relationship in which the presence of one makes a pleasurable difference to, *affects*, the other.[1] Each party considers the other not an object to be used or avoided as in the patriarchal model of social life as conflict but a subject whose active presence affects one's senses, brings pleasure (or displeasure), a subject with power to affect my senses and my feelings in a positive way. Being affected positively can be an empowering experience. Sociable relationships may be more or less pleasurable, more or less affecting, more or less stimulating. As such all sociable relationships are erotic relationships. I mean this not necessarily in the narrow sense relating to sexual intercourse but in the broad sense of social intercourse that includes all kinds of mutual pleasuring, mutual stimulating and mutual empowering. Relationships of erotic sociability stimulate creativity; or, as Weber himself relates, and as salon culture depends on, erotic interest is "valuable as a creative power" (Weber, 1946, p. 346); it is "an embodied creative power" (ibid., p. 347).

A definition of eros that goes beyond the narrowly sexual is: the totality of "pleasure-directed life instincts whose energy is derived from libido." The word "libido" derives from the word "libere" meaning "to please." Pleasure in its original and primary form, before sublimation and symbolization, is bodily pleasure. Hence erotic interests refer to interests in bodily pleasure. But the body is never divorced from the mind. As the body-mind of the infant and child develops, the nature of pleasure correspondingly develops. Erotic interest always has a mental and emotional dimension as well as a physical one, although one or another dimension may take precedence in any erotic interest.

Emotional interest, physical, sensual or aesthetic interest, intellectual interest, or explicitly sexual interest, or all of these may be aroused by another. And by "interest" I mean the promise of making a pleasurable difference. According to the etymology of "interest," the meaning, "to make a difference," comes from the literal meaning of "inter esse," to be between or to concern. That which is an interest to me, a concern, is that which links me to something else. The dictionary synonym for "interest," "concern," comes from Middle English, "com cerner," literally to sift together, to mingle. What is between us makes a difference to each of us; that is, it links us and differentiates us from each other. We learn from what is between us, who we are: how we are similar, how we differ. What is between us brings us together, sifts us, mingles us, but also stays between us revealing our essential separateness and difference. What is between us is not simply our bodies as it is in narrow patriarchal notions of eros.

If each party is capable of responding to the other, and if the other's response makes a difference in terms of one's own pleasure or pain, then one must care about the other's response. This means that each must care about the effects of his or her own actions on the other, the kind of response the action will evoke.

The ways that cultures have devised for ritualizing social encounters to make them more or less pleasurable (or at the minimum as painless as possible) take the form of expressions of caring for the other and the other's response. The ritualized expressions of concern for the other that accompany self-expression may take the form of requesting permission to act, apologizing for one's actions – voluntary or involuntary – expressing one's gratitude to the other, one's subservience and unworthiness in relation to the other, and so forth. In these ways, the one who engages in self-expression informs the other that s/he intends no harm or offense, that s/he would proceed only if the other is agreeable and not offended, that s/he would not dare to impose or take advantage of the other, that s/he would willingly defer to the other, that s/he would be greatly regretful and would seek to make amends if s/he did unintentionally harm or offend the other. In other words, the initiating person informs the other through these ingratiating and self-effacing rituals that s/he would subordinate her/his own desire to the sensibilities of the other. Thus each person is expected to communicate that s/he cares about the other and the other's response even more than s/he cares about realizing or expressing her/his own desire.

Implicit then in sociable relationships is a receptiveness to and respect for the other. Awareness of each other's receptiveness and regard makes trust and hence social life possible. Social life is founded on the capacity to express both desire and self-restraint, self-expression and self-abnegation, self-indulgence and self-denial, assertion of self and caring about the other, as internal to the same act. We arrive at the image of people as both separate, independent, self-motivated and attached, dependent, caring. Both self-interest and caring are internal to sociable action and sociable relationships.

214

Society as sociability

Georg Simmel makes some interesting observations about sociability. He formulates sociability as the play form of human association. By this he means that human society becomes separated from and valued over and above any instrumental purpose or interest that might bring people together. In fact, he relates, in all European languages the term, society, refers to a sociable gathering. Although there are various purposive forms of society – political, economic, and so on – only the sociable society is "a society" without qualifying adjectives. "It is this, precisely because it represents the pure form that is raised above all contents" (Simmel, 1950, p. 44). Kurt Wolff explains that the word *Gesellschaft* means both "society" and "party" in the sense of "social or sociable gathering" (ibid., translator's note).

Because the term "society" refers to a sociable gathering, and because all other forms of social gatherings presuppose some qualifying adjective, I would argue that sociability is necessary for and prior to any particular form of society. I would argue that sociability is not just another drive or interest. Rather it is an essential foundation for all social life and all societies. This means that no understanding of social life and society is possible without an understanding of sociability as core.

As part of his analysis of sociability, Simmel notes the importance of etiquette or tact. "It is no mere accident of linguistic usage that even the most primitive sociability, if it is of any significance and duration at all, places so much emphasis on *form*, on 'good form'" (ibid.). He claims that without the reduction of personal expression brought about by tact, the gathering itself would not be possible. Where shared interests in co-operation determine the social form, "it is these interests that prevent the individual from presenting his peculiarity and uniqueness in too unlimited and independent a manner." Where no such interests "direct the self-regulation of the individual in his personal relations with others, it is tact that fulfills this regulatory function. Perhaps its most essential task," he suggests, "is to draw the limits, which result from the claims of others, of the individual's impulses, ego-stresses, and intellectual and material desires" (ibid., p. 45).

Although social life is characterized by self-interest of all kinds and involves conflict, coercion and violence, as well as desire, as Weber describes, it also involves "good form" and tact or what I call responsiveness to and respect for the other. Thus the pure form of society presupposes as a condition of its possibility the mode of relating and kind of attitude that I described above and that Simmel calls good form and "tact." Furthermore, I would argue, it is impossible to claim that self-interest takes priority over interest in "society."

Simmel describes sociability as creating "an ideal sociological world in which the pleasure of the individual is closely tied up with the pleasure of

215

the others." This means that "in principle, nobody can find satisfaction here if it has to be at the cost of diametrically opposed feelings which the other may have" (ibid., p. 48). Therefore there is a need inherent in sociability and hence in society to ensure the satisfaction of the other. This dimension of social life is underplayed in Weber's analysis.

Even Simmel considered sociability a thing apart from practical life, a separate sphere. He acknowledges that the pleasure of being with others can emerge in any social activity. Nevertheless, he seems to believe that individual interests precede the social interest; that is, individual interests bring people into contact which they may then find desirable in itself. He does not treat the pleasure of relating to others, sociability, as the essential core of social life, that which provides the grounds for ethical behavior (tact, good form, etiquette as well as more explicitly moral behavior) and co-operative action.

Just as purposive association involves some sociability, some consideration of the other, a sociable gathering such as a party also involves some purposive, instrumental behavior. A party that excludes all self-interest must be a highly formal one. That seems to be the kind that Simmel has in mind when he discusses sociable gatherings and notices the emphasis on form and the exclusion of anything too personal.

Simmel identifies one other aspect of sociability that has bearing on this argument. In sociability, one "does as if" all were equal. . .The strong and extraordinary individual not only makes himself the equal of the weaker, but even acts as if the weaker were the more valuable and superior" (ibid., p. 49). This is done in order for sociability to work. In other words, sociability requires that each make the other feel valuable and superior, that no one devalue or diminish the other. Thus there is an inherently ethical character to sociability – mutual respect, even mutual veneration or the pretension of it.

I have argued that self-expression which involves imposition is one side of sociable action; concern for and receptiveness to the other's response is the other side. Weber sees this two-sided nature of sociable action in dualistic terms: one either expresses, struggles, opposes or one submits, complies, appeases. This dualism takes the form of a choice between brotherly love where the actor represses his or her own desires, or erotic love where the actor imposes his or her desires on the other.

Weber seems to be arguing that all of social life is tainted with ethical guilt. There is no form of life that can escape it, not even the intimate relationship of erotic love. Although conflict and coercion are irremediable features of social life, Weber's conflict theory is one-sided. His notion of interests does not include the interest in society itself, in sociability, as a fundamental social interest. He seems to recognize only individual interest and conflicts of interest. He does not emphasize enough the sociable nature of the human being: his or her pleasure in, need for, and rootedness in relationships ("societies") that are desired because they are pleasurable and valuable in themselves.

Essential to sociability is a mutual willingness to forgo the use of power out of mutual regard and respect and out of desire for the pleasure of the relationship. The willingness to renounce power and violence entails a willingness to suspend self-expression that may offend. In formal relations of sociability, personal self-expression is replaced by "good form." Substituting good form for personal expressions of self-interest reduces the likelihood of offense, but it also reduces the likelihood of intimacy. The more that formalities predominate, the less that personal self-disclosure occurs and the more superficial the relationship remains

Erotic love: the agony and the ecstasy

Whether or not erotic love or intimacy involves sexual activity, intimacy introduces the risk of offense and hence violence (at the very least to the sensibility of the other). Violence (offenses of all kinds) remains an ever-present threat within interactions that promote self-expression. As we have seen, sociability minimizes the risk of offense and violence, but it introduces the risk of dissembling and hence deception. The deception that accompanies dissembling (replacing self-expression with good form) remains an ever-present possibility that itself can do violence (to the trust that is constitutive of sociability). Intimacy makes the formalities of sociability seem suspect while sociability makes the self-expressions of intimacy seem offensive. Sociability inhibits intimacy while intimacy inhibits sociability. Thus sociable intimacy requires continual balancing, a back and forth movement between expression of self and concern for the other.

One can pretend to take pleasure in the other's pleasure in order to facilitate a social encounter – good form. But for true mutual pleasuring and mutual empowering each of the parties needs to know enough about the other(s) to be able to affect the other(s) in their uniqueness. This requires a certain amount of intimacy or self-disclosure that goes beyond mere good form.

Because intimacy breaks down the barriers that formality provides, intimacy promotes vulnerability. Intimacy can be dangerous; one's trust can be betrayed, one's weakness exploited, and one's esteem or desire unreciprocated. In other words, one can be hurt and humiliated. On the other hand, intimacy can be protective and intensely pleasurable. Trust can be met with care, vulnerability with tenderness, exposure with recognition and affirmation, esteem and desire reciprocated. In other words one can be nurtured, affirmed and exalted. Because erotic love involves more or less intense desire as well as exposure and disclosure, erotic love involves the greatest personal risk but also the greatest possibility of communion. Hence erotic love can produce the most intense agony and ecstasy.

217

Erotic desire for the other can result from perceiving in the other one's ideal image of oneself. When we see our idea(l) of ourselves mirrored in another who affirms our self-idealization – "Yes, what you see in me, I see in you; what you find most valuable and precious in (my, your) life, I do too" – we feel ecstatic; we are able to find ourselves outside of ourselves in another. Similarly when we see in another our idea(l) of the self we miss in ourselves, and the other sees their idea(l) of the self they miss in themselves – "Just as you love the way(s) that I am different from you, I love the way(s) that you are different from me" – we also experience an affirmation, a mirroring of our differences that enhances ourselves, our uniqueness.

Mutual recognition is possible only when the barriers that separate and protect are removed. But removing one's protective barriers immediately grants a power advantage to the other. Allowing ourselves to be vulnerable in this way serves to "prove" our regard for each other as we acknowledge each other's power to affect us. We each prove ourselves and the value that the relationship has to us in our mutual willingness to refrain from doing violence, from taking advantage of the other's vulnerability, and in our sensitivity to the other who is in this vulnerable state. This is generally what we mean by intimacy. The proving of ourselves by renouncing power and revealing vulnerability and the risking of humiliation and indifference contributes to the agony of erotic love, while sharing and responding to each other's feelings and desires, interests and needs with sensitivity and tenderness contributes to the ecstasy of erotic love, whether it be heterosexual, homosexual or non-sexual.

I consider this "proving" to be the culmination of an erotic interest which, along with the need for co-operation, is a fundamental element in society. I mean society in the pure sense of a group whose primary ties are predominantly erotic in the sense of involving a pleasurable feeling of interest, each in the others, which means predominantly sociable. Because we are embodied beings, all sociable relations have an erotic dimension (the body and senses are affected); all sociable relations are erotic relations. We all find the actual presence or some trace (written missive, verbal message, even memory) of another more or less pleasurable, more or less affective.

Subjectivity

From a patriarchal masculine conception of social life as conflict and erotic love as coercion, it follows that the subjectivity of the other must be rendered powerless, the other's will conquered. After eliminating the other's will and hence difference from self, the body alone remains as the only kind of difference that can be a possible object of desire. Hence patriarchal relations of erotic desire focus almost exclusively on the body. The other's subjectivity is distracting and threatening; it must be denied, rendered innocuous or controlled.

In a feminist conception of social life and erotic love as sociability, the other's subjectivity or will remains powerful. The other remains a desiring subject even as s/he becomes an object of desire. Each becomes both subject and object of desire. Each treats the other as a desirable other and a desiring other. Erotic love as sociability includes an interplay between desiring the other as one that will yield and surrender to my desires allowing itself to be used as an object for my own pleasure and wanting to surrender to the desiring other who finds me desirable. Erotic love as sociability includes an interplay between relating to the other as a willful desiring subject – an active, feeling person – and relating to the other as object of desire – a pleasing, desirable and yielding mind or body. Neither remains only subject or only object of the other's desire.

Within an individual and between individuals the active, feeling, thinking subject (mind) can always interject itself, interrupting a blissful communion in which mind and body lose themselves (oneness of mind and body, self and other) just as the passive presence of the other (body) can always distract one from the thoughts and sentiments in which both (self and other, mind and body) had been losing themselves. Knowing that the unity can be disrupted at any moment makes it that much more special and precious. The interplay within the person of mind and body creates the human spirit as we know it: spirited bodies and embodied spirits. Similarly the interplay between two people as both subjects and objects, mental and physical subjects and mental and physical objects of each other's interest, creates the spirit of the relationship.

The recognition that while the self or the other is appearing to be a subject, an initiating, affecting person, s/he can also be an object, a receptive, affected person, makes for the playfulness of sociable interactions. A phenomenology of playfulness reveals suspension of commitment to be the key feature (Bologh, 1975). Commitment is suspended not to other persons, the community, but rather to the shared meaning that the act usually has. Playfulness creates the possibility of community based on suspension of shared norms or purposes. Hence playfulness becomes a universal source of community and source of universal community. Neither party need take seriously his or her position as object or as subject; neither remains only desiring subject or only object of desire; each undergoes continuous metamorphosis from being primarily a subject (and secondarily an object) to being primarily an object (and secondarily a subject) and back again.[2] (See Table 14.1 for the four kinds of relationships that exist simultaneously as possibilities within erotic relations of sociability.)

Types of sociable relationships

A sociable relationship of subject to subject (#1 in Table 14.1) takes the form of active, mental, physical or emotional interplay, a play of difference. It is

Table 14.1 Harmonious relationships of erotic love.★

	#1		#3	
ME	me	you	me	you
Primary mode: SUBJECT (Secondary mode: object)	s → s (o) → (o)		s → o (o) → (s)	
	s ← s (o) ← (o)		s ← o (o) ← (s)	
	#2		#4	
Primary mode: OBJECT (Secondary mode: subject)	o → s (s) → (o)		o → o (s) → (s)	
	o ← s (s) ← (o)		o ← o (s) ← (s)	

Combinations beneath the broken lines indicate the response of the other (you).

★   All are harmonious with the exception of #1. That one may be harmonious or it may not. See below.

1   I relate as subject to you as subject = active, mental, physical, or emotional interplay, a play of difference; mutual assertion of, appreciation of, and resistance to each other's difference(s) (with secondary possibility of us both surrendering as objects to some other subject, such as the family, community, or God, see below #4).

2   I relate as object to you as subject = femininity, luring, yearning to be desired by, pursued by, affected by you, to surrender to you (with secondary possibility of my actively affecting, controlling you).

3   I relate as subject to you as object = masculinity, lusting, pursuing, persisting, insisting, conquering, and desiring you and your surrender (with secondary possibility of my yielding and surrendering as object to you as subject).

4   I relate as object to you as object = mutual surrender to some other subject, such as the relationship, the community, God. We see each other as objects in relation to some other subject(s) (with secondary possibility of our relating to each other as subjects (see #1 above).

characterized primarily by mutual assertion of and resistance to each other's differences with secondary possibilities of mutual surrender and reconciliation of difference. The relationship of erotic love as sociability that I am sketching here takes the form of movement back and forth from mutual assertion, appreciation and resistance to mutual surrender. It is this movement back and forth that distinguishes the feminist model of erotic love as sociability from the patriarchal model of erotic love as coercion.

A relationship of formal sociability that I have been sketching takes the form of alternating between my being primarily subject to your being primarily object and your being primarily subject to my being primarily object (#s 2 and 3). Each avoids expressing too much subjectivity – interests or emotions that are likely to provoke the subjectivity of the other – and each responds politely and agreeably as a more or less passive but affirming object to the limited subjectivity that the other does express.

A relationship of object to object, platonic friendship or spiritual love (#4), may take the form of shared surrender to some other. (An object requires an other as subject.) We see each other as primarily objects in relation to some other subject. We both desire surrender to some other but not to each other, and we can enjoy our shared (but not mutual) yearning and shared (but not mutual) surrender, our common condition as objects to something other, including the community which we help to form.

Because each individual can change at any moment, the relationship can change instantaneously from one to another of these possibilities. Furthermore, the relationship can take an asymmetrical, discordant form in which case either playfulness occurs or friction develops (See Table 14.2). For instance, I can be relating as subject to you as subject, while you respond by not taking me seriously as a subject but by relating as subject to me as object. I can respond by not taking you seriously; you can respond in kind by not taking yourself seriously, in which case playfulness occurs. I can respond with confusion, irritation, anger, in which case friction develops. I can respond by suspending my subjectivity and becoming an object to you as subject, or I can suspend my interest in you as subject and instead relate as subject to you as object, in which case we have a new asymmetry. If you relate to me as if I am an object and I respond as subject to you as object, if friction is to be avoided, then either you change and yield as object to my interest or I change and yield as object to your interest – or we alternate back and forth. Or we both suspend serious interest and become playful.

The ability to treat the other as object even while the other is treating himself or herself as subject creates possibilities for playfulness, new understanding and humor as well as for serious tensions, misunderstandings and resentments. I can be telling you something of interest to me or articulating or ventilating my feelings and instead of responding actively to me or remaining a passive object to my rantings you can tell me something that is of interest to you or ventilate your feelings about something that is entirely unrelated to what I have been saying. We can continue to talk past each other or at each other, mutually using each other as presences (objects) without substance, or we can stop and laugh at ourselves and respond to each other, re-establishing mutual subjectivity.

As subject one is the affecting, imposing self; as object or body one is the affected, imposed-upon other; as both subject and object of desire, both can

221

Table 14.2 Discordant relationships (playful or tense).

	YOU	
	Subject (s)	Object (o)
ME	**#1**	**#3**
	me you	me you
Subject (s)	s → s	s → o
	---------	---------
	o ← s	o ← s
	s ← o	s ← s
	o ← o	o ← o
Object (o)	**#2**	**#4**
	o → s	o → s
	---------	---------
	s ← s	s ← s
	s ← o	s ← o
	o ← o	o ← o

Combinations beneath the broken lines indicate all possible unreciprocal responses on the part of the other. For instance: in #1, to my relating as a subject to you as a subject, you can relate as a subject to me as an object; you can relate as an object to me as a subject; you can relate as an object to me as an object. All of these responses create asymmetrical, unreciprocal relationships.

affect and both can be affected. Instead of subjects *or* objects, both are agents of mutual affection, mutual pleasuring, and mutual impressing. The impressing is important. It is that which affects the other; the impression creates attraction and evokes desire. To be able to impress means to have some power that the other finds compelling. Mutual impressing means mutual attraction, mutual power, mutual compulsion. In sociable relationships we become agents of our own mutually created relationship, embodiments of its spirit.

Recognizing both self and other as both subject and object, both powerful and vulnerable, means that one does not treat all that seriously the self or the other as *either* desiring subject *or* as desired object. One treats both seriously and playfully with attachment and detachment the self and the other as *both* desiring subject *and* desired object. When one knows and accepts oneself and other as both, one can move playfully between being a desiring subject and a surrendering object without succumbing to either and without being too threatening to the other or too threatened by the other. The threat is mitigated by awareness that the other is neither powerful *nor* vulnerable but both powerful *and* vulnerable. Each is capable of resisting desire and surrendering to desire, one's own or the other's.

Power and empowerment

But since a relationship is never perfectly balanced, the threatening nature of the relationship is never entirely absent. One or another may remain or feel more vulnerable than powerful in relation to the desired other; this feeling of vulnerability may arise any time the other asserts himself or herself, his or her power, in the relationship. That is why there is an obligation within sociable relations for both parties not only to make a show of surrendering and deferring to the other, but to actively draw out the other, to recover the subjectivity of the other, in order that the more fearful or threatened one can be en-couraged to express his or her feelings and desires and have them respected.

Such a relationship, of course, requires a subjective renunciation of violence but it requires as well an objective renunciation, a renunciation of those external objects that create an imbalance of power and vulnerability. A subjective renunciation of violence is only a partial solution. If the objective resources for sustaining the life of the relationship or of the parties to the relationship remain the legal or official property of one and not the other, then the other remains more vulnerable than powerful in the relationship. This is the case for example where the man has the right to control the moneys coming in to the household. It is also the case where the man has the right to use violence against members of "his" household (or where the office holder has the right to the means of administration). These objective conditions subvert and distort sociability even where both parties subjectively desire a sociable relationship.

Even if the man subjectively renounces control over the moneys or sub-jectively renounces using force to impose his will (or if the office holder willingly shares the means of administration), the fact that the woman or child (colleague or client) has no objective right to the moneys, no right to the sanctity of her person (no right to the means of administration), a right backed up by community sanction, means that she or the child remains objectively dependent on the good will of the man, more than does the man remain objectively dependent on the good will of the woman. That is, the man can objectively count on the submission and compliance of the woman (because of her objective dependence, her absence of objective rights) *more* than the woman can count on the submission and compliance of the man.

223

That is why a sociable relationship ultimately requires relative equality or balance of power with regard to the resources necessary for sustaining the relationship and the parties to the relationship. Otherwise, sociability is a suspension from everyday life, a momentary pretense, as Simmel suggests. One pretends to be the equal or servant of the other, but the other remains objectively the inferior or dependent one. This is the case even if the more powerful one is sincere in the avowal of servitude to the other or the avowal of equality. Only if the avowal is backed up by some external communal sanction such as enforceable legal rights protecting the person from violence by the other, establishing joint property rights or the right of each one to sufficient property to meet her needs, can the avowal translate into an objective relationship of equality.

At the same time that a person can be objectively dependent, s/he can also be subjectively powerful. The person with independent means of his or her own may be unable or unwilling to make use of these objective resources; s/he may need or desire to be primarily an object in the relationship, despite legal status. Similarly, the relationship may be one of subjective equality within an objective context of domination. That is, each may treat the other as both subject and object, despite the patriarchal realities of the situation. Nevertheless, despite a subjective desire for a relationship of mutuality, without objective conditions that can support mutuality, the relationship tends to degenerate into one of coercion (patriarchal relations of "devotion"). Furthermore, internalization of the objective realities results in feminine adoration and masculine chivalry, woman as primarily object, man as primarily subject. Weber is sensitive to the coercion inherent in (patriarchal) relationships of erotic love, but he does not analyze the social conditions that produce this reality. He more or less treats the reality of coercion in erotic love as natural and not social and historical.

A sociable relationship requires mutual empowerment in addition to mutual renunciation of power. By serving your pleasure while you serve my pleasure, we each learn to affect the other. My ability to give you pleasure empowers me, and your ability to give me pleasure empowers you. This mode of relating – pleasuring – represents the feminine side of sociability, a feminine mode of power. My ability to give you pleasure depends on my sensitivity to your feelings, needs, interests, my ability to enjoy, appreciate, affirm and thus en-courage your difference, your uniqueness. My en-couraging you enables you to develop, assert and realize your difference; you become empowered. I empower you. Your power to assert yourself, to express your interests, your self-realization, constitutes a masculine mode of power. Your masculine power impresses me; it attracts and compels me; it moves me to want to impress you. This is the masculine side of sociability. Feminine power makes masculine power possible – and the reverse holds as well. Mutuality overcomes the one-sidedness of feminine power and masculine power. Mutual pleasuring makes for mutual empowerment.

Socializing patriarchal relationships

In patriarchal relationships of (heterosexual or homosexual) erotic love, in which each partner can be only masculine or only feminine, the feminine partner (female or male) strives to make herself (himself) attractive; s/he desires to attract the active desire of the other to whom s/he can surrender. S/he desires to become a desired *object*; to surrender to the other's desire. Erotic desire takes the form of desiring the other's desire. The masculine partner desires to overcome the subjectivity of the other, to conquer her (his) will and to reduce her (him) to an object, a thing or body that serves the pleasure of the masculine partner's desire.

Unlike the sociable relationship that takes a flexible if not playful attitude toward being subject or object, in the sure knowledge that each is and knows the other to be both subject and object and that either can change at any time, the patriarchal relationship is rigidly asymmetrical. Each can be only subject or only object. Nevertheless, despite and because of the asymmetry, there is a mutual power play going on. That is because beneath the rigid roles of subject and object remains a subjective being that resists being only an object.

The feminine (yielding, surrendering, vulnerable) partner strives to gain power over the other by making him desire or need her. (I use feminine pronouns, but the feminine partner can be either male or female.) She strives to get the other to reveal himself, to make himself vulnerable and dependent on her for affirmation and acceptance, in this way redressing the asymmetry. (I am using a patriarchal model of heterosexual relations; the same dynamic can apply to patriarchal homosexual relations.) She readily engages in self-disclosure as an appeal for his protection and loyalty, a means of binding him to her.

The masculine partner strives to retain power by remaining distant and independent. He readily engages in protective, chivalrous behavior as a show of power and control. When she has succeeded in getting him to disclose himself and become vulnerable and dependent on her for her regard and affirmation, she has won. When he has succeeded in getting her to admire his strengths and surrender herself to his charge, he has won. Because of the rigidly asymmetrical nature of the game, it is possible for both to win if each submits to the other. The one who submits first takes the risk that the other will not reciprocate and submit to his or her wish. The power play gets acted out in a contest between her wishing to engage in conversation with a strong dose of self-disclosure, an attempt to disarm him, and his wishing to display his strengths and win her over, to engage in conquest.

In a patriarchal relationship of erotic love, woman is reduced to an object. Erotic desire takes the form of lust, a strong desire for the woman as body or object without independent spirit or subjectivity, a desire to conquer the otherness of the woman, to overcome her subjectivity and reduce her to an object that serves the pleasure of the desiring subject. Recognition of the unethical and destructive nature of patriarchal erotic love that treats the other as an object to be used for one's own pleasure can result in an equally one-sided patriarchal alternative, the renunciation of erotic desire and a turn to spiritual brotherly love.

In patriarchal social relations, either erotic desire tends primarily to become reduced to lust and the other reduced to an object *or* erotic desire tends primarily to become elevated to spiritual love in which the self becomes only an object of some divine subject – a loving or wrathful God – and the other similarly becomes object of the divine Other. A spiritual universalistic brotherly love that reduces both self and other, reduces all, to objects of some divine subject means that the uniqueness of both self and other(s) make no difference, must not *matter*; all are equally objects of an undifferentiating, indiscriminate, universalistic, spiritual Love. A patriarchal spiritual perspective perceives the sexual attractiveness of women as a temptation and women as temptresses, tools of the devil, distracting men from their duty and luring them away from the greatness that is their birthright, greatness through union with or service to the divine. Or else from this spiritual perspective men perceive women as chaste virgins (whose ultimate love is reserved for the spiritual Other) inspiring men to strive for some noble or spiritual ideal.

In the feminist model of erotic love as sociability each relates to the uniqueness of the other as spirited body, embodied spirit. The particularity of the other does *matter*, does make a difference. Woman is neither object nor subject; man is neither subject nor object. The relationship is not a relationship of subject to object (patriarchal love). Nor is it a relationship of object to object (patriarchal spiritual love). It is rather a relationship of subject-object to subject-object, sometimes stressing the subjectivity of self or other and at other times the objectivity of self or other.

In patriarchal relations the actors play institutionalized roles in which one party remains only object and the other only subject. The role-playing takes this rigid form because it is backed up by institutionalized force that upholds the superordination of one and the subordination of the other. Participants are *forced* to play these one-dimensional roles. Each party remains objectified and repressed by its fear of violence or force, including violence to the spirit through derision, humiliation, rejection and including the force of social pressure. This fear can coexist with feelings of erotic pleasure in being an object to a desired subject, as well as the erotic pleasure of regard or approbation from desired others in the community that such role-playing may bring.

These ways of socializing the person to accept fixed roles, and the oppression of the spirited body and embodied spirit that such role-playing entails, constitutes the *tradition* that supports patriarchal relations. Without such socialization, the subjectivity of the subordinate might insinuate itself into the relationship and incur the violent reaction of the superordinate. Hence the spiritual violence and social force that is *traditionally* employed in everyday life within patriarchal societies serves to protect the next generation from overstepping its bounds and engaging in potentially dangerous and self-destructive self-assertion, an assertion of the self as a *unique* thinking, feeling, desiring, acting, interest-ing person.

Playfulness and mutual pleasuring recede from such relations. The controlling subject becomes as incapable of playfulness as the object of his will. Without another subjectivity to respond in kind, playfulness becomes mere toying with the other – a kind of sadism.

An asymmetrical relationship of subject to object should not be considered an ahistorical natural relationship that undergoes transformation only under certain historical conditions. Rather, that kind of relationship seems to be the product in the West of patriarchal warrior society. The knightly societies of feudalism with their relatively isolated, autarchic household economies dependent on the pillaging and plundering of the warrior knight and the labor of peasants, servants, slaves and women remained unrestrained by interdependence and mutuality. Such societies produce and require patriarchal social relations.

Consider the following description of feudalism: "Almost everywhere the lord of the manor remains a brutal and rapacious cutthroat" (from Luchaire, cited by Elias, 1982, p. 71). Elias further recounts: "There is mistrust towards women, who are essentially objects of sensual satisfaction, delight in plundering and rape, desire to acknowledge no master, servility among the peasants on whom they live" (ibid., pp. 70, 71, 72). Also "[Wherever] a warrior class or a class of landed gentry has strongly influenced the overall behavior of society . . . forms of purely male social life with its specific eroticism and a certain eclipse of women, are to be found" (ibid., p. 80).

These patriarchal cultures undergo transformation in the civilizing process that occurs with the development of interdependence within the courts of the greater feudal lords and with the development of monetary interdependence in the towns. "As happens wherever men are forced to renounce physical violence [as occurred in the courts of the great lords to which many of the minor lords repaired themselves when their own resources proved inadequate], the social importance of women increased." Without the fear of violence, women could assert themselves as active, thinking, feeling, desiring subjects. "[It] was about women that the first circles of peaceful intellectual activity were established" (ibid., p. 81). These circles of intellectual activity around women were forms of erotic sociability, relations of mutual interest, interactions that make a pleasurable difference.

227

Vanity or love

In Weber's patriarchal model of social life, the hero must tame his soul by forcibly suppressing his own vanity, his desire for self-glorification, his desire for recognition, his desire in other words to be loved or esteemed. How does this notion of vanity differ from the desire that motivates sociable relations? In the feminist model of erotic love as sociability, the (passive) desire to be loved or found interesting or desirable by a particular other means that one (actively) values, desires or finds the other interesting. Conversely, that one (actively) values the other, means that one (passively) desires to be loved or esteemed by that other. To value the other is to value the other's judgment of oneself.

The more one desires to be esteemed by a particular other, the more the person will be concerned with learning about the other, learning how to please and not hurt the other and in this way winning the favor of the other and enjoying the other's pleasure. The giver of pleasure identifies with the pleasure of the other. Enjoying the other's pleasure enhances one's own pleasure. Hence each gets pleasure from giving pleasure to the other and each gets pleasure from the other's pleasure in giving pleasure to oneself. Although this may sound complicated it is the simple experience of mutual identification with each other's pleasure. Each one discovers his or her own pleasure mirrored and echoed in the other.

The pleasure of each can be enhanced by anticipating how that pleasure will bring pleasure to the other. Sharing my pleasure is a form of giving pleasure. In this way my pleasure is enhanced by the pleasure that the other takes in my pleasure. Similarly my distress is lightened when I can unburden myself to another who cares.

Achieving the recognition of another requires affecting the other, "moving" or "touching" the other, in other words making a difference, *mattering*. If I make a difference to the other, this means that the other recognizes me as someone who is "interesting." We all look to make some kind of difference in the world, to feel that our lives have significance, just as we look for things to make a difference to us, to feel that the world has meaning. Making a difference makes us feel both separate and connected. It makes us feel alive.

Vanity resembles desire for recognition, but for vanity it matters little from whom the recognition comes. The vain person imagines that qualities or achievements in themselves are sufficient for inspiring admiration and adoration. The vain one vainly believes that regard comes from one's being or one's accomplishments alone, not from one's way of relating and responding to the other(s).

The vain person turns indiscriminately to others for recognition. Vanity is indifferent to the particularity of the other. Being indifferent means that the other's difference does not make a difference which means that the other's pleasure is not pleasing or painful, the other's pain is not painful or pleasing. Because identification with the other is missing the other's pleasure in myself does not enhance my pleasure. Recognition by the other does not satisfy. The more a person needs and desires recognition and response from another without being able to recognize and respond to the needs and desires of the other, the more susceptible the person is to the flattery and manipulation of indiscriminate others and the less able to find satisfaction or enhanced pleasure. Consequently, the more the person will need to engage continually in external exploits and turn to external rewards as a source of pleasure and recognition in an unending search for pleasures and satisfactions that ultimately fail to please and satisfy.

The ethics of sociability

A feminine ethic of attachment and responsibility assumes a relative lack of power with a corresponding sense of vulnerability. A masculine ethic of independence and commitment (to a cause) assumes power over the environment and a sense of control.[3] Different from both the feminine and masculine ethics of responsibility, a feminist ethic of responsibility assumes the mutual power and mutual vulnerability that accompanies sociability. This mutuality derives from the desire of each for the other which makes them each vulnerable *and* powerful to the other. Feminine vulnerability comes from desiring union and surrendering oneself to the other; masculine power comes from desiring independence and withholding oneself from the other.

Although vulnerability is a form of weakness, it requires courage and strength to take the risk. Although independence is a form of strength, it deprives one of the pleasure and empowerment that comes from community. Desire assumes separateness, the separateness of the other with its own desires, interests, idea(s), ways, style, posture and body. Desire also assumes attachment, an emotional bond that ties one to the other, sensitizes one to the other and creates identification and empathy. Desire for another presupposes passion and produces compassion.

Sociability and ethics in this feminist model of social life are premised on erotic interest, an interest in the uniqueness of the other's embodied spirit or spirited body. A feminist ethic of responsibility that is inherent in this model of erotic love as sociability is expressed neither as self-determined, self-willed, independent action, masculine ethics, nor as compliant, submissive subservience, feminine ethics, but as both self-determined and compliant. Action would be determined on the basis of dialogue in which each of the parties expresses interest in understanding the other by expressly trying to draw out the other and by responding with care to the other's interests while also attempting to articulate his or her own interests. Acknowledgment of the views, feelings, needs and interests of each by the other and responding to these views, feelings, needs and interests constitutes a feminist ethic of responsibility.

Weber strongly suggests that ethics as a value needs to be replaced with that of rationality. He substitutes rules of the game for abstract ethical principles. One acts rationally by following the rules of the game (understanding the objective and the means for achieving that objective) which Weber calls the "ethic" of the particular sphere of life. This ethic is not the same as "ethics." Only with regard to personal relations do ethics *per se* constitute a rule of the game, but this rule applies to the private sphere and not the public sphere. As long as people act "rationally," as long as they follow the rules and logic of the game – striving for success as defined by the particular game, considering alternative moves available in the game and anticipating consequences – then concern for the effects on other(s), one's opponent(s), plays no part in determining action except in so far as the other's response to one's actions may have consequences that affect one's success.

A sociable form of life in contrast with Weber's adversarial form of life requires that one be sensitive to the effects of one's actions on the other, that one heed the other's speech, actions and feelings in every game, in every sphere of life. In other words, every game, whether in public or private life, must be subjected to the rule of sociability. If social life is premised on sociability and sociability on caring or the mutual display of caring, mutual attentiveness and responsiveness to each other's needs and feelings, then acting in an uncaring, unheeding, unsociable way is a betrayal of social life. One can be accused of being unsociable.

If sociability is the foundation of social life upon which co-operation and all forms of social relations rests, such an actor can be accused of acting irresponsibly. His or her actions threaten the very foundations of social life. Sociability requires mutual consideration, a balance among different needs and interests. However, arriving at a balance may be difficult, and once achieved the balance can be upset.

Injustice and renunciation

For a just social order, one committed to sociability, to be institutionalized, a self-conscious orientation to balance in social life, a recognition and responsiveness to both individuality and community, self and other(s), must become the core value to which institutions and their members are accountable. This means that procedures must be established for restoring balance. This requires the right to charge the institution or its members with unsociability, with indifference to a member's needs and interests or to the needs and interests of the whole. Both must be considered and balanced against each other. However, there is no static arrangement by which balance can be institutionalized or automatically restored. The balance that constitutes social justice is never static. The possibilities for both social justice and social injustice are inherent in sociability. Sociability is always a movement back and forth between assertions of power and feelings of vulnerability, between one's own interests and interest in the other(s).

When coercion and indifference, as opposed to sociability, are institutionalized through an impersonal administration of violence (patrimonial rule) or through the use of money (capitalism) and justified in ideology, then those who suffer have no recourse, they can expect no responsiveness or sense of responsibility from the powerful and indifferent other(s). The resulting sense of outrage, despair, meaninglessness and futility that comes from having one's participation in social life betrayed without hope of rectification, a sense of injustice, leads either to revolutionary sentiment or to self-blame – or a combination of both. With self-blame come attempts to overcome or compensate for one's weaknesses, mistakes or failures (the attempt to correct one's failings and compensate for them by correcting those "failings" in one's children), or it may lead to renunciation. In either case, the children become the victims and the carriers of the parents' feelings about themselves and the world (Miller, 1983).

Renunciation may take one of several forms. One may simply renounce or lose all desire (succumbing to a life of routine without meaning or pleasure). One may detach oneself from others, cultivate one's own power and strive after the possession of things that cannot betray, placing the personal, separate, individual self and well-being above all else or one can teach this mode of survival to one's children. However, the sense of futility that results from the pursuit of power and things as substitutes for mutual pleasuring, and the sense of despair that follows, may lead to the substitution of some impersonal ideal for personal material things, or substitution of attachment to a spiritual Other for unsatisfying material attachments.

This then raises the problem to a different level – how to account for undeserved suffering in an unjust world created by an omniscient and loving Other. Weber claims that there are three logically consistent answers to this problem: predestination, dualism, and the most complete formal solution, *karma* (Weber, [1921–2] 1978, pp. 522–5). In order to find meaning in a loveless world without turning to an external purely spiritual source of love and meaning, one must replace attachment to others and things with attachment to an idea(l). That is Weber's solution to the problem of meaninglessness that derives from undeserved suffering caused by human indifference.

Weber never considers the possibility of a society that is revolutionized not in the name of brotherly love (which he does consider and dismisses) but in the name of erotic love in the sense of sociability, a society committed to transforming and continually reforming the state into a sociable community. The possibility of a social order based on the principles of sociability presupposes a social world in which ethical irrationality, social injustice, is not an institutionalized and irremediable feature but merely a recurrent possibility that can be anticipated and challenged.

In this feminist model of erotic love as sociability, violence and power are but one side of social life; desire and interest in others is the other side. However, violence and power are only the other side of desire and interest; the former ultimately prove meaningful only as a means for achieving some sociable end such as recognition, the protection, promotion and prestige of culture or the economic well-being of a nation.

Weber's patriarchal thought fails to value sociability. It rules out a world in which the life of the individual takes on meaning and is enhanced by both identification with and differentiation from, affirmation of and resistance to, others. In short, for Weber, such a world of attachments and separateness is not real. Weber's realism requires a renunciation of attachments, a presumption of injustice – ethical irrationality.

Communion and the problem of difference

Weber does acknowledge, wonderingly, that in the erotic love relationship "is displayed the unique meaning which one creature in his irrationality has for another" (Weber, 1946, p. 347). We see here a change of great magnitude in Weber's own view. In his essay on politics he refers to the worthlessness of the creature and hence the necessity of serving some cause outside the self. Here he refers to the unique meaning that one creature can have for another. Having discovered erotic love, the meaninglessness of life and its irrationality no longer has to be overcome.[4] Instead, a life which is meaningless and irrational in itself takes on unique meaning in relation to another. This is a remarkable admission for one who champions a heroic life as the only one worth living, the only one that provides meaning. Although he has not discovered in erotic love an alternative model for a meaningful world, Weber has discovered in the communion of erotic love an alternative to the warrior ethic as a source of meaning in life.

But communion cannot preserve the uniqueness of the other. A feminist perspective recognizes that in order for each to have unique meaning for the other, each must retain his or her difference and not merge with the other. Weber's patriarchal perspective romanticizes erotic love as a communion, a fading of the thou, but does not acknowledge the other side, the necessary preservation of the thou in order that there be a thou that can affirm the self and give meaning to life.

Nevertheless, Weber acknowledges the conflict and domination inherent in relationships of erotic love. Within patriarchal relationships of erotic love, the mutual devotion of the lovers serves to mystify and legitimize the domination and submission that occurs. Patriarchal relationships of erotic love do not self-consciously acknowledge the need for both mutual resistance and mutual affirmation. Instead, as Weber so astutely observes, they profess a "devotion" that conceals domination. Weber presents erotic love as either a relationship of domination (imposing of will or desire on one side, surrender on the other) or one of communion (mutual desire and mutual surrender). Patriarchal relationships of erotic love give rise to an extremely romanticized view of erotic love as communion and a thoroughly cynical view of erotic love as coercion. Weber holds both. He never accomplishes an integration or reconciliation among these alternatives. Yet he prides himself on his realism.

Weber seems to assume that the experience of communion can be maintained as a prolonged moment. On the other hand he recognizes that the ecstatic experience of erotic love as it occurs in extramarital affairs (which offer an escape from the rational routinized everyday life that gives to erotic love its heightened value in the modern world) can occur only outside of ordinary life and hence cannot be maintained as part of an on-going everyday life.[5] Unlike a feminist view of erotic love, Weber does not see the communion of erotic love as a moment within a movement from communion to differentiation, from attachment to separation and back again within the same relationship.

There is a certain amount of tension between maintaining difference, one's own soul or integrity, the expression of one's own desire or interest, and the "boundless giving" of oneself to the other, the devotion and surrender of the soul. Affirmation of one's difference can only be won; it cannot be coerced. It can be won only when the other is not threatened by the difference. For this reason a show of reassurance, of respect and affirmation of the other's difference, must accompany a display of difference or separateness, different interests or other attachments. In games of sport, this may be a handshake, a comment of "good game," a refusal to indulge in emotional outbursts of gloating or anger which would indicate that one was taking the game too seriously, transforming the contest into a conflict. The aim is to reassure the other that asserting one's difference does not entail dominating or humiliating the other.

In relationships of mutual regard and mutual respect the partners reassure each other that each is valued and that neither wants to make the other into an extension of the self. This requires making certain that neither party dominates or coerces the other or feels suppressed or humiliated by the other. Each must reassure the other by acknowledging and affirming the other when expressing one's difference or when expressing one's devotion. Just as contestants in

233

sporting contests may more or less comply with the rules of the game which include rules of courtesy, conventions of good sportsmanship, people in everyday life may more or less comply with the rules of courtesy and conventions of respect. Greater or lesser compliance produces either games of good will or those that resemble combat more than contest. These rules and conventions reduce the threat that arises with expressions of detachment and desire and with expression of attachment and devotion. Sociability requires a balance between interest and pleasure in the other and separate interests and pleasures.[6]

In discovering erotic love, Weber has discovered that life can have value in itself and that life in itself can be a value. This means that not just an impersonal cause, but a personal one, relationships to other human beings, may give meaning and value to life. He has learned that life can have meaning without having to be rationally directed as an instrument for achieving some goal and without having to require continuous self-discipline, detachment, and distance from things and people. Although, rather late, he discovered the value of erotic love in giving meaning to life and inspiring creativity, Weber never integrated that knowledge into his social or political thought, his theory of social life. Mitzman suggests that had Weber lived longer, this might have happened. On the basis of both his one-sided romanticization of communion and the ambivalence contained in the essay where he acknowledges the value of erotic love[7] – his stress on the incompatibility of politics and economics with love – I am skeptical.

The meaningfulness experienced in sociability and the ecstasy of erotic love can substitute for *both* the meaningfulness of a rational life directed toward the achievement of some external cause – asceticism – *and* the ecstasy of a life that is at peace with and one with all others, the All Other, the All One – mysticism. Erotic love as sociability can substitute for both because it acknowledges, affirms and includes both individual striving and communal surrender. Weber never considers this because he never considers sociability as such. Both asceticism and mysticism as Weber describes them produce dualistic worlds of body and spirit, requiring an unending one-sided struggle again desire and the temptation of material things. Mysticism resembles the patriarchal version of erotic love as communion, a one-sided, unitary vision. Similarly, asceticism resembles the patriarchal version of heroic greatness as human detachment, another one-sided unitary conception. A feminist spirituality affirms both body and spirit, just as a feminist model of erotic love affirms both attachment and detachment, striving and surrender, as two sides of one whole.[8]

Only within community can differences create the pleasures that come from desire and contest. Without community, differences create conflicts that may involve some of the pleasures of contest but that also involve the violence of combat. The latter tends to extinguish the pleasures of contest – at least for the vanquished if not for the victors. The pain of combat becomes confused with the pleasures of contest by a warrior hero who substitutes for mutual erotic love a lady's approbation, who substitutes for sociable community the greatness of a national community.

The tensions between independent self-determination (individual differences, self-affirmation) and commitment to the relationship (communal identity, mutual surrender) is a real tension. Making choices, decisions and determinations that are good for the self often causes tension in relating to other(s). This tension occurs either because a divergence in goals and interests takes people in separate directions and therefore threatens the relationship, or because the realization of one's interests conflicts directly with the realization of the other's.

Conflict and community

Given human differences and the finitude of space and resources, including that of time, there are likely to be conflicts over these. There is always a movement back and forth from concern for one's own separate needs to concern for the needs of the relationship, from desire for independence to desire for attachment and back again. The notion of balance involves no end-state.

In the feminist model of erotic love and society as sociability there may be conflict and dynamism but it is one in which each side tries to assert itself without eliminating the possibility of community. In the patriarchal model of erotic love and society as conflict and coercion, struggle ends with the victor trying to eliminate the possibility of future conflict by creating an end-state without movement, a monistic world of domination and submission, a repressed and repressive state with neither ecstasy nor agony.

A feminist model of erotic love and society as sociability is not a utopian model of love and good feeling. Violence can occur within the relationship of erotic love when one betrays the trust of another and destroys the grounds of the relationship. A sociable relationship requires on-going displays of good faith, the resolving of differences, the proving of good will. In order to minimize the dangers, the frictions and the negative passions provoked by these sensitive interpersonal dynamics, there must be as much space and resources for each of the parties as possible. The fewer resources that have to be shared, the fewer the sources of conflict, but also the fewer the interests in common.

Unlike the feminist model of sociability, the patriarchal model of "rational" reciprocal use of each by the other for reciprocal benefit does not provide any means for resolving conflicts of interest. In this unsociable model of social life the eruption of conflict can be resolved only through the use or threat of violence and hence a reversion to a coercive world order in which

235

strength dominates. In contrast, mutual commitment to sociable community or communion makes possible the resolution of conflict through the renunciation of power. The renunciation proves one's commitment, one's sincerity, one's trustworthiness. Only a form of life based on commitment to sociable community can obviate relations of domination and submission, egoism and altruism.

When conflicts of interest arise, they would have to be resolved responsibly. This means each must be responsive to the other's needs. There must be attempts for both sides to understand what the sacrifice to the other entails. Whoever's interests did ultimately prevail would not feel triumphant but sad over the cost to the other and determined to make it up in another way. And the side who sacrificed would not feel that they lost, but would feel that they were doing some good for the other (as well as feeling sad about the sacrifice), and would trust that at another time the other would do the same for them.

On the macro-level of society erotic interest in others takes the form of interest in different cultures or peoples, a desire for and commitment to a community of separate and different interests, independent and interdependent peoples and nation states. An international community involves the same frictions, the same movement back and forth between independence and dependence, attachment and separation, identification and diversification, empowerment and surrender of power.

Community requires an interplay between shared collective identity and divergent individual identities. A patriarchal perspective sees only unitary community or adversarial society.[9] For Weber difference and diversity mean conflict (which includes peaceful competition and compromise as well as coercion and violence) not community, just as community means a subjectively shared sense of belonging together as a unit, a commitment to some common cause or identity, an absence of diversity, difference and erotic interest.

Weber also describes the associative relationship which rests on "rationally motivated agreement" or "rationally motivated adjustment of interests" and which often consists in "compromises between rival interests." Weber's distinction between communal and associative relationships[10] resembles the distinction I make between sharing a common interest and sustaining individual interests. However, Weber makes a characteristic pronouncement that distinguishes his understanding from my own. He asserts that with the associative relationship "outside the area of compromise, the conflict of interests, with its attendant competition for supremacy, remains unchanged." Like the model of adversarial democracy, associative relations are constrained only by rational self-interest.

Weber acknowledges that conflict can be contained by rationally motivated compromise, but not by rationally motivated self-conscious desire for community. Similarly he acknowledges that, within community, self-interest

236

often operates. However, self-interest within community does not result in the mutual enhancement of individuality and hence of the relationship, rather it results in coercion. He reports that the members of a communal relationship such as a family group may "exploit the relationship for their own ends." Although "the communal type of relationship is, according to the usual interpretation of its subjective meaning, the most radical antithesis of conflict, [this] should not, however, be allowed to obscure the fact that coercion of all sorts is a very common thing in even the most intimate of such communal relationships if one party is weaker in character than the other" (Weber, [1921–2] 1978, pp. 40–2). In other words, if one party is unable to articulate and stand up for his or her own interests, she or he will end up being coerced by the other.

Weber does not investigate the circumstances that produce people with "weak character," people who are unable to give voice to and stand up for their own interests. Nor does he explore how communal relationships could maintain their communal character if both parties are able to stand up for their interests. Must the relationship change into an associative one in which compromise occurs, while outside the compromise the conflict of interests, with its attendant competition for supremacy, remains unchanged?

Weber recognizes that rational associative relationships can give rise to sentiments and that community can give rise to conflict. "Conflict and communal relationships are relative concepts" (ibid., p. 42). For Weber, there is either coercion or there is identity of interests, either conflict or community, and each can shade into the other.

Weber does not discuss the possibility of renouncing power, of surrendering one's self to the other, one's interests to the other's interests, out of desire for the pleasure that one gets from the pleasure of the other. For Weber, conflict is resolved if not by coercion then by "rationally motivated agreement or rationally motivated adjustment of interests." Unfortunately his notion of rational motivation does not include aesthetic and erotic desires for sociability.

A feminist perspective

In Weber's patriarchal perspective the only value is individual autonomy, mastery and control, and the only warrant for that value is an impersonal cause or the aesthetic appeal of that lifestyle. In a feminist perspective the ultimate value is life itself, and the warrant of that value is other lives. Hence the community of human life is the ultimate warrant of all value. In other words, any particular life has meaning and value in itself as body, spirit and mind only in relation to other lives and to the human community. Only in and through relationships, community and humanity, does life itself have meaning. This realization distinguishes women's traditional practical values (the values that are embedded in the traditional practices of women's everyday lives) from men's. Nevertheless, women's traditional feminine values or those ascribed to or associated with femininity and women, the value of devotion to persons, the serving and nurturing of the life of another with all that entails, is similarly one-sided.

Only when some idea, interest or passion that gives direction or uniqueness to one's own life, separate from the life of another, is nurtured, developed, recognized and affirmed – empowered – can the individual be both subject and object of a relationship with another, capable of both affirming and being affirmed, of both realizing her own value, her full humanity and contributing to the human community and of appreciating the unique value and contribution of other(s) and promoting their full humanity.

Erotic interest creates sociability as mutual empowering and mutual pleasuring through the playful move back and forth between assertion of difference and surrender to oneness, an on-going conversation of self-assertion and self-surrender among individuals, communities and nations. A feminist model of society as sociable community explicitly recognizes a tragic side to social life, that tensions, repression, and differences are inevitable. But the same feminist model recognizes also a triumphant side, that reflection, collective struggle and erotic interest are also inevitable. Reflection makes it possible to recognize the sources of tension; collective struggle makes it possible to overcome repression; and erotic interest makes it possible to reconcile differences and be ironic and playful about them.

Notes

1 Here and in what follows I use the words "affect" and "affective," as opposed to "effect" and "effective," to convey the sense that the effect we are talking about occurs with respect to affect.

2 I have adopted the idea of primary and secondary modes of relating from Lynn Chancer (1988).

3 I draw here not just on Gilligan's (1982) work which suggests this difference, but on the cultural associations of femininity with compassion and care for the vulnerable and of masculinity with integrity and respect for independence.

4 Max Weber is reputed to have had an affair with Else Jaffe which, because of his marriage to Marianne, must have caused him inner conflict and which appears to have influenced his thought. His article, "Religious Rejections of the World and their Directions," in which he discusses the clash between brotherly love and the other life orders, contains Weber's most mature writings on erotic love. The latest version of this article (he wrote several revisions) he gave to Else Jaffe, who was responsible for its ultimately getting published.

5 It should be noted that Weber's extramarital relationship challenged the views that he had enunciated so strongly before about the value of marital fidelity and the unethical character of extramarital affairs (Thomas, 1985).

6 Ferguson refers to a similar interplay between defining a situation for oneself (freedom and individuality) and taking the role of the other (compassion and community).
7 The essay in question is, of course, "Religious Rejections of the World and their Direction" (1946, pp. 323–59).
8 Starhawk's work represents a leading example of feminist spirituality.
9 These concepts come from Jane Mansbridge's work, *Beyond Adversary Democracy*.
10 Weber defines community and association in *Economy and Society*, Vol. 1, pp. 40–2.

15

Women's world:
an alternative rationality

Erotic love as sociability is elaborated in everyday life through the practices of women in the domestic sphere. The practices that constitute the reality of women's domestic world include: the recreation of community, homemaking, childraising and intimate friendship. I stress here the aesthetic and rational nature of these practices. I equate aesthetic rationality with female rationality and equate both of these with domestic rationality. I explain each of these below.

Aesthetic rationality, aesthetic practices

Aesthetic rationality is the kind of thinking necessary for accomplishing the objectives of domestic and private life as opposed to calculating rationality which is necessary for success in market and political life. Aesthetic rationality, the kind of thinking necessary for domestic sociability, is essential (although not sufficient), I will argue, to a fully rational way of life.

By aesthetic I mean appreciative of and responsive to beauty – not just visual beauty, but anything that affects the senses and enriches our lives internally. Beauty refers to something whose presence attracts our attention and affects our feelings in a way that we deem desirable; hence there is a subjective element. Beauty refers to the power of a thing to affect our feelings not by what it does but by how it does it. The affect comes from the play or interplay of its elements or features. Beauty is erotic because it is the affect of one body (some objective thing) on another body (a subjective, human, feeling being).

Rationality refers to thinking that makes sense in light of some objective and that does not refute itself or undermine its objective. Aesthetic rationality joins together mind and body, thinking and feeling, intellect and senses. By aesthetic rationality I mean thinking that aims at re-creating beauty in our everyday world, re-creating a world that attracts and affects us, a world that re-creates, enriches and empowers us.

Aesthetic practices refer to those practices that re-create our world and ourselves in this way. These practices, of course, are not limited to women, but they are inherent in the work that women do in the home. Feminist spiritualists[1] and others have explicitly developed aesthetic practices that inspire and empower people, helping people to get in touch with what gives them pleasure and power. From colors to music to imagination, these powers can be called on to affect our spirits and sometimes heal our bodies. Discovering this inner power requires getting to know ourselves, getting to know how we feel about things in our everyday lives, what meaning our dis-ease has for us, and what things make us feel good. Through exercises or rituals involving movement, touch, song, these spiritualists and healers bring together sensual modes of being and relating to the world which modern life tends to suppress and replace with cognitive, calculative thinking. Through these methods, people are helped to get to know themselves and their world in a way that is not primarily cognitive. It is knowing in a holistic way that involves all the faculties and senses.

The magic that such feminist (and other) spiritualists and healers do (and they often refer to their work as magic) is a magic that brings people more in touch with all of themselves so that they can live more fully and feel more fully alive, a magic most often associated with women and female practices of everyday life – including such mundane, everyday practices as preparing meals in ways that appeal, tending to the body in physically sensitive ways, decorating a room to create a particular atmosphere, invoking memories and symbols that are specific to a person's life, using music, lighting and colors to create a mood that can affect the spirit. Feminists who develop practices for empowering women and helping women to get in touch with themselves and get to know themselves in ways that are not primarily or solely cognitive are often considered witches, dangerous women capable of stirring up trouble – not only because of what they say and do (magic), but because of how they say and do it, their outrageous sense of inner power.

Repression and oppression

Just as the modern world separates household and firm, producing a public world of production and circulation and a private world of reproduction and consumption, it also produces a corresponding split between male practices and female practices and between what I call male (cognitive) rationality[2] and female (aesthetic) rationality. Often unnoticed is that the relationship between the two worlds is one of repression.

The private sphere of life traditionally has been the domain of women; public repression of the private realm implies the repression of women and the repression of the mode of rational action that characterizes life in the private sphere and that is associated with women.

241

Weber's conception of rationality is based on (psychological and intellectual) repression of female rationality, just as public life is based on (political and economic) repression of private life. This repression entails oppression as well. As with all repression, that which does the repressing fails to recognize or confirm the other and thus conceives of itself as autonomous and independent of the other – while it lives off the labor of the other. It, therefore, constitutes a one-sided, distorted, self-contradictory, repressive and oppressive form of life. Repression requires force or energy expended in denying the other while simultaneously assuming the other – and the work that the other does for the one that is repressing. Repression and oppression ultimately rest on fear of violence to the spirit or to the body.

Our very conception of what it is to be a man, to engage in men's activity and to do it in a manly way presupposes repression: a certain conception of and relationship to women, a relationship in which women are expected to fulfill men's personal and domestic needs, needs which are then not recognized as essential to being a man. If anything they are viewed as weaknesses, needs that actors in the public world, men, ought not to take seriously. The very existence of the public world as we know it, and of man who is defined in terms of that world, presupposes, yet denies that it presupposes, the private world and the kind of person, woman, who is defined in terms of that world. This is not the same as saying that the two are separate and complementary. Rather they are forcibly divided and the division is maintained by repression.

The relationship of public to private, man to woman, is an internal relationship; each is essential to the other. Nevertheless, the public sphere denies that which it requires; it treats the private sphere as other and itself as independent just as man treats woman as other and himself as independent. Marx makes a similar analysis of capital. Capital treats labor as other and itself as independent. These relationships are repressive ones, and the consciousness that the public world has of itself, that man has of himself and that capital has of itself are repressive consciousnesses, self-denying and hence self-deluding consciousnesses, false consciousnesses, forms of ideology.

The present work challenges the taken-for-granted acceptance of Weber's conception of rationality and rational action. That Weber's formulation has not been challenged or questioned but accepted in a taken-for-granted manner as merely a description and not a formulation reveals a good deal not only about the state of modern social theory but about the nature of modern social life.[3]

Re-creation of community

Rational action for Weber is action that is freed from the constraints of tradition and community. To the extent that women live their lives within the family,

242

neighborhood and community, women's lives are subject to the surveillance and constraints of community and tradition that are typical of family, neighborhood and community life. The money economy does promote "rational" action on the part of domestic women with regard to managing the household economy. However, women often remain the (re)producers of community – of tradition, customs and convention, as well as of human beings. Women become informal creators and enforcers of tradition, custom and convention, informally meting out sanctions to those who transgress.

Although community has a negative, constraining, restricting, sanctioning dimension, it also has a positive, liberating, empowering, celebratory dimension. It is through community that individuals are able to lose themselves and discover themselves anew, to recreate themselves as social beings, members of something larger than themselves. Women's activities within neighborhood communities recreate the human being as a social being who is integrated within a larger social order. In their everyday work of recreating home and family life, women create informal social networks. They talk with each other about the exigencies of everyday life and learn from each other essential information for coping with a common environment.[4]

Discovering common problems and learning from each other's experience liberates people from a sense of isolated individuality. Through sharing information that is vital for surviving the contingencies of everyday life, they empower each other. Finally, through community events, they celebrate and recreate themselves as people with something in common – their common life within a shared socio-physical environment. It is through community that traditions are created and re-created, as people develop ways in common for surviving and re-creating their world.

However, women today have been loosening their ties to community and tradition and becoming more mobile. To the extent that women are freeing themselves from community, community itself ceases to be so constraining and restrictive. That is, community becomes weaker. In part this liberation from community on the part of women is a result of urbanization and a transformed economy that demands a certain amount of mobility. In part it is a result of women's continuing education and their continuing in the labor force during childbearing and childraising years when earlier generations of women were confined to home and community. Their ties to community become less extensive and less intensive. In place of the constraints of community, they now face the constraints of the workplace: domination by the boss and exploitation by capital.[5]

Nevertheless, women also retain primary responsibility for childcare and housework. What reveals Weber's rational actor as male is that women must, I contend, employ a mode of rational action in the private realm that is not encompassed by Weber's two concepts of rational action: calculating and technically rational action aimed at achieving some goal, exemplified by

243

business practices and politics; and ethically rational, value-rational action aimed at manifesting one's values, exemplified by living according to some absolute (religious, for instance) principle.

Although Weber argued for the historical significance of the separation of firm and household, he failed to recognize the repression and oppression that creates this separation. Weber largely ignored the fact that public life as it is structured by modern political and economic realities is founded on the repression and oppression of another sphere of life with another mode of rationality. I use the term "repression" here in its political as well as psychoanalytic sense. The public life of political and market realities and relations simultaneously creates and represses the private life of home, family and personal relations, the reality of women's domestic world with its own practices and relationships.

Excursus on terms

Because the public world with its mode of rational action has traditionally been run by men, and the private world with its mode of rational action by women, I call the two modes of rational action "male rationality" and "female rationality." I use the term "male" rationality as distinct from "masculine" rationality. I employ this distinction following a similar one between female and feminine (both of which differ from feminist), suggested by Keohane, Rosaldo and Gelpi (1982, pp. vii–xii). Male rationality refers to modes of consciousness and action that are associated with the public world of men's lives but not to the emphasis on physical strength or dominance or physical difference from women. The latter aspects I designate as "masculine." Similarly, I use female rationality to refer to those modes of consciousness and action that are associated with the private world of women's lives but not to physical weakness, subservience or physical difference from men. The latter I designate as "femininity."

This may seem like a strange reversal of the traditional feminist distinction between male and masculine, female and feminine. Traditionally feminists have distinguished between sex, such as maleness and femaleness, and gender – masculinity and femininity – claiming that the first is biological and the second social. Following Keohane *et al*, I prefer to use the term "feminine" to refer to the characteristics of women's lives that derive from a direct relationship to men and the term "female" to refer to those characteristics of women's lives that derive from women's own distinctive activities in their own realm, their experiences as active subjects or agents of their own world.

Although I distinguish between female modes of action and consciousness and feminine modes, between male modes and masculine ones, the distinction is a fluid one. As other feminists have claimed, the distinction between physical differences and social ones (sex and gender) cannot be sustained.[6] I employ the distinction at the outset of my analysis, however, because "feminine" resonates with aspects of sexuality (particularly heterosexuality) and subservience, elements that are not so salient to "female," at least not at the outset.

A similar distinction applies to the differences between "masculine" and "male," with the former suggesting force or violence, the display and celebration of physical strength and muscle power. David and Brannon (1976) provide a useful summary of the four elements that constitute masculinity in our culture. The first is an aura of violence, aggression and daring. Another is an air of strength and toughness, including confidence and self-reliance. The others include success, status and the need to be looked up to and the stigma of anything vaguely feminine, including openness and vulnerability. Doyle (1983) adds to the four elements of David and Brannon a fifth, the sexual, with masculinity associated with sexual "conquest," sexual initiation and control.

I defend the distinction I make between "male" and "masculine," "female" and "feminine" by reference to common American usage. The sexual difference associated with the terms "male" and "female," and the differences that these imply regarding reproductive capacities, generally extend to and are used to refer to a *social* division of labor that treats childcare, for instance, as women's work or female work. The "masculine/feminine" distinction, in contrast, tends to refer to differences regarding behavior or attributes that are socially defined (male defined and heterosexually defined) as *sexually attractive* or appealing in one sex but not in the other.

Thus, as I understand it, "feminine" refers to qualities or behaviors that are considered by patriarchal society to be desirable in women and attractive to men. The term "masculine" refers less to behaviors or qualities that are considered attractive *by women* than to behaviors or qualities that are considered *by men* to be desirable for men and attractive to women. Women are assumed to desire strong, powerful men. In a patriarchal world that accords women little power, this assumption is likely to be true. Both "masculinity" and "femininity" are patriarchal categories. They presuppose a world of male domination, power and superiority and female subordination, powerlessness and inferiority. These patriarchal categories deny the fluidity, ambiguity and open possibilities of human behavior. They serve to fix and limit human possibilities. In so doing they assume and require repression.

Through my analysis I show how male rationality (a mode of consciousness and action associated with the public world of politics and economics) turns out to be masculine, how instrumental and value rationality turn out to presuppose and require physical force and the ability to impose one's will on others.[7] Similarly, my analysis will show how female rationality (a mode of consciousness and action associated with the private world of home and family) is feminine; that female rationality turns out to presuppose and require relations of dependence and subordination.

I reserve the term "feminist" for consciousness and action that is aware of and opposes the repression of female modes of consciousness and action as well as opposes the political repression and oppression of women, "the pervasive patterns of subordination, limitation and confinement that have hampered and crippled the development of the female half of humankind" (Keohane, Rosaldo and Gelpi, 1982, p. x). As indicated earlier, feminist rationality requires reflection and contemplation, a questioning of the taken for granted. I include also under "feminist" those modes of consciousness and action that affirm the strengths (defined by male culture as weaknesses) of female consciousness and action, that reject the weaknesses of feminine consciousness and action and that oppose and expose the weaknesses (defined by male culture as strengths) of male consciousness and action. In other words I mean, by feminist, speaking up on behalf of a repressed female voice.

This means challenging the male definition of reality, including definitions of rationality and irrationality, weakness and strength. It means challenging the repressive male voice. In parallel fashion, I would define as "masculinist" those modes of consciousness and action that affirm the (male-defined) strengths of male ways and oppose the (male-defined) weaknessses of female ways while relegating them to women. Jessica Benjamin provides a nice summary of a feminist perspective: "to redeem what has been devalued in women's domain, to conquer the territory that has been reserved to men, and to resolve and transcend the opposition between these spheres by reformulating the relationship between them" (1986, p. 78).

I do not attribute the difference in what I call male and female rationality to some inherent feature of male or female biological constitution, but consider the difference in rationality to be grounded in the different worlds that men and women inhabit and reproduce. However, a key feature of these different worlds is their relationship to each other. In order to understand male rationality one must understand the nature of the public world and its relationship to the private world.

Repression of female practice

The segregation of public and private has enormous consequences. One is fear by the public sphere of contamination by the private sphere. Repression always involves fear. There is a fear of being childish or womanly rather than adult and manly, a fear that the personal feelings and sympathies that motivate private life might enter into and corrupt the public, impersonal mode of "tough-minded," "rational" action and deliberation. There is the fear that the particularism of the private sphere (considering the particular needs, feelings and interests of particular individuals) will corrupt and sabotage the universalism of the public sphere (considering only abstract universal principles or criteria without concern for particularities that could introduce bias or prejudice, sympathy or antipathy).

To be "rational," according to Weber's definition, one must set aside one's personal feelings. Rational action is explicitly defined as not emotional action. Emotions interfere with rational deliberation over the most effective way to realize one's ends. Similarly, one must set aside personal ties and sentiment in order to be rational. One must, instead, employ universalistic criteria or principles. Only then can action be rational, free from "irrational" forces and constraints. This conception of rationality presumes a goal or end that is independent of the individual's own feelings. In other words the end is external to the person. The end cannot be a subjective state, a sense of well-being, but something objective – something tangible outside of the self.

The dialectic of repression

We can better see the limits of male rationality by contrasting it with female rationality. Out of the contrast and opposition between these two modes of rationality, we can better understand the limits and the possibilities of each. This new understanding is accomplished by resisting and challenging, from a woman-centered perspective, the Weberian formulation of "rational." I will focus on essential practices of social life that Weber excludes from his conception of rationality.

These essential practices of social life, associated with women and the private sphere, are discarded by Weber as "irrational" or remain undeveloped theoretically. They include feelings, the development and maintenance of personal relationships, and the reproduction of human life, culture and community. Weber's "theory" of rational action constitutes an ideology of a repressive form of life. Because in practice these essential aspects of social life cannot be excluded, yet in theory they must be excluded for the action to qualify as "rational," the theoretical formulation of rational action functions as ideology: it is a cover for repression.

The repression is not simply a matter of forgetting or of mental denial. The repression is *essential* to male "rational" action and modern "rationalized" society. The problem is not simply a theoretical problem in conceptualization, but a practical problem of social life and its organization. Modern society and "rational" action require repression.

One theory of repression holds that a repressive form of life produces its own self-destruction; it produces its own gravediggers. From a Freudian psychoanalytic perspective what is repressed exerts an opposing and counteracting pressure. The pressure of the repressed for release gets expressed in the form of symptoms and crises. The Hegelian-Marxist perspective is similar. The contradictions inherent in the repression result in an internally conflicted form of life, a self-denying form of life.

The struggle of opposing forces (the clash between thesis and antithesis, the contradiction between what is posed or posited and the opposed or opposite, the struggle between repressor and repressed) makes possible but not inevitable a new form, a synthesis. The pressure for release or recognition of what is being suppressed or denied, but which exists nevertheless and is essential, takes the form of symptoms, contradictions, conflicts and crises.

By resisting and opposing from a woman-centered perspective the given definition of the rational, we arrive at a new understanding of rationality, an understanding that includes the irrational (responsiveness to feelings), as part of the rational, and an understanding that the one-sidedly rational by itself is irrational. With this dialectical analysis, we achieve a more transcendent, synthetic, rational and self-conscious conception: transcendent because it recognizes the need to go beyond the limits of each of the opposing versions, synthetic because it recognizes that each includes the other within itself, rational because it is not self-contradictory, and self-conscious because the experience of mutual recognition of the two opposing forms provides a heightened sense of each (of each one's limits and possibilities) as opposed to the illusory sense that each one has of itself (as the whole). Whereas mutual recognition makes for self-consciousness, repression makes for one-sided, distorted or false consciousness.

The public sphere is associated with a mind that is uncontaminated by the "irrational" impulses of the body; the public actor, especially as defined by Weber in his conception of the ideal politician, is a curiously disembodied actor. The private sphere is associated with the body – a form of life that must be transcended by men and and left to women and children. The actor of the private sphere responds to his or her own private sensations and impulses (including emotions).

The public sphere defines itself and its mode of deliberation and action as superior. From the perspective of masculine rationality the lives of women and children are inferior because they cannot transcend the body and the private sphere. However, the assumption of superiority is not simply a matter of definition. The superiority is grounded in the actual material relations between the private sphere and the public sphere. The private sphere is controlled and dominated by the public. The latter monopolizes the means of production (capital) and the means of administration (bureaucracy). The private sphere is deprived of the capacity for sustaining itself.

The public sphere keeps the private sphere dependent and relatively helpless at the same time that it relegates to the private sphere tasks of maintenance and sustenance without which the public sphere could not exist. The relationship is not one of responsiveness and mutuality, but repression and domination, which gives rise to both accommodation and resistance, and, when the resistance is self-conscious, to feminism.

Dimensions of domestic life and female rationality

I call female rationality the rationality that characterizes the domestic sphere as that sphere has developed with the separation of business from household, and political administration from kinship and personal ties. Female rational action, the rationality of home, family and personal relationships, is personified by the traditional middle-class woman defined as homemaker, mother and wife. This mode of rationality always presumes an orientation to particular concrete human relations, not universal abstract principles or convictions.

The female perspective makes for a different kind of actor with a different version of rational action. In order to understand the female version of rationality, we must examine the context to which it applies and from which it derives. In other words, it is not something that comes from women's nature that can be described in the abstract apart from the conditions that give rise to it. Weber, in contrast, treats what he calls rational action as natural, just as emotional and habitual action are considered natural. Historical social conditions (such as the traditions and world view of the West or the East) merely facilitate or obstruct the actualization of this "natural" mode. I argue that the very conception of rational action as separate from and independent of feelings and embeddedness in community and its traditions comes from a historical sundering of social life into private and public domains.

HOMEMAKING

A central dimension of the private domain is homemaking, the desire to remake or re-create a part of the world as one's own. Such re-creation transforms the alien and disturbing, unknown and unpredictable, disordered and threatening, unsettled and distressing experience of nature into the known and familiar, settled and secure, ordered and harmonious, comfortable and pleasurable. To make oneself at home in the world by making a home out of the world may be thought of as self-consciously and intentionally non-alienating activity.

I distinguish here between homemaking and housekeeping. Housekeeping refers to on-going maintenance based on the realization that nothing stays the same; things deteriorate; the order created must continually be reachieved.

Unlike instrumental, technical action, homemaking is not engaged in as a means toward some external end. Three major objectives *intrinsic* to homemaking are *security*, *comfort* and *pleasure*. Unlike abstract values that characterize male rationality such as honor, duty or courage, the ideals of homemaking cannot be realized without a concern for the body and spirit of both self and other.

Actions in the name of homemaking that make others in the home feel upset, disturbed or distressed, directly and immediately undermine one's own feelings of security, comfort and pleasure as long as the others remain in the home, and hence cannot qualify as successful homemaking. In contrast, to achieve honor, duty or courage requires that the action meet only one's own or some abstract ideal standards or objective to qualify as such; the feelings of particular, concrete others are irrelevant, and so are one's own feelings and one's own body. Renunciation as opposed to responsiveness is necessary and essential.

I conceive of the female mode of rationality neither as value rationality in Weber's sense (striving to live according to some value regardless of consequences) nor as instrumental, calculating, technical rationality (concern with achieving success without concern for values). Rather, I conceive of female rationality as aesthetic rationality, a concept that holds promise of providing an alternative holistic notion of rationality, in contrast to Weber's dualistic notion. Weber's notion of value rationality in which beauty becomes the absolute value seems to resemble my notion of aesthetic rationality. However, for Weber, beauty becomes an abstract, individualistic value. A relationship with others is not intrinsic to the determination or experience of beauty. According to Weber's definition, absolute value rationality, in contrast with calculating or technical rationality, cannot be concerned with consequences. One merely tries to exemplify a life of beauty according to the dictates of one's own aesthetic conscience, one's own aesthetic sensibilities and standards, regardless of consequences other than aesthetic ones.

In contrast, aesthetic rationality of home and family cannot be separated from a concern with the effect of one's choices or actions on others. Female aesthetic rationality assumes embeddedness in communal life – the community of home and family life and a concern for the effects on community. Hence aesthetic rationality brings together what Weber separates into two opposing individualistic rationalities: value rationality and calculating rationality. Aesthetic rationality of home and family life means striving to realize certain values that require a concern for consequences, a concern for the body and spirit of others.

Although the concept of aesthetic rationality holds promise of a holistic notion of rationality that can transcend Weber's dualistic one, this promise cannot be realized as long as the domestic world and its rationality is subordinated to and repressed by the market world of political economy and its rationality. I will address this point below. Only by overcoming its subordination and repression can this alternative mode, aesthetic rationality, realize itself. Only then can aesthetic rationality holistically include and transcend Weber's limited dichotomy.

Weber did consider and reject something that resembles the notion of aesthetic rationality when he compared judging something to be in bad taste with judging something to be morally wrong. He emphatically rejected the reduction of moral judgment to a matter of taste. However, one could turn the argument around and say that by denouncing something as disgusting, repugnant, repulsive, and so forth one can have an aesthetic response to ethical matters that does not reduce or trivialize either the matter at hand or the judgment of it. Probably the strongest condemnation of an immoral act takes the form of emotional, aesthetic judgments of this kind. But of course, a rational justification for the response would be necessary for the judgment to qualify as aesthetic *rationality*.

MOTHERING

Mothering, the second aspect of domestic female rationality, is also neither instrumentally (technically) rational nor value-rational action, although it contains aspects of both. Here I draw on Sara Ruddick's description (1982) of maternal thinking which involves, as I interpret it, three objectives: preserving life, fostering growth, and working with nature. The last involves developing, fostering, or nurturing the nature of the child. Although mothering does involve making choices about alternative courses of action, it is not the same as instrumental rationality. It does not choose the least costly, most profitable means for achieving a calculable goal, because the goal, raising the child, is not calculable in quantitative terms. The goal of childraising is itself subject to interpretation both with respect to means and end. For some, childraising can mean raising physically able, obedient children; for others, raising educated, independent children. The ends and means of childraising are subject to historical, traditional, communal and patriarchal influence and values.

Mothering is also not value rational in the sense of commitment to an abstract value without concern for consequences because inherent in the idea of mothering is a concern with consequences for the child. These consequences also include consequences for others; socializing the child means helping the child to become a "competent" member of the family, community or society, with "competence" itself being subject to interpretation.

Mothering is grounded in a sensual, erotic relationship. The cuddling, holding, touching, nursing, grooming and dressing of the infant and child involves sensual and emotional feelings as does making sounds and talking, making eye contact and playing with the child. An important dimension here, too, is the aesthetic. Mothers enjoy and respond to the beauty (aesthetic, sensual appeal) of their children and strive to re-create that beauty. Through

251

washing, grooming, dressing they attempt to enhance their children's appeal to themselves and others. Through holding, touching, nursing, playing, they realize the erotic pleasure of the relationship and in so doing stimulate the senses and faculties of the child.

Research shows that very significant and essential interaction and play goes on between parent and infant just in the simple activity of making and letting go of eye contact as an activity of mutual responsiveness (Stern, 1977). A sense of empowerment, a sense of self, develops in relationship to the mother through these interactions, a self that is capable of attunement with another – making contact, holding on and letting go. Through these early, unself-conscious, seemingly simple activities, significant mental, physical, emotional interactions and mental, physical, emotional development occurs. An unself-conscious sense of self-in-relationship, a self that is capable of attachment and separateness, develops. Mothering cannot be reduced to a set of formal or strategic procedures or abstract values to be applied regardless of context but is itself developed in the context of responding mentally, physically, emotionally – aesthetically – to the uniqueness of each particular child and with regard to the social context in which the relationship emerges.

INTIMACY

Finally, we may consider the rationality of wife, intimate friend or lover. Action here too expresses an aesthetic appreciation for a particular other. Caring expresses itself as a desire to please and to be pleasing to the other. This kind of action may be compared to instrumentally rational action to the extent that pleasing the other pleases the self, and any harm to the one ultimately harms the other. Yet although seemingly instrumental in this sense, self-interest cannot be calculated or conceived of *independently*, that is, without concern for the interests of the other.

Such love may also be compared to Weber's concept of value rationality – commitment to caring or loving as an end in itself. However, unlike value rationality, the act of loving is not a commitment to loving as an abstract value in itself but to loving particular others. Similarly, loving is not a personal or individual value that one adheres to because it is good and right as an end in itself regardless of consequences. Rather, inherent in the conception is a recognition that consequences for the other have consequences for the self. Caring and loving are not matters of abstract conviction or belief but of appreciation for a particular other. A major distinguishing feature of love is the enhancement of pleasure and the amelioration of pain that occurs with mutual sharing.

These three modes of action – homemaking, mothering and loving – constitute a traditional, aesthetic, female form of life: creative, nurturing, and intimate.

Subordinating domestic rationality to market rationality

These three female modes of action presuppose and (re)produce a typically female perspective, that of attached and responsive individuals, within a relationship, who care for and nurture each other, as opposed to separate and indifferent individuals who either use or avoid each other in order to achieve their own individual ends. Yet, like value rationality's degeneration into instrumental rationality, female rationality becomes irrational in a context of male domination, a context in which female rationality must be subservient to male rationality.

Homemaking, for example, becomes subverted if it serves instrumental rationality which views the home solely in terms of its exchange value as a means for some ulterior end – increasing, realizing and accumulating monetary wealth. Homemaking, which has the intrinsic aim of creating security, comfort and pleasure, becomes subverted and contradicted, hence irrational, when it subordinates itself to the aim of making or (conspicuously) spending money. A concern with making a home for purposes of selling it or for status display contradicts the very aim of homemaking to create an environment that reflects and responds to the particular needs and sensibilities of the self in order that it may settle there comfortably.

To focus on exchange value means to deny the self in favor of what others (a potential market or audience) might be willing to purchase or admire, hence to deny precisely the most idiosyncratic, unique needs, desires, pleasures of the self. Although homemaking may draw on something called taste or aesthetic sensibility that is shared or developed in common by members of a society, this sensibility is expressed through the individual's own unique aesthetic sense as it is formed historically in interaction with social or collective standards. Realizing those unique needs, desires and pleasures – unique aesthetic sense – is the very essence of homemaking. Hence homemaking conceived instrumentally as a means toward an external end such as moneymaking or status display contradicts the essence of homemaking.

The more something is used or worn, the less exchange value or status it generally has. However, the more something is used or worn, the more use value it has, and the more comfortable it becomes. To deny oneself the *pleasures* of using in order to maximize exchange value contradicts one aim of homemaking. To deny oneself *comfort* in order to maximize exchange value similarly contradicts another aim of homemaking. And to treat the home as exchange value, something to be used for purposes of status or for accumulating wealth, means being alert to changing fashions or changing market conditions. Therefore one can never feel *secure* with one's home as one may "want" to or "need" to change (update) it (or sell it if it is owned) based on market considerations. Thus instrumental rationality contradicts and undermines homemaking defined in terms of its three objectives of pleasure, comfort and security.

253

Aesthetic rationality, if it were not dominated by market rationality, would maintain a self-conscious balance between seemingly objective, collective values or standards and seemingly subjective, idiosyncratic values and desires; it would involve a playful appropriation of the collective tradition. But within modern capitalist patriarchal society, aesthetic rationality becomes serious conformist status display. There is a desperate desire to make one's home and one's self presentable and acceptable, something that is difficult to achieve under conditions of limited resources and late capitalism, with its own desperate need to keep changing fashion, and using non-durable materials.

Just as aesthetic rationality in the form of homemaking (including personal displays of style) become subverted by market rationality, similarly, mothering becomes subverted when it subordinates itself to instrumental, calculating, technical rationality. The aim of mothering, to foster the development and growth of the individual child in its relationship to the mother, family and community, becomes self-contradictory when as part of its objectives it prepares the child for membership in a divided community (patriarchal, class society). The aims of mothering are subverted when the community of which the child is a member is divided so that the interests of some dominate, conflict with and repress the interests of others, resulting in one group using another group instrumentally to achieve its own ends. The community treats the child, then, only as a means to be used for some end that is external to the child's own interests or feelings (instrumental rationality), such as producing or reproducing for others or enforcing the division between those who produce or reproduce and those who live off that labor.

Instead of mothering being a playful relationship between tradition and the future, between communal interests and individual pleasures, it becomes the serious business of training the child for a society that is not communal (treating each member as valuable and essential to the whole). I call this patriarchal parenting. Or it becomes the serious (feminist) business of fighting and resisting domination of the child's spirit by societal demands. I call this feminist parenting. A community that appropriates its members in order to reproduce the division between those who (re)produce and those who live off that (re)production embodies an instrumental, means–end rationality that opposes aesthetic rationality, the appreciating, valuing, and treasuring of things and each other in all their particularity and universality. The objectives and practices of such a divided community, with its instrumental rationality, oppose in principle and subvert in practice the objectives and practices of mothering, aesthetic rationality. This subversion of mothering constitutes patriarchal parenting.

The essence of intimate friendship and love, mutual appreciation and enjoyment, also becomes subverted when the other whose qualities and strengths one appreciates and enjoys and from whom one desires recognition, affirmation and pleasure, puts his or her own individual self-interest, pleasures or abstract values first regardless of the consequences for the friend/lover and hence for the friendship or relationship itself. In other words, relating to the other in an instrumental way – out of an orientation to one's own pleasure, interests or principles only – subverts the relationship. Intimate friendship also is corrupted when the material needs of one depend on the largesse of the other, so that the dependent one must try to use instrumental means (feminine wiles) of coaxing, nagging, threatening, feigning, complaining, seducing and so on in order to get those needs met.

The split between instrumental, technical and value, ethical rationality that characterizes the male form of life is mirrored in the female form of life. The dependent woman exhibits both instrumental rationality in her use of the man to provide for and protect her, and value rationality in her commitment to love and to the caring of others. However, the ideal of love conflicts with the need to use the other for her own self-interest. Thus, economic and political dependence, institutionalized in the traditional marital relationship, makes for instrumental manipulation by the wife which corrupts and undermines the intimate friendship that is supposed to be the basis of the relationship. Economic dependence produces female instrumental manipulation which undermines the values of intimate friendship.

In female rationality, the individual conceives of herself in relation to particular others. She is not separate and distinct but related and attached to the other. Her self-interest merges with that of others; her well being is linked up to their fortunes and good will. Decisions cannot be made decisively on the basis of calculating the best means for achieving her own individual ends and then acting with confidence, determination and courage on the basis of those calculations. Rather, she sees her actions as affecting others who might get hurt or resentful (or thrilled and inspired) in a way that distresses and threatens her (or enhances and empowers her) because she does not see herself or, therefore, her self-interest, as separate and independent of theirs.

In male rationality, the individual conceives of himself as separate and distinct from others; his needs are those of a separate and independent self. He relates to others and to the world as separate and distinct things to be used for his own self-interest (instrumental, technical rationality), modified only by some set of universalized values, rules or principles (substantive, ethical rationality) that limits the operations of self-interest.

Male indifference and self-interest, female sensitivity and concern for others are both one-sided; neither is able to sustain itself independently of the other; hence each by itself is irrational. Neither learns to both value the other for the ability to affirm the self and to develop a self that can be affirmed and that can affirm.

The division between the world of business and politics and the world of home and love, the division between instrumental, materialistic, individual self-interest and substantive, idealistic, communal interest produces a dualistic, internally divided and repressive world. It also produces dualistic, internally divided and repressed people. It produces a dualistic conception of "man" as one who acts either out of self-interest or abstract universal principles. It produces a dualistic conception of "woman" as one who manipulates the other for her own self-interest or one who subordinates herself and her interests to the other and the other's interests.

Another contradiction, internal to female rationality itself, results from denial of what female rationality requires in order to realize itself. Female rationality assumes attachment to another; yet in recognizing the other, it implicitly presumes both self and other are separate and have independent, individual needs and idea(l)s.

Hence, female rationality is *implicitly* premised on separation and independence, individual needs and idea(l)s, in short, personal attachment based on attraction to difference. Nevertheless, by stressing attachment and denying separateness, by denying or repressing the actor's own individuality, her own separate and independent needs and idea(l)s, by requiring devotion to the other's needs and idea(l)s, (or devotion of the other to one's own), female rationality denies its own premises (attraction to and affirmation of difference) and hence is self-contradictory and self-defeating. As soon as a relationship of devotion is achieved, the difference that created the attraction disappears, and so does desire. The devoted other ceases to be a different other whose affirmation is desired and who in turn desires affirmation for her difference.

As long as the relationship between men and women is a relationship premised on female responsibility for the private, domestic world, and as long as that world is one-sidedly dependent on an external public world, the relationship between men and women will not be mutual and the values and practices of women and men will differ. Women will remain dependent on or dominated by agents of the public world. These agents do not have to be men; they can be the officials of a public bureaucracy. The nature of the relationship between the public world and the private world influences women's "nature."

The dependence of domestic life on market life, of the private world on the public world, belies the ideology of separate but equal and complementary spheres of life. Even the most personal dimensions of mothering are not divorced from politics and the ideology of the state and capital. Political and ideological struggles occur over defining good mothering, the reproduction of "good" children or citizens. The definition of good citizen influences the definition of good mothering. The struggles over these definitions influence such "private practices" of mothers as when and how best to respond to an infant: demand versus scheduled feeding; method of toilet training; expressions of affection, and so on.

Homemaking, too, is not divorced from the public sphere and the manipulation of consumption and desire by capital. Intimate relations of sensual and aesthetic pleasure are shaped by ideology. Attractiveness and desirability are conditioned by the needs of capital and a patriarchal state. The need to control the private, domestic world belies the independence of the public, market world, just as the need to control the body belies the independence of the mind, and the need to control women and female sexuality belies the independence of men and male rationality.

The making of a home, the caring for children, and the intimacy of erotic love constitute a typically female form of life. These activities lend themselves to a different mode of rationality than that of rational calculation. The man engaged in the public world of economics and politics, who personifies traditional virtues of manliness, gets his sense of self from doing, from achieving some external goal by means of instrumental rationality. The woman engaged in the domestic world of homemaking and childcare, who personifies traditional virtues of womanliness, gets her sense of self not from accomplishing discrete goals but from the way in which she accomplishes them, from her way of integrating those goals into the holistic goal of homemaking: creating pleasure, comfort and security, and childraising, her way of relating to the world and to others, not so much from what she does as how she does it, an aesthetic rationality.

Instead of serving an abstract ideal, women serve the concrete needs and desires of embodied human beings. Ironically, the human beings that they desire to serve are "heroes" who are unwilling to subordinate themselves to anybody else but who are not averse to subordinating themselves to abstract ideals. Idealizing a hero occurs out of the repressed desire to be one's own hero – to go out and make one's way in the world, to conquer one's own dragons.

Male perception of female rational action

Responsibility for home and family life fosters an orientation that differs from the orientation required in the public world. From the perspective of the latter, women appear irrational and emotional. According to a male perspective, women's emotionality gets in the way of rationality. Because women's feelings for others obstruct "rational" action, they are too "soft." They are unwilling or unable to make the hard decisions that are necessary for achieving the goal. They fall into the "compassion trap;" they rely on intuitive judgment; they are concerned with "the relationship" or others' feelings. Women, who *by definition* orient to the maintenance of relationships and the sustenance of human life, "do not know what the 'real' world is like," that hard decisions have to be made, that people have to get hurt, that if one is unwilling to hurt others, then others will take advantage.

Young boys are taught by their football coaches: "It's a dog eat dog world. Trample or be trampled. Kill or be killed." The "rational" male actor sees the danger of admitting "real women" to the public world. Real women (domestic women) cannot function in positions of responsibility in the real world. Of course there are exceptions; biological women can act as men do and enter the real world, but then they cannot remain real women. They must suspend their womanliness. And then who will be available to provide soothing, caring, and nurturance? Segregation allows a public world that is indifferent to such needs to function. In other words, the modern public world with its indifference to human needs and feelings requires a separate private world that is supposed to cater to those needs and feelings.

But is this real world any more real than the world of women's domestic responsibilities? Is the orientation that characterizes action aimed at carrying out domestic responsibilities any less realistic than the orientation necessary for succeeding in a "dog eat dog" world?

Women are often characterized as emotional because they let their emotions get in the way of thinking and choosing rationally. But this accusation usually means that women allow themselves to empathize and sympathize with others. Empathy and sympathy are essential to personal, sociable relationships and to the very possibility of social life. However, these capacities obstruct the ability to make "tough," impersonal decisions that involve hurting others. That sociable caring about others conflicts with rationality means that the goal to be rationally achieved is separate from one's feelings and relationships with others; one's goal is separate from and independent of a subjective sense of well-being; well-being is objectified in an external thing – fetishism. Female aesthetic rationality rejects in principle any goal that requires *as a condition of its realization* an indifference to human welfare. This is not to say that female aesthetic rationality is not corrupted or undermined by male instrumental (market and political) rationality.

In an impersonal world requiring indifference to people's needs and pains, a "real woman" would find it difficult to determine and carry out the most "rational" (technically rational) way to achieve an instrumental goal because her sympathy for those who will get hurt intervenes. It takes a "real man" to do that. In other words, she could not carry out with indifference what Weber considers the inevitabilities of rational political and economic action.

Female rationality, in contrast, finds its ultimate goal in the realization of a subjective sense of well-being. This requires concern for the well-being of those who do or could make a difference to oneself. It requires responsiveness, empathy and compassion for others as well as responsiveness to one's own feelings and needs, interests and desires. Because female rationality assumes an encompassing goal that is both objective and subjective, external and internal, female practices seem irrational to a male rationality that assumes a partial goal, one that is objective and external to the individual and his or her subjective sense of well-being.

Female rationality challenges male rationality. A self-conscious female rationality would question the rationality of a world that is premissed on indifference to the pain and hurt of others as well as to one's own feelings. Max Weber would respond: "Be realistic; be rational; be manly. Renounce the concern for your own and others' feelings." From the perspective of domestic women's lives as homemakers, mothers and intimates, female rationality is realistic, while male rationality is not. Female rationality would question whether the world to which Max Weber points is any more real and rational than a world premised on desire for well-being and responsiveness to needs and feelings. The question becomes: what are the grounds of this "real world" to which Weber refers? I would suggest that this real world is grounded in the repression of the domestic world.

Another referent of woman's emotionality is the quality of effusiveness. Women seem to employ hyperbole more than men, to please and flatter, as part of the stereotypical characteristics of expressiveness. Women, like unrepressed children, are expected to express enthusiasm, liveliness, sympathy, delight, whereas men and repressed children are reserved, self-controlled and uncommunicative about such sentiments. Men allow themselves to express negative emotions towards others: hate, anger, resentment, contempt, hostility, competitiveness; their characteristic stance is that of steadfastness, boldness or aggressiveness as opposed to the flighty, unassuming, conciliatory stance of women.

To assume a stance of steadfastness means to resist being moved by others. It means not allowing oneself to feel or express sentiments of sympathy or joy over another's situation or experience. Such sentiments might weaken or interfere with one's resolve, or they might make one vulnerable to appeals by the other that interfere with the singleminded determination that sustains steadfastness. Similarly, hopes and enthusiasms can easily be dashed, for they presume a certain amount of trust in the environment and in others. But if those sentiments can be hidden behind or beneath a resolve and commitment to use all one's energies and faculties to attain the object of those hopes and enthusiasm, without having to depend on and trust others, then there follows a feeling of strength and lack of vulnerability.

Women are identified as being emotional also because they are expected to succumb to fear. Whereas men, in conformity with the myth of masculinity, must suppress if not repress their fear; women, like children, are supposed to be protected, warned about dangers, and comforted when hurt or fearful. They do not learn to take physical risks as a way of proving sexual or adult status. They do not learn to "take it like a man."

Furthermore, women's personal responsibility for others, especially helpless infants and children, makes risk-taking seem foolish and irresponsible.

Historically, childbirth always involved physical risk and pain, but childbirth was mostly not a matter of choice; one did not choose to take the risk or to expose oneself to pain just to prove oneself. It was rather a matter of enduring unavoidable risk and pain. (This is not to deny that there were often active attempts, overt and covert, to avoid pregnancy and childbirth.)

Men, on the other hand, readily choose to take risks, and they do so for two reasons. First, they may feel relatively confident and prepared in which case the risk is a challenge, fun and exciting. Secondly, willingness to risk physical safety becomes a way of proving themselves, of showing that they are capable of putting something else ahead of mere physical survival, a way of showing their manliness, their ability to conquer and master external threats and internal doubts which might obstruct or paralyze action and make for ineffectualness.

Rather than taking risks and acting courageously, domestic women, who must depend for their well-being on others, are encouraged to develop an attitude of trust. Because they are supposed to be protected and provided for by others, domestic women are deprived of the resources for self-provision and self-protection. Without such means, they are in no position to take action that involves risk. Furthermore, they lack the confidence that comes from being prepared. They may, however, react against their position of passive dependence and become rash, acting impulsively (a weak, negative, version of the feminine virtue of spontaneity) without consideration for their lack of resources or for possible negative consequences.

In sum, from the perspective of a public world of instrumental and value rationality and independent men, women appear as emotional, indecisive, cowardly, fatalistic and irresponsible. They are emotional because they let sympathy interfere with goal achievement; they are indecisive because they are open to the views and needs of others rather than rationally determining a course of action and then sticking to it; they are cowardly and passively fatalistic, because without means of self-support and self-defense, they are reluctant to take a course of action that might incur disapprobation or entail physical risk; they are rash and irresponsible because they will commit themselves without considering the availability of resources or the negative consequences, instead trusting in fate or in others.

From the perspective of male rationality and the world of business and politics, women appear to be irrational. However, from the perspective of female rationality and the world of women's responsibilities, including homemaking, mothering and relationships of caring and commitment to well-being, the male modes of rational action appear to be irrational. Nevertheless, female rationality, like male rationality, cannot stand alone and hence is inadequate as a mode of rational action. Each rests on a repressive relationship with the other. Because of repression which creates one-sidedness, each degenerates

– one into the cult of masculinity and heroism, the other into the cult of femininity and domesticity.

Our contemporary form of life stunts our growth, forcing us into one-sided creatures of a repressive political economic system and a repressed domestic life. Overcoming the repression of domestic life by political economy makes possible a more rational form of life in which human beings could grow and develop in less one-sided, repressed and repressive ways. This would mean a public world of production and politics that is responsive to private needs and personal feelings as well as a private world of reproduction and consumption that recognizes and affirms differences in needs and interests, a world in which no one party caters exclusively to the needs and interests of the other while denying or subordinating her own. In other words, the public world and the private world would begin to resemble each other. The difference would be one of emphasis not one of kind; neither would be seen as radically other, a complete negation of the other.

Female practices and femininity

Just as men have not only accommodated themselves to the male public world but have actively resisted and struggled to transform it, women too have not only accommodated themselves to their situation but have also resisted and created within their world sources of pleasure and meaning, often in their relationships with each other (Smith–Rosenberg, 1975). The differences in actual situation among women have been great; the responsibilities they have assumed as part of being a woman have also varied greatly. These responsibilities have fostered strengths, skills, and sensibilities not encompassed by the idea of femininity.

Women who have children to care for and who are not economically dependent on a personal relationship with a man, especially women who are not from middle- or upper-class families, may find themselves dependent on the welfare state itself. These women of the lower classes may not develop many of the stereotypical aspects of femininity. Middle-class dependent women, who, often through divorce and childraising, "fall" into the lower classes, similarly, and often with great pain, come to repudiate a feminine orientation to the world. In fact femininity is most likely to occur among young women interested in attracting a man.

Married women often have no need to be feminine in their daily work activities; much feminine behavior is a way of relating to men. Women who have had major responsibilities in the private world or the public world are not as readily likely to adopt feminine ways, at least not while carrying out their responsibilities. Even mothering involves more than just serving and nurturing others; it involves power and competencies that are not particularly feminine.

261

However, with extreme polarization of women's work and men's work and with the dependence of the former on the latter, we find a vast difference between women's one-sided practices of pleasing, serving and nurturing others (femininity) and men's one-sided practices of striving for power, wealth, position or heroism (masculinity). We find a difference between women and men similar to a difference between alien cultures or different species. The different life situations create different ontologies – in the sense not only of different ways of being, but different reasons for being.

We have seen how feminine expressiveness signifies attached, dependent, trusting individuals whereas masculine reserve signifies separate, controlled, invulnerable individuals. These differences, in keeping with the general connotations of femininity and masculinity, enhance the heterosexual attractiveness of those women and men who display these sex-appropriate qualities.[8]

It should be noted that the attractiveness and desirability of these qualities in each sex are not transferable to the other sex. The vicarious pleasure that a "man" may take in a woman's spontaneity and joy is often premissed on the inability to allow himself such behavior or sentiments. To the extent that revealing one's feelings of pleasure and pain derives from the situation of being protected and provided for, such behavior is seen as unattractive and undesirable in men; they indicate an inability to survive and succeed in the public realm where nobody can expect others to protect and provide for him.

Similarly, the admiration that a woman feels for the qualities of strength, confidence and self-reliance in a man is often premissed on an inability to take such stances herself. To the extent that she can and does, these qualities may make her heterosexually unattractive and undesirable; they indicate an unwillingness to remain dependent and deferential. It should be noted that femininity and masculinity take on different colorations according to social class and situational differences. A competent, self-sustaining woman may be a threat to some men but quite desirable to others. Where a self-reliant, self-sustaining woman is considered desirable, we can expect that the relationship between men and women differs from one in which the desirable woman is supposed to be dependent and subservient.

Women, femininity and authenticity

I have been stressing the difference between women and men with respect to power and dependency. However, as indicated above, mothering involves power and control; it involves protection of and provision for the home and dependent children. It requires other competencies in addition to the qualities of nurturance and responsiveness. Thus, as a mother, a woman is not feminine in the ways indicated above.

262

However, the mother, as such, has no direct control over her own destiny. She is oppressed. Jessica Benjamin says of mothers: "Their power over their children is not to be mistaken for the freedom to act on their own wishes and impulses, to be author and agent in their own lives" (1986, p. 84). The mother as mother cannot be responsive to herself alone. She cannot separate herself from her relationship to her child. As mother, she is defined and defines herself in terms of her relationship and responsibility to her children. Again it must be stressed that this is an ideological description. Such real-life women may never have existed or may have existed but with all kinds of qualifications and modifications. Real women are not solely mothers; they do have selves that are independent of their mothering relations with others. But these selves are oppressed by a patriarchal society that relegates the needs of mothers to a private sphere that is, none the less, dependent on a man–centered public sphere.

Similarly the image of men as willing agents of a public world characterized by human indifference is an ideological one. In fact men, too, have varied in their actual conformity to the idea(l). Nevertheless men and women have upheld the ideology as the only proper version of men and women given the realities of the public and domestic worlds.

The analysis of male rationality with its denial or repression of female aesthetic rationality reveals internal contradictions and hence irrationality. Female rationality, with its dependence on and subservience to that which denies and represses it, male rationality, similarly turns out to be irrational. In order to be fully rational, female rationality must be true to itself. It must overcome its subservience to that which denies it and become "for itself." Such a fully rational mode of action we call authenticity. Authenticity means refusing to support whatever negates one's own reason for being, whatever denies one's rationality.

Female rationality that is for itself involves standing up and fighting for one's home against the encroachment of market rationality; it means opposing and working to transform a community that denies, represses and threatens the growth, development and uniqueness of each individual child; it means recognizing the separateness and independence of one's own needs and idea(l)s and struggling to realize them.

Thus, a fully rational, authentic female rationality incorporates the strengths of male rationality: willingness to stand up and fight on behalf of itself and its values; acting to oppose and resist all conditions, including a market rationality, that deny and threaten human growth and development; demanding a right to whatever is necessary for sustaining life.

A female rationality of this kind, strengthened by features of male rationality, requires overcoming repression and oppression by gaining access to the resources of the public world, political and economic. This means that female rationality must be recognized by and in the public world. Recognition of female rationality within a sphere premised on its repression requires struggles of opposition. Therefore, overcoming one-sidedness is not simply a matter for consciousness, a matter of adding female rationality to male rationality. It is, rather, a matter of resistance and struggle that results in transformation of a public world and a rationality that is premised on the repression and oppression of the domestic sphere which includes the work and rationality of women in that sphere. Right now, the work and rationality of women (and some men) in the private world is repressed and oppressed by one-sided dependence on the work of men and women in and for the public sphere with its own repressive rationality.

To stand up and fight on behalf of female aesthetic rationality presupposes a self-conscious awareness of and pride in female aesthetic rationality as an idea(l) and value rather than an unself-conscious way of relating to the world. Struggling for recognition of and realization of one's life as the manifestation of an idea(l) requires and develops pride, competence and confidence. Instead of idealizing others who are strong and competent, independent and proud, instead of romanticizing a relationship to one who embodies such qualities and lives a heroic life of struggle on behalf of some ideal, the struggle for recognition and responsiveness to female rationality would mean becoming a hero to oneself, rescuing oneself, an alternative version of heroism.[9]

Only freed from relations of domination and dependence can female rationality and the domestic sphere be true to itself (authentic) and not merely turn into male rationality or degenerate into a cult of domesticity and femininity. Female rationality represents an implicit critique of a male public world that is indifferent to human needs and human suffering, a critique of pure instrumental rationality with its external and abstract goals. With awareness of its lack of resources and its consequent inability to stand up for itself, provide for itself and be self-sustaining, female rationality also becomes self-critique, critique of a separate and dependent female world which keeps female rationality separate and dependent and produces feminine subservience. Making explicit the implicit critique of both male and female worlds transforms female rationality into feminist rationality.

A "rational" transformation

Feminist rationality, female rationality that is for itself, requires resistance and opposition to the domination and repression of domestic life by political economy. It requires resisting and overcoming the domination and repression of female rationality by male rationality, resisting and overcoming the silencing of the female voice by the male voice. It means transforming political economy and the public sphere by compelling it to recognize and acknowledge its dependence on the private sphere and to be responsive to the needs, interests and values of the private sphere. The rationality of public life would have to recognize and respond to the rationality of domestic life.

Such transformation of political economy and male rationality entails a corresponding transformation of domestic life and female rationality. By resisting and opposing their own repression, domestic life and female rationality cease being subservient. In recognizing their own power, importance and efficaciousness, they take on and acknowledge the value of the attributes associated with the public sphere and male rationality.

Thus both public life and private life, male rationality and female rationality, would be transformed by a female rationality and a domestic world that refuses to remain subservient, that is, by the struggles of female rationality to stand up for itself.[10] Female rationality would include instrumental and value rationality as part of itself, just as male rationality would recognize its grounding in the aesthetic rationality of erotic, sociable, domestic and communal life.

Notes

1 Starhawk is an influential feminist spiritualist.
2 For a work that traces the association of maleness with rationality from the time of the ancient Greeks to modern Western philosophy, see Lloyd (1984).
3 Description assumes a taken-for-granted reality whose characteristics are available for anyone to see and know. There is no question of different ways of seeing or knowing a reality. Formulation assumes that the object being formulated is not immediately knowable and in fact is only known in and through the formulation of it.
4 This discussion of women as (re)producers of community draws on Terry Haywoode's (1988) work.
5 The publication, *Women in the Global Factory* by Fuentes and Ehrenreich (1983), provides an overview of the exploitation of women's labor by global capital.
6 Gayle Rubin's (1975) analysis of the sex-gender system provides an insightful discussion about the relationship between sex and gender.
7 See Chapter 8.
8 The connotations of femininity and masculinity differ by class, race, ethnicity and historical period.
9 See Pearson and Pope (1981) on the female hero.
10 Iris Young (1987) provides an outstanding revisioning of public life based on a feminist perspective. Gould (1984b) and Elshtain (1981) also provide feminist discussions reconceiving the public sphere.

16

Marx and Weber: an alternative perspective

Marx's work offers an alternative to that of Weber. Marx's alternative seems to have much in common with a feminist alternative; his critique in some ways resembles a feminist critique. In this chapter I explore the relationship between Marx's thinking and feminist thinking. I do this by re-examining Marx's thought in relation to Weber's. I focus on the gendered nature of both Marx's thought and Weber's. Although the thought of both of them is flawed by a patriarchal masculine bias, nevertheless each of them in different ways has a complex and interesting relationship to feminist thinking.

Marxism, like feminism, challenges Weber's conception of the individual actor. Feminism emphasizes the relational nature of the individual. Marxism rejects any reduction of social life to the level of the individual; it focuses instead on social relations and their embeddedness in a mode of production.

Feminist reflection on the life situation of women, especially women as mothers, their way of relating to the world, has resulted in a critique of the man-centered view of the lone independent individual competing with others and rationally seeking his own self-interest. Such reflection reveals that the idea(l) of a public world of lone independent individuals is a masculine idea(l). Furthermore, it presumes a private world of attached, dependent, vulnerable human beings. The idea(l) of the former is premised on the repression of the latter.[1] This repression includes the oppression of women and the work they do in the home to maintain the taken-for-granted reality (illusion) of a public sphere composed of lone, independent individuals.[2]

Feminist psychoanalytic observation of early childhood development has similarly confirmed a connection between masculinity and independence, an independence that is premised on domination.[3] Here, too, repression plays a role. It is the repression within the psyche of any identification on the part of the male child with the feminine.[4] (The female child must similarly renounce identification with the masculine.) Feminist theory on both the micro and macro levels have identified a connection between masculinity and the idea(l) of the separate, independent individual. It has also identified a connection between this idea(l) and the striving for domination and mastery[5] on the one side and the ethic of individual rights and an impartial public sphere on the other.[6]

Without implicating masculinity, Marx, too, challenges the notion of individualism that is central to capitalism. Furthermore, Marx suggests an alternative that speaks to the concerns of feminism, an alternative that stresses caring and support of each individual rather than rapacious competition, conflict and domination.

Marx's feminine values

Whereas Weber takes the approach of facing up to the fate of the times, the nature of public life, like a man, Marx takes the approach of changing that fate and the public world in a way that accords with feminine values[7] – a feminine transformation. If socialism means a mode of production characterized by people co-operating with and caring about each other, then Marx's conception of socialism may be considered a feminine form of life. That Marx's socialism resembles a feminine form of life suggests a problem. Marx may be insufficiently critical; he may be guilty of romanticizing community and the "feminine." Feminism, unlike Marx, takes a critical perspective on the feminine.

For Marx, socialism was made possible by communal control of the means of production. However, community, like family, may be a gloss for relations of repression in which weaker individuals are dominated and coerced by stronger ones. Marx does not acknowledge that there are tensions involved in communal control. Failure to acknowledge the inevitable tensions, and to consciously address them, necessarily results in relations of domination and oppression that resemble those under patriarchy and capitalism.

Not only is there a problem about Marx being insufficiently self-critical with respect to his goal, socialism; there is also a problem regarding the means that he advocates for attaining the goal. He adopts a masculine emphasis on heroic action, the overcoming of an external enemy. Feminism treats both femininity and masculinity as one-sided, repressed and repressive patriarchal categories and forms of life. Emphasis on external action as a means without continual internal reflection on the realization of socialism in one's everyday life is likely to reproduce a masculine, patriarchal, repressive form of life. Thus, despite a kinship between feminism and Marxism there is an important difference – one that may be summarized in the term "unself-conscious masculine thinking."

The difference reveals a shortcoming of Marx's work that seriously undermines his theory of socialism and of great radical and revolutionary social change. Marx, the most radical critical theorist of the modern world, is insufficiently self-critical. While probably the most dialectical theorist of the West, when it comes to his own goals and means, Marx is insufficiently dialectical. I take the position that both Weber's and Marx's theorizing about the modern Western world, their formulation of the problem and their respective solutions to the problem, represent a one-sided and, therefore, flawed perspective, a masculine perspective. They focus almost exclusively on the public world of politics and economics, the world of men. In itself there is nothing wrong with that. The problem arises with their not acknowledging the necessary and essential relationship between the public world and the private, a relationship that is premised on repression.[8]

In spite of and because of his celebration and advocacy of a feminine form of life, socialism, as a replacement for the masculine individualism of capitalism, Marx's work comes close to resembling and recreating patriarchal repression. He assumes that without private ownership of capital, community can be had without self-destructive conflict and without political repression and coercion backed by force. The self-reflection on femininity that constitutes feminism reveals that ideas like "love" and "community" can conceal social relations of repression and coercion. Not acknowledging the essential tension and conflict between community and individual, unity and diversity, results in a dangerous tendency to treat difference and divergence as subversive of community and hence to be rooted out.

The ever-present and irremediable tension between individual and community in the context of a belief that the two must be one produces a need for ever-present surveillance and forcible repression, neither of which are conducive to a liberating and liberated form of life. The failure to recognize the inherent nature of the tension produces an internal division that undermines community, a division between those who see themselves as representing the interests of the whole (the patriarchal head) and all those individuals and their particular interests that make up the whole (the childlike, feminine body in need of protection and guidance).

Failure to acknowledge the necessary and fruitful tension between individual and community produces a society that requires (childlike, feminine) subordination and surrender of all those who make up the community to those few who speak for the community. Denial of the inherent tension also produces a positivist mode of theorizing, one that stresses external causal relations instead of internal relations of social change through the working out of internal tensions.[9]

That is the failure I attribute to many students of Marx; they treat his work as a theory of external causal relations. The failure, however, originates in Marx's own failure to treat the domination of labor by capital as a historically specific particular manifestation of a universal tension inherent in social life: the internal relation between object and subject, community and individual. He treats the relation between capital and labor as a historically specific totality, which of course it is. Therefore, he stresses external heroic action that aims at ending once and for all the domination of human subjectivity by the objectification of human labor in the form of capital.

However, he does not see the struggle against human objectifications (social categories and symbols, norms and mores) that come to dominate human subjectivity as an on-going struggle internal to every human being and every social formation, an on-going struggle requiring continual self-reflection and self-change or else self-control, self-discipline and self-repression. He does not see the tension between objectifications (social categories and symbols, norms and mores) and human subjectivity as inherent in language and social life itself, a tension that continually (re)produces strain and struggles. He focuses only on one particular manifestation of this tension and struggle: that between capital and labor.

But every social objectification, every social arrangement and social category – not just capital – is both a realization of human possibilities, the creation of an objective identity, and a limitation on human possibilities, a repression of human subjectivity. Tension is inherent in every identity. Struggles against limitation and repression make possible the liberation of human subjectivity and make possible internal growth and development. Struggle against external repressive conditions of public life must include struggle against the internalized repression that is inherent in private life, the repression inherent in one's internalized objective identity, one's subjective identity and one's personal relationships.

Marx's feminist method

Despite the substantive problem inherent in Marx's feminine vision, Marx's *method* of theorizing corresponds to a feminist method of theorizing. Common to both Marx's analysis and feminist analysis is the focus on social relationships rather than individuals as the foundation of social life. This leads both feminism and Marxism to be critical of the individualistic bias inherent in much social thought, including the social thought of Max Weber. Marx's method of theorizing consists of what I call a relational approach.[10] By Marx's relational approach I refer to his method of revealing how what appears to be an independent thing in itself, as well as a category of political economy – money, commodity, gold, capital – is really a social relationship.

A relationship of repression makes it appear that capital is an independent thing or power. This appearance is not a matter of mistaken knowledge; it is a matter of active repression. We could make the same analysis of the repressive nature of patriarchal relations which result in men's lives and masculinity appearing to be independent of women's lives and femininity. If W. E. B. DuBois moved the oppressed of the world from margin to center, the relational method of feminism as well as Marx does the same.

Marx's analysis of capital is an example *par excellence* of theorizing that is relational and sensitive to repression. However, Marx's work is generally not taken as an exemplar of a relational, dialectical mode of theorizing. Unfortunately, Marx's theorizing is taken as a thing – a theory – whose categories are appropriated and used, applied to all aspects of social life. His work, as I have pointed out elsewhere (1979), is not treated as a mode of theorizing, a way of doing analysis that uncovers the repression inherent in any linguistic category, any language or discourse that treats itself as the whole, a given thing in the world that fails to ground itself in historical, social relations and purposes.

However, I no longer consider, as I once did, this reception and conception of Marx's work to be solely a failure of reading, a failure attributable to a positivist bent on the part of students of his work. I now consider it to reflect a failure in his theorizing as well. Marx theorizes as one who has found the problem, and it is out there – capital; now we have only to rectify it and then all will be well; we will be liberated to live happily ever after. Feminists are wary of fairy tales that end with the heroic overcoming of some external problem and a heroine who has been liberated to live happily ever after, usually with the hero to whom she is grateful. We want to know how living happily ever after is to be achieved as an on-going practical accomplishment; in other words, what will the relationship and the work be like from day to day. A female hero, as opposed to a male hero, is one who discovers that the dragon to be slayed is not solely out there, but is inside as well. Liberation occurs not solely by freeing the heroine from some external bondage but by her freeing herself from internal bondage as well (Pearson and Pope, 1981).

Masculine bias in theorizing

Both Marx's theorizing and Weber's are one-sided and man-centered. Both are limited by a patriarchal masculine ideology. Weber celebrates manliness and rejects femininity along with domesticity and depoliticization. Marx invokes masculinity and manliness while romanticizing a domestic, communal and feminine form of life.

Materialists recognize only one side of the dialectic – the necessity for changing external conditions and hence an emphasis on action. The change in external reality becomes the means for change in subjective character or personality. Marxism does not generally acknowledge the importance of struggle as an on-going process of self-change. Marxism does not perceive the relationship between self-change and social change, subjective feelings, (gender) identity and objective social conditions. Marxism does not stress that the process of internal subjective self-change requires and (re)produces external objective social changes just as the process of external or objective social change requires and (re)produces internal subjective self-change.

I attribute this one-sidedness to a masculine bias in favor of action over interaction, doing over conversing, producing over contemplating, a bias in favor of changing the nature of impersonal things over changing the nature of personal relationships, overcoming external objective repression over overcoming internal subjective repression, objective reality over subjective identity. Instead, a feminist perspective stresses that struggle against external objective reality must be a struggle also against internal subjective reality if the struggle is to be genuinely liberating and transforming rather than one that reproduces the same domination with different personnel.

A similar masculine bias in favor of external heroic action is responsible for a flaw in Weber's theorizing. Weber does not acknowledge community or relationship as an end in itself; he sees only the individual as an end in itself. Because he recognizes the inadequacy of individual personal self-interest for providing meaning and purpose to life, he must posit some external impersonal cause with which the individual may identify. Interestingly, the external cause that he chooses as most ennobling is that of enhancing the power and glory of the nation state, a form of community.

As Marx and Weber both agree, the objective reality of modern social life has meaning only in relation to subjective identity, the kind of human being that is presupposed and reproduced. Marx emphasizes "feminine" caring, co-operation and commitment to the community. Weber emphasizes "masculine" political action and commitment to an impersonal cause. Nevertheless, both emphasize external decisive action, external struggle and external objective change to the exclusion of internal contemplation, internal struggle and internal subjective change. Both emphasize action, doing, accomplishing, a masculine orientation, to the neglect of being, relating, growing, a feminine orientation.

To the extent that action is stressed as a means to an end without continual public reflection on the end, in Marx's case, socialism, and what it means to realize socialism as an on-going form of life in the here and now, we have a mechanical notion of change. A materialist theory assumes that change in external reality will automatically cause change in internal reality, a theory that external objective change is necessary and sufficient for accomplishing internal subjective change – once and for all. Such an orientation corresponds well with the masculine, heroic orientation of the modern Western world – a men's world.

The distinctive character of modern "man"

Reading Weber's analysis of the modern world in order to illuminate the distinctive character and subjective identity of modern "man" is not out of keeping with Weber's own intent. Marianne Weber informs us that, for

Weber, the main question to which "all questions should ultimately relate" in analyzing social phenomena is "How do those phenomena influence the character of modern man. . .?" (Weber, 1975, pp. 422–3). Similarly, regarding radical social change, she reports that "the ultimate criterion for a social reformation was the question of what *type of personality* it promoted" (Weber, 1975, p. 415).

Both Marx and Weber are critical of the modern world and modern "man." However, it is questionable whether the characteristics that they ascribe to modern "man" could describe the women of modernity.[11] Weber recognized this; he feared and opposed the rationalization of women's lives and of the relationship between men and women. He opposed the socialist and radical feminists who advocated "free love." He believed that separating erotic love from marriage would reduce the former to a mere valuing of the erotic sensation – eroticism. Furthermore, and most seriously of all for Weber, stripping marriage of its mystification and replacing it with a rational contractual relationship for reproduction and child support would transform marriage into a rationalized relationship that would destroy the last remnant of enchantment left in everyday life.[12]

The distinctive features of the rationalized (in Weber's terms), capitalistic (in Marx's terms) modern public world that Weber and Marx analyze give rise to the characteristics that sociologists of gender today attribute to modern bourgeois masculinity: instrumentally rational, competitive, aggressive, self-controlled, reserved, inexpressive, oriented to achievement, success and impersonal rules that protect individual rights and freedoms. In contrast, the distinctive features of the private world give rise to the characteristics associated with modern bourgeois femininity: emotional, responsive, expressive, co-operative, caring, oriented to personal well-being (including bodily, spiritual and emotional aspects), to relationships and community.[13]

Objective social reality is (re)produced by subjective (gender) identity just as subjective (gender) identity is (re)produced by objective social reality. Objective social reality and subjective social identity, the object of knowledge and the subject of knowledge, do not exist separately and independently of each other. Political economy and political economic changes are interpreted in culture, justified in ideology, internalized in consciousness and, most important, embodied in personal gender identities.[14] That is, political economy, including social class relations, are embodied, personified and gendered. Manliness is, I contend, a central dimension of modern life and modern social classes. However, modern bourgeois manliness presupposes the repression of and oppression of women as a group. That both Marx and Weber call unself-consciously and uncritically on an idea(l) of manliness signals the sexism inherent in their thought.

Perhaps the most unique aspect of the modern public world, from the perspective of both Marx and Weber, is its distinctive ethics, or lack of ethics.

272

Although Marx and Weber agree in their analysis of the (un)ethical nature of the modern world, they differ sharply with respect to the solutions that they offer. Weber's are more in keeping with certain masculine ideals, and Marx's with certain feminist ideals. Paradoxically, Weber was an outspoken feminist while Marx subordinated feminism and feminist issues to class struggle.

Weber's commitment to feminism is related to his sensitivity to situations of dependence and powerlessness and particularly to any hint of servility. This sensitivity, coupled with his "realism," results in a political position that is consistent with that of liberal feminism. Marx's commitment to the cause of achieving socialism, the identity of particular and universal interests in a universal class, through a kind of heroic revolutionary action leads him to subordinate feminist struggle to class struggle. Despite strong affinities with feminism, both theorists, I argue, adopt an unself-conscious masculine perspective.

Weber was more self-conscious and explicit about his commitment to manliness than was Marx. Weber supported women's struggles for rights that would enable them to be more "manly;" Marx supported efforts that would allow men to be more "womanly." However, neither went very far in exploring the issue of gender. Weber remained attached to a notion of natural differences that must be segregated in separate spheres, manliness in the public and political worlds, womanliness in the domestic and private worlds. Marx's method of achieving change and even his conception of socialism assumes masculine notions of external heroic action and of work conceived as the production of things, not the (re)production of (social) human life.

Ethical irrationality: Weber

Both Marx and Weber analyze the modern world in terms of its ethics. Marx elucidates the difference between its surface ethics, expressed in the values of freedom, equality, and enlightened self-interest, and its underlying reality of domination, inequality and class conflict. Weber formulates the dilemma of modernity in terms of the conflict between a rationality that stresses means and a rationality that stresses ends. I summarize Weber's argument below.

In the modern world, technical rationality tends to suppress ethical rationality. Weber refers to this situation as the ethical irrationality of the modern world. Where impersonal market relations obtain, rational capital accounting must exclude considerations of "primeval norms" or ethics, under pain of economic failure and economic ruin (Weber, 1978, p. 585). Thus the modern world of capitalism excludes in principle considerations of an ethical nature. It operates according to rational accounting principles not ethical accounting principles. Politics, too, comes into conflict with ethics. "For public political activity leads to a far greater surrender of rigorous ethical requirements than is produced by private business activity" (ibid., p. 593).

Bureaucratization with its technical, formal rationality stifles political dynamism just as it does economic dynamism; it threatens society with ossification. It eliminates all passion just as it eliminates all ethical values. Instead of heroic political leaders, bureaucracies produce officials and functionaries. The bureaucratization of the political sphere was the aspect of modernity that most disturbed Weber.

Ethical irrationality: Marx

Like Weber, Marx concludes that "ethics" is external to the logic of political economy. "It stems from the very nature of estrangement that each sphere applies to me a different and opposite yardstick – ethics one and political economy another" (Marx, [1844] 1978a, p. 97).

Marx attributes the separation of political economy from ethics to the condition of alienation, to alienated activity and an alienated relation of each activity to the other. If socialism prevailed, political economy would itself be an ethical science and economic activity an ethical activity. There would not be a separate sphere called ethics and another called the economy. Marx claims that the opposition between political economy and ethics is only a "sham" opposition. "All that happens is that political economy expresses moral laws *in its own way*" (ibid.).

In reviewing these "moral laws," Marx anticipates in an incredibly similar description Weber's thesis on the Protestant ethic.

> Political economy, this science of *wealth* is . . .simultaneously . . .a true moral science of. . .self denial. . .The less you eat, drink and read books; the less you go to the theatre, the dance hall, the public house; the less you think, love, theorize, sing, paint, fence, etc., the more you *save*. . .The less you *are*, the more you *have*. . .You must also spare yourself. . .all sympathy, all trust, etc. (ibid., pp. 95–6).

In a world that is not characterized by alienated labor, there would be no separate sphere called ethics, nor a separate ethic for economic relations. The problem derives not simply from individual immorality or unethical behavior on the part of individual economic actors or political economists. The problem derives, rather, from alienation of production from human life as a whole. I conceive of this alienation as the alienation of production from human reproduction, of the production of things from the reproduction of human social life.

Weber considers politics, like economics, to be an independent sphere of life with its own laws and ethics. Marx takes a different view. He argues in the "Critique of the Gotha Program" ([1875] 1978b, p. 537) that the state is not an "independent entity that possesses its own *intellectual, ethical and libertarian bases*" but that *present-day* states are based on modern, more or less capitalistically developed bourgeois society.

Marx recognized an internal relationship between the public sphere of the state and the private sphere of civil society. However, he did not acknowledge that civil society itself is divided into public and private spheres, the reproduction of capital and its impersonal relations of indifference and the reproduction of the human being and the personal relations of nurturance that such reproduction presupposes.

While Weber and Marx both acknowledged the ethical irrationality of the modern public world, the significant divergence comes from their respective solutions to the problem of ethical irrationality. Here we can again see the relevance of gender.

Conflict theory and masculinity

Max Weber adhered to a conflict theory of social life in which struggles for power are considered to be an inescapable and fundamental fact of social life. This view corresponds with a masculine perspective. He advocated a world in which conflict and struggles for power continue because it is out of conflict that strengths are developed and greatness achieved. Greatness involves bold decisive action and risktaking, a form of heroism. Bureaucracy precludes heroism and the attainment of greatness. Weber believes in a manly heroic ethic of daring and decisive action which he distinguishes from the religious "feminine" ethic of brotherly love (1978, pp. 591–2).

Given his view of social life as inevitably and irremediably involving conflict and domination, Weber affirmed and upheld an ethic of manliness, a notion of separate, independent, contending individuals. On the political level, the world is and should be composed of separate individual states all vying for power; on the economic level the world is and should be composed of separate, independent enterprises all struggling for economic dominance; on the social level, the world is and should be composed of separate individual spheres of life all struggling to assert their primacy; and on the personal level, the world is and should be composed of separate souls struggling to realize their own subjective values (Weber, 1949, pp. 17, 27; 1946, pp. 323–57). These competitive struggles make for a dynamic world and life of individual choice and hence rational action and freedom.

Socialist theory and feminism

Marx's solution to the ethical irrationality of capitalism was socialism – a mode of production that eliminated the domination and exploitation of

275

workers by owners of capital. In contrast to Weber's view of social life as composed of struggles for power and conflict among individuals and groups over self-interest, Marx adhered to a view of social life as composed historically of social classes and class conflict with self-interest derived from membership in a particular class. With the socializing of the economy, society would lose its class character, and class conflict and class interest would give way to community. Collective interest and individual interest would coincide.

Socialism would be composed of co-operative, caring relationships, a community in which the free development of each is recognized as the basis of the free development of all (Marx, [1848] 1948, p. 31). This view resembles a feminist ethic, an emphasis on relationship and community modeled on erotic love as sociability, a view of each individual as contributing to the enhancement of the relationship or community and the development of the relationship or community as contributing to the enhancement of the individual.

Contrary to the approach of some Marxists who focus only on workers as workers, and contrary to some vulgar interpreters of Marx who conceive of communism as the attempt to eliminate all inequality, Marx criticizes a form of communism in which unequal individuals ("and they would not be different individuals if they were not unequal") are "regarded *only as workers* and nothing more is seen in them, everything else being ignored." In this society equal rights correspond to bourgeois rights. Marx explains the importance of personal differences: "Further, one worker is married, another not; one has more children than another, and so on." If all are treated equally and differences not acknowledged, equal rights will inevitably result in the very disparities that the emphasis on equality is intended to prevent. Marx concludes: "To avoid all these defects, right instead of being equal would have to be unequal" ([1891] 1978, pp. 530–1). We can see a similarity between Marx's concern for the differences among individuals and the "feminine" particularistic ethic of care and responsiveness to the singular needs of particular individuals as distinct from the "masculine" universalistic ethic of equal rights. Consider the following by Marx:

> If the worker's material condition improves and he can devote himself more to *the raising of his children,* when women and children no longer need to go into the factories, and when he himself can *improve his mind* and *devote more care to his body,* then he will have become a socialist, without noticing (Marx, [1869] 1986, pp. 497–8, my italics).

Although Marx acknowledges the importance of particular needs, he does not adequately consider the relationship between particularism and universalism. In a feminist post-patriarchal world, particularistic concerns and practices would remain in tense but acknowledged relation with universalistic considerations and procedures; actors would be held responsible and accountable for considering and weighing both. Today particularistic concerns often operate but are not acknowledged; they are considered illegitimate and kept hidden. Particularism usually operates by and for those with power, but *sub rosa* under the guise of universalism.

In today's world people with power or influence may use their power or influence on behalf of particular others whom they know personally. The tension between particularistic and universalistic considerations is not made into a topic to be addressed. In a humane, sociable, feminist society that has overcome the repression of private life by public life, personal concerns that one has for oneself, one's family, friends, neighbors, colleagues would also be considered legitimate communal, societal, public and political concerns.

This is not to say that there would be no difference between public and private life. It is to argue that the difference should make a difference, and each should be conscious of the difference that the other makes. Each should recognize its relationship with the other, and that relationship should be able to be made into a public and private topic, a topic of and for both public and private life. But the difference and separateness between public and private spheres would remain. The tension between individual choice, individual freedom and individual privacy and collective rules, collective constraints and collective needs and interests would not disappear. This would be recognized as a real, inevitable tension that creates recurrent strains and conflicts that must be continually readdressed and re-solved. The difference produces not only tensions and conflicts but pleasurable difference as well: the pleasure, comfort and excitement of old and new personal relationships of intimacy, and the pleasure, comfort and excitement of routinized and non-routinized impersonal relationships of work and politics.

Weber's utopian individualism, Marx's utopian socialism

Weber's commitment to individualism and the subordination of the individual and the personal to the universal and the impersonal reflects an ethic of manliness. However, this ethic is ultimately utopian. (I am using the term, utopian, with the negative connotation of impractical, unrealistic, self-contradictory idealism that Marx gave to it.) I consider it utopian not because a manly, heroic leader cannot achieve greatness, but because of its conception of the great leader and the great cause (for example, the great nation state).

Weber viewed the leader as an individual who is divorced from his body, his personal interests and needs, an individual without attachments or for whom attachments are always subordinated to the cause, an individual without any loyalties or concerns that might interfere with goal attainment and instrumentally rational decision-making. In this respect Weber idealized the Protestant ascetic who denies the body and the self out of devotion to some higher cause. Similarly, Weber conceived of the needs and goals of the cause (the state) as separate and distinct from, and often involving a denial of, the personal needs and goals of the people that the cause is supposed to serve or represent, the people that compose the state (Beetham, 1974, p. 42).

Just as the individual is conceived as an independent monad competing with other individuals in a struggle for power, the nation state, too, is conceived as an independent entity competing with other nation states in a struggle for power. Each individual, each state, strives to be in a position to realize or impose its own will over the resistance of others – supremacy – or at least able to resist the imposition of will by the other – a balance of power. Individuals are not conceived as embedded in mutual relationships; nation states are not conceived as embedded in an international community.

Marx's solution to the contradictions of capitalism involved a communal, caring form of life in which concern for the individual would be the basis of human community just as contribution to the human community would be the basis of individuality. I consider his view to be utopian as well, not because communal decision-making and consideration of both individual and community needs is impossible. Rather, Marx is utopian because he appears to believe that the abolition of private control over the means of production will result in an unproblematic sense of community and human caring, a sense of responsibility of one for the other, of the community for the individual, the individual for the community, and that this sense of community will not only prevail but will suffice to resolve any issues, problems or conflicts that arise, without reproducing relations of exploitation and alienation.

As Weber suggests, even relationships of mutual devotion can and do involve coercion to the soul of the "less brutal" partner, and democracy often means domination of the majority by a minority. According to Weber there is always conflict of some sort, either repressed or expressed, that takes the form either of competition or coercion. Devotion to the person of a leader means the loss of the followers' souls, which Weber calls psychic and intellectual proletarianization. Weber accepts this as the price to be paid for leadership. The alternative to leadership is rule by professional politicians or bureaucrats. Marx, however, opposes proletarianization and therefore must confront the question of leadership.

Applying Weber's insight to Marx's vision suggests that a world in which the "free development of each is the condition for the free development of all" (Marx, [1848] 1948, p. 31) needs to acknowledge and be sensitive to the subjective dimension of social life, "the soul" in Weber's terms. Otherwise those who are least assertive and least powerful will have their souls coerced, their individuality repressed, often without consciously realizing it. We have learned from Freud, the women's movement and the black power movement, and would learn if we were to listen to the voice of "the worker," that the effects of such coercion and repression or feelings of "psychological oppression" (Bartky, 1979, pp. 33–41) are as destructive as, although not independent of, material exploitation or the threat of physical harm or violence.

With his assumption that conflict is ubiquitous and irremediable, Weber was more sensitive to this unacknowledged or repressed form of conflict and its subjective experience than Marx with his assumption that the elimination of capitalism will be sufficient for the liberation of women and all oppressed and exploited people. Although Weber was more sensitive to this issue, he accepted dehumanizing proletarianization as necessary. Marx, who rejected proletarianization, was more sensitive to the objective, historical, material conditions that give rise to the subjective experience of oppression than to the subjective experience itself and the need for self-reflection, self-change and struggle within the psyche and within the interpersonal relationships of everyday life in order to avoid reproducing the subjective experience of oppression.

Marx implies that the socialist personality, the new human being that will replace the bourgeoisie and proletariat, will emerge after the revolution when the new mode of production is in operation. As people participate in a socialist society, they will develop a socialist character. But first must come the revolution. William DiFazio refers to this as the "big bang theory of revolution."[15] The kinds of human problems involving subjective fears and the silencing of certain voices that arise in democratic communities such as collectives and town meetings which Jayne Mansbridge analyzes in *Beyond Adversary Democracy* remain unaddressed in Marx's vision of socialism.

Weber's conflict theory reduces communal life to individuals banding together to realize their own individual ends. He does not see community, relationships or sociability as essential ends in themselves. He reduces social life to the practices and motives of self-interested individuals or collectivities, all of whom are engaged in struggles for power.

Marx's conflict theory, on the other hand, reduces conflict and egotistical self-interest to capitalism or class society. He does not see that conflict and repression are inevitable even in loving communities. Or, if he does see this, he does not consider the on-going struggle to discern and overcome repression as essential to socialism as a dynamic process. For somebody who is keenly aware of the difference between appearance and reality, he is surprisingly uncritical about the nature of community and interpersonal relationships and the continuing need for self-reflection, self-criticism and self-change.[16]

I attribute this failure to his conception of unity. Marx failed to be critical about (comm)unity, to subject (comm)unity to a critical analysis. Marx treated (comm)unity as a thing to be achieved by and through the struggle to resist and overcome capitalism. However, he implied that (comm)unity is achieved once and for all with the abolition of the private ownership of capital. Socialism as the self-conscious awareness of the social nature of human life will take

279

the form of an on-going, unproblematic sense of social (comm)unity. He did not treat (comm)unity as an on-going movement and struggle or tension between separation and attachment, difference and identity, diversity and unity, individual and community, public and private.

Ironically, Marx did not have a dialectical theory of community, and hence he did not have a dialectical theory of socialism. Consequently his dialectical theory of social change is flawed by a one-sided commitment to manly heroic action. The big-bang theory of revolution leads him to treat socialism as an end-state to be achieved once and for all with the transformation of private property into social property.

Feminism as sociable community

Rather than a masculine, Weberian either–or choice, or a feminine, Marxian identity of one and the other, I suggest that there is an inevitable play or tension between individual and community although – and because – each is irremediably and inextricably tied to the other. Concern for the individual and concern for the relationship or community and hence for the other(s) that constitute the relationship or community must be recognized as equally legitimate concerns that cannot be entirely separated from each other. Neither can they be treated as completely identical or reducible to one another.

Only a social arrangement that acknowledges and affirms the legitimacy of both and that does not posit or deny the primacy of either protects both. The personal and subjective, that is, the needs and interests of individuals including their feelings and attachments, are understood and stipulated to be a legitimate concern for public and political decision-making. Similarly, community interest and needs have a legitimate call on the person and a legitimate place in personal decisions. The difference between the individual and the collective makes for tension and on-going struggles of social life. These in turn make possible continuing social and personal change.

Marx recognized that the relationship between the human being and human objects is a dialectical relationship of subject to object; each presupposes and (re)produces the other. Marx ([1844] 1978b, pp. 88–9) discusses the relationship between subjective human senses such as a musical sense and objective human products such as music and shows how each requires and (re)produces the other. But he does not talk about any tension between the subjective sense and the objective products.

However, others such as Simmel talk about the tension between objectification as formalization and the constraints of form or objectification on creativity and subjectivity, on freedom. Marx, of course, was quite sensitive to the process by which an object (such as objectified labor) becomes subject (capital) and the human subject (labor) becomes an object (wage labor or labor power). Nevertheless, he limited his analysis of this phenomenon to commodities and exchange value (also religion).

Despite the unity between the subjective and the objective, which Marx describes, there is a difference and separation that makes for tension and conflict. Marx acknowledged the tension and conflict with respect to capital, religion and class, the last defined in relation to the mode of production. He did not treat the tension and potential conflict between the human subject and the human object or between the community and the individual as universal and inevitable.

But socialism must be self-conscious about and acknowledge the mutual but tense relationship between subject and object, between the reproduction of objective wealth and the reproduction of subjective wealth, between public life and personal life, a relationship in which each recognizes its unity or identity with the other, but also its separateness and difference. In place of the separation and repression that we now have, with the (re)production of things repressing the (re)production of human life, the public world repressing the personal, the political repressing the domestic, each would recognize and respond to the other.

The development of a responsive form of life as opposed to a repressive one requires that each sphere of life, each aspect of (re)production, and each human being, struggles to discover, articulate and assert its own interests, and to listen, draw out and be responsive to those of the other. The on-going struggle to overcome repression and discover one another's interests, one another's soul, makes liberation an on-going achievement. The achievement involves the discovery and creation of interests through informal sociable conversation, reflection, organization, etc.

Marx does not consider as necessary for socialist practice the institutionalization of practices or arrangements that facilitate informal relationships; the institutionalization (institutionalized encouragement) of discovering through informal discussion those interests that are developing or being repressed or not yet recognized; and the institutionalization of procedures and practices for articulating those interests and getting them recognized. He does not indicate that socialist practice requires a self-conscious interaction between institutionalization and deinstitutionalization, formal social structure and informal relationships, repression and its discovery and overcoming. It is as though socialism ends all repression or, in Weber's terms, as though socialism ends all conflict.

By not acknowledging the inevitability of conflict and repression, socialism can only reproduce conflict and repression. Only by recognizing its inevitable character can social life be reconceived as an on-going movement of discovering repressed interests, separating, struggling for recognition, and reachieving community as well as individuality.

281

Feminists such as Mansbridge (1983) suggest that the notion of interests is more complex than either capitalism or Marxism recognizes. Individuals, workers, women, blacks – male and female – discover and create their own interests through being together and talking with each other. Mansbridge emphasizes a dialogical process of interest formation. Objective interests and their repression are discovered through subjective reflection and informal as well as formal discussion within and outside of organized group life. Informal, personal, sociable relations are essential to a dynamic public sphere.

Similarly, through sociable conversation not just (repressed, undeveloped or conflicting) interests but ideas emerge, creative possibilities surface and people become inspired.[17] In the feminist model of sociability, relations of erotic interest, which include conflict and competition as part of community and sociability, inspire individual and collective human greatness. This contrasts with Weber's one-sided patriarchal masculine model of social life in which only relations of conflict and competition foster individual and collective greatness. It contrasts also with Marx's one-sided patriarchal feminine model of social life in which only communal relations of (brotherly) love foster individual and collective greatness.

Feminism as sociable socialism

A feminist sociable community that is sensitive to the issue of repression recognizes the importance of conversation, personal relationships and community formation for the discovery and articulation of needs and interests, both the general (public) interest and particular individual (private) or minority interests. However, transforming a public body into an informal community does not guarantee that interests become articulated and considered. Mansbridge (1983) finds that the personal nature of conflicting and competing interests within consensual, communal contexts can make for personal anxiety and distress that serve to intimidate and silence. Her findings resemble Weber's observations regarding the coercive nature of relationships of erotic love.

Collectives that begin among friends with shared interests, values and commitments often dissolve with the development of internal tensions and conflicts. In each instance, particular individuals or personalities tend to be blamed. Mansbridge argues persuasively that it is not so much an individual or personality problem as a problem with social structure, one that does not develop explicit, formal procedures for dealing with the problem of difference and conflict of interests. Her work suggests that impersonal, universalistic procedures, including the use of personal advocates or representatives who bargain with other representatives over conflicting interests, can serve an important need within a communal context or socialist society, a collectivity larger than a small group of friends. In today's non-socialist societies, a form of adversarial democracy prevails in which representatives bargain but without the constraint of an explicit communal commitment. On the other side, in societies in which adversarial democracy does not exist, conflict of interest and hence individuality is repressed.

Feminist sociable life would, therefore, stress both communal, consensual, participatory decision-making based on the model of friendship and commitment to communal interest, but also liberal, formal, procedural, representative democratic decision-making based on a model of adversarial democracy with its commitment to abstract universal principles of individual rights and freedom to pursue particular interests.

Each by itself, communal, participatory, consensual democracy and impersonal, representative, adversarial democracy has the potential for being repressive. The inherent tension between these two forms must be recognized and treated as internal to communal political life rather than having the tension expressed as an either–or choice or conflict with either one or the other attempting to establish itself as supreme while repressing the other.

Weber takes a dualistic position that the world must be based on one or the other, either personal relationships (community and traditionalism) or impersonal ones (modern society and rationalism). He believes that basing social life on the former which he identifies with "altruism" (his conception of community as an end in itself) is not realistic. In contrast, I am proposing that social life is based on both an identity of interests between community and individual, public and private concerns, and a divergence of interests. A world that fails to recognize this, a world that emphasizes the first to the exclusion of the other (a world of private, competing interests), or that assumes the two are identical (a solidary, national unitary state), is a repressed and repressive world. I disagree also with Weber's designation of these interests as egoistic and altruistic; I prefer to conceive of them as desire for independence and distinction (individuality) and desire for attachment and love (community).

Capitalism, with its class divisions, obviates community and makes it impossible to realize a communal model of democracy. Impersonal market considerations and formal, universalistic rules and procedures repress personal, individual needs and differences (inequalities of situation) and thereby perpetuate injustice and inequity. But communal socialism, to the extent that it assumes only identity of interests between the individual and the collectivity and no difference and no potentially destructive conflict between the two, makes it impossible to safeguard individual rights, to discover repression and to resolve conflicts through universalistic procedures and impersonal relationships.

283

Weber's insight regarding the value of struggle and conflict holds good. But I substitute for his view that conflict results in the imposing of one's will over others, the strong dominating and repressing the weak, a feminist vision of conflict as on-going struggles of liberation from repression in which conflict results in liberation from repression. In this feminist view, however, repression is as inevitable and as irremediable a feature of social life as conflict is for Weber. Struggles of resistance and liberation are likewise an inevitable and irremediable feature. However, the movement of liberation from repression is a progressive movement. Changing the nature of a repressive relationship by liberating the repressed engenders changes in the parties to the relationship – the repressed and the repressor both change. Changes in the parties in turn engender changes in the relationship.

Feminism adds to Weber's conflict theory a recognition that, along with conflicts and struggles over self-interest, there is also the desire for community and sociability. The latter includes a willingness to sacrifice or subordinate individual interests to the community's interest, to the interests of the other(s). Weber, for the most part, fails to recognize the desire for community that is inherent in social life, yet he implicitly draws on that desire. He calls for heroic self-sacrifice for the honor of the nation. In this feminist view, conflicts and struggles over self-interest are limited by an equally strong and equally legitimate desire for community, and vice-versa. Neither interest vanquishes the other, but the tension and play between them makes for the dynamism of social life.

Just as Weber's insight regarding the essential nature and value of conflict and struggle holds good but undergoes transformation, Marx's insight regarding the essential nature and value of community likewise holds good, but undergoes transformation. Marx views community as one with individuality; the individual is but a particular manifestation of the communal; the community is but the totality of relations among individuals. I replace Marx's one-sided view of social life as an identity of community and individuality with a vision of social life as a dialectic of community and individuality, the dialectic of sociability.

A feminist socialism, as distinct from a masculine socialism, would constitute an institutionalized commitment to sociability which explicitly acknowledges an inevitable internal tension between individual and community, differentiation and identification, separation and attachment, a tension that must be lived with and recognized rather than denied and repressed. Socialism as a mode of production characterized by people co-operating with and caring about each other and each other's needs, feelings and uniqueness requires a commitment to sociability if it is not to degenerate into coercion. Socialism must ground itself in sociability – a mutual play of difference between whole and part, community and individual, and between and among groups and individuals.

284

Gender, sex and reproduction

A feminist analysis generally focuses on gender and sex. From the perspective of any repressed group the world appears to be divided into one absolutely fundamental division, the division between that group and all others. Thus to a black person in a racist society, a Jewish person in an anti-semitic society, a foreigner in a nationalistic society, a disabled person in a world of temporarily able-bodied people, a lesbian or homosexual in a heterosexual society, the world appears to be based on a single fundamental division. Not only does it appear that way but, in actual practice, in that person's lived reality the world is based on that fundamental division. It is the fundamental division affecting that person's life. That division is the source of the person's subjective and objective identity.

Differences in subjective identities and tensions among those different identities may derive from historical relations of political and economic oppression. Socialism requires overcoming the conditions that produce these forms of oppression. But to assume that these differences in identity do not continue to exert an important subjective force that reproduces destructive relations of oppression, including internalized oppression, is a mistake of which Marxism may be guilty. Struggles over racism and sexism have made this clear.

Marx assumed a class-divided world; feminism a gender-divided world. Both are correct. (And there are other significant divisions, to which the present argument applies as well, but I focus here on these two.) However, to treat either one as accounting for the whole is a mistake. By failing to consider sex and gender, Marx ignores that aspect of social life that deals with the reproduction of the social human being. Without consideration of this dimension, Marx implicitly leaves child care and personal nurturance to women and treats this arrangement and these skills as natural.

If economic dependence on individual men is not to be replaced by economic dependence on a political community of men, as is happening today in welfare state capitalism, then concern for the work of reproducing the human community must be a top priority for the whole community. Otherwise, a situation of exploitation, oppression and alienation between men and women will persist. It is not enough nor is it possible or necessarily desirable for women to participate "equally" in the public world of politics and production if some equitable arrangement is not made for child care, one that is sensitive to the needs of children for more than just physical care and material support.

Not only does Marx disregard the private realism of reproduction, he has no recognition of how the division between patriarchal femininity and patriarchal masculinity presupposes and reproduces the kinds of social relations that are incompatible with socialism and that preclude or distort the development of socialism. An exclusively masculine person regardless of biological sex would be unable to share equally in the reproduction of the social human being and the reproduction of communal life, because s/he would be too repressed to identify with, empathize with and nurture others. This failure obviates the sexual equality that is supposed to be implicit in Marx's vision of a liberated society.

An exclusively feminine person would be unable to share equally in political and economic decision-making. S/he would be overly wary of establishing and being subject to impersonal (and hence personally indifferent) universalistic rules and procedures. A feminine person presupposes and depends on personal good will, personal care and personal protection by others. In so doing, s/he perpetuates relationships of dominance and dependence under the guise of personal relationships of love, friendship or community. It follows, then, that the development of a socialism predicated upon equality and liberation from political and economic repression is precluded by the development of exclusively feminine and exclusively masculine actors. Such actors presuppose and reproduce repression and inequality.

Gender, sex and sexuality

To the extent that compulsive patriarchal heterosexuality promotes masculinity and femininity as we know them, then compulsive patriarchal heterosexuality[18] obstructs the development of feminist socialism – a socialism that is liberating of women as women and not just as "workers." Without a change in gender identities, women will remain "socialistic" and particularistic; men, individualistic and universalistic, and the latter will continue to dominate the former. Under patriarchal heterosexuality the development of certain "masculine" possibilities is denied women if they are to remain "women" and hence sexually desirable to men, and the development of certain "feminine" possibilities is denied men if they are to remain "men" and hence sexually desirable to women. Nevertheless, as indicated above, only if each is free to recognize and develop the possibilities of both and to recognize and overcome the limitations of each is feminist, as opposed to patriarchal, socialism possible (socialism that is not based on rigid gender roles, sexual inequality and women's oppression).

For such transformation to occur, our images of sexual attractiveness, our erotic desires, would undergo change along with our subjective (gender) identities. I am suggesting that relations of sexual attraction both presuppose and reproduce social and historical relations of domination. We saw something of this in Weber's and Kelly's historical treatment of erotic love relations.[19] Already today with more women participating equally with men in the public world the very terms "masculinity" and "femininity" seem outdated. Nevertheless, they continue in force, particularly with regard to sexual attractiveness.

In his early philosophical writings Marx describes how we speak a language that is so permeated by market relations, a language in which we make demands and speak to each other through the medium of money, that we could not understand a genuinely human language. I make the same claim regarding a language that is so permeated by patriarchal gender relations of superordination and subordination (relations that are eroticized and idealized) that we could not understand a different, more human language. By a human language Marx means one in which we would relate to each other directly as one human being to another without money (or, I would add, patriarchal gender) mediating our mutual need for each other.

Marx suggests that, so long as we live in an alienated society where money talks, "we would not understand a human language, and it would remain without effect." Our expression of need and desire "would be felt and spoken as a plea, as begging, and as *humiliation* and hence uttered with shame and with a feeling of supplication." Or, on the other hand, "it would be heard and rejected as *effrontery* or *madness*. We are so much mutually alienated from human nature that the direct language of this nature is an *injury to human dignity* for us." In contrast, the language that we do speak, "the alienated language of objective values [such as money] appears as justified, self-confident and self accepted human dignity" (Marx, 1986, p. 124, italics in original).

In other words, a human language would be one in which we could express our feelings, needs and interests with a sense of entitlement – a sense that our feelings make a difference to others and will be taken seriously and respected. In today's world, for men to expect their needs, feelings and interests to be fulfilled without offering money is seen as madness or effrontery – except in relation to women in the private sphere.

We could make a similar claim about a genuinely human language that has not been permeated by patriarchal conditioning. So long as we live in a patriarchal, gendered society the idea of men and women relating to each other in non-patriarchal ways remains incomprehensible – it could only seem to us as unmanly on the one hand and unwomanly on the other.

I am not proposing a public world run according to feminine principles to replace the currently "masculine" public world nor a domestic world run according to masculine principles to replace the currently "feminine" private world. That is, I am not recommending a reversed heterosexual world in which women and feminine principles dominate men and masculine principles. Neither am I recommending a world that is totally feminine or a world that is totally masculine, a homosexual world, to replace a heterosexual world in which the domestic sphere is feminine and the public sphere is masculine.[20] Rather, I am recommending a sociable world in which we learn through struggle and pleasure to appreciate both masculine and feminine aspects of the self and of social life, to acknowledge both aspects and the tensions between them in both public life and private life.

The tension and play between "masculinity" and "femininity" must be maintained within a single identity. Rather than segregating masculinity and femininity in separate spheres and separate identities, each sphere of life, each person, group and institution, must come to terms with both. This means consciously acknowledging the value of both. The aim is not some new non-gendered static identity. The aim is freedom to move beyond; to explore and play out different possibilities. In such a world, masculinity and femininity would have different meaning; they would refer to different starting places and hence different journeys; they would refer not to different ways of being, but to different ways of becoming.[21]

Men and women may have different journeys to undergo, different selves to explore and different strengths to develop. For instance feminine persons need to learn to take power over their lives which means participating as an equal in making decisions that affect their lives, even when the temptation is to surrender and say, "Take care of me. You decide. I'll trust your judgment and your personal loyalty and good will towards me. I don't want conflict." Masculine persons need to learn to give up power over others which means accepting and helping others to have power over their own lives, accepting their inexperienced attempts, however wrong-headed they might seem, and helping them to enjoy their own power and to face and learn from the difficulties it brings forth. Feminine persons need to become empowered, and masculine persons need to become maternal. Marx never considers these kinds of changes.

Sometimes universalistic considerations must deny particularistic needs; other times particularistic considerations must suspend universalistic needs. Sometimes individual needs will take precedence over communal interests; other times communal needs will require the sacrifice of individual interests. As an illustration, an early Israeli kibbutz had established a rule that proscribed the conceiving of children because the community needed to devote all its resources to establishing the viability of the kibbutz. After a while, a couple announced that the woman was pregnant and that they intended to keep the child. The kibbutz met to discuss the matter. The community decided to support the couple and develop child-care arrangements. Here is a case where individual interests took precedence over the communal interest.[22] The tension between the two is a fruitful one contributing to reflection, social change and self-change. Marxism needs to recognize this.

Conclusion: repression in Marx and Weber

There is a major flaw, I contend, in the thinking of both Weber and Marx. The flaw consists in the failure to take an interactive, relational perspective with respect to the values and practices of public and private worlds.

Two of the greatest theorists of the modern condition, Marx and Weber, have been relatively unself-conscious with respect to a major aspect of the modern condition, a major division of modern life – the repression of the private world by the public world, a repression that derives from the oppression of women by men. By failing to be self-critical with respect to this relationship and its embodiment in the gender identities of masculinity and femininity, Marx and Weber unself-consciously reproduce the patriarchal repression of women's lives and women's reality.

To the extent that their works unself-consciously reproduce this repression, their works re-present unself-conscious gendered thought – masculine patriarchal thinking. This masculine patriarchal thinking reproduces the split between love (relegated to live with women and children in the private sphere) and greatness (reserved for life among men in the public sphere) and corrupts both.

Notes

This chapter is based on an essay that first appeared in Wiley (ed.) (1987), *The Marx Weber Debate, Key Issues in Sociological Theory* (Sage).

1 Jean Bethke Elshtain (1981) describes the repression of the private sphere by the public sphere and calls for bringing the values of the former into the latter. However, she does not seem to recognize that transforming the relationship between them requires that both the private sphere and the public sphere become transformed.
2 Dorothy Smith (1979) makes this point.
3 Jessica Benjamin's work (1988) analyzes the connections between gender and domination from a psychoanalytic perspective.
4 Nancy Chodorow (1978) draws this connection between masculinity and the repudiation of identification with the mother.
5 Evelyn Fox Keller (1985) has shown the connections between masculinity and the idea(l) of mastery in science.
6 Carol Gilligan (1982) makes the connection with ethics; Iris Young (1987) with impartiality in the public sphere.
7 Now that I have shown (Ch. 15) how female rationality (under modern patriarchal capitalism) by itself constitutes a feminine form of life – subordinate, servile, subservient – I use the terms female and feminine interchangeably.
8 Marx follows the classical tradition and distinguishes between the state as the public world and civil society, which includes the economy, as the private world. He disregards the realm of home and family life. I adopt the feminist distinction between public and private worlds and consider both the economy and the political sphere as part of the public world while referring to the domestic life of home, family and personal–communal relationships as the private world. I also use the term private life to refer to internalized (class and gender) identities that make up the psyche.
9 Bertell Ollman (1971) introduces the idea of a theory of internal relations as the distinguishing feature of Marx's work. Bologh (1979) explicates further the theory of internal relations.

10 Bologh (1979) offers an interpretation of Marx's method of theorizing based on a reading of *Grundrisse*.

11 Janet Wolff makes the same argument regarding the literature of modernity in general which she claims describes the experience of men but not women. Women's lives, which were essential to men's lives and to the public world, were invisible in this literature (1985, p. 45).

12 According to Thomas (1985), Max and Marianne Weber believed that freeing erotic love from marriage and replacing the latter with a rational contractual relationship for reproduction and child support would also redound to the disadvantage of women and would reduce erotic love to a mere valuing of the erotic sensation, eroticism.

13 We would expect that these characteristics would vary by class and particular social relations and experiences, such as might affect race and ethnic groups.

14 The work of Willis (1977) and Acker (1983) explore the connections of gender to class.

15 William DiFazio (1985, pp. 22–3) contrasts a "big bang" theory of revolution with a theory of continuous revolutionary process that centers on the dialectic of resistance and accommodation in the everyday lives of working people.

16 In his early writings of 1844 and in 1852 Marx does stress the necessity of critical reflection including self-criticism. (1978a, pp. 13, 15, 597). But he does not explicitly include self-reflection regarding internalized feelings of oppression, powerlessness, fatalism. He does not treat the achievement of class consciousness, community or socialism as other than a problem of overcoming external obstacles; he does not see it as an on-going struggle for self-change and social change through continuous self-reflection and self-critique.

17 Habermas (1984) conceives communicative rationality on the model of (male) argumentation. That model differs from (female) sociable conversation with its relation to erotic interest, mutual pleasuring and mutual empowering. Habermas seems not to know how to achieve emancipatory reflection and emancipatory communication, both of which are essential to the emancipatory interest he had identified as central to critical theory.

18 See Adrienne Rich's article (1980) for a challenging account of the origins and psychodynamics of heterosexuality as well as the concept "compulsory heterosexuality."

19 Chapter entitled "Brotherly Love and Culture."

20 Linda Glennon (1979) similarly distinguishes between four logical possibilities regarding gender and social change: instrumentalism, expressivism, polarism and dialecticalism.

21 I develop this idea in Bologh and Fischer, 1985.

22 I am grateful to Delilah Amir of Tel Aviv University for this illustration.

17

Love and greatness: an alternative vision

For Weber love and greatness were incompatible. Nevertheless, greatness requires passion.

Power and passion

For Weber passion was essential to greatness and to a manly life. Weber asserted that without a great passion, man becomes "prematurely old and all too wise" ([1895] PS, p. 7, cited by Eden, 1983, p. 16). Weber hoped to inspire his audience with political passion. "It is not age that makes a man senile: he remains young, so long as he is able to experience the *great* passions with which nature has endowed us" (ibid., pp. 24–5, italics in the original, cited by Eden, p. 48). Here in his Freiburg Address of 1895, Weber self-consciously contrasted age with youth. Weber felt keenly the absence of political passion among the liberals of the older generation. Passion was linked for him with potency and virility, with action as opposed to contemplation or intellectualism. As late as 1918 in "Science as a Vocation" (1946, p. 152) Weber reported that he hated intellectualism as the worst devil. In that same speech of 1918, he repeated the theme of his youth: "For nothing is worthy of man as man unless he can pursue it with passionate devotion" (ibid., pp. 134–5).

Like the individual man, the nation state, too, needs passion to give it life, to give meaning and purpose to its existence. Within the individual, this great passion (commitment to an impersonal cause) must dominate, subordinate and repress other petty passions. In this way, the individual rises to a heroic level. Similarly, the nation state must rise above a "flabby eudaemonism," a concern with mere well being (PS, p. 5, cited by Eden, p. 21). The nation state must affirm some great passion to which all other petty passions can be subordinated, something which can stand as the national cause.

Weber affirms the need for domination on both the intrapsychic and the political level. The need is the same: to dominate, suppress or repress the baser passions – concerns with individual comfort and pleasure, the self-interest of the individual or the group. Weber asserts that liberals "must learn that in politics, domination is the name of the game and take their maxim from the Junkers: Landgraf werde hart! – 'a politician must become hard.'" Literally, a baron must become hard (Eden, 1983, p. 26). This speech raises questions that go beyond Weber. We can ask ourselves, what kind of audience would be receptive to this speech; what historical, social and cultural conditions would make for a receptive audience; how are gender images assumed and influenced by such talk?

Weber opposes hardness to flabbiness, passion to eudaemonism, youth (virility and potency) to age (senility and impotence). These metaphors of masculinity suggest that for Weber and his audience notions of manliness were at issue. These notions and metaphors informed individual, cultural and political thinking of the time. Masculinity here requires hardness, the willingness and ability to suppress and to repress, to dominate and subordinate, all in the name of some great passion.

Just as petty self-interest on the individual level must be subordinated to the development of "human" greatness,[1] self-interest on the part of the Junkers or some other class must be subordinated to the development of national greatness. Weber does not, however, argue that national self-interest should be subordinated to a great international order that has as its reason for being the development of human greatness. The reason for this is that Weber's notion of human greatness is tied to the idea of great passions that not only inspire action but that require agonistic struggle (competitive contest). A world order without nation states struggling for power and dominance is for Weber a world without passion, greatness, or vitality.

This view of life and what gives meaning to life – agonistic struggle – continues today to motivate many men, including "policy intellectuals" in Washington DC. Following the changes within the Soviet bloc toward democracy and a market economy, Fukuyama (1989) celebrated the seeming triumph of the West as "the end of history." However, he concluded his highly publicized article with an appraisal of this final stage as "a very sad time" because "the meaning of life lies in the causes we fight for, and in the future there won't be any" (Atlas, 1989, p. 42). In Fukuyama's view:

> The struggle for recognition, the willingness to risk one's life for a purely abstract goal, the worldwide ideological struggle that called forth daring, courage, imagination and idealism, will be replaced by economic calculation, the endless solving of technical problems, environmental concerns and the satisfaction of sophisticated consumer demand (quoted by Atlas, 1989, p.42).

In other words, we are heading for a time of "boredom" (ibid.). Agonistic conflict, heroic struggle against an opponent, appears to be the only alternative to a world of boredom, petty self-interest and passionlessness. This alternative to the boring bourgeois way of life is not one that draws on images associated with women or femininity, nor is it one that is welcoming of women, nor one that women would be likely to propose as an alternative to boredom. It is not a feminine image.

Eden discerns a concern with impotence in both Weber's and Nietzche's thought, "The constraints that limited government imposes upon self-assertiveness, according to this Nietzschean interpretation, are constraints that keep us in premodern impotence. Bourgeois democracy coopts our natural leaders and princes, diverting them into administration and commerce, relaxing their natural political drives" (Eden, 1983, p. 52).

According to Eden, "Weber found it necessary to rediscover or invent 'the heroic age of the European bourgeoisie,' an age in which its guiding ideal was hard, ascetic, disciplined and cruel, not least toward the bourgeoisie itself" (ibid., p. 53). Weber wrote in a letter of 1906, "But the fact that our nation has never gone through the schooling of hard asceticism in *any* form, is on the other hand the source of everything which I find hateful in the nation *as in myself!*" (italics in original, cited by Eden, 1983, p. 262, n.60; quoted in Mommsen, "Universalgeschischtliches und politisches Denken bei Max Weber," p. 292, n.48). We see here an idealization of hardness, discipline and asceticism, a warrior-hero image that resembles his mother's idealized image of her father.

We can see something similar operating in Weber's stress on the need to choose one's own fate, the meaning of activity and existence, and to distinguish one's life from an event merely running on in nature (Weber, 1949, p. 18). We see here a fear of surrender to life that may be understood as a fear of surrendering to desire, a fear of the desire to surrender. Such "feminine" desire must be renounced; a man must be hard and not allow himself to give in to such feelings and desire; he must conquer and master them, take charge of himself and his world.

Eden reports that "The Freiburg Lecture was on its face the most warlike and Nietzschean of Weber's formulations. . .'Politics as a Vocation' is clearly less offensive to liberals, because it is far less abrasive of their moral sensibilities" (Eden, 1983, p. 42). Weber's admirers were profoundly offended by Wolfgang Mommsen's analysis of Weber's politics because "the pathos of Weber's attempt. . .to make the major institutions of the liberal democratic regime worthy of the heroic efforts of greathearted men, is transformed by Mommsen into an unintentional and misguided propaeduetic for Hitler's regime" (ibid., p. 185). According to Eden, Weber used Nietzsche's rhetoric in support of those same bourgeois liberal institutions that Nietzsche saw as making men soft and impotent. However, Eden concludes that "Weber's rhetorical gestures will not withstand critical scrutiny. . .Weber's framework does not go beyond Machiavellian reason of state" (ibid., p. 244).

293

Weber "turned the Nietzschean rhetoric of a 'master people' to the service of the liberal cause by defining a *Herrenvolk* as a self-commanding, self-governing nation, a people governing itself by an ethic of responsibility rather than the bureaucratic ethic of obedience" (ibid., p. 200). Eden likens the ethic of responsibility to the ethic of matter-of-fact power politics, to independence and the art of command. He likens the absolute ethic to the Christian ethic which is reminiscent of Nietzsche's type of slave mentality, while the ethic of responsibility parallels Nietzsche's master morality (ibid., p. 201).

Although Weber does not directly combat Nietzsche's appeal to a sovereign self, Weber attempts to deflect that demonic self toward professional work (ibid., p. 202). At the heart of every profession, there is a god or demon that corresponds to a specific drive or ruling passion on the part of the individual. Weber distinguishes between a "'spiritual aristocracy' of genuinely inspired or 'called' individuals. . .and the banausics, the specialists without spirit or vision" (ibid., p. 203). The distinction is between men without passion who accept the idea of obedience and duty to external authority, personal or impersonal, and those who seek to find and obey their own inner gods or demon. In a world of many gods and demons one must be willing to fight to preserve and assert one's passion, one's god or demon, one's inner self, against the threat of competing passions, either one's own base passions that tempt one away from the one great passion or the demonic passions or gods of others. In this way Weber retains a heroic warrior ideal.

By stressing the polytheism of gods, values, passions, Weber shows a respect for individual differences, the unique genius or passion of each individual. We see here an implicit commitment to liberal, democratic values: respect for the individual. This commitment is expressed more explicitly as well. I tend not to stress Weber's liberalism because that does not seem to be Weber's passion. Rather, liberalism is a *means* for promoting heroic individuals who are passionate actors. Liberalism is not an end or cause to which he devotes himself passionately. That which evokes his great passion is the idea of passion itself, passionate commitment to something. The passion must be a great passion, which is to say it must be a passion that transcends the individual and individual self-interest. Such a transcendent value or passion makes for "human" (manly) greatness. For Weber, the one value that transcends the individual and excites his passion is the greatness and power of the nation state.

The desire to overcome suffering, the search for edification, can lead to a kind of wisdom that represents a form of greatness – what Weber might consider an exemplary way of living – but Weber rejects this kind of greatness. It requires too much inwardness, reflection and contemplation. He wants action – great deeds – not insight.

By reinterpreting political leadership as passionate serving of a cause, Weber departs from the principle of representative government and endows the political actor with a right to rule (Eden, 1983, p. 209). Hence Weber's liberalism, as others have remarked, shades into something else. Eden grants that Weber was attempting to attract the best and most politically talented to politics at a time when the social and political situation together with the ideas of Marx and Nietzsche were propagating a contempt for liberal democratic politics (ibid., p. 210). But the rhetoric Weber uses to affect his audience is a rhetoric that has disturbing resonances.

Fascism, nihilism and liberalism

Eden makes clear that "there is a profound weakness in Weber's remedy," an "inability to prevent his initiative from developing into a frankly nihilistic politics" (ibid., pp. 210–13). Turner and Factor suggest that from a critical perspective the Weberians of the 1920s, who held that there could be no rational ordering of human values, that values conflict with each other, and that commitment to one set of values as opposed to another is a matter of faith not reason, a non-rational "decisionism," must be judged as celebrating irrationalism in morals and politics, in this way heralding the irrationalism that was to come (Turner and Factor, 1984, p. 129). This is not to suggest that the rise of Nazism can be blamed on this kind of thinking. Weber's mode of thought and his attitudes were part of a public scholarly, literary and cultural tradition (Turner and Factor, 1984; Stern, 1975). Nevertheless, the rhetoric of the Nazis drew from the rhetoric of this tradition, a rhetoric that apparently was not alien to a large public.

Eden's view of the nihilistic implications of Weber's thinking is shared by other scholars (Strauss, 1953; Turner and Factor, 1984). Eden is concerned with the nihilism and the turn away from liberal values that is implicit in Weber's position. Eden sees the problem of ranking values and of articulating what is higher than mere political leadership as a permanent problem (Eden, 1983, p. 227). For Weber, neither reason nor science can rank values. This would mean that there is no rational basis for holding to the liberal cause rather than any other cause as a matter of ultimate commitment (ibid., p. 217).

Eden notes that Weber defends liberal democratic institutions, but not the liberal cause. Weber defends these institutions (of rational, legal authority with a bureaucratic staff) in terms of instrumental rationality: these institutions are the most efficient and successful forms of administration or political domination. Eden contends that "the liberal cause critically understood [which includes 'returning to the constitution for limits to leadership'] is possible only if the ascent to a governing reason or a recovery of modern liberal politics at the level of [social] science or philosophy is possible" (ibid., p. 241).

Eden asks why Weber shares with Nietzsche the celebration of great passions and the contempt for all pettiness, including values that are not conceived as "holding the fibers of one's very life." The possibility that there may be "intelligible transcendent values," a governing reason or philosophy that transcends politics, is repugnant to Weber and inspires his indignation and contempt, in Eden's view, because "it implies that reason could ascend to a height from which our tragic struggles with our 'demons' – and the grave seriousness with which we surround those struggles – look comic. . .It is our . . . all-too-human response to [defense against] irreverent laughter" (ibid., p. 228). According to Eden, the turn toward governing reason, which for me would mean self-reflective, interpretative reasoning that gives us distance from and perspective on our passions and struggles, disenchants politics more fully than Weber could bear. But Eden's insight moves the question to one of why Weber needed to maintain his commitment to politics over and above a commitment to reason, why he needed to liken both life and politics to a war among gods and demons, competing absolutes. I suggest that Weber needed the idea of gods and demons in order to retain and legitimize the importance of passion over reason; passion for Weber implied life, vitality and virility. One of the greatest threats to passion is moralistic reasoning, something that his mother relied on in her mothering. Weber identified the loss of passion with the stifling of the *soul*.

Morton Schatzman's (1973) work, revealingly entitled *Soul Murder*, like Alice Miller's work discussed above (Chapter 1) suggests that the concern to protect the soul or the will may be understood as a reaction to a patriarchal authoritarian tradition that aims at stifling or subordinating the will of the child.[2]

Weber's key terms, passion and power, may be understood as a masculine reaction to a patriarchal, authoritarian tradition of childraising set within a patriarchal, authoritarian political culture (in crisis), both of which threaten men with emasculation. Defensive concern for passion and power may be understood as a masculine reaction to threat of castration, the denial or cutting off of feeling, desire and potency.[3] The terms, passion and power, form the core of a masculine life philosophy that differs from a life philosophy that emphasizes eros and creativity. The difference between an orientation to passion and power and an orientation to eros and creativity represents the difference between Weber's vision of greatness, grounded in masculine reaction to a patriarchal authoritarian culture in crisis, and an alternative vision that I stress here.

Eros and creativity

Weber divides life into action and contemplation, striving and surrender. Action and striving are associated with greatness and power; contemplation and surrender, with love and powerlessness. Although there is an obvious kinship, there is a world of difference between greatness conceived in terms

296

of power to impose one's will over against a given reality – the resistant will of another – and greatness conceived in terms of power to (re)create reality through a play of difference between self and other, self and world.

Simmel considers both art and sociability to be play forms. He even includes science as a play form – the removal of cognition from its role in the struggle for existence and its treatment as a value in itself (Simmel, [1910] 1950, p. 41). He explains the value of play forms such as art, science and sociability: "we cannot be relieved of life by merely looking away from it, but only by *shaping* and experiencing [it] . . . in the . . . play of its forms." These play forms "present all the tasks and all the seriousness of life in a sublimation and, at the same time, dilution" (ibid., p. 57, italics added). Yet it is in these play forms that human greatness resides.

I would go further than Simmel and consider all of culture a playing with and shaping of nature; hence all of culture can be analyzed sociologically as sublimated forms of life. This means conceiving of social and cultural life as a playing with the forms of nature; it means analyzing social life as a sublimated and creative interplay among different forms of human nature. Creative and heroic greatness, in this view, involve uncovering and overcoming the history of repression (conflict) that stifles this creative interplay and produces rigidified, reified forms of life. This version of greatness contrasts with Weber's which involves struggles for power among conflicting, mutually exclusive wills, desires and values.

The view of social life as composed of mutually antagonistic values and ago-nistic struggle produces and assumes a dualistic, either–or world of polar oppo-sites among which a decisive choice must be made. (Hence both epistemology and ontology are implicated.) A theory of social life as creative interplay differs from a theory of social life as conflict. But the difference is not merely one of each accentuating different aspects of social life. Stressing one to the exclusion of the other produces a distorted picture and dangerous outlook.

Weber assumes a world of conflicting, mutually resistant, mutually exclu-sive wills and disembodied values, a world of mutual hostility as opposed to a world of mutually interested, mutually stimulating, embodied human beings, a world of mutual desire, mutual recognition and creative interplay among differences. The world is neither one nor the other, but both, an unsettled (comm)unity of conflict and sociability, identity and difference, attachment and separation, eros and power, resistance and yielding, rigidity and creativity.

Creative generativity[4] is a non-patriarchal way of conceiving of greatness – the power to transform and transcend a given reality, the power to produce a new reality through a play of difference between self and other. Weber does allude to creative greatness when he talks of the "idea" (see Chapter 7). But he sees the "idea" as a gift of nature, a private possession, a matter of predestination that distinguishes the elect from all others. Instead, I conceive

297

of the "idea" as one product of a stimulating interplay between self and other (object, world, person). A mutually stimulating, challenging, facilitating, affirming interchange is what I mean by erotic sociability.

A world of erotic sociability is not a world of boredom, nor is it a world devoid of passion. Creative intensity involves both passion and discipline but these are focused on shaping and playing with forms rather than maintaining rigid boundaries and segregating differences. It is ironic that Weber's one-sided accentuation of conflict among interests and values assumes and perpetuates rigid identities and forms of life. Weber was most concerned about the ossification of social forms; he valued dynamism above all. But he located dynamism in conflict (assertion and defense of oneself and one's values against others) and not in erotic sociability.

Weber does appreciate the importance not only of creativity (the "idea"), but of intersexual conversation in stimulating creativity (Chapter 13). In that model men compete with each other for the attention and approbation of women (a means of proving themselves). Instead, I propose a world in which men compete both among themselves and with women. Women, too, compete both among themselves and with men. In addition, men and women not only compete with each other but applaud and support each other. There is no fixed audience (women), no fixed set of competitors (men), no fixed set of supporters (a brotherhood).[5] All is open and in flux; the distinctions among supporter, competitor and audience, friend, enemy and stranger, are fluid.

Erotic sociability is not limited to only "intersexual" conversation. All "others" have the potential for stimulating creative interplay. When that happens we experience erotic sociability: mutual stimulation, mutual pleasure and mutual empowerment.[6] All is not conflict and domination, struggles for power in order to impose one's will against a resistant other. When the mutual struggle for recognition becomes a struggle for mutual recognition, then a world of sociability instead of hostility, of creative generativity instead of domination and subordination, in short, a world of mutual desire, mutual understanding and mutual empowerment becomes possible.

Within patriarchal society, the desire for power and greatness – creative generativity – takes a perverted form of a world of nation states vying for the power to dominate others and a world of "men" and groups struggling for power to dominate each other and society. The world is seen as one of scarcity; (human) nature, the (m)other, is seen as withholding and threatening, in need of mastery and domination by one who is more powerful, a "man." In contrast, a world of creative generativity is one of fecundity and hence abundance; (human) nature, the (m)other, is seen as promising and bountiful, if nurtured, cared for and treated responsibly by one who is a partner. A world that orients to greatness conceived as creative generativity does not yet exist; it is a historical possibility premised on

298

social, political, economic and technological transformation, a world in which power and greatness are conceived as directly human ways of relating to the world.

In today's world, human relations (among people and between people and their world) are mediated by objects that take on a power over and above people – the alienation of people from a world that they (re)create. This alienation and the insecurity that it engenders, particularly economic insecurity, in turn produces "normal" psychopathologies. When people are alienated from the reality that they (re)create and this reality takes on a power that directly affects them in an unsettling way, people turn to external objects (scapegoats and saviors) as the cause to be eliminated or the answer that will settle their troubles.

People who are alienated from their own reality-creating activity and hence from each other as co-producers of that reality have no awareness that their activity collectively (re)creates the reality that they experience individually as coming from outside. They do not know how to control a reality that seems to have lost control of itself. Even without widespread economic crisis,[7] alienated activity produces insecurity and psychopathology (such as narcissism and the sado-masochism of everyday life) that appears normal because it is necessary for surviving and succeeding in an alienated world.[8] This work has traced the normal psychopathology (alienation from desires, needs and powers) inherent in modern gender polarities along with the normal social pathology (imperialism, bellicosity, self-aggrandizement) inherent in the bifurcation of love and greatness.

The political economy of patriarchal capitalism with its alienation of people from the reality that they (re)create occurs with the mediation of (re)creative activity by objectified value – a thing out there – which replaces human value – the subjective determination of value. There is always a tension between objective measures and subjective value. The former tends to replace the latter.

In a world that conceives of power and greatness as creative generativity, power and greatness are not conceived of as objective things out there that can be possessed or taken away: things that mediate activity. Instead, power and greatness inhere in the activity itself, in the creative relationship of people to their world. Marx asks if, when the limited bourgeois form is stripped away, wealth (power and greatness) is other than the

universality of individual needs, capacities, pleasures, productive forces, etc. created through universal exchange?. . .The absolute working out of. . .creative potentialities. . .the development of all human powers as such the end in itself. . .[Striving] not to remain something [one] has become, but is in the absolute movement of becoming ([1857–8] 1973, p. 488).

299

Marx recognizes an alternative notion of power and greatness, but despite his commitment to human power and wealth in the form of creative generativity, and despite his sensitivity to oppression and repression, he is, like Weber, blind to patriarchal gender and the oppression and repression on which it rests. Moreover, despite his analysis of exchange value and its objectification in the form of money and capital, Marx does not address the inevitability and universality of power and wealth being objectified and as such mediating human relations – even if not in the form of capital as we know it; he does not stress the need for on-going struggle against oppression (alienation) even under socialism.

Marx, Weber and Freud on love and greatness

Whereas Weber sees an incompatibility between love and greatness in the public sphere, Marx sees the possibility of harmony and unity between love and greatness. For Marx, a socialist world would (lovingly) promote the greatness of each individual and the greatness of each would (lovingly) contribute to the greatness of the whole. For Weber, public greatness requires the sacrifice or suspension of love in the public realm. Freud shares this view.

Weber, Freud and Marx see love and greatness as either separate and in tension with each other or united and in harmony. They do not see the two as both separate and united. Freud sees the difference and tension and, like Weber, he takes the position of keeping the two separate from each other: love at home, greatness at work. Hence Freud and Weber see only the difference and tension between them, Marx only the identity and harmony. From a feminist perspective both of these views are correct, but neither by itself is correct.

While Weber addresses the subtleties, complexities and difficulties of greatness in the public sphere, Freud addresses the subtleties, complexities and difficulties of love in the private sphere. But neither of them see the distortion that results from forced segregation, the repression of love (private life) by greatness (public life). In accepting and advocating the segregation, they accept and advocate a patriarchal repressive reality. Moreover, by failing to see the repressive relationship between political life and personal life, masculine lives of greatness and feminine lives of love, they (re)produce a distorted, repressive patriarchal vision of each.

Freud takes the radical position of making intensely personal and private matters into public concerns but does not see the necessity for treating public issues as matters of intense and profound personal significance. This failure constitutes the great sexist flaw in his work. Marx takes the radical position of transforming work into (a labor of) love but fails to recognize that this means transforming love into (the labor of) work. That is, he does not recognize that love takes work; the kind of emotional, interactional work that women do

300

(Fishman, 1982; Cancian, 1987). That Marx fails to see this constitutes the great sexist flaw in his theorizing. That Weber must deny love in favor of greatness, that he must segregate love in the private realm in order to strive for greatness in the public realm, constitutes the great sexist flaw in his theorizing.

Weber's paradox

Weber emphatically chooses masculinity over femininity, striving over surrender, action over contemplation. Weber sets up as an end in itself ceaseless striving as a way of proving oneself and realizing one's potential for greatness. Weber's desire to strive for something worthy, a worthwhile cause, some value, as a way of proving himself contains a paradox. This paradox creates a dilemma that keeps reappearing in his work.

He conceives of life as a heroic struggle to prove oneself by striving on behalf of some value or cause that is external to the self. The paradox is that the worth or value of something comes from valuing (desiring) it; it does not inhere in the object itself. Hence its value comes from the desiring subject. We arrive at a dilemma, however, if the desiring subject is conceived as a lone, independent, unitary individual, a masculine individual who defines for himself his own values, his own object of desire. He has no way of proving to himself that those values or desires are worthy ones. If he cannot prove to himself that his values are worthy, how can he prove his worth in terms of those values?[9]

If the value comes from outside the self, it must be received or affirmed by the self – Weber's notion of elective affinity. However, this process of arriving at one's value can only be accomplished by means of contemplation, faith (trust) or surrender. All of these represent the feminine dimension of life that Weber renounces as unmanly. Implicit in Weber's masculine need or desire – ceaseless striving to prove oneself – is this unacknowledged, repressed feminine dimension.

Weber ostensibly denies the feminine ethic of faith, surrender and contemplation that he himself implicitly assumes – faith or trust (in his cause), surrender (to his cause) and contemplation (of the world and of life, which gives rise to the cause). Faith, trust, surrender, contemplation, which he has tried to banish from public life in order to devote himself rationally and realistically to his cause, turns out to be essential to the very having of a cause.[10]

Marx's paradox

Marx's thinking also contains a paradox. Marx's goal – socialism – may be understood as feminine. Yet the means he advocates for achieving that

301

goal are masculine. He must suspend and subordinate his feminine goal – the realization of socialist ends – to his masculine means. In other words, Marx explicitly denies the masculine capitalist spirit that he himself implicitly embodies – the desire to prove oneself through competitive struggle for power and dominance, the desire for heroic conquest and appropriation of the spoils (capital) by a victorious proletariat.

Marx's goal denies the masculine means that Marx implicitly values. Weber's goal – ceaseless struggle and striving – denies the feminine means that Weber implicitly relies on. Marx is feminine in his goal but masculine in his means. Weber is masculine in his goal but feminine in his means. Neither acknowledges the repressed side of his thinking.

How can the masculine and feminine, the desire to strive and the desire to surrender be reconciled? A form of life that reconciles the two would be premised on recognition of and responsiveness to both – an unresolved unity. I liken this form of life to capitalism within socialism or socialism within capitalism. As in Marx's notion of socialism in which love and greatness are in harmony, the striving and uniqueness (greatness) of each would be recognized as serving the (greatness of the) whole. Each individual would desire to prove himself or herself (his or her love) by contributing to the whole. However, unlike Marx's notion of socialism, but like Weber's notion of competitive capitalism, this form of life would be premised equally on the desire to assert difference and uniqueness, to prove oneself through contest and competition. This form of life, competitive capitalism within socialism, encourages striving within limits. These limits are determined collectively out of shared commitment to the good of the whole. This means that the individual striving of some cannot lead to the defeat and emiseration of others.

This capitalism within socialism, individuality within community, can also be likened to socialism within capitalism. Within capitalism the goal is continual striving and increase in wealth. However, if such a world is not to be repressive and restrictive of the production of wealth it must support, nurture and empower each individual so that s/he can become capable of striving and contributing to the increase in wealth. To paraphrase Marx, the wealthy individual is simultaneously the needy individual, one whose human faculties, various sides of the self, have been developed and hence are in need of realization. Analogously, the wealthy society is one that has many sides of itself developed and in need of realization.

In recognizing the need for promoting diversity and individual striving in order to avoid the tyranny and lack of both economic development and dynamism of a unitary state, a self-conscious capitalism must support the development of each individual (person and group) that comprises that state – socialism within capitalism. This means not just a minimal subsistence policy, but a policy aimed at reinvigorating, strengthening and enhancing each individual. This requires, of course, limiting, constraining and appropriating the objectified wealth and power of some individuals on behalf of the need to support, care for and nurture others – living wealth or human wealth. Thus, whether conceived as a socialist state within capitalism or a capitalist state within socialism, this form of life would constitute a sociable society: sociable socialism or sociable capitalism. As in sociable sports,[11] the striving and competing would take place within a collective that serves to nurture and promote the individuality and greatness of each individual member as well as the uniqueness and greatness of the collectivity. However, unlike Marx but like Weber, such a form of life would recognize that the striving of some could come into conflict with the striving of others, the needs and desires of the individual with those of the collective.

Striving and surrender

A world that promotes greatness and power is one in which one's own desire, one's own striving for distinction and recognition from other(s), would be matched by the desire of others, the striving of others for distinction and recognition. If there is conflict between the striving of one and the striving of the other and neither is willing to surrender to the other – a patriarchal model of manliness – then we have an outer world of conflict, competition and striving that never brings fulfillment and an inner world that remains untouched and unmoved.

This description conforms with the image of a public world of greatness, competitive capitalism, that Weber advocated, a world of ceaseless striving, conflict and competition. For Weber, one either surrenders and becomes dependent and submissive or one strives and preserves one's integrity and independence. For Weber life is a choice between being a warrior hero or being subjugated and submissive.

However, if one is unable to surrender distinction and power to other(s) (to suspend taking oneself and one's interests seriously), then striving (greatness) ultimately becomes empty and meaningless; self-development and self-change become impossible. If our striving and desire do not evoke striving and desire by the other, but stifles it, if we cannot surrender ourselves and suspend our striving when it inhibits, impedes or impairs the other, then, to paraphrase Marx, our striving is impotent and a misfortune.

On the other side, if we do not assert ourselves or our interests, preferring only to subordinate and surrender our needs and interests to those of another (an inability to take ourselves and our interests seriously), which is the only kind of intimate relationship one can have with somebody who is unable to suspend his or her own interests, then surrender is also a misfortune; it means stifling the self. Striving without surrender, surrender without striving, comprise the patriarchal situation of masculine greatness and feminine love. A post-patriarchal world, in contrast, is a world of mutual striving and surrender and, through these, self-change and self-development, social change and social development. A patriarchal social order denies developmental (dialectical) process. It forcibly prevents one side from being recognized. The basic social nature of the collective whole and the individual human being appears fixed in a one-sided patriarchal cast – striving without surrender, movement without change.

Surrender does not mean yielding to the other without retaining one's own difference. Just as defensive rigidity must give way to playful elasticity, solidity to fluidity, self to other, similarly all that is fluid must take shape, must take on some form that can contain it, some identity that can withstand an encounter with another, if it is not to seep away and disappear. The values, needs, interests of each must be retained even as each surrenders to the other, if the former are not to dissolve into the other. It is the integration of resistance and yielding, solidity and fluidity – the striving of greatness (capitalism) and the surrender of love (socialism) – that makes for the play of difference that is life itself. The play of difference makes for internal dynamics (change from within) as opposed to external dynamics (change brought about by external forces).

The relationship between part and whole, individual and collectivity, is one of both (comm)unity and integration of individuals (Marx's image) and also disunity and friction among individuals and groups (Weber's view). The whole is not only the sum of its parts (Weber's image). The individual is not merely the embodiment of the whole (Marx's view). Despite the unity of part and whole, individual and community, particular and universal, self and other, there are differences between them that cause tensions and divide the (comm)unity. The achievement of a sociable (comm)unity out of diversity must continually be reachieved as new tensions emerge. These internal tensions and divisions make for unresolved and unsettled unity. The achievement of (comm)unity depends on our acknowledging the inevitable, inherent, unavoidable strains and tensions that are eternal and internal to (comm)unity, to any collectivity, even the unity and collectivity (of desires) that is the self. (Comm)unity is always an on-going accomplishment ever subject to disruption and reconstitution.

There is always some difference, some play, between individuals and the collective as well as between and among individuals and within individuals. This difference can create friction, tension and disunity; it can also lead to new possibilities. The aim is not to overcome, suppress or repress difference but to allow difference to move us and change us, to learn from the encounter with difference.

Separate spheres

Conflict caused by difference can create the need for a separate space (or separate resources) in order to maintain a sociable relationship. However, it is important to distinguish this notion of separate space from that of separate spheres. The notion of separate spheres has been used to refer to the assignment of women to one sphere of life and men to another, with women and the domestic sphere subservient to men and the public sphere, while men and the public sphere (which controls the means of violence and the means of production) presumably take responsibility for the protection and provision of women and the domestic sphere.[12] That is the patriarchal reactionary notion of separate spheres.

Weber advocates another version of separate spheres, social differentiation. Social differentiation refers to the separation of cultural forms such as art, science, economics, politics from religion and from each other in order that they may develop on their own as ends in themselves. The development of separate spheres in this sense represents the distinguishing hallmark of modernity and the core of liberalism. For Weber, the importance of separate spheres lay not solely in the liberation of various dimensions of social life from the rigidity and absolutism of religious dogma and church control, but in the separation of different ultimate values – truth, beauty, goodness – and their cultural forms – science, art, ethics – from each other.

Because of the unresolvable nature of the potential conflict among values, in Weber's view, there is an ever-present danger that one value could come to dominate and repress the others. The result would be lack of dynamism and development, the ossification of society that presumably characterized other periods and other societies, particularly those non-modern societies where all spheres of life were subordinated to religion and religious values.[13] For Weber, the notion of separate spheres refers to non-interference of one value by another. The (ethical) values of the private sphere with its orientation to personal relationships of human need should not interfere with the (political and economic) values of the public sphere with its orientation to impersonal relationships of money and power.[14] This perspective on the relationship between the public sphere and the private sphere and their respective values, its disregard for the asymmetrical relationship of power (control over resources) and dependency between the spheres and hence between the individuals who represent and personify those values, suggests the patriarchal nature of this modernist version of separate spheres.[15]

A post-patriarchal, postmodern feminist notion of separate space stresses a sociable relationship among values and spheres with no impermeable boundaries. Weber advocates segregating cultural values in separate spheres in order to avoid the negative consequences that otherwise could occur: ethics could undermine political and economic values; by extension, politics could undermine art; science could undermine ethics; and love could undermine greatness.

The greatness of modernity, for Weber and most modernists, consists in the separating of spheres and values so that they can develop independently. Debate can occur over cultural values: which policy is more effective or efficient, which works of art are of greater or lesser aesthetic value, which scientific theory or method has more validity, and so forth. Dialogue should occur within each sphere over means and ends in relation to its own ultimate value; but dialogue should not occur among spheres.[16] In this way rationality can prevail. Because of their incommensurability, differences among spheres and among ultimate values cannot be resolved through (calculative) rationality. But there is another version of rationality that orients to human relatedness and human differences (see Ch. 15).

Values do not engage in conflict with each other; only individuals, groups or nations committed to those values engage in conflict. It is important to make that distinction in order to avoid reifying categories. Weber talks about conflicts among values, meaning that adhering to one value can require stifling another value. Weber does not seem to have a notion of individuals, groups, nations, coming to terms with their different desires, values, interests; no notion that differences can be resolved in some tentative (comm)unity that neither suppresses nor segregates difference.

Feminism, too, stresses the need for a separate space and resources in order for each individual, group, nation to develop its own values, interests, talents, powers, *not as an end in itself*, as Weber argues is the case with modernity, but *in order to make a difference* to an other, to a particular other, to a generalized other (society), to a universal other (humanity). We can think of this as the development of individuality within community. In other words we need separation and independence in order to develop our values, powers and greatness. But our desire to develop those values and powers is one with our desire to make a difference and to have our difference recognized. Thus separation and independence occur within a relationship (community) held together by mutual desire for recognition.

Mutual recognition among (adherents of) different values is not only possible but desirable. Each of the values can enhance and inform each of the others; (adherents of) each can give recognition to the other: (adherents of) art can recognize the beauty of science; science, the truth of art; and ethics, the goodness of each. Such appreciation of identity within difference makes for sociable relations and a sociable (comm)unity. Similarly, we can appreciate and respect the different sides of ourselves, the different values and desires that we hold; differences within identity.

Although conflicts do emerge over boundaries where the development of one value, the fulfillment of one desire, seems to impinge on that of another, such conflict is healthy and necessary. For example, there are times when

306

science, politics, economics and art should be subject to ethical considerations; science, art, ethics and politics to economic considerations; art, science, economics and ethics to political considerations; science, economics, politics and ethics to aesthetic considerations; and so on.

Weber sees difference as a threat to identity. He does not see identity within difference or difference within identity. He does not see identity as a tentative unity of differences; a being that is simultaneously a becoming. He recognizes the differences among values and the value of differences, but he feels that if values and differences are not segregated in separate spheres and separate beings, the conflict that emerges results in the domination and repression of one by another. It is assumed here that the stronger will impose on the weaker. That is why he recommended that his bride take up the arts of housekeeping so that she would have a sphere of her own and not become dependent on the fluctuations of his temperament, as would be the case, he feared, if she tried to maintain "a companionship in the 'intellectual' sphere."[17] The differences between them (his "richer resources") would lead to domination and dependence.

For Weber, only separate spheres protect one value or person from another. However, as feminists, people of color, the Third World and other marginalized groups are aware, separate is not equal nor is separate the same as independent. In direct contradiction with Weber's world, where those with less power must surrender to those with greater power, a world of sociable relations assumes and requires that those (individuals, groups, nations) with greater power (resources, wealth) use that power (those resources) to empower others. Surrendering, in the form of giving, in order to nurture and empower others (as distinct from self-sacrifice), makes possible a sociable world of mutual recognition. An empowered other is able to engage in mutual recognition, mutual pleasuring and mutual empowerment. A powerless dependent (even with a sphere of his or her own) cannot give recognition, only deference.

As emphasized throughout, surrender for Weber means submission and subjugation. He does recognize compromise as a solution to the problem of opposing wills where neither is strong enough to coerce the other, but he does not understand surrender born of desire for and faith in relationships of mutual recognition and mutual respect, relationships that are mutually enhancing and mutually empowering.

Contemplation and action

Surrender, if it is not to be submission, subjugation or self-sacrifice, requires the ability to become detached from one's desires and values in order to be receptive to and achieve unity with an "other," to realize one's identity with an "other." The achievement of detachment from oneself requires contemplation. Weber contends that the contemplative life of total detachment from all worldly desires and values (the Buddhist empty mind) and the inner contentment and peace that such detachment or surrender brings, eliminates striving and in so doing obstructs development.

However, we could make a very different argument based on a different interpretation of contemplation and its relationship to action. Through contemplation we can gain self-consciousness. Instead of seeing value and power as residing exclusively in something outside of the self which we desire, we can discover that such external, objective values and powers are false (fetishes). We create their value and power. By reclaiming our human value and (re)creative power, by recognizing and accepting our desires and fears freed from their false projections (fetishes), we become at one with ourselves. We can recognize and accept our human desires and fears and respond to those instead of reacting to externalized, objectified desires and fears (our projections and fetishes) – things out there.

A unity of contemplation and action, action grounded in contemplation, differs from calculative or strategic ("rational") action. After bringing to bear strategic, calculative thinking, concentrating one's rational faculties on some object of concern or desire, one may relax one's efforts and take a receptive attitude, allowing the object to work on one's consciousness, to affect one's being. This contemplative or receptive attitude towards the object and towards one's concerns or desires often brings with it a "solution" that had been eluding one or an illuminating insight, a new idea or new perspective, a new way of perceiving and relating to the object (and to one's own being), and a new way of being in the world.

Contemplation produces detachment from false, objectified desires (fetishes) and recognition of their falseness. This recognition is both liberating and empowering. It fosters an openness to the world that corresponds to an openness to oneself, to one's own feelings, to one's universality. An openness to the world and to oneself generates creativity and inner power. This inner power then informs action.

Contemplation requires a holding environment in which one can feel safe enough to reflect on, contemplate and play with reality as opposed to defending against it. Freedom within a safe, secure, protective environment allows for contemplation and creativity, openness to the self, to the other, and to the world.[18] This openness to the other in turn fosters a relationship of mutual trust, a new safe space, a holding environment for both self and other.

Weber prefers to believe that only self-control and ceaseless striving after something that remains forever beyond one's grasp makes for greatness. He does not see that striving requires surrender, that creative greatness requires some trust or faith in an other, in the world.[19] The difference between the two kinds of greatness marks the fundamental difference between us. Like W. E. B. DuBois, I believe the kind of striving that Weber identifies with greatness makes for a one-sided development (based on repression) that ultimately threatens the greatness of the whole – personality, relationship, society, world.

Detachment from false desires can make for attachment to the activity, person or stimuli at hand, a true enjoyment of that which is other. Conversely, attachment to (immersion in) some object, action or being can be a means for achieving detachment – a state of unself-consciousness in which one loses oneself and one's egoistic concerns and fears. Total detachment from the self in the form of total attachment (self-less involvement) makes for striving that is one with surrender, consciousness that is one with action, self that is one with other, greatness that is one with love.

Weber describes this experience with regard to intellectual work. He conveys his intense ambivalence about surrender while acknowledging its power as a creative force:

> The scientifically most useful *new* ideas, in my experience, have always come to me when I was lying on the sofa with a cigar in my mouth and was cogitating *con amore* [with love] – that is, not as the result of real work. I regard this truly intellectual production in the narrowest sense only as a product of free hours, as a sideline of life. . .The great marital happiness of our Westphalian relatives is. . .based on the fulfilling and satisfying *practical* work of the men (Marianne Weber, [1926] 1975, pp. 186–7).

Great ideas come from cogitating *con amore*, but he must resist this particular unity of work and love – creative generativity – in favor of the kind of greatness he associates with the "real" practical work of men. He does not see that being able to surrender oneself to the object at hand, whether in the form of contemplation or practical activity, makes for fulfilling, satisfying and productive accomplishments.

Emptying the mind of egoistic (fetishized) desires and fears, so that it is totally open to experience, enhances one's experience. One becomes free of egoistic concerns by gaining deep insight into them and accepting them for what they are. This acceptance transforms them from particularistic egoistic desires for and fears of something out there to universalistic human desires and fears. Such self-consciousness makes for a new consciousness of things out there as things that derive their value, power and meaning from our subjective human relationship to them, a socialist aesthetic appreciation of value instead of capitalist fetishism.

Such self-consciousness also makes for a new consciousness of others, a consciousness that allows us to see and appreciate a particular (human being) as an embodiment of a universal (human being), a person as a particular embodiment of universal human feelings and desires. Only when we are able to appreciate the universal human being in ourselves are we capable of greatness, of touching the universal in everybody.

In losing ourself in an activity, in an other, in surrendering to our activity or in becoming attuned to an other while maintaining our separateness and difference, we are able to experience and relate to an other, to the world, relatively unimpeded by egoistic (fetishized) concerns. This state of being outside ourself may be likened to ecstasy. In becoming one with the world, in losing ourself in the activity, the other, we are able to see, feel and act differently, we are able to come up with new ideas, new understanding, new insight – new power. The experience of suspending egoistic desires and becoming receptive to the other, to the world, surrendering or losing ourself, requires active practice, the practice of reflecting on our experiences and relationships, our desires and fears, a form of self-discipline (detachment from and contemplation of what is going on rather than just reacting).

Weber does not realize that contemplation is itself active, that receptivity requires a form of discipline. Furthermore, contemplation inspires and empowers creative action in the world. Weber fails to see the unity between contemplation and action and thus has to choose between them. Weber's vision of (masculine) modern Western rationalism is that of excessive, one-sided attachment, action, and striving; his vision of (feminine) traditional Eastern mysticism is that of excessive and one-sided detachment, contemplation and surrender. These visions (and these realities to the extent that they are realities) are dehumanizing and repressive, especially because they are presented as mutually exclusive choices.[20] As such they deny the unresolved unity that characterizes all human life.

Weber believes that a life of contemplation and detachment, a life of contentment and fulfillment, prevents striving, desire, dynamism and development. In other words, a life of love precludes a life of greatness. The dichotomy he sets up resembles the dichotomy between socialism and capitalism. Instead of such dichotomies, I argue that greatness requires love, striving requires surrender, action requires contemplation and capitalism requires socialism. However, these exist in an unsettled unity. A self-consciously sociable world recognizes and accepts the nature of these unsettled unities of self and other, striving and surrender, contemplation and action, individual and community, as on-going accomplishments that make for individual and societal greatness – creative generativity.

Power and desire

Wealth and power enable one to have a major impact on other people and on the world. Wealth and power can be conceived of as internal to an individual, inner power, inner wealth; or as external power, external wealth; or as both. People desire power and wealth as means for affecting other(s) and themselves. In striving for power and wealth one is striving to make a difference in the world, a difference to some other(s). Similarly, what is desired in a relationship is confirmation that one does make a difference. Because of the objective power of some to make a powerful and pleasurable difference to others, it is not unlikely that power evokes desire.

The ability to affect the world makes for vitality and desirability. Power stimulates the desire to be like the powerful one and recognized as such. This desire therefore stimulates striving to emulate the powerful one. Power also stimulates the desire to surrender, to give oneself up to the care and love of the powerful other. If the powerful one responds to the other's desire for power and desire for surrender, then desire produces both greatness (striving to be like the powerful one) and love (giving oneself to the other).

Power evokes desire (love). The response of the powerful to those whose love they inspire can have momentous consequences, not only with regard to the psyche (consider, for example, the effects on the development of gender identity) but with regard to society if we recognize the power of charismatic leaders.

It is not unusual for children to fall in love with their parents, for novices to fall in love with their mentors, for students to fall in love with their teachers, for analysands to fall in love with their analysts and for less powerful women to fall in love with more powerful men. (Patriarchal heterosexual desire seems premised on asymmetry of power.) The relationship (protective holding environment) that develops can be a potent force for creative change and development.

On the other side, it is not unusual for parents to love their children, for powerful men to fall in love with vulnerable women, teachers with their students, analysts with their analysands, and so on. In such relationships, the powerful one has his or her own power confirmed while at the same time vicariously experiencing the vulnerability of the other, just as the powerless one has his or her powerlessness confirmed while at the same time vicariously experiencing the power of the other. Both sides of the self, powerful and powerless, both desires, to be powerful ("like the man") and to be cared for ("like the other – the woman"), are evoked in a relationship of love between a relatively powerless and relatively powerful other. Moreover, erotic relationships of power and dependence are always symbiotic; the more powerful needs the other in order to have his or her power recognized (desired) or realized and hence is not all powerful in relation to the other. Thus, although relationships of erotic sociability may be asymmetrical in power, they are never unambiguously so. This ambiguity also makes possible creative movement within the relationship.

311

Falling in love occurs with the reawakening of one's desire. A relationship with the "other" represents an opportunity to re-enact an earlier drama of desire: the desire to be recognized and affirmed as both powerful and vulnerable, as one who is able to affect and make a difference to the world, the other, and as one who is in need of surrendering to and being cared for by the world, the other. In a reconstruction of Freud's view, repressed desire, either to be powerful in the world or to surrender to a powerful other, may continue to exert its force indefinitely, creating, on the one side, "men" who strive for power and greatness in the world and, on the other, "women" who substitute for their own lack of power and greatness desire to merge with a powerful man or (male) child.

Power, wealth and beauty

A feminist, non-patriarchal world committed to the empowerment and enhancement of its participants, a world committed to sociability and the play of difference, is not a naive, utopian vision of a world devoid of the inequalities of power and wealth and free of conflicts and repressions. The latter result from the striving for and appropriation of power and wealth, attachment to and striving for things in the world.

Objectified power, wealth and, for women particularly, beauty seem to be the surest ways of realizing unfulfilled, repressed desire – the means for giving and receiving love, for giving and receiving pleasure, the means for asserting self and affecting the world. It is not surprising that people desire to be in positions of power even if only to be free of control by other(s) who have the power to disregard their feelings, needs and interests. People strive for external power, wealth and beauty in good part to assure themselves of their potency and desirability, their ability to make a difference in the world and attain the respect and love (recognition) that they desire. External power, wealth and beauty represent objectified means for affecting the lives of other(s). Instead of affecting others by the manifestation of one's being in relation to other(s) (inner powers), one can affect others by employing these external, objectified means.

However, objectified means such as money, power and beauty bring with them the danger that the means can come to replace the end. Desire for money, power and beauty can replace the dual desire to make a difference to and be cared for by other(s). On the other hand, the striving for and accumulation of money, power and beauty can enable one to make a difference in the world and to elicit care from others.

For Marx, the desire to make a powerful, pleasurable difference to other(s), the desire for love and greatness, would be realized not by the mediation of money or external sources of power but only by actually and directly affecting others. In the world of direct human relations envisioned by Marx, a person who wishes to have a positive impact on others must be "a person who really has a stimulating and encouraging effect upon others." In this human world, "every one of your relations to man [*sic*] and to nature must be a *specific expression*. . .of your *real individual* life" (Marx, 1986, p. 115, italics in original). In a world mediated by objectified values, "Our *mutual* value is the value of our mutual objects for us. Man himself [*sic*], therefore, is mutually *valueless* for us" (ibid., p. 124, italics in original). Where mediation in the form of objectified exchange value comes to replace the direct relationship between people, value is given up to the object (money or the commodity) and the human being becomes valueless.

In contrast, in a world in which we produce and relate as human beings, in your satisfaction and use of my product, "I would have been affirmed in your thought as well as your love" (ibid., p. 125). On the other hand, "if you are not able, by the *manifestation* of yourself as a loving person, to make yourself a *beloved person*, then your love is impotent and a misfortune" (ibid., p. 115, italics in original). This failure cannot be compensated for or substituted for by the possession of objectified forms of wealth and power. The desire for recognition (love) from others requires that one act with love toward them. An economy that self-consciously founds itself on human desire for recognition (love) would enable people to produce directly for each other, the world, humanity, instead of for exchange value.

The young Marx envisioned a directly human world of immediate social relations among human beings – socialism, as opposed to a world in which human relations are mediated by money and external power – capitalism. "Let us assume man to be man, [*sic*] and his relation to the world to be a human one. Then love can only be exchanged for love, trust for trust, etc." (ibid., p. 115). A human relation to the world and to one another is one of mutuality unmediated by the objectification of social relations (money, power, position, norms). But this state of affairs can never obtain; it remains an idea(l). There will always be a tension between means and end, between objectifications and subjectivity. The aim must be to remain self-consciously sensitive to the human relationship and to the tensions caused by mediation.

Instead of envisioning a utopian Marxian reality in which means, such as money, power, bureaucracy, never become ends, and instead of facing up to the Weberian reality in which means always become ends, my alternative vision is of a world that encourages people continually to confront the reality that means tend to become ends and to continually strive to rectify the situation, to reconstitute and recreate the whole (self or society) by calling into question the relationship between means and end, and recalling how means become ends.

Instead of a continual struggle to obtain external power and wealth, a struggle against others for limited resources, a struggle for domination or superiority, life would involve continual struggle to confront and challenge externalized, objectified forms of power, wealth and beauty in order to recover subjective forms of power, wealth and beauty – creative generativity, abundance, vitality. The recovery of subjectivity requires replacing relations of coercion and domination with relations of erotic sociability.

If we recognize the impossibility of a world unmediated by objectified relations of power (Marx's vision) and therefore anticipate the inevitability of the latter (Weber's "realism") while recognizing the undesirability of it – the human needs, desires and feelings that are denied by it (Freud's insights, the humanism of both Weber and Marx), we can take measures to facilitate the uncovering of repression and the recovery of subjectivity.

We always find ourselves in the midst of some already established, on-going, objectified relationships. We always objectify each other (as teacher, bus driver, nurse, mother, dentist); we always see each other as embodiments of something – power, position, wealth, love – and relate to each other in terms of these objectifications instead of as one subjectivity (feeling, acting, desiring, powerful, fearful being) to another. Our relationships are always mediated by objectifications.

The aim of a genuinely sociable world would be to avoid reifying these objectifications, to avoid treating them as thing-like ends in themselves and to recover the human subjectivity (human feelings and desires) that are denied in and by those objectifications. Given the pervasive control of external objectified power and wealth in our lives, the recovery of subjectivity becomes a profound, revolutionary act.

Liberation as objectification

Objectification *per se* is not necessarily oppressive; it is also a liberating form of creativity. Both self and society (including social relationships and social institutions) experience conflicts among desires, needs, interests and obligations. Sometimes the tensions and conflicts can be overwhelming and paralyzing. The process of identifying and objectifying the conflicting, competing elements helps us clarify and deal consciously with them instead of being confused and overwhelmed. By recovering the repressed, naming the confusing, conflicting, contradictory elements, we taken possession of them instead of being possessed by them. Contemplation and reflection enable us to achieve this self-liberating experience.

By naming or re-presenting our experience, we objectify our subjective feelings; by finding a universal that collects and communicates the experience, we identify it, give it a social identity, re-collect ourselves, rescue our identity and ourselves from immersion in an amorphous whole. Objectifying the experience, we can take hold of it, talk about it, think about it, imagine it, prepare for it, refashion and re-create it. Instead of it existing within and about us, an amorphous feeling that engulfs us and wells up in us, we are able to step outside it and look at it, examine it, consider it, in much the same way that artists take possession of their material. We can take possession of our feelings and hence of ourselves. Naming our feelings enables us to become self-possessed. By naming an unidentified feeling, an ambiguous emotion, we become like the artist who takes unformed material and gives it form and meaning. The act of objectification, of naming or redefining subjective experience, can be a creative, empowering, liberating, meaningful act.

It is necessary for me to objectify and universalize my inchoate experience, to find some shared language or identity of which my own experience is but an instance, some universality or identity in terms of which or in the name of which I can re-present myself, some universality or identity that can re-collect us. In this way, I can discover the universal in myself and myself in the universal. I can speak, not only as a single, subjective, personal, relatively powerless being in the face of the whole, but as one who represents some objective, universal condition, a particular instance of the human condition. By naming in language that which is repressed – unrecognized and unidentified – I liberate it. As a liberating member of the repressed, I feel empowered; in speaking and struggling with and for the repressed, I speak and struggle not just as a particular individual but as a member of the collective whole, a particular embodiment of some universal. In so doing, I am empowered and empowering. I challenge the collective whole to re-member and re-collect itself.

Particular subjective experience can be translated into a universal objective form. The universal objective form collects those of us or those aspects of us that identify with that subjective experience. In this way we re-collect our universality; we re-member and re-create our collective identity.

An alternative thinking and practice

Every identity, however, creates an "other" that it excludes and denies. Hence, every identity is simultaneously repressive, even as it is also liberating and empowering. In this dialogue with Max Weber and masculine thinking I have striven to identify the missing other, the repressed side of patriarchal thinking and action: the private, domestic world of love and life associated with women. I have shown how identifying greatness with a public world that is based on the repression of love and the private world (re)produces a repressive, patriarchal greatness that is destructive, limited and mean.

In keeping with the method of dialectical phenomenology,[21] I have striven to show how existing conceptions of any whole, any identity, any category, any objectification must be re-examined in order to identify its relationship to its other (side), the negation that is repressed by it and (re)produced by

315

it. Recognition and liberation of the repressed makes for development of the whole, movement to a fuller and greater form of life. That is the kind of analysis that constitutes emancipatory, liberating thinking and theorizing. As this book has aimed to show, a liberating form of life requires identifying the repressed and identifying with the repressed.

Inside the psyche and inside the polity, inside any social organization of human beings, the same process can be identified of uncovering repression and reconstituting the whole in a way that gives recognition to the repressed, the unrecognized aspect(s) or part(s) of the whole. Through the process of recognizing the repressed, the whole reconstitutes itself with more vitality, the vitality that comes with the freeing up of powers that had been stifled. The polity and the person can re-create themselves as more complex, more vital, and more interesting multifaceted wholes. A world committed to overcoming repression, a world premised on self-conscious mutual desire for recognition, desire to make a difference in the world, would constitute an alternative world of love and greatness.

This work has focused on liberating the repressed side of masculine thinking: the side associated with femininity. But, as we have seen, liberating the repressed does not mean replacing masculine greatness with feminine love. Both are one-sided repressed and repressive patriarchal forms. Liberating the repressed means transforming both by transforming the relationship between them. Hence the patriarchal masculine notions of public greatness and the patriarchal feminine notions of private love would undergo transformation as would the repressive relationship between them. The relationship would be transformed into one of unresolved unity. Love and greatness, inspiration and materialization, subjectivity and objectivity, private and public, although retaining their difference from each other (with the potential tension, friction and creative possibilities that such difference generates), would cease being mutually exclusive, repressive, patriarchal categories.

In uncovering a relationship of repression and replacing it with a relationship of mutual recognition, the repressed experiences its own creative powers and vitality. A relationship of mutual recognition is exciting and empowering; it constitutes a holding environment (recognition of common identity), but also a stimulating environment (recognition of difference), a safe space for exploring, playing, creating. Within this new relationship, new dimensions of being can be unfolded, new feelings and desires acknowledged, new powers discovered, new projects undertaken.

Overcoming repression

The struggle to overcome repression differs from the kind of struggle Weber describes. For Weber, struggle involves the attempt to obtain some end against

316

any and all resistance. The resistance could come from outside or it could come from within. The image is that of calculating the most effective trajectory to follow in order to arrive at the goal; the struggle is to eliminate obstacles that might interfere with achieving that goal. It is a linear, instrumentally rational, monistic model of an actor who determines the most efficient method of achieving a goal and then attempts to follow that method. If any temptations or obstacles appear, one must struggle to overcome them. There is no room for playful creativity here; there is no intersubjective moment.

Despite his emphasis on *Verstehen*, itself a form of intersubjectivity, Weber is known as a methodological individualist. He conceives of social life as essentially individual struggle aimed at achieving some self-determined end within a cultural context of values that provide the meaning to such action and such ends. Weber's emphasis on *Verstehen*, his desire to both understand (become one with) the other and to resist and retain his difference from the other, a relationship that may be understood as one of erotic sociability, contributes to his intellectual greatness. Despite his self-conscious and explicit reliance on *Verstehen*, Weber does not understand social life as *intersubjective* relationships of erotic sociability and creative generativity.

Weber's model of struggle aimed at overcoming obstacles to the achievement of some external goal inevitably has as its end result a master–slave relationship. Either one is successful and becomes master of oneself and one's world, successfully achieving one's goal, or one fails and ends up succumbing and becoming a slave to one's own impulses, sentiments, emotions or to the superior force of another. The struggle to overcome repression differs from this model; consequently, the end result of this struggle likewise differs. In Weber's model, mastery consists of repressing the forces of resistance.

Overcoming repression, instead, requires confronting the origin and source of repression in social relationships of force, violence, fear and desire. In the struggle to overcome repression, the aim is not the attainment of some predetermined end. Rather the struggle is to recover one's subjective feelings, desires and powers that have been suppressed or deflected by a relationship based on fear. Hence, mastery is not the result of a conflict between opposing forces, with one coming out the victor and the other defeated. Instead of mastery as domination and repression, mastery, here, means self-recovery and self-knowledge. The aim is not domination nor the attainment of some predetermined end, but a transformation in one's way of relating to the world, to other(s), and hence to one's desires – a way of being attuned to oneself, to the world, to others, a relationship of mutual recognition, sociability and creative generativity which by definition has no predetermined end.

How can repression be overcome? If, by employing superior force to subdue and subordinate the repressor, the repressed succeeds in overturning the repression and becoming, itself, dominant and master, we do not have an overcoming of repression but merely a reversal of the original repressive relationship. How can violent denial – the intransigence of the repressor – be overcome? Overcoming repression requires acknowledging fear and the origins of the fear in some original relationship of power and desire. Fear (of destructive power – one's own or the other's) leads to denial or deflection of desire (repression).

In attempting to overcome repression, the violence and intransigence of the repressor can lead to a need to destroy or separate from the repressor, a fight to the death. This is the tragedy of patriarchal masculinity. Can an intransigent other be overcome without a fight to the death? Can intransigence be over-come? Can a repressor be forced, compelled or induced to confront the nature and origins of the fear and desire that produce repression – the fear and desire that constitutes the essence of the repressor as such? Can a repressor be forced, compelled, or induced to engage in self-reflection? The very act of treating one's self as an object of contemplation, reflection and re-cognition transforms the repressor and makes possible a relationship of mutual recognition.

While patriarchal masculinity requires each "man" to strive to resist and overcome the other "man" and to refuse surrender, a fight to the finish, patriarchal masculinity is premissed on patriarchal heterosexuality, erotic desire for the repressed feminine. Patriarchal masculine struggles for rec-ognition are premissed on a repressive desire to be powerful in the world "like a man," that requires repudiating and splitting off from itself a differ-ent "feminine" desire. The masculine refusal to recognize "feminine desire" constitutes repression.

The origins of this repression lie in a social order and public world premissed on a refusal to be responsive to and respectful of people's needs and feelings, their vulnerability and desire for care and nurturance, a holding environment – the indifference of a market economy and the violence of a warrior state. Because of its denial of personal needs and feelings, its exclusion of care and nurturance and its relegation of these to a subordinate, dependent, subjugated private sphere where these become women's domain and women's work, this social order and this public world must be considered "patriarchal." To succeed, actors must deny their own and others' personal feelings and needs. Moreover, the nature of the care and nurturance that women provide in the private sphere is itself distorted and perverted by the asymmetry of power between the public and private worlds. A desire for the survival and success of one's "man" (child or adult) in the public world, and hence of oneself in the private world, influences women's work in the private sphere. In addition, women are exhorted to inculcate certain values and behavior patterns. The public world intrudes, imposes and intervenes.

With the women's movement (itself a consequence of historical political, economic and social developments) and the ambivalence, inability and unwill-ingness of women to continue representing the repressed feminine, we have a challenge to patriarchal repression. Women now refuse to represent men's repressed desire. Men cannot sustain their repression without the collusion of women. Men who can no longer project their repressed desire onto women must now confront themselves and their fears. They must come to terms with their repressed desire just as they must come to terms with women and feminism.

As women *en masse* enter the public world, obtain some economic independence and wield some power, they cease to represent only the repressed feminine: vulnerability, surrender, responsiveness to needs, and so on. They now also represent self-reliance, independence, striving. As women cease being the embodiment of men's split off and projected desire, repressed femininity, women begin to envision and struggle to fashion new relationships of desire, new worlds of sociability in which both desires, for striving and for surrender, for love and for greatness can be realized.

A feminist movement that seeks to overcome repression of "the feminine" must struggle to have both desires recognized and affirmed in both the private world of the psyche and personal relationships and the public world of impersonal relationships. A transformed private sphere is not possible without a transformed public sphere. If the public sphere is not transformed, women who enter will simply become like men. But, like men, they will seek a haven in the home, a place where their desire for care and nurturance can be realized, a place, however, that along with the traditional housebound woman no longer exists; it certainly does not exist for women. Only by transforming a public sphere premissed on struggles for power into one of social relations premissed on sociability can the private sphere likewise be transformed.

As women struggle to realize their desires, men must confront the repressive character of their own desire and the repressive character of their masculine world. As men are confronted with women's dual desire, women's refusal to represent only the repressed "feminine," men must come to terms with their fear of surrender, their fear of the repressed "feminine desire." As women cease to be "castrated" or powerless, as they cease to represent the repressed feminine, men can begin to face the origins of their fear of castration, of being treated like a powerless "woman." They can begin to learn that the reality of castration is not grounded in nature (biology) but in repressive patriarchal social relationships and a repressive patriarchal social order.

Overcoming repression is not a matter of only changing the psyche or personal relationships; nor is it one of only changing society; it is a matter of both, of transforming a patriarchal social order that expresses itself (its repressiveness) both psychologically and socially, in both psychic reality (gender identities of patriarchal masculinity and femininity) and social reality (repressive political and economic institutions and repressed personal and domestic life). A women's movement that demands recognition of repressed feminine desire challenges such patriarchal reality.

On-going struggles to overcome patriarchal reality and patriarchal repression must take place on the personal level (of the individual psyche), the interpersonal level (of social interaction), and the impersonal level (of institutions and spheres of life). The individual and the collective continually re-create each other. Just as struggles for power and recognition occur on all levels, struggles to overcome repression must occur on all levels.

A self-conscious world of feminist rights

The desire for power and greatness that motivates social action, the striving to affect and re-create the world, to make a difference and be recognized in the world, represents one side of human desire. The desire for surrender and contemplation that allows oneself to be affected (moved, touched, tickled, awed, informed, educated) by the world represents the other side of human desire. The unsettled unity of both desires, for striving and surrender, action and contemplation, the desire to both know and be known, to affect and be affected makes possible mutual recognition, mutual power and mutual pleasure; it makes possible creative generativity.

Marx proposes a new universal – communism – that promises a relatively non-repressive, harmonious whole of mutual recognition, empowerment, productivity and aesthetic creativity. Weber rejects this as another false promise, another false universal, and advocates instead a world of particulars – a universe of contending, competing and conflicting individuals, groups and unitary nation states all struggling to survive and succeed and in the process developing strengths and greatness. Where Marx sees the possibility of universality and unity, Weber sees only the possibility of particularity, conflict and domination. I propose an alternative, post-patriarchal, feminist vision of sociability that orients to the former while recognizing the possibility of the latter.

A world committed to the reality and value of sociability with its play of difference would institutionalize ways to protect the basic rights of each individual, group, nation: not just the right to *positive objective means* for (making a) living, for reproducing oneself and one's world – feminine socialist rights; and not just the right to *negative subjective means*, non-interference by others, and *negative objective means*, the protection of self and property from violence by others – masculine capitalist rights; but also the basic right of each individual to the *positive subjective means* for making a difference, both pleasurable and powerful, to particular others (individuals, groups, nations), to the generalized other (society or world) and to a universal other (humanity, science, art, life, and so forth) – feminist rights of sociability. Positive subjective means for making a difference refer to the abilities and qualities that others find pleasurable and empowering.

320

In other words, we need to reconstitute our world with a new set of rights that goes beyond the *negative* human rights stressed now (rights of protection from abuses that are sanctioned actively or passively by a government) to *positive* new human rights of entitlement. These rights would entitle individuals, groups and nations to resources (including the kinds of social arrangements, human relationships and subjective experiences) that enable them to make a powerful and pleasurable difference in the world. This entitlement would consequently give people, groups and nations the right, and en-courage them, to challenge social arrangements and relationships that repress, degrade, oppress or exploit, social arrangements and relationships that prevent people from making a positive difference in the world.

That the modern patriarchal world is premised on negative rights of protection suggests that an assumption (perception) about the aggressive, rapacious, and violent nature of "man" underlies this world. We have seen (Chapter 1) how this assumption takes hold in a patriarchal masculine psyche that must fear and repress (its own) "feminine" desire. But the masculine psyche itself presupposes as well as produces a masculine public world of violence and struggles for power, an indifferent market and a military state. A post-patriarchal world would integrate masculine and feminine assumptions, perceptions and desires. For these to become integrated, the public world itself must change.

Because these masculine and feminine assumptions, perceptions and desires appear contradictory, integration of opposites requires a transformation of both. An integration of opposites cannot be accomplished by merely adding one to the other; such integration requires a struggle against repression. The struggle to liberate the "feminine" values, methods and rationality of domestic and personal life, for example, requires a struggle against the repressive "masculine" values, methods and rationality of public and political life. Out of this struggle, the very character of masculinity and femininity, of public life and private life, and of rationality itself, undergoes trans-formation. A new post-patriarchal masculinity and post-patriarchal public life would acknowledge and be responsive to the "feminine" values, meth-ods and rationality of domestic and personal life. Likewise, post-patriarchal femininity and post-patriarchal domestic life would acknowledge and be responsive to the "masculine" values, methods and rationality of public life.[22]

Ultimately, the development of a sociable, empowered person, group or nation able to take pleasure in affecting and being affected by the world, able to surrender to the other while retaining and asserting difference from the other, derives from *subjective* experience with others who are capable of taking pleasure in and empowering the person, group or nation through recognition, support and affirmation (post-patriarchal relationships). Such persons, groups and nations differ from the heroic individualists that Weber wished to see. But, as I have argued, such persons, groups and nations would be more capable of both greatness and love than Weber's heroic individuals.

The development of empowered, sociable individuals capable of greatness and of love requires a different kind of public and private world – a post-patriarchal feminist world. The latter would protect and promote the basic rights of each individual person, group or nation to be treated as (if he, she, it were) one that makes a powerful and pleasurable difference to other(s), to a generalized other, and to a universal other. Each individual (self or society) would be more impressed with the desire of the other(s) to empower and give pleasure to and take pleasure in oneself or society than impressed with the capacity of the other(s) to hurt or be hurt. A feminist world of sociability would promote the former and protect against the latter. A feminist world would recognize, celebrate, protect and promote in all of us the power to make a pleasurable difference to the world and to make a home out of the world – the capacity for greatness and love, creativity and generativity[23].

No greatness without love

Not only in a post-patriarchal world, but even in patriarchal society, greatness requires love. But in a patriarchal society the need for love is denied, renounced, repressed by the desire for greatness. Ironically, the modern Western public world of independence and greatness that denigrates and forcibly excludes love and dependence must turn to the latter to give meaning and value to its own existence. The patriarchal public sphere of politics and the market justifies its own unloving, violent, destructive struggles for power in terms of serving to support, defend and protect a vulnerable private sphere that is the locus of love and nurturance.

The modern public sphere needs the private as its *raison d'être*. Furthermore, the public world implicitly assumes the very values and practices of the private sphere that it explicitly denies. The values of love, mutual dependence and mutual support are implicit in the solidarity that the public world advocates as its other *raison d'être*: solidarity and unity of the political group, the nation state, the combat or corporate group or the men's community. Action in the public world requires renouncing needs and feelings of love, care, nurturance in order to strive for greatness. At the same time the unloving, uncaring, unnurturing actions that characterize the public sphere call on the idea(l)s of love, care and nurturance in the form of loyalty and (comm)unity in order not only to justify but to make possible the striving for greatness.

In other words, greatness requires love; yet within a patriarchal social order, greatness must deny what it presupposes and needs, creating a self-contradictory, self-defeating, self-destructive form of greatness and form of life. The desire for patriarchal power and greatness requires renunciation of the desire for love at the same time that it presupposes and produces a yearning for love. The kind of love that it produces as its negated other is itself as one-sided and self-contradictory as this kind of greatness. It is the love of self-abnegating, self-sacrificing, subservient beings unable to truly recognize or be recognized.

We have seen the same paradox in Marx's writings, in Weber's writings, in Freud's writings. In each case, alienated consciousness in the form of masculine thinking displays a yearning for the feminine that it explicitly denies either in practice (Marx), in principle (Weber) or in rationaliza tion (Freud). Within patriarchal thinking masculine desire for power and greatness justifies itself as serving to protect a world of love, loyalty and nurturance, a world in which creativity and culture – civilization – can flourish. Nevertheless, masculine desire for power and greatness must renounce, deny and destroy in its practices the love, loyalty and nurturance that it purports to preserve or support. Repressive masculinity threatens to destroy the very civilization that it claims is its reason for being.

The problem of repressive masculinity is not a quantitative matter of too much or surplus repression;[24] it is a qualitative matter of human relations characterized by fear and violence, domination, oppression and exploitation; repression that, as such, is dangerous and destructive – a denial of desire for relations of erotic sociability. Freud rationalizes the need for repression, claiming that repression, which he equates (mistakenly, I have argued) with instinctual renunciation, is necessary for productive work and hence civilization. From a feminist perspective such rationalization amounts to nothing less than patriarchal ideology.

It is to Weber's credit that he explores patriarchal reality and instructs us as to its nature. Modern patriarchal greatness – the world of politics and wealth – requires the exclusion of love. On the other side, modern patriarchal love – the world of erotic desire and devotion – must deny the soul, the uniqueness and hence the greatness of the other. These repressive, mutually exclusive forms of greatness and love are ultimately self-contradictory, self-destructive and oppressive of women. Hence, overcoming the oppression of women requires overcoming these patriarchal forms of greatness and love, patriarchal forms of public life and private life.

I am arguing here for a feminist movement based on the vision of a sociable world of mutual recognition in which the dual desire to be recognized as powerful and independent like "the man" and as vulnerable and dependent like "the woman," the desire for "masculine" greatness and "feminine" love, the desire for action and excitement and for contemplation and well-being, for striving and surrender, for attachment and detachment, for individuality and for community, is retained and acknowledged as an unsettled unity within the public world of political and economic life (nationalism within international-ism, internationalism within nationalism, socialism within capitalism,

capitalism within socialism) as well as within the private world of the psyche and personal relationships.

This unsettled unity can give way to either repressive unity in which one or the other desire is denied or to disunity characterized by inner and outer struggles and conflicts. Or it can be sustained in the form of mutual recognition and sociable (comm)unity. A world committed to mutual recognition and sociable community would see a transformation in the nature of love and the nature of greatness. From mutually exclusive categories they would become united in a synthesis that transcends both: creative generativity.

Mutual recognition, erotic sociability, a relationship of I and Thou, is itself a creative, generative experience – mutually affecting and mutually inspiring. To recall the words of DuBois on "the strong man," a patriarchal masculine form of greatness means "the advance of a part of the world at the expense of the whole; the overweening sense of the 'I' and the consequent forgetting of the 'Thou.'" An alternative feminist vision moves from margin to center the ever unsettled creative interplay between I and Thou.

Notes

1   Weber's notions of human passion and human greatness seem to be notions of manly passion and manly greatness. We can easily replace the terms human passion with manly passion, human greatness with manly greatness, and convey quite the same meaning that Weber seems to intend. But we cannot so easily replace these terms with the terms womanly passion and womanly greatness, and still retain Weber's meaning. The meaning becomes ambiguous. What is womanly passion, womanly greatness? Is it the same as "human" passion and "human" greatness? Does it differ from manly passion and manly greatness?

2   Schatzman traces this tradition back to the nineteenth century in the writing of Daniel Gottlieb Moritz Schreber (1808–61). Schreber's views in turn resemble those of Johann Gottlieb Fichte (1762–1814), the German philosopher and educator who, according to Schatzman, is considered a philosophical forefather of Nazism and whose influence was strong in the years when Dr Schreber was being educated. Schreber was renowned as a great pedagogue whose activities Freud credited with exerting "a lasting influence on his contemporaries" (Schatzman, p. 159). His books went through many editions and translations (Schatzman, p. 161).

Schreber thought his age to be morally "soft" and "decayed." He proposed to "battle" the "weakness" of his era with an elaborate system aimed at making children obedient and subject to adults. In 1862, it was written, "Every age produces its man who expresses its spirit as if with the power of Providence. . .the generation of our century demanded and created a man like Schreber" (Schatzman, p. 159). Schatzman analyzed the consequences of the elder Schreber's childraising philosophy and practices on Schreber's own sons, one of whom went mad and committed suicide, the other of whom was analyzed by Freud as the classic model of paranoia and schizophrenia. Freud never linked the strange experiences of Daniel Paul Schreber, for which he was thought mad, to his father's totalitarian childrearing practices despite the fact that those childrearing practices and the philosophy behind them were not only known but widely promulgated.

3 Schatzman questions Freud's theories of castration anxiety which Freud draws on in his analysis of Schreber. Because of the widespread existence of the threat of castration that his research uncovers, Schatzman finds unnecessary Freud's theory that boys' dread of castration derives from their discovery of the female genitals. Similarly, Schatzman challenges psychoanalytic theory that a boy's fear of castration by his father is based on a projection of the boy's wish to castrate his father, i.e., the denial of the boy's wish and its displacement onto the father. Like Miller (see Chapter 1 above) Schatzman argues "This view does not consider the possibility that a boy's unconscious wish to castrate his father might be a response to his father's behavior towards him" (p. 123).

4 I am grateful to Lenny Mel for this term.

5 Alan Blum and Peter McHugh (1979) in their "Introduction" discuss a similar congerie in relation to theorizing: "friends [supporters], enemies [competitors] and strangers [audience] represent the various kinds of hearing. . .among which the thoughtful speaker must compose himself" (*sic*) (p. 5).

6 Marilyn French (1985), especially ch. 7, discusses the need to go "beyond power" to pleasure. Audre Lorde (1984) discusses "the erotic as power."

7 Karl Mannheim (1940) discusses the role of economic insecurity in creating social and psychological pathology, particularly fascism.

8 Christopher Lasch (1979) discusses narcissism, but see Jessica Benjamin's critique of Lasch and her alternative analysis (1988). Alice Miller also analyzes narcissism and its prevalence (1981). Lyn Chancer (1988) discusses the sadomasochism of everyday life. Evelyn Fox Keller (1985) links pathological cognitive, emotional and moral development to patriarchal social structure while Michael L. Schwalbe (1988) links pathologies of cognitive, social and moral development to the social conditions and social structure of capitalism and postmodernity, including the effects of power and oppression on ability to take the perspective of another. See also Schwalbe (1986).

9 The dilemma of the masculine individual tends to resolve itself into a cult of masculinity (discussed in Chapter 8) where worth derives not from the values or ends for which one fights but from the fight itself.

10 Alan Sica (1988) details Weber's "compulsive dependence on the rationality–irrationality dichotomy, a biopolar conceptualization which apparently held for him some great private meaning, and which became, one might argue, an incantation" (p. 194).

11 Sociable sports would differ from the way sports today are currently organized. "Masculine sports" emphasize an exclusively instrumental orientation. Mary E. Duquin (1978), in an insightful and illuminating article, analyzes the instrumental nature of sports and suggests that they be transformed by emphasizing as well the expressive nature of sporting activity. Instead of an exclusive stress on the end results, there would be equal stress on the process: attunement with one's body, the pleasure of movement, control over one's body and the development of skill.

12 That men and the public sphere are to protect women and the domestic sphere finds expression in the early English Factory Acts. These were introduced to protect the welfare of children and women in the factories who were viewed as incapable of free contractual activity. Men were considered free to dispose of their labor power as they chose (MacGregor, 1989). Nancy Fraser (1987)

discusses the denigrating, patriarchal attitude towards women that is embedded in contemporary social welfare practices and policies.

13 Weber (as well as Marx) may be accused of "Orientalism" in Edward Said's sense (Bryan Turner, 1981, p. 264). Orientalism interpreted the Orient as a static, unchanging society attributable to the absence of Western institutions or beliefs (ibid., p. 264).

14 Despite his history of great strictures against the idea(l) of "ethical politics," with Germany's defeat at the end of the First World War, Weber participated in a "Working Group for Ethical Politics." The group, soon renamed "Toward a Politics of Right," had as its aim a propaganda campaign abroad in favor of "peace of right" not "a peace of force" (Roth, 1989, p. 7). Weber's endeavor "to shift the focus from 'guilt for the past' to the allied governments' 'responsibility for the future'" must be seen in light of Weber's unwillingness to acknowledge Germany's war guilt (ibid.).

Weber's position on "ethical politics" was so well known that a leader of the conservative women's movement, Gertrud Baumer, castigated Marianne Weber for distancing herself and her circle from the Nazi program by citing Max Weber's own philosophy that the political and the moral can never coincide (Roth, 1988, p. li–lii).

Weber was not blind to the asymmetry with respect to control over resources. He strongly opposed the injustice of men controlling the property and income of their wives, the situation that prevailed in his childhood home. He also advocated the "inner freedom and independence of women." Nevertheless, Marianne Weber and presumably her husband as well fought against the more radical feminists of the time, followers of Charlotte Perkins Gilman, who advocated the economic independence of women (Roth, 1988, p. xxvii).

In keeping with the patriarchal idea of separate spheres for love and greatness, morality and politics, Marianne Weber, concerned about "the war's brutalizing impact" on men, assigned to the "cultured" woman the special task of "rebuilding morality and shaping the immediacy of existence through love and beauty" (Roth, 1988, p. xxxvii). Despite her horror at the "global catastrophe," she could, in the early days of the war, write of the war that "one. . .can yet feel even as a woman that mankind would be emptied without the opportunity for, and challenges inherent in, such tests of ethical greatness" (cited by Roth, 1988, p. xxxvi).

16 Habermas (1984) seems to accept this version of separate spheres, despite his commitment to rational dialogue. His notion of communicative rationality occurs only within spheres not among spheres.

Habermas and I agree that Weber's notion of instrumental rationality is repressive and seek an alternative principle for orienting social life. But because his alternative, communicative rationality, excludes feeling, sentiment and desire as irrational emotions which must be segregated into their own separate sphere – aesthetics – I consider his notion of communicative rationality repressive. (See Young, 1987, for a similar postmodern, feminist critique of Habermas.) Habermas makes an important break with Weber by stressing the intersubjective dimension of social life in contrast with Weber's methodological individualism. However, for Habermas, the intersubjective dimension consists of coming to an agreement (rationally). For me, as for Jessica Benjamin, it is mutual recognition or what I call erotic sociability.

17 Marianne Weber reports that when she and Max were engaged, he wrote her that he wanted her to have a domain in which he would not compete with her, an area that he could not touch – "a housewifely sphere of duty and work."

He feared that a "companionship in the 'intellectual' sphere could jeopardize [his wife's] position" (Weber, 1975, pp. 187–8).

18 D. W. Winnicott has written on the relationship between creativity and a holding environment or transitional space (1965 and 1974). Jessica Benjamin (1988) draws on his ideas of a holding environment in her attempt to formulate women's desire.

19 Weber does talk about commitment to a cause as based on faith. But it is not a matter of faith in others or in humanity; it is a faith in one's choice.

20 For critiques of this setting up of "ideal types" as polar opposites, see note 7 above and also note 2 of Chapter 9.

21 I spell out an early formulation of this method in *Dialectical Phenomenology: Marx's Method*.

22 Jessica Benjamin (1988) develops the idea of more flexible gender identities.

23 Creativity is not simply a matter of innate talent. Environments can encourage and foster creativity or they can stifly it. As a theorist of creativity reminds us, "when cultures value it, creativity flourishes" (Mihaly Csikszentmihalyi in Roark, 1989).

24 Herbert Marcuse (1962), also concerned about the repressive character of modern capitalist society, draws on Freud's drive theory in order to formulate a notion of surplus repression. Jessica Benjamin (1988), sympathetic to Marcuse, nevertheless faults his reliance on Freudian drive theory as opposed to a theory of intersubjectivity – desire for mutual recognition.

References

Acker, Joan (1983), "Gender and the Construction of Class," paper presented at the 78th Annual Meeting of the American Sociological Association, Detroit.

Alexander, Jeffrey C. (1987), "The Dialectic of Individuation and Domination: Weber's Rationalization Theory and Beyond," in Whimster and Lash, op. cit., pp. 185–206.

Aron, Raymond (1971), "Max Weber and Power-politics," in Stammer, op. cit., pp. 83–132.

Atlas, James (1989), "What is Fukuyama Saying?" *New York Times Magazine*, October 22.

Bartky, Sandra Lee (1979), "On Psychological Oppression," in Bishop and Weinzweig, op. cit., pp. 33–41.

Beetham David (1974), *Max Weber and the Theory of Modern Politics* (London: Allen & Unwin).

Bendix, Reinhard (1960), *Max Weber: An Intellectual Portrait* (Garden City, NY: Doubleday).

Benhabib, Seyla, and Cornell, Drucilla (eds) (1987), *Feminism as Critique: On the Politics of Gender* (Minneapolis: University of Minnesota Press).

Benjamin, Jessica (1986), "A Desire of One's Own: Psychoanalytic Feminism and Intersubjective Space," in de Lauretis, op. cit., pp. 78–101.

Benjamin, Jessica (1988), *The Bonds of Love* (New York: Pantheon).

Bishop, Sharon and Weinzweig, Marjorie (eds) (1979), Philosophy and Women (Belmont, Calif.: Wadsworth).

Blum, Alan, and McHugh, Peter (eds) (1979), *Friends, Enemies and Strangers, Theorizing in Art, Science, and Everyday Life* (Norwood, NJ: Ablex).

Blum, Larry, Homiak, Marcia, Housman, Judy, and Scheman, Naomi (1973–4), "Altruism and Women's Oppression," *Philosophical Forum*, vol. 5, nos 1–2, pp. 222–47.

Bologh, Roslyn Wallach (1976), "On Fooling Around: A Phenomenological Analysis of Playfulness," *Annals of Phenomenological Sociology*, vol. 1, pp. 113–25.

Bologh, Roslyn Wallach (1979), *Dialectical Phenomenology: Marx's Method* (London: Routledge & Kegan Paul).

Bologh, Roslyn Wallach (1984), "Max Weber and the Dilemma of Rationality," in Glassman and Murvar, op. cit., pp. 175–86.

Bologh, Roslyn Wallach (1987), "Marx, Weber, and Masculine Theorizing: A Feminist Analysis," in Wiley, op. cit., pp. 145–68.

Bologh, Roslyn Wallach, and Fischer, George Uri (1985), "Gender, Repression and Liberation: An Alternative Feminist Theory, Method and Politics," paper presented at the 80th meeting of the American Sociological Association, Washington DC.

Brubaker, Rogers (1984), *The Limits of Rationality* (London: Allen & Unwin).

Cancian, Francesca M. (1987), *Love In America* (Cambridge: Cambridge University Press).

References

Chancer, Lynn (1988), "Sado-Masochism and Everyday Life," unpublished ms, City University of New York.
Chodorow, Nancy (1978), *The Reproduction of Mothering* (Berkeley: University of California Press).
Cohen, Lorraine (1987), "Reinterpreting Rosa Luxemburg's Theory of Social Change: Consciousness, Action and Leadership," PhD thesis, City University of New York.
Collins, Randall (1986), *Max Weber* (Beverly Hills: Sage).
Coltheart, Lenore ([1986] 1987), "Desire, Consent and Liberal Theory," in Pateman and Gross, op. cit., pp. 112–22.
Cooper, Sandi (1980), "The Impact of Nationalism on European Peace Movements and Liberal Internationalists 1848–1914," *Peace and Change*, vol. 6, nos 1–2, pp. 23–36.

David, Deborah S., and Brannon, Robert (1976), *The Forty-Nine Percent Majority* (Reading, Mass.: Addison Wesley).
de Lauretis, Teresa (ed.) (1986), *Feminist Studies/Critical Studies* (Bloomington: Indiana University Press).
DiFazio, William (1985), *Longshoremen: Community and Resistance on the Brooklyn Waterfront* (South Hadley, Mass.: Bergin & Garvey).
Doyle, James A. (1983), *The Male Experience* (Dubuque, Iowa: Wm C. Brown).
Dronberger, Ilse (1971), *The Political Thought of Max Weber* (New York: Irvington).
DuBois, W. E. B. (1965), *The World and Africa* (New York: International).
DuBois, W. E. B. (1970), *W. E. B. DuBois Speaks*, ed. P. S. Froner (New York: Pathfinder).
Duquin, Mary (1978), "The Androgynous Advantage," in Oglesby, op. cit., pp. 471–83.
Durkheim, Émile (1965), *The Elementary Forms of the Religious Life* (New York: Free Press).

Eden, Robert (1983), *Political Leadership and Nihilism, A Study of Weber and Nietzsche* (Tampa, Fla: University Presses of Florida).
Elias, Norbert (1982), *The Civilizing Process*, Vol. 2: *Power and Civility* (New York: Pantheon).
Elshtain, Jean Bethke (1981), *Public Man, Private Woman* (Princeton, NJ: Princeton University Press).
Elshtain, Jean Bethke (1986), *Meditations on Modern Political Thought: Masculine/Feminine Themes from Luther to Arendt* (New York: Praeger).
Erickson, Victoria Lee (1989), "A Feminist Critique of the Sociology of Religion," PhD thesis, City University of New York.
Evans, Richard J. (1976), *The Feminist Movement in Germany 1894–1933* (London: Sage).

Ferguson, Kathy E. (1980), *Self, Society and Womankind* (Westport, Conn.: Greenwood).
Ferguson, Kathy E. (1984), *The Feminist Case Against Bureaucracy* (Philadelphia: Temple University Press).
Fishman, Pamela M. (1982), "Interaction: The Work Women Do," in Kahn-Hut, Daniels and Colvard, op. cit., pp. 170–80.
Flax, Jane (1983), "Political Philosophy and the Patriarchal Unconscious: A Psychoanalytic Perspective on Epistemology and Metaphysics," in Harding and Hintikka, op. cit., pp. 245–81.

Foner, Philip S. (1970), "Editor's Introduction," in DuBois, op. cit., pp. 1–11.
Fox Keller, Evelyn (1985), *Reflections on Gender and Science* (New Haven, Conn.: Yale University Press).
Fraser, Nancy (1987), "Women, Welfare and the Politics of Need Interpretation," *Hypatia*, vol. 2, no. 1, pp. 103–21.
French, Marilyn (1985), *Beyond Power, On Women, Men and Morals*, (New York: Simon & Schuster).
Freud, Sigmund, *The Standard Edition of the Complete Psychological Works of Sigmund Freud*, trans. and ed. by James Strachey in collaboration with Anna Freud, assisted by Alix Strachey and Alan Tyson, 24 vols (London: Hogarth Press and Institute of Psychoanalysis, 1953–74) (abbreviated in the following entries as SE followed by vol. no.). The dates given are of first publication.
Freud, Sigmund (1910), "The Future Prospects of Psycho-Analytic Therapy," SE 11, pp. 141–51.
Freud, Sigmund (1914), "The Moses of Michelangelo," SE 13, pp. 211–38.
Freud, Sigmund (1921), *Group Psychology and the Analysis of the Ego*, SE 18, pp. 69–143.
Freud, Sigmund (1923), *The Ego and the Id*, SE 19, pp. 12–66.
Freud, Sigmund (1927), *The Future of an Illusion*, SE 21, pp. 5–56.
Freud, Sigmund (1928), "Dostoevsky and Parricide," SE 21, pp. 177–96.
Freud, Sigmund (1931), "Female Sexuality," SE 21, pp. 225–43.
Freud, Sigmund (1937), "Analysis Terminable and Interminable," SE 23, pp. 216–53.
Freud, Sigmund (1939), "Moses and Monotheism: Three Essays," SE 23, pp. 7–137.
Freud, Sigmund ([1930] 1961), *Civilization and Its Discontents* (New York: Norton).
Fuentes, Annette, and Ehrenreich, Barbara (1983), *Women in the Global Factory* (Boston, Mass.: South End Press).

Gilligan, Carol (1982), In a Difference Voice (Cambridge, Mass.: Harvard University Press).
Glassman, Ronald M. and Murvar, V. (eds) (1984), *Max Weber's Political Sociology: A Pessimistic Vision of A Rationalized World* (Westport, Conn.: Greenwood).
Glennon, Linda M. (1979), *Women and Dualism* (New York: Longman).
Gould, Carol C. (ed.) (1984a), *Byond Domination* (Totowa, NJ: Rowman & Allanheld).
Gould, Carol C. (1984b), "Private Rights and Public Virtues: Women, the Family, and Democracy," in Gould, op. cit., pp. 3–20.
Green, Martin (1974), *The von Richthofen Sisters* (New York: Basic Books).

Habermas, Jurgen (1984), *Theory of Communicative Action*, Vol. 1 (Boston, Mass.: Beacon Press).
Harding, Sandra, and Hintikka, Merrill B. (eds) (1983), *Discovering Reality: Feminist Perspectives on Epistemology, Metaphysics, Methodology, and the Philosophy of Science* (Boston, Mass.: Reidel).
Hartsock, Nancy (1983), *Money, Sex and Power* (New York: Longman).
Hartsock, Nancy (1984), "Prologue to a Feminist Critique of War and Politics," in Stiehm, op. cit., pp. 123–50.
Haywoode, Terry (1988), "Working Class Feminism," unpublished ms, City University of New York.
Held, Virginia (1973–4), "Marx, Sex, and the Transformation of Society," *Philosophical Forum*, vol. 5, nos 1–2, pp. 168–84.
Held, Virginia (1987), "Non-contractual Society: A Feminist view" *Canadian Journal of Philosophy*, supplementary vol. 13, pp. 111–37.

References

Hennis, Wilhelm (1988), *Max Weber, Essays in Reconstruction* (London: Allen & Unwin).
Hooks, Bell (1984), *Feminist Theory: From Margin to Center* (Boston, Mass.: South End Press).

Kahn-Hut, Rachel, Daniels, Arlene Kaplan , and Colvard, Richard (eds) (1982), *Women and Work* (New York: Oxford University Press).
Kalberg, Steven (1980), "Max Weber's Types of Rationality: Cornerstones for the Analysis of Rationalization Processes in History," *American Journal of Sociology*, vol. 85, no. 5, pp. 1145–78.
Kandiyoti, Deniz (1988), "Bargaining With Patriarchy," *Gender and Society*, vol. 2, no. 3, pp. 274–89.
Keller, Evelyn Fox (1985), *Reflections on Gender and Science* (New Haven, Conn.: Yale University Press).
Kelly, Joan (1984), *Women, History and Theory* (Chicago: University of Chicago Press).
Kent, Steven (1983), "Weber, Geothe and the Nietzschean Allusion: Capturing the Source of the 'Iron Cage' Metaphor," *Sociological Analysis*, vol. 44, no. 4, pp. 297–320.
Keohane, Nannerl O., Rosaldo, Michelle Z., and Gelpi, Barbara C. (eds) (1982), *Feminist Theory: A Critique of Ideology* (Chicago: University of Chicago Press).
Kohlberg, Lawrence (1971), *The Philosophy of Moral Development* (New York: Harper & Row).
Kohlberg, Lawrence and Kramer, R. (1969), "Continuities and Discontinuities in Childhood and Adult Moral Development," *Human Development*, vol. 12, pp. 93–120.
Koonz, Claudia (1986), "Some Political Implications of Separatism, German Women Between Democracy and Nazism, 1928–34," in Judith Friedlander, Blanche Wiesen Cook, Alice Kessler-Harris and Carroll Smith-Rosenberg (eds), *Women in Culture and Politics: A Century of Change* (Bloomington: Indiana University Press).
Koonz, Claudia (1987), *Mothers in the Fatherland: Women, the Family and Nazi Politics* (New York: St Martin's Press).

Lasch, Christopher (1979), *The Culture of Narcissism* (New York: Norton).
Lazreg, Marnia (1988), "Feminism and Difference: The Perils of Writing As a Woman on Women in Algeria," *Feminist Studies*, vol. 14, no. 1, pp. 81–107.
Lerner, Gerda (1986), *The Creation of Patriarchy* (New York: Oxford University Press).
Lloyd, Genevieve (1984), *The Man of Reason: Male and Female in Western Philosophy* (London: Methuen).
Lloyd, Genevieve (1986), "Selfhood, War and Masculinity," in Pateman and Gross, op. cit., pp. 63–76.
Loewenstein, Karl (1966), *Max Weber's Political Ideas in the Perspective of Our Time* (Minnesota: University of Massachusetts Press).
Lorde, Audre (1984), *Sister Outsider* (Trumansburg, NY: Crossing Press).

MacGregor, David (1989), "Marxism's Hegelian Blind Spot: The Theory of the State in Hegel and Marx," *Current Perspectives in Social Theory*, vol. 9, pp. 143–75.
MacPherson, C. B. (1962), *The Political Theory of Possessive Individualism, Hobbes to Locke* (Oxford: Oxford University Press).

Mannheim, Karl (1940), *Man and Society in an Age of Reconstruction* (New York: Harcourt Brace & World).

Mansbridge, Jane J. (1983), *Beyond Adversary Democracy* (Chicago: University of Chicago Press).

Marcuse, Herbert (1962), *Eros and Civilisation: A Philosophical Inquiry Into Freud* (Boston, Mass.: Beacon Press).

Marx, Karl ([1857–8] 1973), *Grundrisse*, trans. Martin Nicolaus (New York: Random House).

Marx, Karl ([1844] 1978a), "Economic and Philosophic Manuscripts of 1844," in Marx and Engels, op. cit., pp. 66–125.

Marx, Karl ([1875] 1978b), "Critique of the Gotha Program," in Marx and Engels, op. cit., pp. 525–42.

Marx, Karl (1986), *Karl Marx: The Essential Writings*, 2nd edn, ed. Frederic L. Bender (Boulder, Col.: Westview).

Marx, Karl, and Engels, Friedrich ([1848] 1948), *Communist Manifesto* (New York: International).

Marx, Karl, and Engels, Friedrich (1978), *The Marx-Engels Reader*, ed. Robert C. Tucker (New York: Norton).

Miller, Alice (1981), *The Drama of the Gifted Child*, trans. Ruth Ward (New York: Basic Books) (originally published in 1979 as *Prisoners of Childhood*).

Miller, Alice (1983), *For Your Own Good, Hidden Cruelty in Child Rearing and the Roots of Violence* (New York: Farrar, Straus, Giroux).

Miller, Alice (1984), *Thou Shalt Not Be Aware: Society's Betrayal of the Child* (New York: New American Library).

Mitzman, Arthur (1971), *The Iron Cage* (New York: Grosset & Dunlap).

Mommsen, Wolfgang J. (1984), *Max Weber and German Politics 1890–1920* (Chicago: University of Chicago Press).

Oglesby, Carole A. (ed.) (1978), *Women and Sport: From Myth to Reality* (Philadelphia: Lea & Febinger).

Ollman, Bertell (1971), *Alienation: Marx's Conception of Man in Capitalist Society* (Cambridge: Cambridge University Press).

Parsons, Talcott (1954), "Democracy and Social Structure in Pre-Nazi Germany," in *Essays in Sociological Theory*, pp. 104–23 (New York: Free Press).

Pateman, Carole (1980), "Women and Consent," *Political Theory*, vol. 8, no. 2, pp. 149–68.

Pateman, Carole, and Gross, Elizabeth (1986), *Feminist Challenges, Social and Political Theory* (Boston, Mass.: Northeastern University Press).

Pearson, Carol, and Pope, Katherine (1981), *The Female Hero* (New York: Bowker).

Pitkin, Hannah Fenichel (1984), *Fortune is a Woman: Gender and Politics in the Thought of Niccolo Machiavelli* (Berkeley: University of California Press).

Portis, Edward Bryan (1986), *Max Weber and Political Commitment: Science, Politics, and Personality* (Philadelphia: Temple University Press).

Reiter, Rayna R. (ed.) (1975), *Towards an Anthropology of Women* (New York: Monthly Review Press).

Rich, Adrienne (1980), "Compulsory Heterosexuality and Lesbian Existence," *Signs: Journal of Women in Culture and Society*, vol. 5, no. 4, pp. 631–60.

Roark, Anne C. (1989), "Tracking the Roots of Genius," *The Standard Star*, Gannett Westchester Newspapers, October 1, pp. 9–10.

Roth, Guenther (1981), "Introduction," in Schluchter, op. cit., pp. xv–xxvii.
Roth, Guenther (1988), "Marianne Weber and Her Circle, Introduction to the Transaction Edition," in Weber, op. cit., pp. xv–lxi.
Roth, Guenther (1989), "Max Weber's Political Failure," *Telos*, vol. 78, Winter, pp. 1–14.
Rubin, Gayle (1975), "The Traffic in Women: Notes on the 'Political Economy' of Sex," in Reiter, op. cit., pp. 157–210.
Ruddick, Sara (1982), "Maternal Thinking," in Thorne, op. cit., pp. 76–94.

Said, Edward W. (1979), *Orientalism* (New York: Vintage).
Schluchter, Wolfgang (1981), *The Rise of Western Rationalism, Max Weber's Developmental History*, trans. with an introduction by Guenther Roth (Berkeley: University of California Press).
Schwalbe, Michael L. (1986), *The Psychosocial Consequences of Natural and Alienated Labor* (Albany, NY: State University of New York Press).
Schwalbe, Michael L. (1988), "Role Taking Reconsidered: Linking Competence and Performance to Social Structure," *Journal for the Theory of Social Behavior*, vol. 18, no. 4, pp. 411–36.
Seidman, Steven (1985), "Max Weber: A Classic Analyzed," *Contemporary Sociology*, vol. 14, no. 6, pp. 673–7.
Seidman, Steven (1986), review of Wolfgang Mommsen, *Max Weber and German Politics 1890–1920*, Society, vol. 23, no. 3, pp. 86–8.
Sherman, Julia A. and Beck, Evelyn Torton (1979), *The Prism of Sex: Essays in the Sociology of Knowledge* (Madison: University of Wisconsin Press).
Sica, Alan (1988), *Weber, Irrationality, and Social Order* (Berkeley: University of California Press).
Simmel, Georg (1950), *The Sociology of Georg Simmel*, ed. Kurt H. Wolff (New York: Free Press).
Smith, Dorothy (1979), "A Sociology For Women," in Sherman and Beck, op. cit., pp. 135–87.
Smith-Rosenberg, Carrol (1975), "The Female World of Love and Ritual: Relations Between Women in Nineteenth Century America," *Signs: A Journal of Women in Culture and Society*, vol. 1, no. 1, pp. 1–29.
Stammer, Otto (ed.) (1971), *Max Weber and Sociology Today*, trans. Kathleen Morris (New York: Harper & Row).
Starhawk (1982), *Dreaming the Dark: Magic, Sex and Politics* (Boston, Mass.: Beacon).
Stern, Daniel (1977), *The First Relationship (The Developing Child)* (Cambridge, Mass.: Harvard University Press).
Stern, J. P. (1975), *Hitler, The Führer and the People* (Berkeley: University of California Press).
Stiehm, Judith H. (ed.) (1984), *Women's Views of the Political World of Men* (Dobbs Ferry, NY: Transnational).
Straumanis, Joan (1984), "Duties to Oneself: An Ethical Basis for Self-Liberation," *Journal of Social Philosophy*, vol. 15, no. 2, pp. 1–13.
Strauss, Leo (1953), *Natural Right and History* (Chicago: University of Chicago Press).

Thomas, J. J. R. (1985), "Rationalization and the Status of Gender Divisions," *Sociology*, vol. 19, no. 3, pp. 409–20.
Thorne, Barrie (ed.) with Yalom, Marilyn (1982), *Rethinking The Family* (New York: Longman).

Tormey, Judith Farr (1973–4), "Exploitation, Oppression and Self-Sacrifice," *Philosophical Forum*, vol. 5, nos. 1–2, pp. 206–21.

Tucker, Robert C. (1978), *The Marx-Engels Reader* (New York: Norton).

Turner, Bryan (1981), *For Weber: Essays on the Sociology of Fate* (Boston, Mass.: Routledge & Kegal Paul).

Turner, Stephen P., and Factor, Regis A. (1984), *Max Weber and the Dispute Over Reason and Value* (London: Routledge & Kegan Paul).

Van Herik, Judith (1982), *Freud on Femininity and Faith* (Berkeley: University of California Press).

Weber, Marianne (1975), *Max Weber: A Biography* (New York: John Wiley & Sons, Inc.).

Weber, Marianne (1988), *Max Weber: A Biography* (New Brunswick: Transaction).

Weber, Max (1946), *From Max Weber. Essays in Sociology*, trans. and ed. H. H. Gerth and C. Wright Mills (New York: Oxford University Press).

Weber, Max (1949), *Methodology Of the Social Sciences* (Glencoe, NY: Free Press).

Weber, Max (1951), *The Religion of China* (Glencoe, NY: Free Press).

Weber, Max (1958), *The Protestant Ethic and The Spirit of Capitalism*, trans. Talcott Parsons (New York: Scribners).

Weber, Max ([1922] 1964), *The Sociology of Religion* (Boston, Mass.: Beacon Press).

Weber, Max (1978), *Economy and Society*, ed. Guenther Roth and Claus Wittich (Berkeley and Los Angeles: University of California Press).

Weber, Max (1981), *General Economic History* (New Brunswick: Transaction).

Whimster, Sam, and Lash, Scott (eds) (1987), *Max Weber, Rationality and Modernity* (London and Boston, Mass.: Allen & Unwin).

Wiley, Norbert (ed.) (1987), *The Marx Weber Debate, Key Issues in Sociological Theory* (Newbury Park, Calif.: Sage).

Willis, Paul (1977), *Learning to Labor, How Working Class Kids Get Working Class Jobs* (New York: Columbia University Press).

Winnicott, Donald Woods (1965), *The Maturation Process and the Facilitating Environment* (New York: International Universities Press).

Winnicott, Donald Woods (1974), *Playing and Reality* (Harmondsworth: Penguin).

Wolff, Janet (1985), "The Invisible Flaneuse: Women and the Literature of Modernity," *Theory, Culture and Society*, vol. 2, no. 3, pp. 37–46.

Wrong, Dennis (ed.) (1970), *Max Weber* (Englewood Cliffs, NJ: Prentice-Hall).

Young, Iris Marion (1987), "Impartiality and the Civic Public," in Benhabib and Cornell, op. cit., pp. 57–76.

Index

Love or Greatness